At the Limits of ...e

At the Limits

CRITICAL GLOBAL HEALTH:
EVIDENCE, EFFICACY, ETHNOGRAPHY

A series edited by Vincanne Adams and João Biehl

# of Cure

BHARAT JAYRAM VENKAT

Duke University Press   Durham and London   2021

© 2021 Bharat Jayram Venkat
Printed and bound by CPI Group (UK) Ltd, Croydon, CR0 4YY
Text design by Drew Sisk
Cover illustration and design by Jonathan Yamakami
Typeset in Portrait Text, Canela Text, and Folio by Westchester Publishing Services

Library of Congress Cataloging-in-Publication Data
Names: Venkat, Bharat Jayram, [date] author.
Title: At the limits of cure / Bharat Jayram Venkat.
Other titles: Critical global health.
Description: Durham : Duke University Press, 2021. | Series: Critical global health:
evidence, efficacy, ethnography | Includes bibliographical references and index.
Identifiers: LCCN 2021009365 (print)
LCCN 2021009366 (ebook)
ISBN 9781478013792 (hardcover)
ISBN 9781478014720 (paperback)
ISBN 9781478022022 (ebook)
ISBN 9781478091776 (ebook other)
Subjects: LCSH: Tuberculosis—India—History—20th century. | Tuberculosis—
Treatment—India. | Tuberculosis—India—Prevention. | BISAC: SOCIAL SCIENCE /
Anthropology / Cultural & Social | HISTORY / Asia / India & South Asia
Classification: LCC RC317.14 V465 2021 (print) | LCC RC317.14 (ebook) |
DDC 362.19699/500954—dc23
LC record available at https://lccn.loc.gov/2021009365
LC ebook record available at https://lccn.loc.gov/2021009366

This book is freely available in an open access edition thanks to TOME (Toward
an Open Monograph Ecosystem)—a collaboration of the Association of American
Universities, the Association of University Presses, and the Association of Research
Libraries—and the generous support of Arcadia, a charitable fund of Lisbet Rausing
and Peter Baldwin, and the UCLA Library. Learn more at the TOME website, available
at:openmonogr aphs.org.

Awarded the Joseph W. Elder Prize in the Indian Social Sciences by the American
Institute of Indian Studies and published with the Institute's generous support.
AIIS Publication Committee: Susan S. Wadley, Co-chair; Anand A. Yang, Co-chair;
Deborah Hutton; Diane Mines; Ramnarayan S Rawat; Tulasi Srinivas

For Patti and Thatha

CONTENTS

This is a book about how we imagine cure, and how cure comes up against its limits. It is a book about the unexpected shapes and even more unexpected peregrinations of science and medicine. And it is, finally, a book about tuberculosis treatment in India.

It's ironic—and, as I've come to realize, entirely fitting—that a book about curative imaginations has its origins in the incurable. In 2006, I began to investigate the vexing influence of American philanthropy on HIV interventions in India. Despite the protestations of stalwart figures in public health and medical anthropology, HIV prevention and treatment continued to be viewed as separate sorts of activities.[1] Under the sway of McKinsey consultants, the Gates Foundation gambled heavily that prevention was the right way to invest their fortune in India, given the high cost of treating an incurable condition. The provision of antiretroviral drugs was left to the state, and to the many medical practitioners who operated along the porous borders of government hospitals.

To begin to understand how treatment worked in India, I traveled in 2011 to the city of Chennai, where the first diagnoses of HIV in the country had been made twenty-five years earlier. I spent my days in a small HIV clinic with doctors and nurses as they deftly rounded the inpatient wards, and with counselors who offered reassuring catechisms to patients and their families. I learned patiently about treatment in this clinic and in other, larger, government-run facilities. I learned about a way of life, which was also a mode of survival, built around the idea of a normalcy attained and maintained through dogged adherence to antiretroviral drugs. I even wrote an article about it.[2]

1. Among those advocating for approaching prevention and treatment conjointly, perhaps most notable are Paul Farmer and Jim Kim of Partners in Health.

2. Venkat, "Scenes of Commitment."

Looking back, what strikes me now is the dissonance between a promise and its fulfillment. With the introduction of antiretrovirals, I was repeatedly told, HIV had become a livable, chronic condition. I could see that this was often the case. Even so, people died. I remember a man on a gurney, rolled one morning into the inpatient ward with great haste, comatose, his family clinging to the sides of his bed. By evening, he had passed away, his family still clinging, now wailing. Many patients came in these moments of extremis, otherwise resistant to the discipline demanded by the clinic. Many other patients died despite their strict discipline.

Other than the patients themselves, the usual culprit blamed for these deaths was tuberculosis, described to me as a particularly opportunistic infection. Patients were warned that they must maintain what was described in Tamil as their *noi ethirppu sakthi*: literally, a disease-opposing power, but used by physicians as a translation for "white blood cell count" or "immune system." Tuberculosis paid little regard to such power, manifesting even in patients who registered high white blood cell counts.

As I would learn, tuberculosis was in fact the most common cause of death for those with HIV.[3] At the time, I was baffled. Tuberculosis, I was repeatedly told by the doctors at the hospital, was eminently curable. Why, then, were patients dying from it? Here, too, a dissonance between promise and fulfillment. At the same time that my research was shifting to tuberculosis—to what was purportedly a curable condition—strains of the disease described as "totally drug resistant" started to appear in Mumbai and elsewhere. In many conversations I had across the country, people began wondering aloud whether they were now living in an India after antibiotics. Had tuberculosis, a seemingly curable condition, become incurable once again? If so, it hardly made sense to ask why people continued to die from a curable condition.[4]

This book represents my effort to sort through this ambivalence or near contradiction, an attempt to understand a condition that is sometimes curable and sometimes incurable, sometimes both, and sometimes not quite either. I stopped asking why people were dying from a curable condition, and I began to ask another question, one that is at the core of this book: what does it mean to be cured in the first place?

3. The inverse is not true: the majority of people with tuberculosis in India are not HIV positive.
4. And yet this is a question that many have asked and continue to ask, a question grounded in both a humanitarian moralism and a public health pragmatism.

In our present moment, tuberculosis is a particularly appropriate condition through which to think about cure precisely because its status as a curable condition has become increasingly suspect. Back in mid-twentieth-century India, as government-operated pharmaceutical factories began churning out the antibiotic streptomycin, it was prophesied that tuberculosis would soon become a thing of the past. In this sense, a curable disease was a disease waiting to become history.

Yet, in India today, tuberculosis is both history and present, and as many have pointed out, most likely also the future.[5] At the time of my fieldwork for this book, conducted primarily in the years between 2011 and 2016, there were estimated to be just under three million new cases of tuberculosis in India—about a quarter of all new cases worldwide, more than anywhere else in the world. During that period, the government reported about 400,000 deaths from the disease each year—the sixth leading cause of death in the country.[6] Looking beyond India, the World Health Organization has estimated that a third of the world's population harbors the bacteria that cause tuberculosis—what's referred to as latent tuberculosis—but only about a tenth of that number go on to develop active symptoms of the disease.[7]

5. As Christian McMillen puts it, "History's most deadly disease remains so in the present and very likely will remain so in the future." McMillen, *Discovering Tuberculosis*, 1.

6. World Health Organization, "Global Health Observatory Data Repository." Numerous commentators have noted that such numbers are reminiscent of Western Europe in the nineteenth and early twentieth centuries. Such comparisons, while common, foreclose as much as they reveal, fueling further diagnoses of India's backwardness, organized around a figure of universal history that is imagined to culminate in a hygienic utopia.

7. In India, about 40 percent of the population is estimated to have latent tuberculosis. In general, people do not know that they have latent tuberculosis. It operates more as an epidemiological category than as a clinical or experiential one. At present, latent cases are not pursued, as physicians wait for symptomatic patients to appear at clinics and hospitals (what is often described as "passive case finding"). I was told by government physicians and bureaucrats that treating patients who are asymptomatic—who are not (yet) sick—is a poor use of limited resources. Yet the divide between latent and active tuberculosis is porous, as a latent condition might nevertheless produce effects in the body, and might eventually manifest in active symptoms (at present, it remains exceedingly difficult if not impossible to predict who will develop active tuberculosis). For this reason, the persistence of a latent reservoir of infection ensures the failure of any efforts toward eradication predicated on treating only active cases. As Erin Koch puts it, "Latency is not a biological state, but one that emerges through human-microbe social relationships. In some ways, the 'active'

Despite its global enormity, the uneven distribution and visibility of tuberculosis mean that it remains for many both vanquished and forgotten, not only curable but—having been relegated to other people in other places and times—practically eradicated.[8] But as cases of tuberculosis pop up in places where it had been thought banished (in Paris and Berlin, for example) and as drug resistance traverses bodies and oceans (as in the case of a traveler from India arriving at Chicago O'Hare Airport), tuberculosis has resurfaced as a problem for Europe and North America.[9]

Telling the story this way, in terms of a disease of the past that returns from elsewhere, risks trapping us in an entrenched pattern of thinking about both geography and history.[10] In the pages that follow, ethnography and history meet film, folklore, and fiction to tell a story that stretches from the colonial period—a time of sanatoria, travel cures, and gold therapy—into the postcolonial present, in which eugenicist concerns dovetail uneasily with antibiotic miracles. I began to turn to history in a former tuberculosis sanatorium on the outskirts of Chennai, one that teetered on the brink of existence with the rise of antibiotics before finally regaining a sense of purpose in the 1980s as a treatment center for HIV. Now, the former sanatorium treats patients harboring TB-HIV coinfections as well those with drug-resistant variants of either condition. When I arrived at Tambaram Sanatorium, as it is popularly known, I still intended to write a monograph on HIV treatment, grounded in the ethnographic present of my experience. But I couldn't shake this curiosity about where the sanatorium had come from, and none of the physicians I met there could satiate my curiosity. This was not the Swiss Alps. There was no *Magic Mountain* to behold.

My curiosity led me to the Tamil Nadu State Archives and Roja Muthiah Research Library in Chennai, and then to the National Library in Kolkata, and later to the India Office Records of the British Library in London. I would learn

---

and 'latent' opposition suggests a false—or at least a forced—dichotomy that obscures the ways in which the microbe, the social context, and the body are all 'in motion.'" Koch, *Free Market Tuberculosis*, 192.

8. For example: each year, there are estimated to be approximately nine thousand new cases of tuberculosis in the United States and about five hundred deaths. These numbers suggest one reason why tuberculosis has largely fallen off the radar of both US-focused health researchers and the broader American public, as compared, for example, to a seemingly ubiquitous condition like cancer.

9. On the idea of tuberculosis as a disease banished from Europe and returned as a revenant, see Kehr, "Blind Spots and Adverse Conditions of Care"; Kehr, "Une Maladie sans Avenir"; Kehr, "The Precariousness of Public Health"; Kehr, "'Exotic No More.'"

10. On other places as metonymic of other (past) times, see Fabian, *Time and the Other*.

about the founder of Tambaram Sanatorium, David Chowry Muthu, a Tamil Christian tuberculosis specialist with a handlebar mustache and a hatred of alcohol, and I would track down his descendants in India, Britain, and the United States by following the flourishing branches of the many new sites of internet genealogy. Eventually, I would find myself in the graveyard in Bangalore where Muthu had been buried. What began with Muthu quickly became an exploration of the many pasts that have yielded our present conjuncture, an India where tuberculosis and its treatments are more than ghostly remains.

What follows then is less a straightforward ethnographic monograph and more an anthropological history.[11] In both archives and clinics, I worked with an eye to stories that told me something about what it meant to cure tuberculosis. My experiences as an ethnographer could not help but influence how I approached these stories, but they could not shape it wholesale. Sometimes I discovered threads that connected past to present—for example, in the founding of Tambaram Sanatorium—but as my research progressed I was often left with loose ends. Not every past forms part of a history of the present—at least, not in a way that is concrete, genealogical, or causal. Sometimes a story just ends. Sometimes a story refuses, as Nietzsche would insist, to serve the needs of the present. Sometimes a story wants to stay small—neither brilliant nor banal, neither scalable nor representative, but simply singular.[12]

As I've tarried with these stories, they've taught me how to write them, as well as how to read them. Much of this book tends toward a diegetic mode of presentation, one that might have all too easily been papered over by the will to explain, to theorize. For this reason, the theorizing in this book—like cure itself—is fragile, an extended meditation that dissipates as it travels rather

11. My approach to history is deeply influenced by the focus within subaltern studies on minor histories (as found in the work of Gautam Bhadra and Sumit Sarkar, for example), the strong attention to singular figures in microhistories (exemplified by the work of Carlo Ginzburg and many others since), and the questioning by anthropologists of how the past becomes (or fails to become) history (in the work, for example, of Michel-Rolph Trouillot, Ann Stoler, Michael Lambek, Brian Axel, and Mareike Winchell, among many others too numerous to list).

12. Here, my thinking is inspired by the historian Projit Mukharji's discussion of the contrast between metaphysics and pataphysics: "Metaphysics attempts to explain the world and being in terms of the universal and the particular; pataphysics, a term coined by Alfred Jarry, on the other hand, seeks to extrapolate a science of the singular, the unrepeatable and the exceptional. Metaphysics seeks out regularities and explanations; pataphysics seeks out exceptions and limits to explicability." Mukharji, *Doctoring Traditions*, 286.

than a definitive diagnosis that holds fast across space and time. It is a kind of theory that emerges from narrative description, from the juxtaposition of scenes, and from allowing oneself to be lost, at least for a time, in a sanatorium at the foothills of the Himalayas, on a coolie ship returning from a South African plantation, or in a hectic research hospital near the Mumbai coastline—in other words, in the imagination of cure.

The Incurability of Fantasy

All existence is an imagination within an imagination.
—Ibn al-'Arabi, *The Bezels of Wisdom*

The Beginning of the End

In August 1953, a rather immodest proposal introduced into the upper house of the Indian parliament called for the sterilization of those suffering from incurable conditions—and, in particular, tuberculosis. In the debates that followed, a parliamentarian from Madras cautioned that tuberculosis was fast "becoming a curable disease" with the use of new wonder drugs like streptomycin, an antibiotic developed half a world away.[1]

His words rang like prophecy: just a few years later, Madras was to become the site of a major study testing the efficacy of antibiotics for treating tuberculosis. In the wake of the study, sanatoria the world over would shut their doors. Cure—in the form of antibiotics—could now be delivered to the masses. Tuberculosis, a disease that had plagued humanity for millennia, had finally become curable and, with time, perhaps eradicable.

---

1. Rajya Sabha Official Debates, "Resolution Regarding Sterilisation," 556.

The Wrong Kind of End

In December 2011, reports began to pour out of Mumbai of patients suffering from a kind of tuberculosis caused by strains of bacteria resistant to all standard treatments.

By many accounts, the curable had once again become incurable.

Was this the end of the antibiotic era?

That Monstrous Indian Imagination

To study the history of cure is to be confronted at every turn by the imagination. In 1861, the English biologist and naturalist Charles Darwin described the imagination as our ability to combine "images and ideas, independently of the will, and thus creat[e] brilliant and novel results."[2] Imagination, he insisted, was a powerful but unconscious force, one that operated most prominently in the work of dreams. The value of the imagination depended on our conscious capacity to sort through these syntheses, to utilize our reason—for Darwin, the highest of the human faculties—to select certain combinations of images and ideas while forcefully rejecting others that threatened to mislead. To fail to exercise proper discernment was to risk ending up, he warned, like those "superstitious" dogs that bay at the moon, creatures entirely at the whim of their unruly imaginations.[3] Despite the prominent role that he attributed to reason, science for Darwin was a powerfully imaginative enterprise, one that metabolized the world and imbued it with ever greater form, force, and connectivity.[4]

Darwin's vision of the imagination finds an unexpected antecedent in the philosophy of history proposed by the German philosopher G. W. F. Hegel, for whom India was a "land of imaginative aspiration, and appears to us still as a Fairy region, an enchanted World."[5] Imagination, for Hegel, was a necessary but less evolved form assumed by Reason, one that entranced the Indian into

2. Darwin, *The Descent of Man*, vol. 1, 106.

3. Darwin, *The Descent of Man*, vol. 1, 107. Drawing on Houzeau, Darwin notes that dogs are unable to clearly discern what is on the horizon, and therefore "conjure up before them fantastic images" to satisfy their "disturbed" imaginations. Darwin, *The Descent of Man*, vol. 1, 108.

4. On the role of the scientist's imagination in the formation of ideas, see Holton, *The Scientific Imagination*.

5. Hegel, *Lectures on the Philosophy of History*, 139. On Hegel's vision of India, see Hegel, *On the Episode of the Mahabharata*. For an analysis of how Hegel's view fit into a longer tradition of imagining India in the West, see Inden, *Imagining India*.

an immoral disregard of the distinction between self and world. Without a sense of an external reality in which to act, there could for Hegel be only repetition, but no change. And without change, there could be no history: India, he wrote, "has remained stationary and fixed," enraptured, like Darwin's baying dogs, by its own "monstrous, irrational imagination."[6]

For Darwin, imagination required the controlling power of reason to generate novel insight. For Hegel, imagination was at best an unevolved form of reason, one particularly at home in the antihistorical "dream-world" of India.[7] Yet there were other imaginations of imagination that flourished in India—for example, in the thirteenth-century philosophy of the Muslim theologian, mystic, and poet Ibn al-'Arabi, whose words were studied and debated by generations of Indian Sufis. Ibn al-'Arabi taught that "the Imagination deals only in what is sensible."[8] The sensible world, he maintained, was but a manifestation of God, a dream accessible to us only through the synthesis of reason ('aql) and imagination (khayâl). For Ibn al-'Arabi, and contrary to both Hegel and Darwin, imagination was neither opposed to the world nor subservient to reason. Rather than a flight of fantasy away from the sensible world, imagination was instead a path toward it.

A distinct but complementary way of conceiving of the relationship between the imagination and the sensible world can be found in the south Indian Sanskrit tradition of the sixteenth century, in which the imagination (bhāvanā) "can be said to see what is there as it was imagined and, by so seeing and knowing it, to enhance what is there so that there is now more there. In this sense, imagination does create newness. . . . It is not the original image that the imagination finds but, through the finding, something much fuller, something the imagination has itself driven to the surface and then shaped and deepened by seeing or reimagining it."[9] Within this tradition, to imagine is a process of ripening the world that draws on our capacities to recognize, remember, and reshape the stuff in it. Insofar as cure is a mode of responding to an imperfect world, it is one that depends on these capacities to recognize how things are, remember how they might have been, and shape how they might yet be. Understood in this way, to enter into the imagination of cure is not, as Hegel might have it, to freeze time, but rather to attend to the many forms that time might assume.

6. Hegel, *Lectures on the Philosophy of History*, 139, 147.
7. Hegel, *Lectures on the Philosophy of History*, 148.
8. Al-'Arabi, *The Bezels of Wisdom*, 122.
9. Shulman, *More Than Real*, 261.

Take, for example, Rudyard Kipling, a prominent writer of empire at the turn of the twentieth century. The ubiquity of tuberculosis in England under both Victoria and Edward spilled over into much of his prose. And as an Englishman born in imperial Bombay, Kipling would retain his imagination of India in the worlds that he forged through his stories. In 1909, over a hundred years before our threatened descent into an India after antibiotics—and over half a century before streptomycin arrived on Indian shores—Kipling published "With the Night Mail." An early work of science fiction, his story unfolds in a future in which humanity has taken to the sky in giant airships floating high above the highest hills.[10] In the following scene, two of the crewmen aboard a mail transport ship reflect on the workings of history, and on a history long past (but one that is entirely present to Kipling the writer):

> "Funny how the new things are the old things. I've read in books," Tim answered, "that savages used to haul their sick and wounded up to the tops of hills because microbes were fewer there. We hoist 'em into sterilized air for a while. Same idea. How much do the doctors say we've added to the average life of a man?"
>
> "Thirty years," says George with a twinkle in his eye. "Are we going to spend 'em all up here, Tim?"[11]

In the exchange between Tim and George, we see the dogged persistence and malleability of a certain curative imagination. Kipling's lifetime roughly maps onto the period when bacteriological thinking was on the rise, buoyed along by Robert Koch's discovery of a microbial cause for tuberculosis. In the light cast by this imagination of a world suffused with microbes, the colonial hill station, the sanatorium, and other elevated sites of healing did not disappear.[12]

---

10. The relationship between social science (in particular, cultural anthropology) and science fiction (or social science fiction) has been elaborated by Diane Nelson in her essay on Amitav Ghosh's *The Calcutta Chromosome*. In the last line of her essay, she concludes: "Social science fiction is itself a pharmakon, a poison and a cure, a threat and a promise, a warning sign and a how-to guide for postcolonial new humans." If I could steal this line as a description for my book, I would. Nelson, "A Social Science Fiction," 262.

11. Kipling, "With the Night Mail," 333.

12. On the idea of a social reconfigured by the arrival of microbes, see Latour, *The Pasteurization of France*.

INTRODUCTION

Instead, they were refigured by Kipling as sites of "sterilized air" where microbes struggled to survive and humans might thrive.[13]

Looking into the future—"With the Night Mail" takes place in the year 2000—what Kipling imagined was not something like antibiotics but rather a further mutation of the tuberculosis sanatorium, elevated from the hills up into the air. His character, Tim, is struck by the sameness of the new, how the most cutting-edge and novel represents nothing more than a modification of the past, transposed from one therapeutic scene (the hill) to another (the airship).

In reading Kipling's story today, I wondered: what made it possible for Tim to see these airships as simply a refinement of a historical form of therapy rather than a break or rupture, a new form of curative imagination entirely? Or, to take a further step back, what made it possible for Kipling to square bacteriological ideas about disease causation with what went on in hilltop sanatoria? The curative imagination of Kipling's characters—and of Kipling himself—is one in which therapeutic forms survive across time by incorporating "images and ideas" drawn from the sensible world.[14] The past is neither refused nor overcome but constantly refurbished for a new age.

A central contention of this book is that *our imagination of cure shapes our understanding of time*: not only the temporality underlying histories of science and medicine—as we see in Kipling's story—but also the temporality of therapy itself. The two are in fact connected. In our moment, cure is frequently taken to be an ending—to illness, treatment, and suffering more generally. If cure is an ending, then a history of cure (or of a curable disease) is more often than not a history of how we came to that ending.[15] We might think back to the optimistic words of the critic Susan Sontag that first appeared in 1977: "the fantasies inspired by TB in the last century . . . are responses to a disease thought to be intractable and capricious—that is, a disease not understood—in an era in which medicine's central premise is that all diseases can be cured."[16] Medicine in the nineteenth century, according to Sontag, was no better than the baying of dogs at moonlight—the unruly product of an imagination deprived of the

---

13. On the persistence of older ways of understanding disease causality in the face of germ theory, see Worboys, *Spreading Germs*.

14. Darwin, *The Descent of Man*, vol. 1, 106.

15. This helps to explain, at least in part, why we have so many histories of tuberculosis and relatively fewer anthropological studies (although this seems to be changing).

16. Sontag, *AIDS and Its Metaphors*, 5.

guidance of reason. In what we might think of as Sontag's imagination of cure, incurability was primarily a problem of ignorance, what Sontag tried to capture with the word *fantasy*. Such fantasies, Sontag suggested, dissipated once tuberculosis became properly known and therefore curable.

Yet over roughly the last two centuries there has been no shortage of cures for tuberculosis. The antibiotic cure is only one among many, a cure whose future has become increasingly uncertain with the spread of drug resistance. While Kipling glimpsed a future that was, quite literally, an elevation of his present, Sontag looked instead to a past and denigrated its forms of knowledge as pathological fantasy. Their contrasting visions suggest that our imagination of cure—and of historical time—directs our thinking about what counts as proper knowledge, as well as the forms of research and evidentiary production that properly undergird such knowledge. What Sontag overlooked was that medical knowledge in the late twentieth century, when she was writing, was itself a kind of fantasy—dependent on its own imagination of what it meant to be cured. Even today, the complex world-spanning choreography of clinical trials and pharmaceutical research continues to depend on a specific imagination of what sorts of conditions (and what kinds of people) require cure, and how we know whether a cure works.[17] Put simply, the idea that fantasy ever disappears is itself fantastical. It is, in a word, incurable.

How we conceive of the history of cure, as well as what we count as proper research and proper knowledge in the present, delimits the kinds of questions we can ask moving forward and the kinds of ends we can pursue. The imagination is a collective "field of action," one that both draws from the world and transforms it.[18] Within the curative imagination articulated by Sontag, one in which we have finally arrived at proper knowledge of tuberculosis, we might feel an ethical injunction to ask: why do so many people continue to die of a curable condition?[19] The fact of curability is given, a fait accompli rather than

17. On the organization and ethics of transnational clinical trials, see Petryna, *When Experiments Travel*. In the context of India, see Sunder Rajan, "Experimental Values," 67–88. See also Sunder Rajan, "The Experimental Machinery of Global Clinical Trials," 1–55. On the priorities of big pharma, see Dumit, *Drugs for Life*.

18. Benjamin, *The New Jim Code*.

19. The question of why people die of curable conditions, by its very framing, is an unequivocal indictment: someone is to blame. When I first asked myself, and others around me, this question, I was naive enough not to understand that. It speaks to the generosity of the doctors with whom I worked in India that they understood my question in its naïveté, rather than as an accusation meant to highlight their own failures. I had witnessed, for example, multiple episodes during which an Indian American

something to be turned over, examined, and studied in its own right. To begin to ask different questions, we have to stretch our imagination of what cure might be, how it might work, and what it might mean. In other words, we must begin to imagine cure otherwise.

If, as Sontag would have it, the history of medicine is a movement away from fantasy and toward greater enlightenment, then it is an irony that a book about tuberculosis must explain the disease to an audience that might be unfamiliar with it.[20] In India today, as elsewhere, tuberculosis is most commonly diagnosed in its pulmonary form—that is to say, in the lungs—but can appear in various parts of the body, from the spine to the brain to the genitals

———

medical student, who was on fellowship at one of the hospitals where I worked, pointed out the shortcomings of the hospital's infrastructure and its staff, seemingly with little grasp of the underlying situation. The hospital staff responded with a great deal of forbearance. Nevertheless, some of the physicians with whom I worked had their own answer to this question: they blamed the patient, or more broadly, the backward culture of the patient. The medical anthropologist and physician Paul Farmer has consistently worked to turn the question back onto the medical community. Reflecting on his work in Haiti, he writes:

> We encountered no shortage of silliness—again, immodest claims of causality—among people attempting to explain, without alluding to the concept of neglect, why so many people died in places like Haiti from an eminently treatable disease such as tuberculosis. The ranking explanation among Haitian and certain non-Haitian health professionals was that the peasants believed in sorcery and thus had no confidence in biomedicine. We learned, instead, that rural Haitians had no access to biomedicine and that they did just fine, regardless of their views on disease etiology, once we fixed the dysfunctional tuberculosis program. What needed to change was not the cultural beliefs of the patients but rather the quality of the tuberculosis program—and with it, perhaps, the cultural beliefs of part of the medical community. (Farmer, *AIDS and Accusation*, xvii)

Farmer succeeded in reversing the direction of the indictment, by linking the problem of failure to the quality of healthcare provision, to bureaucratic neglect, and to the culture of medicine more generally. For a similar view from an Indian tuberculosis clinic, see Das, *Affliction*.

20. One might object that Sontag was not a professional historian. Certainly, but her work has enjoyed a much broader reach than that of most historians, and for that reason, it reveals how a specific curative imagination shapes ideas about the history of medicine more widely. And of course, even some professional historians of medicine, and of tuberculosis specifically, continue to operate from the vantage of present-day enlightenment.

and kidneys.[21] The possibility of cure has regularly been thought to depend on knowing the underlying cause of a disease. Our present-day understanding of tuberculosis as a unitary, bacterial disease emerged from contentious etiological debates in the late nineteenth and early twentieth centuries that stretched from Berlin to Madras. Through these debates, *tuberculosis* began to refer to a condition brought on by an infection with any bacteria that are part of the *Mycobacterium tuberculosis* complex, regardless of where in the body it takes root, or for that matter, the kind of body in which it appears (European or otherwise, human or not).[22] In place of symptoms (wasting, tubercles), the contemporary classification of tuberculosis is organized around cause. But as I've already suggested, Koch's announcement in 1882 that tuberculosis was engendered by bacteria did not dispel the sense that its causes were primarily environmental, an etiology affirmed by the persistence of sanatorium-based forms of treatment. The shift to construing cause in narrowly bacteriological terms required the emergence of powerful antibiotics in the early to mid-twentieth century. In this sense, the way in which we imagine cure might just as well be said to shape how we conceive of disease and its causes. To put it another way, our understandings of a disease and its causes are consolidated alongside our imaginations of cure.[23] And in the absence of new imaginations of cure, new ideas about disease causality might at best be incorporated into older understandings of causality, or potentially ignored entirely.[24]

21. As Bryder, Condrau, and Worboys have noted, there is a serious dearth of historical (and anthropological) studies of nonpulmonary forms of the disease, undoubtedly related to the fact that such forms are harder to diagnose and more easily confused with other conditions like cancer. Bryder, Condrau, and Worboys, "Tuberculosis and Its Histories," 3.

22. The most common way in which these bacteria are thought to be transmitted is through inhaling what someone else has expelled from their body, usually through coughing, sneezing, or spitting. But these bacteria can also travel in other ways: for example, through injection, as is the case with animals used in experiments. On tuberculosis in nonhuman animals in India, see Venkat, "Iatrogenic Life."

23. In his history of malaria, Rohan Deb Roy similarly argues that "knowledge about a cure and a disease-causing entity, to a considerable extent, shaped one another. In fact, it is not entirely implausible to think about situations in which knowledge about cinchona and quinine preceded, and effected crucial shifts in the history of malaria." Deb Roy, *Malarial Subjects*, 276.

24. The historian Michael Worboys has made a related point, that new ideas of causation did not simply displace older ones, but rather assimilated them. See Worboys, *Spreading Germs*.

Tuberculosis, and the fantasies it has inspired, has not gone away, even if many of its cures have. Perhaps its most powerful fantasy has been that of its end: the fantasy of a cure for tuberculosis, once and for all. As we observe the spread of drug resistance, we are faced with the question of what happens when the curable becomes incurable. When the history of cure is no longer simply the history of how we arrived at an ending, we can end up with what looks like a pendular history, in which we return, as I was told during my fieldwork, "to the dark ages"—that is to say, a time before antibiotic enlightenment. The idea of return is at the center of an imagination of cure grounded in lack or loss. For that reason, it is also, if often implicitly, at the center of medical anthropology, a field that examines the "culturally constructed ways in which various people experience ill health and find ways to 'get back to where they were' before the onset of disease, illness, or pain."[25]

The idea of return has a long genealogy in the history of anthropology, in which cure has what might be thought of as a social function: to normalize the deviant or abnormal subject, to reincorporate them into the social or symbolic order. Much of this work—frequently focused on magical or shamanistic healing—assumes a conservative imagination of cure, one that operates through a return to preexisting norms.[26] Such a vision of therapy has its uses, as a promise that things might be as they once were, that disorder, disruption,

---

25. Alter, "Heaps of Health, Metaphysical Fitness." Alter is less interested in how people return to "where they were" and more in how they become something else, something potentially superhuman. Relatedly, Todd Meyers suggests that, following Canguilhem, we might make a distinction between cure and healing: whereas cure has a sense of return or restoration dependent on external criteria, healing is an opening that allows for the laying down of new norms. Meyers, *The Clinic and Elsewhere*, 9.

26. Returning to a preexisting norm might not always mean returning to the same norm that one had previously inhabited. Cure might instead entail the inhabitation of a preexisting norm that is nevertheless new to you. A telling example of this form of thinking can be found in the work of the French anthropologist Jeanne Favret-Saada. In the 1970s, she conducted fieldwork among peasants in the Bocage region of France. In this region, she argued, witchcraft was a kind of "remedial institution," one that granted bewitched male farmers an opportunity to acquire the violent norms of French peasant masculinity that they had failed to learn in their previous roles as sons subservient to their fathers. Cure, in this sense, was the adoption of those adult male norms specific to the Bocage. This is less of a return to one's previous norms than the adoption of the norms appropriate to a new status, one that parallels what Michael Taussig described when he wrote, in regard to Latin American shamanism, that "the cure is to become a curer." Taussig, *Shamanism, Colonialism, and the Wild Man*, 447. In

or pathology might be remedied by the reestablishment of a preexisting social and biological order. By contrast, a vision of history as return has quite different uses, as a dire warning to the present about an apocalyptic future that resembles a dark past, or as a means of culling lessons from that history in order to shape a dramatically different future.

But therapy and history only appear pendular if we assume that we return to where we began: that to be cured is to be restored to a previous state of health, and that for a condition to become incurable throws us back to an earlier moment, for example, before the ascendance of antibiotics. Yet the ends of cure, and the ends of history, are not so neatly satisfied. Rather than restoring a previously existing set of norms, cure might be transformative—even revolutionary—in its open-endedness, acting to elaborate, widen, or even overthrow existing norms.[27]

------

the Bocage, then, we might say that the cure is to become a man. See Favret-Saada, *Deadly Words*.

27. Questions of norm and status were taken up quite differently—even radically—by scholars of race, gender, sexuality, and disability, many of whom took inspiration from the anthropologist Ruth Benedict and, in particular, from her short essay titled "Anthropology and the Abnormal," *Journal of General Psychology* 10, no. 1 (1934): 59–82 (for an example of this kind of lineage making, see Staples and Mehotra, "Disability Studies," 35–49). In this work, Benedict suggested that the problem posed to society by divergence from the norm might be remedied by a widening of the cultural pattern rather than a disciplining of the abnormal. In other words, social norms might become more capacious, more embracing.

To further elaborate Benedict's own examples, the problem was not non-normativity; the real problem was a form of society, a certain set of political arrangements, and an economic system that made life potentially unlivable (or at least exceedingly difficult) for those who failed to approximate a certain normative ideal. The problem was not disability but rather a lack of accessibility. The problem was not homosexuality but rather a narrow definition of what counts as appropriate desire. The problem was not schizophrenia but rather the crushing weight of discrimination. Such an argument is activist and political, and, to my mind, very much in line with Benedict's vision of redesigning society and producing social change. On the idea of redesign in Benedict, see Modell, *Ruth Benedict*.

The aim then would be to cure society, rather than the individual. Here, the form of cure that emerges is not remedial but rather transformative, acting not on persons but rather on cultural norms. This position might be identified, for example, with the early work of the scholar of disability and activist Eli Clare, who questions a structure of curative expectation in which life in the present is sacrificed for a future to come. For Clare, the narrowly individuated cure of disability is genocidal, an effort to eradicate difference and, in the process, to eradicate the kinds of communities that have emerged on the basis of these differences. On the future-oriented temporal-

Just as one cure is not quite the same as another—in substance, in therapeutic mode, in its distribution and effects, in the kinds of ethical questions it raises, and in the ways in which it is conceived of in its moment (and in our own)— neither is one form of incurability the same as another. What this means is that the incurable is not simply the mirror opposite of the curable, but rather an effect of how we imagine cure in the first place. And if our ideas of cure can change, so too can our ideas of the incurable. Asking about what it means to be cured, and what it means to be incurable, might make it possible to halt the pendulum-swing of therapy, and of history—or at the very least to think critically about what is at stake when we conceive of the conjoined temporalities of therapy and history as pendular at all. The more general point is that how we think about the curable and the incurable shapes how we conceive of history, and of time more generally. This book then offers an anthropological history, by which I mean I approach history itself as an effect of the curative imagination rather than as an explanation for it.

In a World of Pure Kipling

Anthropologists are fond of arrival stories. Let me tell you one—not mine, but that of Edward Selby Phipson, who arrived in India as a physician but became, to the best of my knowledge, the first anthropologist to study tuberculosis in India. Born in Birmingham in 1884 to a family of painters and businessmen, Phipson completed his medical training in 1908 and enlisted in the Indian Medical Service. He was moved every few years, experiencing the far reaches of the Indian colony, which in that moment stretched from Burma in the east to Aden in the west.[28] In 1937, as Aden shed its dependency on India, Phipson was reassigned

---

ity of curative promises, see Kim, *Curative Violence*; Clare, *Brilliant Imperfection*; and Clare, *Exile and Pride*. Relatedly, but in a very different place and time, Frantz Fanon struggled with the near impossibility of psychiatric cure in Algeria in the face of continuing colonial violence. For Fanon, individual cure could not take place without a transformation of the social order. See Fanon, "Colonial War and Mental Disorders."

28. In Burma, Phipson served as deputy sanitary commissioner. During World War I, he found himself in Gallipoli, where, after the death or incapacitation of many British officers, he found that he was the only Britisher left standing with the language skills required to command the 156th Gurkha Rifles over two days of fighting. After the war, he was invalided to India, where he was first appointed assistant medical officer of health in Bombay, and then health officer in Simla, a post that he held for five years. In 1923, he was relocated to Aden, where he served as the port health officer.

to Assam, a region in the northeastern corner of the Indian colony, where he was promoted to colonel and assigned to the post of inspector-general of civil hospitals.

This is where our story begins, in an Assam contending with British efforts at pacification and control. As a physician, an administrator, and gentleman scholar, Phipson was an integral part of this colonial apparatus. He had a reputation for linguistic virtuosity (if obituaries are to be believed, he spoke Urdu, Burmese, Pashtu, Gurkhali, French, German, and Italian) as well as for acting and stagecraft (honed as a participant in an amateur theater group). He lived, as a colleague put it, "in a world of pure Kipling."[29] Such a world was one drawn from the experience of India and filtered through the optics of empire.

Like his compatriot Kipling, Phipson became engrossed by the problem of tuberculosis. He wanted to learn how the tribal peoples of Assam understood the causes of the disease, and what (if anything) they thought could cure it. The spark for his curiosity had likely traveled from British Africa, as anthropological methods and knowledge flowed across colonial networks. In 1930, just a few years before Phipson arrived in Assam, the British Medical Council put together what it called a "Draft Scheme for a Tuberculosis Survey in an African Community," which incorporated both ethnographic and historical approaches to determine the extent of the disease as well as native beliefs about it. The Colonial Development Fund, which supported the draft scheme, surmised that it was "through the sympathetic adaptation of native ideas and methods to the uses of modern hygiene, rather than by the abrupt substitution of European regulations for native customs, that success is most likely to be attained."[30] As we will see, Phipson's strategies paralleled those of his colleagues working in colonial Africa.

Another possible inspiration for Phipson's approach might be found in the work of the British social anthropologist Edward Evan Evans-Pritchard, who published his magnum opus on witchcraft just two years before Phipson arrived in Assam.[31] Based on his doctoral research on the Zande people of north central Africa, conducted in the mid-1920s, Evans-Pritchard's *Witchcraft, Oracles and Magic among the Azande* has become a classic text for thinking through forms of explanation that diverge from natural or physical causality. According to Evans-Pritchard, the Zande frequently explained what he thought of as unfortunate coincidence in terms of witchcraft. This mode of explanation

29. Wolstenholme, "Colonel E. S. Phipson," 720.
30. McMillen, *Discovering Tuberculosis*, 42.
31. Evans-Pritchard, *Witchcraft, Oracles and Magic among the Azande*.

provided a meaningful causal agent, the witch, against whom a stereotyped response might be enacted, either to exact retribution or to facilitate cure.[32]

The critical question for Phipson was whether tribal groups in Assam believed that tuberculosis could be transmitted from one person to another. If the fact of communicability was "embodied in or at least not obviously at variance with tribal beliefs," Phipson wrote, then it might be possible to encourage these groups to act scientifically without realizing it.[33] Put another way, he believed that science might be hidden beneath what he described as the "extraneous trappings of superstition and ignorance."[34] Phipson's goal was to persuade the Assamese people to behave the right (scientific) way, even if it was for the wrong (religious, magical, or superstitious) reasons. He believed, along with his colleagues in Africa, that rationally appearing behavior might be produced even in the absence of an entirely rational belief system.[35]

32. Evans-Pritchard's work prefigured and in many cases directly influenced generations of anthropologists concerned with understanding the rationality of peasants, particularly in the era of postwar development. For example, in 1955, a young anthropology student at Harvard University, Edward Wellin, was recruited by the Rockefeller Foundation to travel to Peru as part of an assignment with the Peruvian Ministry of Public Health. His task was to evaluate the work of a team of hygiene visitors who had been working in Los Mollinos, in the foothills of the Andes. Wellin wanted to find a specific behavior of the local people that might serve as an index of the efficacy of these hygiene visitors. He chose to study the boiling of water. Wellin would argue that to improve public health—in this case, to increase the rates of water boiling—you needed to understand local forms of reasoning. The residents of Los Mollinos might be convinced to boil their water, but might not be convinced by the kinds of reasons that mattered to public health experts. See Wellin, "Water Boiling in a Peruvian Town."

In the 1960s, at the height of what have come to be known as the rationality debates in the social sciences, modern scientific forms of reasoning became increasingly understood as situated, local, and at times provincial. Medical anthropologists in particular turned to the study of competing rationalities, perhaps most prominently in the work of the Harvard-based psychiatrist and anthropologist Arthur Kleinman, who, in the late 1980s, developed a typological distinction between disease (a biomedical diagnosis) and illness (a culturally mediated understanding and experience of that disease). As a result, the proper domain of medical anthropology became illness (rather than disease) and healing (rather than, for example, cure). See Kleinman, *The Illness Narratives.*

33. Phipson, *Tribal Beliefs concerning Tuberculosis,* 39.

34. Phipson, *Tribal Beliefs concerning Tuberculosis,* 38.

35. In his review of the history of medical anthropology, Lawrence Cohen has described this as a form of thinking that considered peasants to be acting *as if* they were rational when their actions served what was construed to be a useful social function,

The first step, however, was to understand what native peoples believed. The existence of some sort of idea of communicability represented, for Phipson, a "rational element in tribal beliefs," one that he hoped might come to "supersede the irrational."[36] He was convinced that the "basic principles of the management of tuberculosis could be grafted on to or interpolated between tribal beliefs, so as to avoid any serious clash between scientific truth and tribal superstitions."[37] Phipson hoped to use his findings to introduce propaganda among the tribes regarding the cause of the disease, as well as how it might be prevented and cured.

Although anthropology as a discipline had become professionalized in universities in Britain, the United States, and, to a lesser extent, France, it was still de rigueur for colonial administrators to engage in an amateur but nevertheless respectable kind of anthropological inquiry.[38] Around 1938, Phipson recruited British administrative officers from across Assam to collect ethnological information from local tribal groups.[39] His team unearthed a range of ideas about the disease. Tuberculosis, he learned, was thought to be the fruit of ancestral sin, passed down through generations; the result of a family member entering into the home of an enemy; the effect of a spell cast by a jealous sorcerer or a covetous neighbor; the penalty for murder or the killing of another's livestock; the price to be paid for eating prohibited food or drink or consuming dirt from a grave; a curse sent by spirits who had been improperly worshipped. Different groups in Assam used different words and focused on different symptoms.

This variability was not unique to India. *Phthisis*, a Greek term inherited from Hippocrates that remained popular into the early twentieth century, was a hereditary condition that rendered one constitutionally *phthisical*. The primary symptom was a body that wasted away, as if consumed by an internal flame. Both *phthisis* and *consumption* referred in general to a disease that had whole-body effects. What we now call *tuberculosis*, a term that originated in the nineteenth century but seems to have really taken off only in the twentieth, originally referred to the finding of tubercles, pale potato-like structures, in the

---

without the need for an underlying rational belief system. See Cohen, "Making Peasants Protestant and Other Projects."

36. Phipson, *Tribal Beliefs concerning Tuberculosis*, 49.

37. Phipson, *Tribal Beliefs concerning Tuberculosis*, 39.

38. On the history of amateur anthropology and the institutionalization of the discipline, see Kuklick, *The Savage Within*; Stocking, *After Tylor*; and Barth et al., *One Discipline, Four Ways*.

39. Phipson, *Tribal Beliefs concerning Tuberculosis*, 38.

lungs of those with the disease. For a time, it was not uncommon for physicians to speak of tuberculosis, consumption, and phthisis in the same breath. While there were efforts to draw clear lines between these and other conditions, many physicians would treat them as virtually synonymous.

Sometimes, potentially different conditions were deliberately superimposed: for example, in the writings of early twentieth-century compilers of Ayurvedic recipes, who maintained that the old Sanskrit term *kshayarogam* referred to the same condition that European physicians called phthisis or tuberculosis.[40] We might think of this as an innocent act of translation.[41] But in fact, kshayarogam could have been translated in many other ways, or simply described in terms of its causes, symptoms, and treatments. In superimposing these conditions, it became possible to say that European medicine and Ayurveda were in a way equivalent, sharing a common understanding of the body and the series of ways in which that body could be deranged. Moreover,

40. This act of translation, in which two conditions were rendered equivalent, required a further set of intellectual gymnastics. Medical conditions never travel alone. They carry with them ideas about the body, the world, and how everything works together, all of which also requires translation. See, for example, the debates surrounding the translation of germ theory into Ayurveda in early twentieth-century Bengal in Mukharji, *Doctoring Traditions*, 169–76. On the history of the continuing encounter between biomedicine and Ayurveda, see Sivaramakrishnan, *Old Potions, New Bottles*; Wujastyk and Smith, *Modern and Global Ayurveda*. In a parallel case, Chinese practitioners of Western medicine in the early twentieth century translated germs as "wasting worms," an idiom drawn from the medical etiologies of the Qing dynasty. Andrews, "Tuberculosis and the Assimilation of Germ Theory in China."

This is not, however, to say that all aspects of science and medicine are infinitely translatable. In attempting to translate the core concepts involved in a randomized controlled trial to Tibetan subjects, for example, the absence of concepts like randomness (and the disposition to regard such matters in terms of fate) poses a limit to the malleability or recontextualization of divergent epistemologies within radically different understandings of the world. See Adams et al., "Informed Consent in Cross-Cultural Perspective."

41. The sociologist of science Bruno Latour disturbs the idea that there can be simple translation between past and present. He examines the case of Ramses II, who is said to have "died of tuberculosis." Latour argues that such a statement can make sense only through the coordination of specific knowledge, skills, and technologies belonging to the twentieth-century scientists who examined his mummy, thereby giving reality to his postmortem diagnosis. Latour's question is not whether the deceased died of tuberculosis, but rather for whom and under what conditions such a tuberculous death becomes meaningful (certainly not for Ramses II's coevals in Pharaonic Egypt). See Latour, "On the Partial Existence of Existing and Nonexisting Objects."

it became possible to claim that India's knowledge of tuberculosis had come first. If European medicine was held up as a standard, it was an anxious one that could be derided as old (Ayurvedic) wine in a new (European) bottle. This was, in a sense, an even deeper sorcery, of a particularly modern form that allowed anthropologists like Phipson to transmute enmity and jealousy, curses and ancestral sins, phthisis and kshayarogam, into the singular condition we call tuberculosis.[42]

The Magic of Juxtaposition

Phipson's research resulted in a study published by the Assam Government Press, with a generous foreword provided by an Oxford-educated anthropologist and colonial administrator named James Phillip Mills, who had written extensively on the Naga people of Assam.[43] In his foreword, Mills distilled from Phipson's findings a more abstract—and more academic—explanation for the perceived cause of tuberculosis among the Assamese tribes: the breaking of a taboo. According to Mills, the sense of identity between self, family, and clan among the Assamese meant that the effects of taboo breaking could spread from the original victim to their family and eventually to the larger group. As Mills put it, "Substitute 'tuberculosis' for 'magic' and it is clear wherein lie the hopes of successful propaganda against this terrible scourge."[44] As with the effects of magic, tuberculosis might be defended against, controlled, and maybe even defeated.

Mills's equation of magic and tuberculosis echoed the evolutionary theories proposed four decades earlier by the Scottish anthropologist James George

42. In other moments, conditions were deliberately held apart. See Bryder, "'Not Always One and the Same Thing.'" In the early twentieth century, for example, a diagnosis of tuberculosis could signal the death knell of a British soldier's career in India, with dire consequences for their state-granted benefits and pension. For this reason, colonial physicians frequently afforded soldiers less severe, more readily curable diagnoses, relying on the fact that many of the symptoms of tuberculosis were shared by other conditions (see chapter 2).

43. From 1913 to 1947, Mills served in the Indian Civil Service in northeast India, where he gathered the information for his several ethnographies of Naga groups throughout the region. Mills served as subdivisional officer at Mokokchung in the Naga Hills of Assam between 1917 and 1924 and deputy commissioner, based at Kohima, during the 1930s. In 1930, he was appointed as the honorary director of ethnography for Assam. In 1943, he was promoted to the position of advisor to the governor of Assam for tribal areas and states, with overall responsibility for tribal matters in northeast India.

44. Mills, foreword, 37.

Frazer, in which magic was a less evolved form of science. For Frazer, magic came in two varieties. The first, which he called imitative or homeopathic magic, operates through the principle of like affecting like, or action through resemblance—what Michael Taussig has described as the "magic of mimesis."[45] By contrast, contagious magic operates through the principle of previous contiguity or contact, through "the notion that things which have once been conjoined must remain ever afterwards, even when quite dissevered from each other, in such a sympathetic relation that whatever is done to the one must similarly affect the other."[46]

At the heart of either form of magic is what we might think of as an efficacy produced through juxtaposition: two things that resemble one another, or two things that were primordially connected but since separated, have an unshakable hold over one another. On both counts, we can understand how the effects of taboo breaking might spread through a family or clan, bound by kinship and perhaps also resemblance. But for Frazer—and we can see this line of thinking as it is inherited by Evans-Pritchard, Phipson, and Mills—the rationality underlying magic is in fact irrational, what he described as a "mistaken association of ideas."[47] This mistake became for both Mills and Phipson a convenient guise behind which scientific principles of disease management could be implemented. Rather than an obstacle to be overcome, native belief became a resource that could be put to use. If Assamese ideas about tuberculosis were, in Sontag's words, a fantasy, they were also, for colonial officials, a convenient and available one amenable to their own functionalist interpretations of culture.

Ironically, Frazer's method, which relied heavily on the juxtaposition of temporally and spatially separate phenomena—"snipping and combining similar customs from wildly scattered societies"—has faced over a century of criticism accusing him of falling prey to precisely the kind of mistaken associations that he described as foundational to magic.[48] The similarity between such phenomena is merely superficial, critics have alleged.[49] There is no real relation, no primordial association, no universal "grammar of the human soul."[50] Yet

45. Taussig, *Mimesis and Alterity*, 48. See also chapter 4 of his book more generally.
46. Frazer, *The Golden Bough*, 37.
47. Frazer, *The Golden Bough*, 37.
48. Graeber, "Remarks on Wittgenstein's Remarks on Frazer," 20.
49. Frazer also had his adherents, those who took inspiration from his work, in particular the surrealists, who in turn have inspired generations of anthropologists, including, for example, Claude Lévi-Strauss.
50. Graeber, "Remarks on Wittgenstein's Remarks on Frazer," 2.

both Frazer and his critics subscribed to a shared belief in something like an a priori true association between ideas and things. But they disagreed on which relations were true, and which were mistaken. Rather than contributing to such adjudications, my interest is instead in the kinds of effects produced by specific juxtapositions, as well as those that they preclude.

A powerful example of the effects of juxtaposition can be found in anthropological writings on what have been termed symbolic cures. Whereas biomedical cures might be thought to work through the manipulation of material connections—artery to heart, for example—symbolic cures operate through the manipulation of symbolic connections, which may or may not have a material substrate.[51] Let's take, for example, the work of the French anthropologist Claude Lévi-Strauss. In 1963, he published his famous analysis of a Cuna shamanic ritual (in Panama) performed in the event of difficult birth. In the course of the ritual, the shaman sings a complex incantation, a narrative of a great quest that allegorizes the challenges of childbirth and their overcoming:

> The sick woman believes in the myth and belongs to a society which believes in it. The tutelary spirits and malevolent spirits, the supernatural monsters and magical animals, are all part of a coherent system on which the native conception of the universe is founded. The sick woman accepts these mythical beings or, more accurately, she has never questioned their existence. What she does not accept are the incoherent and arbitrary pains, which are an alien element in her system but which the shaman, calling upon myth, will re-integrate within a whole where everything is meaningful.[52]

The song, stocked with a mythical menagerie, offers the woman a language for her otherwise incomprehensible pain. Cure, in this sense, is a return to meaning—the swing of the pendulum—made possible through the translation of the woman's pain into the symbolic order of her society. The effect of connecting what is otherwise an arbitrary and alienated pain with these mythical images from her society is to remove that arbitrariness. Critically, her pain has no necessary, a priori relationship to these images, although it might seem to be the case after the fact. Such relationships must be forged by the shaman,

---

51. On these varied forms of therapeutic manipulation, see Lévi-Strauss, "The Effectiveness of Symbols," 198–204.

52. Lévi-Strauss, "The Effectiveness of Symbols," 197.

who is a master of juxtaposition.[53] In connecting an image to her pain, it has become meaningful, and she is cured.

Taken a step further, juxtaposition might be understood as the method of cure writ large. And just as juxtaposition might be taken as the method of cure, it is also the method of this book. In the chapters that follow, I juxtapose scenes drawn from folklore, film, and fiction, as well as ethnographic and historical research, to forge associations and, more precisely, to create contexts. Scholars depend on a variety of well-trodden contexts to make sense of a given phenomenon or situation. For anthropologists, this has often been culture; for scholars of South Asia, religion or caste.[54] Such favored contexts can take on an aura of obvious relevance, so much so that the juxtapositions they require are obscured entirely.[55] To be clear, there is much to be understood by taking seriously such contexts, in discerning the twitch from the wink—and in fact, I frequently draw on these more routinized contexts (for example, the context of India, which constantly threatens to slip into a bounded national territory that doubles as an explanatory device).

But in returning again and again to our usual contexts to explain something, we risk explaining it away. Taken to the extreme, routinized contexts can overdetermine the meaning and signification of the thing to be explained. Through the process of contextualization, a life or event can become an example, effect, or symptom of something larger: a statistical or scholarly trend, a

---

53. This absence of necessity is undoubtedly in the eye of the beholder. It might just as well be said that the relationships forged by the shaman are in fact preexisting relationships that had been broken. As Gerald Bruns argues in his introduction to the Russian formalist Viktor Shklovsky's *Theory of Prose*, a poetic universe operates through the idea of a necessary connection between a thing in the world and the transcendental. Bruns, "Introduction," ix–xiv. By contrast, "a prose universe is just one damn thing after another, like an attic or junkyard or side of the road" (ix). This is a universe of arbitrariness. In the face of this arbitrariness, "the task of reason . . . is to bring things under control—not, however, by poeticizing them, not by allegorizing events into semantic superstructures (theories of chivalry, for example, or of culture), but rather by the construction of plots . . . whose operations do not so much abolish randomness as justify it" (x).

54. See Appadurai, "Theory in Anthropology"; Appadurai, "Is Homo Hierarchicus?"; Inden, *Imagining India*. See also Strathern, *Partial Connections*.

55. I'm reminded here of the words of Gregory Bateson, who teaches that "a story is a little knot or complex of that species of connectedness we call *relevance*." For Bateson, relevance is a property that emerges as a result of story, rather than a prior connection that is merely uncovered or underscored by story. Bateson, *Mind and Nature*, 13.

zeitgeist, a cultural norm.[56] Context can begin to appear as a kind of cure for the messiness of life. The danger, however, is that we succumb to a heavily territorialized form of thinking in which we confront a profoundly naturalized world that has already been carved up, leaving us only to accept our slices. Such a form of thinking is one in which we already know what matters and why, one in which we run the risk of extinguishing the singularity of life, of phenomena, and of experience.[57]

Certainly, a particular juxtaposition will open up specific lines of inquiry and occlude others.[58] But rather than ask which is the right juxtaposition, I wonder instead about what a particular juxtaposition illuminates. What kinds of juxtapositions might be vitalizing, because they force us to rethink taken-for-granted contexts and raise new questions? And what kinds of juxtapositions might lead us to predictable end points?[59] Or, as with Phipson and Mills, to the instrumental production of contexts that suit our own ends, that make the sense we require to fulfill our own ambitions? In writing this book, my aim has been instead to produce juxtapositions that jolt the senses. For this reason, this book was not written for the quick excerption of "theory," for the canny lifting of a term or phrase that can be laid down wherever you may go. The method of the book is a plea for a renewed attention to scholarly form, specifically, to the kinds of juxtapositions (and contexts) we depend upon and demand. In this sense, my method is also an argument about cure itself.

At the Limits

While this book begins in the early twentieth century and ends in the early twenty-first, the reader will be frequently transported across time and space, sometimes abruptly. Threads are dropped, others are picked up. The movement

56. I am indebted here to a conversation with Projit Muhkarji, in which he referred to an "implicit rule of numbers" in historical writing: the more people affected, the more relevant or important a phenomenon.

57. Ronald Inden has made a related point about the contextual taming of the singular text: "more often than not, when my colleagues in anthropology call for context they seem to be asking for a detached, potentially feral, textual practice to be converted into an expression of or, at best, a commentary on this anthropological text." Inden, "Introduction," 10.

58. See Strathern, "Out of Context."

59. I draw here from the work of the anthropologist Naisargi Dave, who has thought carefully about the uses of context in relation to the distinction she draws between vital and sterile contradictions. Dave, "On Contradiction."

from colonial gardening, pension benefits, and philandering milkmen to cosmology and dying wives is an attempt to produce, through juxtaposition, unexpected contexts for imagining cure. What it means to be cured is not "stationary and fixed," as Hegel infamously described India, but rather dependent on the kinds of juxtapositions through which it is imagined.[60] In particular, the question of what is being cured—a disease, a body, a people, a relationship, a society, an attitude, a population, an environment—reveals that cure might inevitably and always be a metaphor with a slippery referent. There is no originary cure that we can turn to as our founding paradigm.

Cure is never panacea, boundless in every direction, ubiquitously and eternally efficacious for everyone, everywhere, at all times. A central claim of this book is that we can better understand cure through its partiality or fragility, through the ways in which it unravels, comes undone, or even fails—in other words, by examining the limits of cure. Those limits come in many forms: in the limits to knowledge (What can we know?), of ethical comportment and action (How should we act?), and—crucially—of expectation (What can we hope for?). Antibiotic resistance might signal one form of limit, organized around the waning power of pharmaceuticals in the face of bacterial mutation. Claims about who needs or deserves cure (and who doesn't) might be thought of as another kind of limit, premised on deeply racialized and classed calculations of human worth and value. Approaching cure at its limits provides a stronger, less idealized foundation for thinking the ethics and politics of treatment, and medicine more broadly.

While tuberculosis has frequently been held up as exemplary of disease more generally, the way in which cures for tuberculosis have been imagined will only ever partially map onto other conditions. The recent development of a functional cure for HIV, for example, must be understood in relation to a transnational history of activism, the unequal distribution of various generations of antiretroviral drugs and modes of prevention, and the fact that this cure remains, at least at the moment of writing, unscalable. Yet, as we shall see, the existence of such a cure contributes to how cure is reimagined in relation to TB-HIV coinfections. Similarly, the forms of curative imagination that have taken shape around mental illness have been inflected by gendered and racialized histories of institutionalization, psychopharmacology, and psychiatry, histories that at moments have run parallel to tuberculosis. For example, the theoretical elaboration of cure in psychoanalysis provides a way of thinking about the problem of recurrence and the role of the clinician's declaration in

60. Hegel, *Lectures on the Philosophy of History*, 139.

the making of cure—which likewise bleeds into how we imagine relapse and remission in the treatment of cancer. To be sure, for certain conditions, like heart disease, we have a difficult time imagining cure at all. And the debates over what it might mean to cure disability take us in an entirely different and more radical direction, forcing us to confront the fact that in imagining cure we imagine certain forms of life as somehow damaged or in need of repair.[61]

This book explores a range of curative imaginations that have taken form around tuberculosis: in debates contrasting idyllic sanatoria and crowded prisons, through which freedom in its many forms became envisioned as a kind of therapy; in the itineraries of ships filled with coolies and soldiers seeking work and treatment across the British Empire; in the networks of scientists who tested antibiotics in India as a means of asking whether poverty really mattered to therapeutic success; in clinics where patients were told that they were cured only to undergo treatment again and again; and in the reworking of midcentury anxieties about population growth in relation to contemporary drug resistance in India's urban centers. In conjoining past and present, *At the Limits of Cure* is an effort to contribute to conversations about the promises and perils of medicine for our collective futures.

My aim in this book is to grapple not only with the history and present of cure but also to lay a foundation from which we can begin to envision what forms of therapeutic promise might be imaginable in the times to come, and to prepare ourselves for the inevitable limits of such therapies. We might think of such a quest for limits as a form of critique, one that reveals the arbitrariness of what frequently appears as "universal, necessary, or obligatory."[62] It is, in other words, a beginning for how we might imagine cure otherwise in a world of fading antibiotic efficacy.

61. I'm referring specifically to the work of scholars who have studied cures for deafness. See Virdi, *Hearing Happiness*. In relation to India, see also the work of Michele Friedner, in *Becoming Normal*, on state-sponsored cochlear implants and the promise of normalcy.
62. Foucault, "What Is Enlightenment?," 45.

Chapter One

The literature of tuberculosis is strewn with
the wrecks of theories once popular, but
now almost forgotten and cast away.

—David Chowry Muthu,
  Pulmonary Tuberculosis

In early twentieth-century India, the force of the colonial imagination profoundly reshaped the relationship between hills and cities, microbes and humans. The environment could be ally or foe, and bacteria could be innocent or sinful. Change, rapid and unsettling, was identified as a potent cause of tuberculosis among the colonized. In accompanying an Indian tuberculosis specialist returned from England as he ventured down the dark alleyways of colonial cities, we learn how Indian bodies were simultaneously constrained and yet exposed to pathogenic environments. Constraint was both physical and metaphorical, an opportunity to think about freedom in all its forms: Indian women's perceived lack of freedom, which provided an alibi for women missionary-doctors to enter into enclosed zenanas, bearing bodily salve and spiritual salvation; or the freedom desired by those who fought the British and thereby lost their freedom—and their health—as they were locked away in crowded prisons. To be free was to be open to the therapeutic power of nature, a kind of mediated openness made possible, for example, by the sanatorium. Cure, like its limits, was thought to depend on the ways in which the colonized body was made strong or brought down by its exposure to and enclosure from the swiftly changing world of the British Raj. In the face of such transformations, to focus exclusively on bacteria would have been like trying

To Cure an Earthquake

with a pill.

A Disorder of the Imagination

Near the end of the seventeenth century, a Swiss medical student named Johannes Hofer manufactured a neologism to describe the consuming pain of separation experienced by his countrymen—soldiers and sailors in particular—who had been banished to the low-lying plains or to the high seas. He called this feeling *nostalgia*: from the Greek νόστος, *nóstos*, "homecoming, to return home," and ἄλγος, *álgos*, "pain, grief, distress."

By dressing what was an ordinary feeling—*Heimweh*, or homesickness—in classical garb, Hofer succeeded in raising it to the status of a nosological category. He conceived of nostalgia as a "disorder of the imagination" that vitiated the vital energies.[1] Stories abounded of nostalgic sailors who, confusing the rolling green seas with the sloping meadows of home, leaped to their deaths. That nostalgia was a real ailment was not in question. But Hofer's explanation of this malady, lacking as it did a material substrate, proved unsatisfying for succeeding generations of scientists and doctors. In the first two decades of the eighteenth century, the Swiss physician Jean-Jacques Scheuchzer proposed an atmospheric explanation for nostalgia, resting on the difference between the light air of the hills and the dense, heavy air of the plains. For Scheuchzer, air provided a more substantial grounding for nostalgia than imagination, precisely because it was outside the mind.

Yet even air was found to be altogether too ethereal. For the Austrian physician Josef Leopold Auenbrugger, the question remained: how might nostalgia be materialized in the clinical encounter? He found his answer through the use of percussion; the pitter-patter of physicians' fingers across a series of points on the chest and back, and the varying qualities of sound produced through these taps, could reveal to the trained ear the specific form of pathological intrigue hidden beneath. In 1761, he attuned his well-honed ears to listen for nostalgia: "While all thought is directed toward ungratified desires, the body wastes away, with a dull sound [*sonitus obscurus*] on one side of the chest."[2] He confirmed his findings via autopsy: "I have opened many cadavers of those who died of this disease and have always found the lungs firmly adherent to the pleura; the lobes on the side where the sound was dull were callous, indurated, and more or less purulent."[3] For Auenbrugger, nostalgia was localized in the lungs. It was something solid, extending beyond the imagination to take root within the organic body. Nostalgia remained tied to longing, but it was

1. Hofer cited in Starobinski, "The Idea of Nostalgia," 87.
2. Auenbrugger cited in Rosen, "Nostalgia," 345.
3. Rosen, "Nostalgia," 345.

also physiological, an audible and visible malformation of pulmonary tissue, a kind of visceral sound-image. Once located in the distance separating the hills from the plains, nostalgia had now taken up residence in the patient's body.

Where Auenbrugger heard and saw nostalgia, scientists and physicians working at the end of the nineteenth century, moved by developments in bacteriology and pathological anatomy, would find tuberculosis.[4] As a medical condition, nostalgia lost its standing as physicians began "chasing after bacilli."[5] Yet tuberculosis remains a profoundly nostalgic condition in both geographic and historical terms. Displaced, with important exceptions, from Europe and America, from the lungs of the elite to those of the poor, tuberculosis is easy to imagine as a condition of a stylized past, an era long gone and far away, replete with artists, philosophers, operatic courtesans, and, perhaps above all, sanatoria.[6]

Historians of the sanatorium have frequently tasked themselves with exorcising nostalgia from the imagination of tuberculosis, piecing together archival residues and oral histories to provide a historicist alternative to a "fictional" or "literary sanatorium," figured as a "romantic ocean liner where middle- and upper-class patients are confined together on a long journey, with ample time for sexual adventures and philosophical reflections."[7] In this sense, nostalgia remains a disorder of a wayward historical imagination, a "disturbing disease of historicity" that can be exorcised only by stringent fidelity to the documentary remains of therapeutic pasts.[8] In writing about India, the danger is doubled, in that we are also confronted by a nostalgia for the imperial past.[9]

While researching this book, I often wondered: Can we ever truly escape from nostalgia? Do we depart from Thomas Mann's marvelously *Magic Mountain*

4. On the transition from nostalgia to tuberculosis, see Rosen, "Percussion and Nostalgia."

5. Starobinski, "The Idea of Nostalgia," 100. As Kevis Goodman has argued, nostalgia migrated from medicine into Romantic-era aesthetic writings, particularly those concerned with poetics. See Goodman, "Romantic Poetry and the Science of Nostalgia," 197.

6. As Andreas Huyssen has argued, "The architectural ruin is an example of the indissoluble combination of spatial and temporal desires that trigger nostalgia." In the latter half of the twentieth century, the sanatorium became emblematic of such ruin, a passé therapeutic form that left behind its shell. See Huyssen, "Nostalgia for Ruins," 7.

7. Condrau, "Beyond the Total Institution," 74.

8. Goodman, "Romantic Poetry and the Science of Nostalgia," 197.

9. See in particular Rosaldo, "Imperialist Nostalgia."

only to arrive at Erving Goffman's terrifyingly total institution?[10] Do we exit from the romance of the British Raj only to find ourselves burdened by the heroism of anticolonial nationalist struggle?

What if, instead, we were to return to Hofer's understanding of nostalgia, a disorder characterized by a longing for return? For Hofer, the cure for nostalgia can only ever be nostalgic, that is to say, a cure that depends on return—if only an imaginative one. In the early nineteenth century, for example, a popular prescription for treating nostalgia involved reading books about one's homeland in the hope of carrying the imagination back to its proper place.[11]

What follows then is my admittedly nostalgic reading of the archival traces of an Indian sanatorium.[12] Because nostalgia, after all, is nothing other than "an elaborated symptom of the waning of our historicity, of our lived possibility of experiencing history in some active way."[13] To enter, then, into the complexities of cure in early twentieth-century India—to treat nostalgia as enabling inquiry rather than endangering it—you need a bit of imagination.

So, now, I ask you to read, and to imagine.[14]

10. According to Flurin Condrau, the romantic ocean liner was replaced by the total institution as a model for understanding the sanatorium. Both of these models, he argues, are idealizations that can be undercut by careful historical attention. See Condrau, "Beyond the Total Institution," 74.

11. On bibliotherapy, see Goodman, "'Uncertain Disease.'"

12. I should note that the documents I have access to largely represent the perspectives of sanatorium staff, physicians, and colonial officers rather than those of patients. Social historians of tuberculosis like Sheila Rothman have provided invaluable studies of patient experience through recourse to patients' letters and diaries as well as family papers. Rothman, *Living in the Shadow of Death*. Unfortunately, I have for the most part been unable to find similar documents in India, having been frequently told by families that papers had been lost or perhaps never existed—especially for those who might not have been literate.

13. Jameson cited in Goodman, "Romantic Poetry and the Science of Nostalgia," 195.

14. The injunction to imagine is one that I borrow from feminist scholars of science and medicine, especially Michele Murphy, Sarah Pinto, and Banu Subramaniam. In reconstructing the sanatorium through the eyes of an imagined traveler of uncertain provenance, I have attended scrupulously to details drawn from archival sources while allowing space for readers to grapple with the limits and possibilities of their own nostalgic tendencies. Murphy, *Sick Building Syndrome and the Problem of Uncertainty*; Pinto, *The Doctor and Mrs. A.*; Subramaniam, *Holy Science*.

Maybe you'd begin in the summer of 1910, on the narrow-gauge tracks of the Kalka-Simla railway line. As your train crosses the Sivalik Hills, the southern sentries to the Himalayas, you crane your neck for a final glimpse of the plains receding behind you.

You had booked your passage all the way to Simla. But as your train navigates the shifty mountain terrain, crossing bridges and threading tunnels, something catches your eye.

There, just outside your window.

And then you remember. You had read something about this in the paper.

Letting your curiosity get the best of you, you abandon the train at the next station, luggage in hand. After proceeding on a brisk hike about a mile and a half east, you come upon a sign: DHARAMPUR SANATORIUM.[15]

Just past the sign, a trail opens up before you, carved through mature *kadam* pines leading up a hill and winding past a medication dispensary, storerooms, wooden cottages, and a terraced garden, before finally arriving at a two-story bungalow surrounded by terra-cotta pots bursting with flowers.

Standing on the veranda of that bungalow, five thousand feet above sea level, you breathe deeply the rejuvenating mountain air. Where has your curiosity taken you?

First, you look: balancing at the edge of that veranda, you take in the sea of white double-fly tents (which you had seen from the train) and wooden cottages before you, flanked on all sides by almost seventy acres of pine-dotted hills. You squint, and you're just able to make out the Lawrence Asylum perched atop one of those hills, a military-style boarding school for European children who had been cast off and forsaken, providing them refuge from the sultry and immoral climate of the plains down below.[16]

Then, you listen: the peal of gunshots echoes from the nearby Dagshai Cantonment, where the soldiers of the British Indian Army practice their marksmanship. This is a matter of great annoyance to the superintendent of

15. A government document from the early months of 1911 refers to the Dharampur Sanatorium as the Edward Sanatorium in Dharampore, most likely after King Edward VII, for whom many sanatoria across India were named. See the Revenue Secretary to the Government of Punjab to the Superintendent, Hill States, Simla, "Consumptives Hospital at Dharampore," December 20, 1910, no. 969-M. & S., *Proceedings of the Home Department,* January 1912, no. 58, British Library India Office Records (hereafter cited as British Library).

16. The historian Dane Kennedy has described the Lawrence Asylums as the "nurseries of the ruling race." Kennedy, *The Magic Mountains,* 117–46.

the sanatorium, who is roused from his morning meditation when he collects himself at the beginning of each day. That superintendent, A. C. Majumdar, is a retired government servant and former homeopath to the poor from Punjab. Majumdar lives in the bungalow with his wife, niece, and on occasion his daughter, a schoolteacher living in Lahore who visits during the holidays.

These three institutions—the boarding school, the military encampment, and the sanatorium—represented in miniature the many faces of state power in India. The colonial government had taken great interest in this little sanatorium, primarily for fear that the illness contained within would spread to the military men stationed at the nearby cantonment. An officer or two had even been sent to inspect the operations of the sanatorium.

Such visits had taught Superintendent Majumdar a great deal of patience. Of course, he also knew that the support of the government could be invaluable. Only last year, he had requested that spare water from the Dagshai Cantonment's pipes be provided to the sanatorium.[17] He had also convinced the railway officials to station a guard over the tracks during the hotter seasons. It had happened before that friction produced by the painful grinding of the train against the tracks had set fire to the dry pine needles that littered the ground, no small threat to a community floating in a sea of pines. And in fact, Majumdar explains to you, some of the patients prefer to sleep out in the open, on a bed of pine needles, to maximize their exposure to the curative powers of nature.

Majumdar's wife, who has just returned from the cowshed, brings you some tea made with fresh milk.

While you sip, Majumdar reaches for his files. Even in retirement, the habits of a former bureaucrat are slow to fade. He presents you with documents of incorporation, as well as the finances from the previous year, showing that 61,000 rupees were received, much of it from the shipbuilding Wadia family. Some of these funds, he tells you proudly, are used to support those patients too poor to pay for their own care. Poverty, he insists, should be no bar to treatment.

Before you have time to ask, Majumdar starts telling you about the founding of the sanatorium, which began as the dream of the Bombay Parsi Behramji Malabari. A man of letters and a fierce social critic, Malabari engaged in contentious debates around issues like widow remarriage and age of consent laws

17. Quarter Master General in India to General Officer Commanding, Lahore Division, "Consumptives Hospital at Dharampore," February 25, 1911, no. 4241-I (Q. M. G.-3), *Proceedings of the Home Department*, January 1912, no. 55, British Library.

for women.[18] As his interests stretched to encompass concerns about health, he set up the Consumptives Home Society in 1907 to begin searching for a suitable location to establish a sanatorium.[19] It was thought that a large swath of land somewhere up in the hills would provide the ideal climate and environment for the sanatorium-based cure. Many locations were canvassed, but most lacked a climate amenable to outdoor living throughout the year. Where the weather was good, the land was prohibitively expensive. The pair of sanatoria that already existed in India, near Ajmer and Almora, were operated by missionaries who received funds from their home congregations.[20] Dharampur was the first sanatorium in India to operate outside of the Christian fold.

Eventually, through the influence of a few well-placed contacts, Malabari's organization entered into conversations with Patiala, a princely state governed under the watchful eye of the British Raj. The maharaja of Patiala, whose many wives and concubines had themselves been afflicted, was sympathetic to their efforts. In June 1909, he granted to the society the kadam pine hills for a pittance, just 5 rupees per year.

But enough about Malabari and the maharaja. At this point, Majumdar refills your teacup and begins telling you about his own background: how he had become involved with the Sadharan Brahmo Samaj, an organization committed to social and religious reform, modernization, and service to the poor.[21]

18. For a fascinating discussion of Malabari as a reformer and travel writer, see Grewal, *Home and Harem.*

19. Honorary Secretary, "Report of the Consumptives' Homes Societies, for the first year ending May 31, 1910," August 2, 1910, Annexure to an order issued by W. S. Meyer, Chief Secretary, Government of Madras Public Department, order no. 675, British Library. This order suggests that Dharampur might serve as a model for a sanatorium proposed for Madras. See also Ramanna, *Health Care in Bombay Presidency,* 89.

20. In 1906, a missionary-run sanatorium was established near Ajmer (in present-day Rajasthan), likely the first in India. Two years later, another was established by the Church of Scotland near Almora (in present-day Uttarakhand), this one exclusively for women patients. The well-known sanatorium at Madanapalle was established in 1915, by a group of Christian missionary societies. As a rule, these sanatoria were frequently segregated along the lines of race, caste, class, gender, and, given their missionary orientation, religion. See Kathiresan, *Kasu Noi.*

21. The Sadharan Brahmo Samaj was founded in 1878 as an offshoot of Rammohan Roy's Brahmo Samaj, established in Calcutta in 1828. The Sadharan Brahmo Samaj was involved in various social activities, running schools, libraries, printing presses, and philanthropic organizations, while also offering aid during famines and epidemic outbreaks. Philosophically, the Sadharan Brahmo Samaj was opposed to a kind of Hinduism organized around patriarchy and caste hierarchy, although its own membership

How he had traveled to the United Provinces during the famine that had ended the lives of millions, and to the Kangra Valley after the earthquake that had swallowed up over twenty thousand souls.[22] How he had ministered to the poor, traveling from village to village armed only with his box of medicines. But from June 1909, he says with some pride as you finish your second cup of tea, patients had begun traveling to him, the first Indian sanatorium director in the country, trickling in from every corner.

After having tea with Majumdar, you go for a stroll around the grounds of the sanatorium. You run into Dr. Banerji, the sanatorium's voluntary physician from Allahabad. He invites you to join him on his daily rounds, during which you meet a high-caste Hindu woman from Ferozepur with advanced-stage tuberculosis. Her husband is far away, studying at an engineering college in England. She herself is well educated. Dr. Banerji notes with great respect in his voice that she has even read the *Yoga Vasishtha* in the original Sanskrit. Although she doesn't say much, a smile lingers across her lips throughout your visit. As you leave, Dr. Banerji notes that she plans to return to Ferozepur within the next week, against his admonitions, uncured.

At this point, the doctor's assistant joins you, a staunch vegetarian and former hospital aide from Bombay, who also happens to be a patient at the sanatorium. As they continue their rounds, he weighs every patient in turn and takes their temperatures, recording each figure in a small notebook that he carries with him. As you walk with them, you meet a Eurasian from Bombay, a Hindu judicial officer from the United Provinces, a Kashmiri Pandit woman who refuses to lie down despite the stern reprimand of the doctor, and a Bengali woman who insists, against all contrary opinion, that she is completely cured.

---

tended to be drawn from upper-caste, English-speaking elites. See Bhatt, "Brahmo Samaj, Arya Samaj, and the Church-Sect Typology."

22. The United Provinces and many surrounding regions experienced famine in 1896–97, resulting in upward of five million deaths in the affected area. The Kangra earthquake struck in 1905, leveling most of the buildings in the surrounding parts of Punjab, including McLeod Ganj and Dharamsala. With regard to famine specifically, the historian Benjamin Siegel has noted that the British tended to view such famines as natural parts of the Indian climate and landscape, and the failure of Indians to survive these famines as evidence of their incapacity for self-rule. Certainly, Malthusian ideas about population growth underscored much of their thinking. Siegel, *Hungry Nation*, 9. For an earlier history of this kind of thinking, see Arnold, "Hunger in the Garden of Plenty."

You also encounter a wealthy Sikh gentleman from Gwailor, sitting out-side his wooden cottage with one of his attendants, concentrating intensely on a chessboard laid out before him.[23] As you study the board with him, another attendant brings out the midday meal for his master, prepared in the kitchen shared by many of the sanatorium's residents. Without looking up from the chessboard, the Sikh gentleman orders the attendant to send an extra portion of food to the man from Poona who lives next door, a destitute Britisher who survives on the charity of his sister and who detests the food prepared by his own servant, a notoriously terrible cook.

Stifling a yawn, the Sikh gentleman from Gwalior asks your leave, as he wishes to curl up with a Marie Corelli novel and take a nap. But he invites you to return to sup with him in the evening, when you meet his friend, a fellow Sikh from Punjab carrying a harmonium. Unfortunately, neither he nor anyone else at the sanatorium knows how to play it. With a hearty laugh, the wealthy Sikh gentleman promises to have a gramophone and a musician brought to the sanatorium. After all, chess is certainly not an entertainment suitable for all of the sanatorium's patients.

In fact, just after dinner, you attend a party thrown by the superintendent for the children at the sanatorium. You listen with great pleasure as a young girl recites poetry in crisp English while her brother, a precocious but fragile youth, sits nearby watching, taking great pride in his sister's virtuosity. Unlike many of the missionary-run sanatoria, you observe that the Dharampur Sana-torium treats an incredibly wide range of people: Hindus, Muslims, Christians, Sikhs, and Parsis, Indian and English, men and women, rich and poor, adults and children. Although each has their own living space and, if they can afford it, their own caretaker and food. After all, the sanatorium remains a part of a larger social world, one rife with rules of division.

Such social distinctions become evident to you that evening. You watch as the sweepers arrive to remove the night soil from the cottages and tents. You watch as they bury paper, cups, and envelopes covered in tuberculous mucous and saliva coughed up by patients. Dr. Banerji tells you that, eventually, an

23. The figure of a wealthy gentleman playing chess is reminiscent of Satyajit Ray's 1977 film *Shatranj Ke Khilari* (The chess players), a period drama organized around two aristocratic men playing chess in the princely state of Awadh under the shadow of the British East India Company, and on the eve of the 1857 Rebellion. Ray's film is based on Premchand's 1924 Hindi short story of the same name. On the story and the film, see Pritchett, "The Chess Players." Death from tuberculosis, figured as a largely incur-able disease, would feature prominently in several of Premchand's works, including the 1921 short story "Maa" (Mother) and the 1928 novel *Nirmala*.

incinerator will be built—more hygienic, more sanitary, he explains—but until then, this is how things are done.

By then, the sun has set, and the supervisor generously offers to put you up for the night. Before heading to bed, you decide to take a walk around the grounds to enjoy the cool, clean air as it whistles through the trees. As you walk, you come upon neat rows of empty iron casks that had carried water from the Dagshai Cantonment, ready to be returned and refilled the next morning. And as you keep walking, you think back to what the supervisor told you, that the grounds of the sanatorium had once been used by the Plague Department for the manufacture of rat poison.[24] Looking around at the well-oiled organization around you, and staring into the night sky, it is hard to imagine that now.

Taken in by all that you have seen and heard—or perhaps there is some other reason?—you wake up the next morning and decide to stay a little while longer, in one of the empty cabins, vacated and sanitized a few weeks earlier after the death of a patient.[25] After all, not everyone can be saved. Especially those who arrive too late, when the disease has already progressed too far.

You come to understand this better just a few days later. While in the midst of a rousing game of chess with the Sikh gentleman, a bedraggled man appears suddenly from behind a clump of trees. His appearance gives you quite a fright, so much so that you jump out of your chair and knock over the chessboard.

No matter, you were losing anyway. After recovering your senses, you help the man stumble the rest of the way to the superintendent's home. A Rajput police inspector, he had trekked through the woods rather than arriving by the path that you had taken just a few days earlier. The exertion demanded by the journey is too much for the man. He begins coughing up blood.

Arrangements are hastily prepared to take care of him, although there is little available room. (You offer your own cabin, explaining that you have no real reason for being there, but oddly enough, neither Superintendent Majumdar nor Dr. Banerji seem to want to take you up on your offer.)

After the police inspector has been settled in, he explains to Dr. Banerji that he had eaten too much pork, which made him ill. That illness in turn led to his consumption.

24. On the history of plague in turn-of-the-century India, see Catanach, "Plague and the Tensions of Empire."

25. At the turn of the century, disinfection likely entailed the use of some combination of Izal (a by-product of the process through which coke is distilled from coal), mercury perchloride, carbolic acid, soap, and sunlight.

Dr. Banerji tries to keep the police inspector calm, explaining that he has nothing to fear. The man responds cheerfully, if weakly: "I am a Rajput and I do not fear death."[26]

By June of the following year, he has passed away.

Cases like that of the Rajput police inspector pose a problem for the sanatorium. The incurable ones, they are called (but never to their faces—that would be utterly demoralizing). After the police inspector dies, you hear from a few of the patients that the old maharaja has big plans to build a consumptives hospital nearby, for those patients who are on their way out.[27] It is a controversial plan; the military brass has begun to complain. Colonel Hedley, the principal medical officer of the Sirhind Brigade, currently stationed at Dagshai, grouses that the sanatorium is already a "menace to the health of the general public."[28] A hospital for the "worst cases," who are according to him "the most infectious," would only make matters worse.[29]

You can't help but think that Hedley has a point. Just below the site of the maharaja's future hospital for incurables is the halting place for draft animals on the Simla Road, a predictably filthy stretch of land plastered in manure and flies. Hedley worries that those flies would feed on the tuberculous sputum of dying consumptives and carry the disease to the nearby bazaar, and then on to the cantonment. Ultimately, though, it is the maharaja's land—even the cantonment was built on land lent by the maharaja to the military. And after all, one mustn't look a gift horse in the mouth.

Eventually—after days, or weeks, or has it been years? It is hard to say how much time has passed—you pack your things and head back through the kadam pines down the hill. As your train departs from the station, you reflect

26. "Report of the Consumptives' Homes Societies, for the First Year Ending May 31, 1910," p. 5, August 2, 1910, British Library.

27. Flurin Condrau points out that in Britain and Germany, great effort was expended to make sure that those patients who were admitted to sanatoria were treatable. Those with terminal prognoses were discharged to die elsewhere. In Dharampur, the proper site of death became the hospital. See Condrau, "Beyond the Total Institution," 81.

28. General Officer Commanding, Sirhind Brigade, to the Assistant Quarter Master General, 3rd (Lahore) Division, "Consumptives Hospital at Dharampore," May 8, 1911, includes "Copy of an office note by the Principal Medical Officer, Sirhind Brigade, to the Brigade Major, Sirhind Brigade," Memorandum no. 3479-R, *Proceedings of the Home Department*, January 1912, no. 59, British Library.

29. General Officer Commanding, Sirhind Brigade, to the Assistant Quarter Master General, 3rd (Lahore) Division, "Consumptives Hospital at Dharampore."

on your days at the sanatorium, the most unexpected people you befriended, those you did not, and above all, the respite that the sanatorium provided you from life in the plains. How did Dr. Banerji describe it, just a few weeks earlier when he too was preparing to leave? He said that it was nature, and the open air more specifically, that restored vitality to tuberculous patients and brought them cure.

And as you descend back toward the lowlands, you're left to wonder: had the sanatorium cure worked on you too?[30]

A Body of Machines and Nerves

For almost a century, the British had scaled the Indian hills to escape the sweltering climate of the plains. But sanatoria like the one at Dharampur offered something more than pearly colonial resorts nestled in idyllic hill stations: not just the climate, but the architecture, the diet, the graduated exercise, the sunlight, the watchful eyes of the superintendent and the doctor, the communal activities, the break from everyday life, the peace, and the rest.[31] Through the coordination of these elements in the sanatorium, the tuberculous body was exposed to the curative power of nature.

This openness was explicitly opposed to the predicament of the Indian body in the colonial city. In the early 1920s, an Indian tuberculosis specialist named David Chowry Muthu stepped away from his thriving sanatorium practice in England to travel across India, a trip that took him "from Bombay to Burma" one way "and from Nepal to [the] Nilgiris" in the other.[32] As he traveled around India, Muthu found tuberculosis everywhere. In all of the major

---

30. Details included in this section have been largely gleaned from the aforementioned "Report of the Consumptives' Homes Societies, for the First Year Ending May 31, 1910," as well as from a letter in which a Major E. Wilkinson describes an unplanned trip he made to the sanatorium on August 22, 1910. Major E. Wilkinson, Sanitary Commissioner, Punjab, to the Secretary to Government, Punjab, "Establishment of Sanatoria for Treatment of Patients Suffering from Tubercular Diseases," October 7, 1910, no. 169-S, *Proceedings of the Home Department*, May 1912, no. 48, British Library. Dharampur Sanatorium is also fleetingly referenced in a variety of other documents, which have provided valuable context for this section.

31. On the sanatorium as a therapeutic technology, see Adams, Schwartzman, and Theodore, "Collapse and Expand." See also Venkat, "A Vital Mediation."

32. Muthu, "Some Impressions of Tuberculosis Problems in India," 118.

cities and towns, he estimated that one in three deaths among adults could be attributed to the disease.[33]

Close to four decades earlier, Muthu had left India behind to become a doctor in London. There, he had trained with renowned physicians, joined the YMCA and the British temperance movement, was nicknamed "the Christian Brahmin" by the papers, married an English woman of minor peerage, and raised a family.[34] Muthu eventually left London to take charge of the Inglewood Sanatorium on the Isle of Wight, a plot of land off the southern coast of Britain renowned for its healthy air and home to some of Britain's first sanatoria. He quickly became dissatisfied with the low altitude of the isle, and after three years relocated to the Mendip Hills, in the west of England. Perched in his new sanatorium, balanced eight hundred and fifty feet above the valley of Wells, Muthu built for himself a comfortable life in a country where he stuck out like a sore thumb.

It was there that he received a rather unexpected visitor, the Indian journalist Saint Nihal Singh. In a glowing review of Muthu's sanatorium, Singh limned for his readership a majestic image of three hundred acres of "woodland and meadow, in the heart of the pine-clad Mendip Hills."[35] Nevertheless, he wondered aloud why someone like Muthu would give so much of himself for the English, and yet do nothing for his own people.

Singh's rebuke found its mark, and Muthu found himself back in India. In the course of his travels around the country, Muthu witnessed the affliction among "all classes and races, from the humbler ranks of coolies, mill-hands, and servants, to the educated and well-to-do communities."[36] From the last group, he singled out "junior clerks with small and fixed incomes, college students burdened with the strain of long hours and a heavy curriculum, and child-mothers badly nourished with poor stamina."[37]

How had the Indian city become so conducive to tuberculosis? And among such a broad range of people? In part, the answer had to do with the organization of urban spaces. Muthu described "cities like Delhi and Lucknow . . .

33. Muthu admitted that there was great variation between Indian cities. "Crowded Bombay presented a higher death rate from tuberculosis than Bangalore with its garden cities," he wrote. Muthu, "Response to 'On the Social Aspects of Tuberculosis,'" 518.

34. *Morning Star*, March 21, 1895, 1.

35. Singh, "An Indian Tuberculosis Specialist in England," 531.

36. Muthu, *A Short Account of the Antiquity of Hindu Medicine*, xcix.

37. Muthu, *A Short Account of the Antiquity of Hindu Medicine*, c.

full of slums, blind alleys, and narrow passages, where the sun never shines and fresh air never penetrates."[38] "Even middle-class and humbler Anglo-Indians," he wrote, crammed together "under the joint-family system . . . find their accommodations more and more limited."[39] Shielded from nature, the Indian city was the antithesis of the sanatorium. Rather than openness, there was enclosure, and enclosures within enclosures, exacerbated by the impact of urban crowding and pauperization. What Muthu observed in his travels was not the planned, modernist city of Le Corbusier, but rather the city built up through a dialectal relationship between improvisatory, ad hoc construction by local interests on the one hand and colonial sanitation and building projects on the other.[40]

In this sense, India was no different than England during the Industrial Revolution, where the density and impoverishment of industrial cities were also linked to increasing rates of tuberculosis. "Factory life," Muthu lamented, "has turned men and women into machines."[41] It was only a matter of time before they were broken beyond repair. Rather than a body plagued by germs, what Muthu imagined was a body that registered its environment as a kind of organic machine. In Muthu's words, we can hear echoes of Karl Marx. The worker, caught within an ever-expanding division of labor, became for Marx involved in an increasingly "one-sided and machine-like type of labour."[42] Writing in the early 1840s, Marx noted that such a worker becomes "depressed . . . both intellectually and physically to the level of a machine, and from being a man becomes an abstract activity and a stomach."[43] Through the merger of mechanical and organic metaphors, the human laborer became a hungry robot engaged in repetitive and meaningless activity.

But could the deprivations of industrial labor adequately explain why such a broad range of Indians—mill hands and servants but also child-mothers, students, and clerks—fell ill? Alongside his vision of the body as organic machine, Muthu also imagined the body as a system of nerves, capable of both vitality and exhaustion.[44] In the early nineteenth century, the delicate body characteristic of the

38. Muthu, *A Short Account of the Antiquity of Hindu Medicine*, cii.

39. Muthu, "Some Impressions of Tuberculosis Problems in India," 119.

40. On the distinction between the high modernist city and the improvisatory, ad hoc city, see Scott, *Seeing like a State*.

41. Muthu, *Pulmonary Tuberculosis* (1922), 7.

42. Marx, "Economic and Philosophical Manuscripts," 285.

43. Marx, "Economic and Philosophical Manuscripts," 285.

44. Much of the historical work on the nervous body has focused on Britain. See, for example, Logan, *Nerves and Narratives*; Bonea et al., *Anxious Times*. Salisbury and Shail's edited volume extends this history into Europe and the United States. See

lady of refinement, once praised for its sensitivity to the environment, became pathologized as a mark of frailty. Sensitivity was reformulated, at least in part, as nervousness.[45] In the face of unceasing labor, relentless poverty, and population growth, and as the tempo of life quickened over the nineteenth and early twentieth centuries, the nervous system became both a barometer and a metaphor for the stress and breakdown of Victorian bodies trapped within "both literal and figurative structures of confinement."[46] With the body, mind, and soul depleted, wrote Muthu, "the nervous system becomes dulled, the thinking powers lose their brightness and activity, the brain gives way under constant dread of hunger, and the man either becomes insane or ends his unfortunate life by committing suicide."[47] Nervousness was more than a problem of the individual; what the nervous body exposed was a weakness that threatened to slide into racial degeneracy.

Whether as an organic machine or a bundle of nerves, the body was clearly figured as an energetic, vital system, one capable of exhaustion through physical and psychic stress. While Britain had undoubtedly been transformed by industrial capital, India's transformation took place under the yoke of colonial rule. What for Muthu distinguished Indian cities from their European counterparts was the severity of this transformative shock. Indians, Muthu claimed, were unprepared for this new way of life. Colonized people were robbed "of their freedom," tempted by "rifles and drink," and forced to endure the "speculators, planters, gold-diggers, convicts, and the refuse of European communities."[48] Their "moral habits" were not, he insisted, "strong enough to stand the strain of such a violent change of environment."[49]

The problem, for Muthu, was the very process of civilization: "The contact of the East with the West has caused great social, economic, industrial, moral, and spiritual upheavals, as seen in the growth of towns and cities, the expansion of trade and commerce, the depopulation of villages, decay of home industries, migration in towns, high rents and dear food, overcrowding and

----

Salisbury and Shail, *Neurology and Modernity*. There is also an expansive literature on neurasthenia, or nervous exhaustion, in the United States. See, for example, Gosling, *Before Freud*.

45. Wilson, "The End of Sensibility."

46. Taylor-Brown, Dickson, and Shuttleworth, "Structures of Confinement," 138.

47. Muthu, "A Discussion on Poverty," 939.

48. Muthu, *Pulmonary Tuberculosis* (1922), 133.

49. Muthu, *Pulmonary Tuberculosis* (1922), 133.

insanitation, poverty, want, intemperance, and degeneration."[50] According to Muthu, civilization had deprived the colonial subject of "the immunity that he enjoyed while he lived in the open air."[51] Among British medical officials and administrators of the time, tuberculosis was frequently described as a disease of civilization, couched in terms of the metaphor of seed and soil.[52] The ubiquity of such a metaphor in the early twentieth century reveals the continued reliance of the science of tuberculosis on a kind of Judeo-Christian agrarian thought.[53] The seed referred to the inciting factor, something that arrived from outside. The soil referred to a (racialized) body or group, or to the environment in which such bodies and groups were located. Scientists and physicians debated over which of the two factors played a greater role in the genesis of disease. Did you fall ill because you were fragile or otherwise vulnerable? Did you inherit a constitutional disposition toward tuberculosis from your family or racial group, or were you exposed to an environment that rendered you weak? Or was it simply that something alien had entered your body?

The idea of soil carried clear racial—and gendered—connotations. Entire colonized populations were classified as "virgin soil," until recently untouched by the seed of certain diseases. Within India, Gurkhas, Pathans, tribal groups, and Anglo-Indians were thought by the British to be most susceptible to tuberculosis, as virgin soil populations with little experience of tuberculosis. As civilization marched triumphantly forward, colonized populations across Asia, Africa, and the Americas underwent the necessary process of tubercularization as they gradually acquired immunity to the disease—albeit at a heavy cost.[54]

Ideas about virgin soil would be applied to understand patterns of tuberculosis-related morbidity and mortality across the British Empire and the United States. To be clear, tubercularization was not an individual process

50. Muthu, *Pulmonary Tuberculosis* (1922), 135.

51. Muthu, *Pulmonary Tuberculosis* (1922), 6.

52. Harrison and Worboys, "A Disease of Civilization."

53. On the naturalization of the metaphor of seed and soil in the context of gender and reproduction, see Delaney, *The Seed and the Soil*, 31. As Delaney has shown, this metaphor must be carefully unraveled to understand the relative contribution and value of each component. For a clear explanation of the metaphor of seed and soil in relation to a rather different condition, see Homei and Worboys, *Fungal Disease in Britain and the United States*, 137–38.

54. On debates concerning tubercularization, see Packard, *White Plague, Black Labor*; Gandy, "Life without Germs"; Bynum, *Spitting Blood*; McMillen, *Discovering Tuberculosis.*

but rather one experienced by entire populations, construed in terms of race. The spread of tuberculosis was taken to be a necessary, if at least partially lethal, step on the path toward modernity, one built on Darwinian notions of natural selection.[55] Weaker representatives of a racial group would be killed by the disease; the stronger would survive.

In India in the 1920s and '30s, debates about the specificity of tuberculosis in India often returned to the metaphor of seed and soil: was tuberculosis in India a tropical disease, and as such, constituted by an altogether different seed or more impaired soil than in Europe?[56] If it was indeed a distinct tropical disease, rather than the same tuberculosis that could be found in Europe, then causal explanations organized around the civilizing process made little sense. Despite his insistence on civilization as a kind of foundational cause for tuberculosis in India, Muthu found the racial logic underpinning the seed-and-soil metaphor unconvincing: "Even the current idea of a virgin soil as being the cause of the rapid spread of tuberculosis among the dark races should be imputed not to an impaired physical soil, but first to a depraved moral environment, brought on by the collusion of two different standards of living and thinking."[57] The problem was not that colonized populations were inherently fragile or weak, waiting to be culled through the process of tubercularization, but that their ways of life were being distorted and reformed at breakneck velocity. For Muthu, then, tuberculosis in India was not the product of a virgin soil, an inherent susceptibility or lack of immunity, but rather—to continue the metaphor further than Muthu might have wished—the colonial devitalization of the soil. The persistence of an agricultural metaphor alongside industrial images of a mechanical and nervous body further demonstrates how colonial medicine was able to draw on the most varied of sources. According to Muthu, colonized peoples were ill prepared for this onslaught of new ideas, norms, and ways of being. The rapid rate at which the physical and moral environments were being reshaped under British rule created a misfit between colonized bodies and their equally colonized environments. The conjoint effects of poverty, malnutrition, overcrowding, climate, and custom could not, at least for Muthu, be untethered from the colonial transformation of the Indian body and its environment.

55. Arthur Lankester, who appears later in this chapter, took a slightly different view, contending that tuberculosis in India was the result of the country being "improperly civilized." In Harrison and Worboys, "A Disease of Civilization," 115.

56. See Brimnes, *Languished Hopes*, 55–56.

57. Muthu, *Pulmonary Tuberculosis* (1922), 133–34.

The Backup Plan

But change in and of itself was not the problem. The environment was always in flux. Change was necessary, inevitable. After all, life was nothing other than a constant process of becoming, an organism adjusting to its changing *milieu*, a concept that referred to the "life-sustaining envelope surrounding an individual" as well as "the space connecting two entities."[58] The precise contents of milieu were open to debate, ranging from the social and biological to the material and the ethereal. Just as bodies adjusted to the milieu, so too did curative interventions adjust to ideas about the milieu.

Both healthy and diseased states were a part of this same process of adjustment. In the early stages of a disease, Muthu argued, the symptoms that manifested represented nothing more than the body's effort to adjust to a changing environment. He conceptualized this relationship between health and disease by recourse to a metaphor drawn from wartime: "If health can be understood in terms of the ordinary plan of a war campaign which a general follows in the course of war, disease can be likened to his alternate plan which he keeps in his pocket to be used should a crisis arise and the first plan prove unsuccessful."[59] Disease was the ultimate backup plan. When all else failed, it provided a circuitous route to victory: "The symptoms which arise in disease are part of the curative process of nature."[60] What this meant was that, at least in theory, tuberculosis carried with it its own cure, in the form of "fever, inflammation, caseation, fibrosis, etc."[61] Health and disease were not opposed states, but rather two means through which the body sought to achieve equilibrium with its surroundings. Disease was not necessarily a bad thing. Disease could be curative—a sign of life's persistence rather than death's approach.

Of course, the backup plan could fail. According to Muthu, it was a risky proposition that could lead back to health or culminate in death. Disease became pathological when the body failed to make the proper adjustments to changes in its environment. But it was more than that. Pathological disease was not just a failure to adjust, but a loss of the very capacity to adjust. Such a loss took place "when the stress of war is continued": when the environment changed and kept changing, in a way that made it nearly impossible to adapt.[62]

58. Tresch, *The Romantic Machine*, 4.
59. Muthu, *Pulmonary Tuberculosis* (1927), 110–11.
60. Muthu, *Pulmonary Tuberculosis* (1927), 111.
61. Muthu, *Pulmonary Tuberculosis* (1927), 111.
62. Muthu, *Pulmonary Tuberculosis* (1927), 111.

In such a state of permanent war, the body was transformed in a deep and lasting way: "The functional adaptive changes pass on to structural changes, and structural to more or less permanent organic changes."[63] The temporary symptoms of disease, which once demonstrated the body's willingness to adapt, became indissoluble, like an affectation repeated often enough to turn to unbreakable habit.

Under such conditions, the signs and symptoms of tuberculosis no longer represented an adjustment to new conditions, but were instead "the surface indications of a greater and more serious bodily derangement."[64] In the process, the body was unmoored from its capacity to change, which was, fundamentally, its capacity for life. As the historian of medicine Georges Canguilhem explained, "Each disease reduces the ability to face others, uses up the initial biological assurance without which there would not even be life."[65] Here, again, we can see an echo of the nervous body, one that is not just temporarily exhausted, but permanently diminished.

Civilization. Modernization. Westernization. Tubercularization. What these terms point to is a process of dizzying and irrefutable change. Colonial rule as a state of permanent war. The chessboard overturned, the pieces scattered on the floor. No more moves to make, the backup plan no longer an option.

Muthu's concerns about rapid social change were not only his own.[66] In the wake of the Indian Rebellion of 1857, dubbed the Sepoy Mutiny by those on the other side, change became a matter of serious philosophical and political reflection. As the territories ruled by the British East India Company were reorganized under Crown rule, colonial administrators like Henry Sumner Maine worried that the source of chaos and disorder in India was to be found in the changes wrought by British intervention.[67] The years following the rebellion witnessed an increasingly conservative approach to introducing change in India, especially in regard to what were thought to be social and religious customs.

63. Muthu, *Pulmonary Tuberculosis* (1927), 111.

64. Ott, *Fevered Lives*, 34–35.

65. What Canguilhem describes here helps to explain why the Rajput police inspector whom we met at the Dharampur Sanatorium explained his tuberculous condition as the result of eating too much pork and falling ill. Canguilhem, "Disease, Cure, Health," 117.

66. Concerns about change were also voiced by other colonial physicians. See Brimnes, *Languished Hopes*, 32.

67. On Maine's conservative vision, see Mantena, *Alibis of Empire*.

Such an approach produced its own set of problems. As rulers over an alien land, how were the British to know what counted as ageless tradition? How could the Indian order of things be ascertained? Were high-caste scholars the appropriate arbiters of Indian custom? Were sacred scriptures the primordial source of tradition? Was Indian society essentially one that was organized around caste hierarchy? Despite its reputation for timelessness, the territory governed under the auspices of the British Indian Empire was a dynamic and diverse place. What was required was the production of knowledge about how things were or, rather, how they had originally been. As the British rulers of India proceeded to tease out Indian tradition from the messiness of life in India as it was actually lived, certain ways of conceptualizing traditional society were privileged over others.[68] Where there was once dynamism, debate, and plurality, the British sought to impose a kind of uniformity. In the name of keeping things the same, everything changed.

Into the Zenana

And then there were the reformers. Those who insisted that things—at least, certain things—must change. Colonialism was a fractured and fragile construct, composed of contending interests that occasionally overlapped or made common cause but often found themselves looking at a matter from rather different angles.[69] This was particularly true in India, where the government, under both East India Company and Crown rule, hesitated to allow missionization in British territories for fear of promoting political instability.

To understand how the controversies around social change were tied to concerns about health, we might look to the Scottish Presbyterian missionary Thomas Smith, who in 1840 penned a controversial proposal in the pages of the *Calcutta Christian Observer*. Smith bemoaned the sequestering of Hindu women, especially high-caste women, in zenanas, those inner spaces within the home shielded from the world of men. What Smith wanted for these women was an education (which of course he hoped would reveal the contradictions of Hinduism and lay the foundation for conversion to Christianity). Smith's proposal received little support, from high-caste Bengali patriarchs or from his fellow

68. On the sanctioning of a largely upper-caste vision of social life over others and the changes it produced in Indian society and politics, see Dirks, *Castes of Mind*.
69. On the misalignments of church and state in colonial times, see Comaroff and Comaroff, *Of Revelation and Revolution*.

missionaries. For the time, the zenana remained cloaked in an imagined dark-ness, impenetrable and, for that reason, something to be penetrated.

Things changed with the arrival in Calcutta of the educator and missionary John Fordyce, who latched onto Smith's proposal and ran with it. In 1854, he began assembling a cadre of ayahs, governesses, teachers, and women mission-aries to educate the wives and daughters of Bengal's most influential families. Many of these zenana missionaries, as they were called, began to receive train-ing as doctors, nurses, and midwives, concerned as they were with both the bodily and spiritual salvation of Indian women.[70] This form of ministry was a kind of Christian therapy, a "blend of medical science, charitable sentiment and evangelical faith."[71] Within this liberal feminist imaginary, Indian women had been deprived of freedom, held captive by Indian men.[72] It was thus the task of the British—and British women in particular—to establish their free-dom by opening up the zenana.[73]

The work of women missionaries became critical to the research of the phy-sician Arthur Lankester. A former medical missionary himself, he broke from his role as the director of the Medical and Sanitation Department for the Nizam of Hyderabad to explore the prevalence of tuberculosis across the subcontinent. His actions were a response to a pair of sanitary conferences that called for an investigation into tuberculosis in India, one in Madras in 1912 and a follow-up in Lucknow two years later.[74] Delegates at these conferences had raised doubts about the statistical rise in tuberculosis in India: was it really a product

70. Burton, "Contesting the Zenana."

71. Hardiman, *Healing Bodies, Saving Souls*, 153.

72. As Inderpal Grewal notes: "What is remarkable in the modernization of In-dian women is the way in which such women began to think of their lives within their homes and the regulations under which they lived as restrictive, as a form of *unfree-dom.* . . . Life in the zenana, considered normal before the British, was reconstituted as pathological in comparison with an abstract and idealized notion of English life, the patriarchal ideas of which became the norm for many English-educated Indians." Grewal, *Home and Harem*, 169–70, emphasis added.

73. A similar colonial logic of opening as freedom can be found across multiple domains in India. For example, colonial officials took the opportunity of plague to "breach the privacy of the Bengali home through enforced searches and removals." See Mukharji, *Nationalizing the Body*, 164. Across the British Empire, enforced libera-tion often targeted women, as in colonial interventions into female genital cutting. See Boddy, *Civilizing Women.*

74. Concerns about tuberculosis were voiced at an earlier sanitary conference held in Bombay in 1911, but the call for inquiry started in Madras. See Brimnes, *Lan-guished Hopes*, 24.

of spreading disease, or simply a reflection of better diagnostic and recording procedures?[75]

To answer this question, Lankester traveled across India from July 1914 to June 1916 collecting evidence. He drew heavily on the accounts of other medical missionaries and physicians—and in particular, women—whose work in the zenanas made them among the vanguard in detecting tuberculosis among the native population. Women medical missionaries played a crucial role, teaching scripture and offering treatment while acquiring valuable information about the lives of Indian women.

What Lankester learned from zenana missionaries confirmed what had long been suspected: that there was "scarcely a zenana . . . which has not some case of tuberculosis!"[76] Lankester noted that women confined to zenanas were usually unable or unwilling to leave their homes to seek medical treatment. In a report on his findings, Lankester clarified that tuberculosis was unrelated to religious, ethnic, or racial grouping. Hindu or Muslim, high caste or low, what mattered was enclosure. Light and air had been traded for privacy. More accurately, open air had been traded for the pathogenic, uncirculating air of the zenana.[77] In Lankester's estimation, it was a poor bargain. The zenana was undoubtedly "the most insanitary part of the house," he wrote, full of "damp, dark, airless corners."[78] Little wonder, he remarked, that tuberculosis "plays havoc in the zenanas."[79]

In 1916, Lankester submitted his findings to the colonial government. His original report was circulated among the provinces for comments, but

75. Lankester, *Tuberculosis in India*, 2.

76. Lankester, *Tuberculosis in India*, 140.

77. Air could be classified in many ways: the uncirculating air of the zenana, and of the city more generally, was frequently opposed to the circulating, vitalizing air of the sanatorium, and of the hill station more broadly. There were other kinds of air that could also be either pathogenic or salubrious: the miasmatic air of the swamp and the devastatingly hot air of the Loo, on one hand, or the bracing air of the sea, on the other. For related conversations, see Yankovic, *Confronting the Climate*.

78. Lankester, *Tuberculosis in India*, 141.

79. Lankester, *Tuberculosis in India*, 141. Lankester aside, the association between the zenana, tuberculosis, and Muslim women was pervasive. For example, delegates at the All-Indian Sanitary Conference in Bombay, held in 1911, expressed particular concern about tuberculosis among Muslim women in Calcutta. See All-India Sanitary Conference, *Proceedings of the First All-India Sanitary Conference Held at Bombay on 13th and 14th November 1911*, 136 (Calcutta: Superintendent Government Printing, 1912), Wellcome Library. For a related discussion of Lankester's views on the zenana and purdah, see Brimnes, *Languished Hopes*, 33–34.

was never released to the public, raising questions about the colonial government's motives in keeping the report under wraps. When Lankester finally published his findings as a book, he received mixed reviews: some agreed that tuberculosis was a serious problem for the health of the Indian population, and others insisted that his findings were overblown.[80] Undoubtedly, Lankester's concern was not only with the Indian population but also with the effective functioning of mission and empire. The spread of tuberculosis posed a danger to those who were involved in the routine operations of colonial governance. In addition to medical officers and missionaries, he underlined the threat to a wide range of government employees, from railway ticket masters, clerks, and schoolteachers to police officers, postal workers, and telegraph operators.

Lankester found his views on tuberculosis in the zenana echoed in official medical circles. In 1923, the director-general of the Indian Medical Service, C. A. Sprawson, attributed the increased mortality of Muslim women from the disease to "the restriction of the zenana which confines women to their rooms and to a narrow courtyard; usually there is no garden. The middle-class Mohammedan woman sees nothing else than this during her life, and within that small and insanitary area are enclosed female relations and children and often one or more servants. I have several times seen tuberculosis run through a zenana and destroy the majority of its inmates in a few years."[81] In an important break from Lankester, Sprawson added that the pernicious effects of enclosure were not only embodied but also passed down hereditarily to the point of becoming a racial characteristic. Environment, race, and bacteria all mattered, funneled through heredity. In other words, one's own susceptibility to tuberculosis in the present could be the result of the enclosure of previous generations.[82] Zenanas were inherently pathogenic, not only to those who lived in

80. On those who agreed with Lankester, see Rao, "Tuberculosis and Public Health Policies," 34. On those who disagreed, see Brimnes, *Languished Hopes*, 29.

81. Sprawson, "Tuberculosis in Indians," 483. The director of public health for the Madras Presidency shared these concerns, noting in 1923 that "among purdah women conditions are even worse [than among nonpurdah women], *tuberculosis* being particularly common." Cited in Van Hollen, *Birth on the Threshold*, 44.

82. The racialized ideas of resistance and susceptibility developed and endorsed by Lankester and Sprawson grew out of the writings of S. Lyle Cummin and S. L. Cobbett in particular. See Cummin, "Primitive Tribes and Tuberculosis"; Cobbett, "The Resistance of Civilised Man to Tuberculosis." On Lyle Cummin's ideas about race-based resistance and immunity, see also McMillen, *Discovering Tuberculosis*, 19–20; Worboys, "Tuberculosis and Race in Britain and Its Empire"; Worboys, "Before McKeown," 159.

them but also for succeeding generations who might themselves live in more salubrious surroundings.

If the zenana was framed as a space where women could be protected from the outside world, it is clear that it was also figured as a highly gendered threat to that world, as a breeding ground or womb for contagion, a reservoir from which tuberculosis could run roughshod through the city and into the outlying areas. "The disease of consumption," wrote Lankester, "has emerged from the quiet of the zenana into the open life of the people."[83]

A Bacterial Theodicy

Let's return for a moment to the metaphor of seed and soil. Lankester, and later Sprawson, emphasized the importance of both seed (that which arrived from outside) and soil (a body or its environment) to explain how and why people fell ill. In the zenana, there was darkness, seclusion, insanitary conditions, and poor ventilation, they argued. But there were also bacteria.

Neither seed without soil, nor soil bereft of seed, would lead to tuberculosis. As Lankester envisioned it, there were "special corpuscles or cells in the blood, lymphatic glands, and other organs, which under conditions of perfect health can deal with the tubercle bacilli, destroying their vitality and their power to multiply."[84] A healthy body (which was an unenclosed body) could render these pathogenic bacteria powerless. The seed was necessary, but it was nothing without the right kind of soil.

Lankester's way of parsing the metaphor of seed and soil was common enough. But it was far from universal. Muthu, like Lankester, had studied the effects of tuberculosis on the Indian population and was strongly convinced that tuberculosis had nothing to do with bacteria. Certainly, bacteria existed. He could see them under the microscope. But seeing something, and knowing how to interpret it, were entirely different matters.

Muthu's skepticism emerged out of his experience treating patients in his sanatorium practice, many of whom showed every sign of tuberculosis—but no bacteria. Other patients continued to harbor bacteria long after other signs of the disease had faded away. If bacteria were truly the cause of tuberculosis, they should be present in every sick patient and absent in every healthy or cured one. Yet evidence of bacteria didn't seem to indicate that a patient suffered from tuberculosis, "any more than the presence of eagles near a corpse

83. Lankester, *Tuberculosis in India*, 15.
84. Lankester, *Tuberculosis in India*, 142.

shows that they are the cause of the dead body."[85] Muthu cautioned against what he thought to be an obsessive and foolhardy hunt for microbes, relating that a patient had once asked him, "I eat well, I sleep well, I feel well, what is this t.b. [bacteria] you are searching for?"[86]

What indeed?

What Muthu observed was that bacteria in general were frequently defined in moralistic terms. He roundly criticized the science of bacteriology for "so persistently calling our attention to [bacteria's] evil ways that we have ignored the fact that myriads of them render priceless service to man, and that life would cease to exist even for a day without their aid and co-operation."[87] Muthu concluded that the great majority of bacteria were either necessary for life or simply harmless. Bacteria, he argued, helped the body work by participating in the "physiological functions of digestion, assimilation, and excretion."[88]

No, bacteria were not evil. If anything, they were victims of their human hosts. "Tubercle bacillus take their virulence from the soil and are poisoned themselves through it."[89] According to Muthu, cells, and particularly bacterial cells, were not specific, stable entities. Their shape, their potency, and their effects were entirely a product of their porosity to their surroundings. If those surroundings happened to be an unhealthy human body enclosed within a pathogenic space, then it was no wonder that things went awry. Bacteria were, in this sense, victims to their hosts, and to their hosts' surroundings.

The picture before us is that of worlds enclosed within worlds.[90] The colonized subject, trapped within the city or confined in the zenana, whose capacity for adapting to the changing environment has been stripped from them. And within the colonized subject, another world of cells, struggling and failing to

85. Muthu, *Pulmonary Tuberculosis* (1927), 56.

86. Muthu, *Pulmonary Tuberculosis* (1927), 68.

87. Muthu, *Pulmonary Tuberculosis* (1927), 46. As Nancy Tomes notes, this "gospel of germs," replete with the moralizing idioms of evil and sin, was far-reaching, taking root not only in the United States and Europe, but in China and the Philippines as well. See Tomes, *The Gospel of Germs.*

88. Muthu, *Pulmonary Tuberculosis* (1927), 45.

89. Muthu, *Pulmonary Tuberculosis* (1922), 67.

90. It's tempting to see in Muthu's vision of the body a kind of proto-microbiome, or even a Cold War defensiveness, as in the figuration of the immune system described by Emily Martin. However, Muthu's vision of the body might be better understood as a response to the emerging body of bacteriology (which prefigures the Cold War body), as well as in terms of the nationalist body and its need for defense from colonial violation. Martin, *Flexible Bodies.*

adjust to the pathogenic milieu of their human hosts. If there was evil to be found, it was at the level of (colonial) politics and power. What Muthu seemed to be articulating was a form of biomoral thought that made it possible to think morality and the question of evil beyond the merely human realm, by drawing the lengthy threads that connected microorganismic life to the form of life engendered by colonial rule.[91] In a real sense, what Muthu was putting forward was a critique of colonialism on microbiological and theological grounds—the two were, for him, inseparable.

What we have then is a tale of shared victimhood. In the same way that human bodies were shaped by their surroundings, so too were bacteria. Muthu drew a moral and theological parallel between the bacterium and the human sufferer: "micro-organisms are not born pathogenic to hurt man," he insisted, because "man is not born to evil and to sin."[92] In Muthu's theologized medicine, God did not create evil beings, so bacteria could not be inherently evil. It was turtles all the way down, a series of nested environments in which the container gave shape to what it contained.

The consequences of this line of thinking were quite striking. Bacteria were not the seeds that caused our illness. They did not make us suffer; they suffered with us. Muthu went even further in suggesting that bacteria were not really bacteria at all. Rather, they were parts of our bodies, normal human cells that had been transformed through their enclosure in the pathogenic environment of the human body. Human cells could mutate into bacteria, while bacteria could mutate into other kinds of bacteria, and potentially, if the conditions were right, back into human cells. There was no stability, no essence; only mutability and openness to being shaped by the milieu. If bacteria did not come from outside, if they were not in fact seeds planted in the body, then they

91. The idea of the biomoral comes from the work of McKim Marriott, who, inspired by David Schneider's work on kinship, wrote of the simultaneously biological and moral substance that composes the Indian "dividual." Marriott, "Hindu Transactions." This idea has been creatively developed by many anthropologists, far beyond those who work on questions of medicine and personhood in South Asia. Of particular relevance is Joseph Alter's extensive scholarship on Gandhian dietetics, in which morality was a problem where "truth and biology were equally implicated." Alter, "Gandhi's Body, Gandhi's Truth," 301. At the same time, it is important to note the ways in which both antistigma activists and those involved in the anti-Brahmin/ anticaste movements in south India have worked to pry apart ideas of morality and biology, under the signs of political and scientific modernity, bhakti devotional movements, and the Tamil Self-Respect Movement (*suya mariyathai iyakkam*).

92. Muthu, *Pulmonary Tuberculosis* (1922), 140.

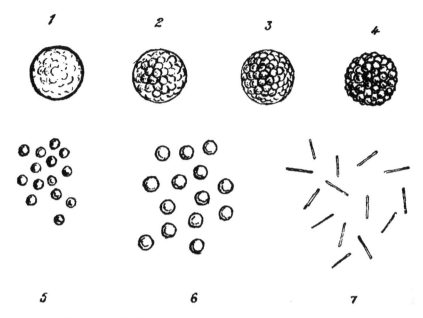

Figure 1.1. This image, which diagrams the mutation of a leukocyte (a white blood cell) into a bacterium in seven steps, was reproduced by Muthu in his book with the permission of C. H. Collings. Collings, Muthu, and many others were continuing the half-century-old debate between two French scientists, Antoine Béchamp and Louis Pasteur. Béchamp had insisted against Pasteur that the body was composed of entities called *microzymas*. These microzymas, Béchamp maintained, were the basic building blocks of the body, and they were inherently unstable (and therefore mutable). Diagram taken from Muthu, *Pulmonary Tuberculosis* (1922), 174.

could not be the cause of disease. They suffer with us because they are part of us. The cure for humans, then, was also the cure for bacteria. In this sense, cure represented a kind of theological intervention that exceeded the human, encompassing worlds both larger and smaller.

Life in the Void

As the years rolled by, those who prioritized soil at the expense of seed in their explanations of the cause of disease found their position increasingly difficult to defend. It all started back in May 1882, when the German bacteriologist Robert Koch announced that he had isolated the true cause of tuberculosis, a rod-shaped bacterium visible only under a microscope. It probably started even earlier, with Louis Pasteur's demonstration that germs live among us. Or even before that, as an inkling about microbial existence slowly became a full-blown

Figure 1.2. Patients engaged in breathing exercises at Muthu's Mendip Hills Sanatorium in Britain. Singh, "An Indian Tuberculosis Specialist in England," 536.

thought. Nevertheless, the events of 1882 certainly moved things along, especially when it came to tuberculosis. With Koch's microbial discovery, hopes ran high among both physicians and sufferers that a cure would soon follow.

Since the time of the Greek physician Galen, knowing what causes a disease had been taken to be a critical step toward finding its cure (an idea we still hold dear in our time of mysterious syndromes and phantom pains).[93] But a cure that specifically targeted bacteria was slow to come. Between the time of Koch's announcement and the development of the first antituberculosis drugs in the 1940s, between these two revolutions in medicine—an etiological revolution premised on knowledge of germs, and a therapeutic one founded on the development of antibiotics—the relationship between cause and cure was thrown out of sync. As the historian of medicine Katherine Ott put it, "Koch's discovery created both a theoretical and technical *void* rather than any insight into therapeutics and prophylaxis."[94]

For Muthu, the solution was not to be found in specific treatments that targeted bacteria, which would be like "administering a pill to cure an earthquake."[95] Even for those like Lankester and Sprawson, who held what was arguably a

93. On the relationship between knowledge of cause and knowledge of cure, see Porter, *Medicine*, 68.

94. Ott, *Fevered Lives*, 53, emphasis added.

95. Muthu, "Some Impressions of Tuberculosis Problems in India," 120.

CHAPTER ONE

more balanced view of the relationship between seed and soil in attributing some part of disease causality to bacteria, there remained no clear means of targeting these bacteria. The only option was to transform the soil. The weakened body was vulnerable to tuberculosis. How then might its vitality be restored?

Vitalism has had many incarnations: as a philosophy, as a means of grappling with the concept of life in all of its complexity, and as a basis for therapeutic intervention. In the early twentieth century, when physicians in India referred to vitality, they had in mind the idea that something distinct from matter—a force, power, or principle—animates and gives life to that matter. Above all, the presence of vitality distinguished the living from the nonliving. In its most polemic forms, vitalism stood against mechanism, a competing strain of philosophical thought that posited that life could emerge from nonliving elements without the infusion of a vital supplement. For the mechanists, life was nothing more than an incredibly complex machine (but as we have seen, the vital and the mechanical could be intertwined, as in the figure of the organic machine).

The enduring place of vitalism in the treatment of tuberculosis can be attributed, at least in part, to the lasting influence of German Romantic *Naturphilosophie*. The first sanatorium, with its focus on the restoration of vitality in the open air, was established in Silesia (now Poland) by the physician Hermann Brehmer in 1854. About thirty years later, when Koch argued that tuberculosis was caused by bacteria, it's tempting to imagine that he was putting the final nail in the coffin of vitalism. Yet vitalism did not simply vanish. Nor did the sanatorium. To the contrary, the sanatorium cure and its vitalist foundations flourished in the void generated by Koch's discovery. Bacteriological modes of understanding, explaining, and treating disease did not simply displace vitalist modes of reasoning.[96] References to bacteria mingled freely with discussions of vitality, resisting energies, vital force, power, and capacity.

In India, the influence of vitalist thought stretched far beyond medicine. After all, Naturphilosophie had drawn heavily on Romantic readings of Indian philosophy and religion.[97] But we might also look to those forms of mysticism that circulated between Britain and colonial India, which led to the formation of the highly respected Theosophical Society, founded by the occultist Madame

---

96. Worboys, *Spreading Germs*. As Craig Gordon puts it, the sanatorium exemplified "the persistence of vitalistic understandings of the disease in the face of the advances in medical science that dominate traditional histories." Gordon, *Literary Modernism, Bioscience, and Community*, 62–63.

97. See Ott, *Fevered Lives*, 33; see also Chakrabarti, *Western Science in Modern India*, 207.

Blavatsky and established in Madras in 1883.[98] Another source of vitalism in India could be found in the work of the Bengali scientist Jagadish Chandra Bose, whose research into metals and plant cells confounded the boundaries between living organisms and nonliving matter by applying physiological categories to inert substances.[99]

Gesturing toward what he took to be more autochthonous sources of vitalist philosophy in India, Muthu claimed that the "ancient Yogis" understood that "breath was life, and that fresh atmospheric air, in its freest state, was charged with a universal principle of life, or vital force, called *prana . . .* through which life manifests itself."[100] By calling on such traditions, Muthu effectively recuperated an Indian history of vitalist thought in medical practice, allowing him to make claims about the precocious knowledge of Indian antiquity. Taken together with the German vitalist traditions, he was able to construct a historically deep and geographically wide-ranging justification for sanatorium therapy. In fact, Muthu had gone as far as to incorporate a kind of secularized yoga practice into the sanatorium treatment he offered in the Mendip Hills of Britain (and most likely in India as well). Despite his references to ancient yogis, the form of yoga practiced in his sanatoria was largely decontextualized from its ancient moorings and reconstituted within the culture of physical exercise emerging in both Britain and India.[101] Such a yoga fit well into Muthu's sanatorium program, which incorporated the British sanatorium's emphasis on graduated exercise with the German sanatorium's focus on open-air therapy.

Muthu also looked to what was called "nature cure," a form of therapeutics with foundations in Europe that had been taken up with much enthusiasm in India.[102] In his correspondence, Mahatma Gandhi, a prominent advocate for

98. On the circulation of Theosophical thought, see Viswanathan, "The Ordinary Business of Occultism"; see also Jones, *The Racial Discourses of Life Philosophy.*

99. On Bose's alternative science, see Nandy, *Alternative Sciences*; Visvanathan, "The Dreams of Reason," 43; Geddes, *The Life and Work of Sir Jagadis C. Bose.*

100. Muthu, *Pulmonary Tuberculosis* (1922), 81–82, 90.

101. On the reconstitution of yoga as modern physical exercise tied to anatomy, and as a form of therapeutics, see Alter, *Yoga in Modern India.* For the use of yoga as a form of physical culture central to anticolonial and Hindu nationalist movements, see Valiani, *Militant Publics in India,* 36, 49–50. On the history of the mainstreaming of yoga in Britain and its de-essentialization, albeit in a later period, see Newcombe, *Yoga in Britain.*

102. On nature cure in India, see Alter, "Nature Cure and Ayurveda." Vitality was a serious concern for many practitioners of the Indian nature cure. One of its main

nature cure, invoked Muthu's work to argue for natural forms of healing that relied on diet and environment.[103] Gandhi had in fact consulted with Muthu about his high blood pressure and digestive problems. In an interview with the Associated Press, Muthu is quoted as saying, "I found that [Gandhi] had injured himself through too much fasting. I put him on a diet which varied goat's milk with salads, vegetables, fruits and nuts . . . but the Mahatma didn't like the salads, so he went back to goat's milk and nuts. . . . He continues to do this even in prison."[104]

In a letter addressed to Muthu from 1928, Gandhi wrote, "As you know I have a horror of drugs and the like. I therefore welcome every honest effort to replace them with drugless and what might be termed natural methods of curing a disease which need never find an abode in this sunny soil of ours."[105] Nature cure and sanatorium treatment provided a means for Muthu to unearth what, to his mind, had already been known within Indian medical and philosophical systems. The centrality of vital forces in the shaping of health and illness was a profoundly universal truth. No, a pill would not do. To cure an earthquake, you had to restore the vitality of the soil itself.

Bone, Muscle, Blood, and Pluck

If the restoration of vitality depended on the body's openness to nature, we can begin to understand why zenanas occupied such a frightful place in the British imagination. Through enclosure and confinement, the women who inhabited zenanas were not only shielded from society but deprived of life itself. Nevertheless, British empathy had its limits. While certain kinds of bodies seemed

----

proponents, K. Lakshmana Sarma, argued that "by excessive attachments one comes to disregard the rules of hygienic living; and this leads to a loss of vitality." In Alter, *Gandhi's Body*, 80.

103. Gandhi's faith in Muthu's philosophy led him to recommend him to friends. He even organized the treatment of the son of a jeweler friend, Revashankar Jagjivan Javeri, by having Muthu travel from Madras to Bombay to examine a tubercular bone. Gandhi also wrote to Rajaji and Nehru about Muthu's ideas. See Gandhi, *The Collected Works*, February 25, 1928, vol. 41, 225; February 27, 1928, vol. 41, 238; February 29, 1928, vol. 41, 239.

104. "Gandhi, Fortified by Goat's Milk, Fit for New Battles," 24.

105. Gandhi, *The Collected Works*, April 5, 1928, vol. 41, 368. Writing in his Gujarati-language weekly newspaper, Gandhi explained "vital essence" as something that "chemists cannot detect by analysis," even though "health experts have been able to feel its presence." *Navajivan*, June 6, 1929, in Gandhi, *The Collected Works*, vol. 46, 124.

to cry out for salvation (at least to those with a certain kind of humanitarian, often Christian sensibility), others demanded enclosure and even imprisonment. What kind of cure could be imagined for those whose freedom had been ripped from them by the state?

The question of tuberculosis in prisons began to emerge in the late 1850s, with the arrival in India of a young doctor named Joseph Ewart, an assistant surgeon posted to the Bengal Medical Service, at a time when India was under the corporate rule of the British East India Company. Ewart was a physician and a researcher. He hungered for information. Records of disease and death among civilian populations in India were notoriously uneven and frequently unavailable. Working with officials from across the Madras, Bengal, and Bombay presidencies, Ewart began collecting information about hospitalizations and deaths. What he found was that there were in fact two populations that were kept under regular surveillance, for whom morbidity and mortality statistics were scrupulously recorded: soldiers and prisoners.

The information he gathered allowed him to make comparisons not only between soldiers and prisoners but also between Britishers and Indians. Among both native and British regiments, Ewart found that phthisis was the fourth leading cause of disease and death.[106] The rates of phthisis were lowest among native soldiers, with their British counterparts suffering at about twice the rate. British officers, who undoubtedly enjoyed a higher standard of living than either of these other two groups, fell somewhere in the middle.

What Ewart documented was a clear difference between the races. He bemoaned this needless loss of "British bone and muscle, British blood, and British pluck" on Indian soil.[107] Governing a colony like a business was an expensive endeavor, paid for in British lives. For much of the nineteenth century, colonial medicine in India was primarily enclavist, focused on the

106. A helpful reminder: throughout the nineteenth century and into the early twentieth, the terms *scrofula, phthisis,* and *tuberculosis* were used to describe a variety of related conditions. Generally speaking, *scrofula* referred to a swelling of the glands, *phthisis* referred to wasting, and *tuberculosis* referred to a condition in which caseous growths, or tubercles, could be found in the lungs. Prior to the establishment of a common bacterial cause for these conditions, their relationship was a matter of much debate.

107. Joseph Ewart, *A Digest of the Vital Statistics of the European and Native Armies in India: Interspersed with Suggestions for the Eradication and Mitigation of the Preventible and Avoidable Causes of Sickness and Mortality amongst Imported and Indigenous Troops* (London: Smith, Elder and Co., 1859), 6, Wellcome Library TRO RAMC Collection, Rare Materials Room.

lives of Europeans stationed in cantonments and behind civil lines.[108] Given this inequality of attention, Ewart began to ask himself why it was that Indians seemed to suffer less than Britishers. For much of the nineteenth century, the general consensus among British medical doctors and colonial administrators was that tuberculosis was not a serious problem in India. Prior to the turn toward theories of virgin soil, the natives of the subcontinent were thought to enjoy a partial immunity to the condition. In part, it was thought that this had something to do with the climate. Even British soldiers, in the early stages of the disease, were advised that travel to India might alleviate their symptoms, if not offer complete cure.

Beginning in the 1840s, reports began to trickle in of tuberculous conditions among Indians examined at hospitals and dispensaries across northern India: in Howrah, Mindapore, Cawnpore, the lower Himalayas, and lower Bengal.[109] In 1854, T. W. Wilson of the Bengal Medical Service forcefully argued against the prevailing notion that the disease was somehow rare in India, and that the Indian climate offered much in the way of cure for the British soldier.[110] Ewart built on Wilson's findings, blaming the scarcity of Indian cases on poor diagnostic skills (specifically, auscultation); the difficulty in making postmortem examinations of native bodies; and finally, the high prevalence of "bowel complaints" among the Indian population, which he noted often carried them away before tuberculosis could manifest itself.[111] Nevertheless, Ewart argued against Wilson that tuberculous conditions were in general rarer in India than they were in Europe.

Except perhaps, among those who were confined to Indian prisons. As in the military, phthisis was the fourth leading cause of death among prisoners. However, Indian prisoners tended to fall ill and die at far higher rates than their compatriots in the army. Ewart was shocked by what he described as the "defective sanitary and hygienic state of Indian Prisons," which produced the

108. The movement from enclavist medicine to something like a more capacious public health concerned with Indian lives began toward the end of the nineteenth century, particularly in the wake of epidemic outbreaks like plague in 1887–88. Rather than simply an extension of sympathy or an assumption of responsibility, this move should also be read as a response to the growing understanding that the shared environment (and the possibility of infection) meant that Indian health inevitably had effects on British health.

109. Joseph Ewart, "On Scrofula, Tuberculosis, and Phthisis in India," *Indian Medical Gazette*, December 1882, 335, Wellcome Library K21780.

110. Wilson, "On Tubercular Diseases in the East."

111. Ewart, "On Scrofula, Tuberculosis, and Phthisis in India," 335.

"most appalling mortuary bills that are to be found among any class of human beings on the face of the civilized world."[112] As things were going, he estimated that it would only take about fifteen years to complete the "annihilation of the criminal population."[113]

As a solution, Ewart proposed that greater powers should be granted to the medical officers of prisons, who held an advisory role and were involved only in "curative" rather than "preventive" endeavors, an arrangement that Ewart described as "fatal to successful sanitary discipline."[114] It's difficult to say whether his appeal bore fruit. But it is clear that, when it came to disease, Indian prisons remained sites of grave concern for decades to come.[115] As late as 1924, a government report compiling data from across the country noted that overcrowding and disease were serious problems in Indian prisons.[116] The report included, for what seems to be the first time, a separate category for "tubercle of the lungs."[117] Yet the great majority of provinces had no data available for prisoners with tuberculosis.[118] Despite this lack of data, many provinces reported that the disease was "rare" and that "very few prisoners contract the disease in jail."[119]

112. Joseph Ewart, *The Sanitary Condition and Discipline of Indian Jails* (London: Smith, Elder and Co., 1860), v, Wellcome Library K21780.

113. Ewart, *The Sanitary Condition and Discipline of Indian Jails*, 2.

114. Ewart, *The Sanitary Condition and Discipline of Indian Jails*, xi.

115. In 1919, the Bombay municipal commissioner reported that 51,525 prisoners were confined in his prisons. However, the *Bombay Jail Manual* clearly stated that each prisoner was to have at least 648 cubic feet of space. By that measure, the number of prisoners should have been about 27,000, about half of the existing population. Cited from *Bombay Jail Manual*, annexure to letter from E. J. Turner to the Public & Judicial Committee, March 31, 1926, 156, R. & S. 2398/20, L/P/J/6/1927, British Library.

116. "Report on the Sickness and Mortality in the Jails of India and Tables Relating to the Jails in British India for 1924: Overcrowding and Tuberculosis in Indian Jails—Report by the Government of India," 1926, P. & J. 409, Public and Judicial Department, L/P/J/6/1927, British Library.

117. "Note by the Public Health Commissioner with the Government of India on the Health of the Jails in India during 1924," with table included as annexure, 1926, P. & J. 409, British Library.

118. Government of India, Home Department, Simla, despatch to Earl Birkenhead, His Majesty's Secretary of State for India, "Jails," May 12, 1927, Subject: "Overcrowding and Tuberculosis in Indian Jails," Enclosure no. 3, Statement B, "Particulars furnished by local Governments of number of cases of tuberculosis admitted to jails and the number contracting the disease after admission," L/P/J/6/1927, British Library.

119. Government of India, Home Department, despatch to Earl Birkenhead, "Jails," May 12, 1927, British Library.

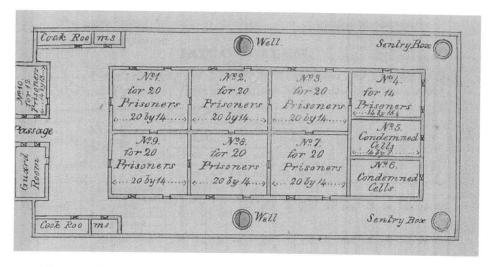

Figure 1.3. Plan for a jail in Salem. Lithograph by B. C. Regel, "Plan of the Jails at Salem, No. 1" (Madras Lithographic Press), in *Report on the Medical Topography and Statistics of the Southern Division of the Madras Army: Compiled from the Records of the Medical Board Office*, 83 (Madras: R. W. Thorpe at the Vepery Mission Press, 1843), British Library.

Even with its incompleteness, we can still learn a few things from the report. For example, prisons in Madras had the highest mortality rate overall (although, again there was no data on tuberculosis).[120] Burma, which did track tuberculosis, had nearly one thousand cases, a third of which resulted in death.[121] We can also get a sense of scale: from the years 1915 to 1924, 586 prisoners were diagnosed with smallpox, of which 57 died (about one-twelfth of the total number of cases). Over the same period, there were 11,553 recorded tubercle cases among prisoners, resulting in 3,494 deaths (nearly one-third of a much larger population). Even with limited records, it is clear that tuberculosis in prisons was both common and deadly. As the report speculated, "Of those who did not die in prison the vast majority would die later of the disease."[122]

The most common approach to dealing with tuberculous prisoners was to transfer them to less crowded facilities. But this was taken to be a "palliative"

120. J. B. Smith, "Enclosure, Note by Medical Adviser," March 22, 1926, included in letter from Birkenhead, India Office London, to His Excellency the Governor General of India in Council, May 13, 1926, Public, no. 44, L/P/J/6/1917, British Library.

121. Smith, "Enclosure, Note by Medical Adviser," March 22, 1926, British Library.

122. Smith, "Enclosure, Note by Medical Adviser," March 22, 1926, British Library.

measure; a more "radical cure," at least according to the Home Department, could only be provided through "an increase of jail accommodation."[123] Then, as now, the proposed solution was to build more jails. With more jails, tuberculous prisoners could be completely segregated from the general prison population. However, many of the provincial authorities felt strongly that the construction of additional jails was either unnecessary or financially impractical.

Ultimately, neither relocation nor segregation were curative measures. J. B. Smith, a medical advisor to the government, questioned the logic of putting people in jail for minor offenses, where they were likely to die of communicable disease. In effect, he argued, jail time was a death sentence. Smith further wondered whether "Indian crime," as he put it, was in fact the result of chronic illness that made it impossible to work.[124] In which case, the prison did not simply confine or punish criminals—it produced them (and certainly did not cure them).

Die Free or Die

> Evil deeds like poison weeds thrive well in prison air;
> It is only what is good in man that wastes and withers there.
>
> —Legislative Council, "Supplementary Estimates"

The function of Indian prisons was a matter of some debate.[125] Were they machines of reform, or did they instead manufacture the criminality they were meant to punish? Or perhaps their function was largely political: a place to sequester freedom fighters from the general population, to prevent the spread of populist sentiment. Political prisoners were frequently jailed for challenging the authority of the British Crown, deprived of their own freedom while fighting for the freedom of the country.

In 1924, in a case that would grab headlines, the colonial authorities alleged that a group of communist leaders in Cawnpore, in the United Provinces, had been engaged in a conspiracy against the Crown: "to deprive the King Emperor of the sovereignty of British India" by violent, revolutionary

123. Government of India, Home Department, despatch to Earl Birkenhead, "Jails," May 12, 1927, British Library.

124. Smith, "Enclosure, Note by Medical Adviser," March 22, 1926, British Library.

125. The quote in the epigraph to this section is from Legislative Council, "Supplementary Estimates," April 2, 1927, transcript of debate, poem quoted by A. P. Dube, p. 1224, L/P/J/6/1927, British Library.

means.[126] Among those convicted in the Cawnpore Bolshevik Conspiracy Case, as it came to be known, was Shaukat Usmani, who would spend sixteen years incarcerated in a series of Indian prisons. Usmani was a recognized leader of the communist movement that had begun to emerge in India from the early 1920s. He had even participated in efforts to secure Soviet support for the Indian freedom struggle against the British. During his many years in prison, he maintained his high public profile by running for British Parliament, twice, in constituencies several thousand miles away across an ocean. He viewed his unwinnable campaigns as a means of shedding light on the undemocratic injustice perpetrated by colonial rule.

During his stay at a prison in Dehra Dun, in the foothills of the Himalayas, Usmani developed tuberculosis. News of his condition made its way to Thakur Majit Sing Rathor, a member of the legislative council of the United Provinces. He attempted to have Usmani transferred to a prison in Almora, which enjoyed a rather more salubrious climate in the Kumaon Hills. Rathor's efforts were thwarted, and it was decided that Usmani would be transferred instead to a rather curious institution located in Sultanpur, also in the United Provinces. This institution was described, rather incomprehensibly, as a "Sanatorium-Jail."[127]

The sanatorium: life in the open air.
The jail: life in confinement.

How might a single institution combine such contradictory elements and functions, simultaneously punitive and curative?[128] This question emerged as the underside of a seemingly innocuous proposal presented to the legislative council of the United Provinces in April 1927. The proposal itself was exceedingly run-of-the-mill: the hiring of a new medical officer for the Sultanpur Prison-Sanatorium.[129] Rather than considering this new hire, the assembled delegates chose instead to focus on the nature of this seemingly paradoxical institution. How could a prison be curative?

126. Section 121-A, Indian Penal Code.

127. Smith, "Enclosure, Note by Medical Adviser," March 22, 1926, British Library.

128. This is in a sense an iteration of an older question that remains with us today—namely, can prison operate simultaneously as a space of punishment and rehabilitation?

129. Legislative Council, "Supplementary Estimates," April 2, 1927, transcript of debate, p. 1201, L/P/J/6/1927, British Library.

T. H. Symons, the director-general of the Indian Medical Service, had provided a partial answer the year before. The ideal jail-sanatorium, he had explained, would be dry, positioned between two thousand and three thousand feet above sea level, and exposed to the air and sunshine. Climatically, then, it would resemble a sanatorium. But to prevent escape, it would also have to be secure.[130] In this way, it would resemble a jail. Somehow, the prison-sanatorium would have to combine the openness to nature exemplified by the sanatorium with the level of confinement ensured by the prison.

Given these parameters, the District of Sultanpur struck the legislative council as a rather odd choice to locate such an institution. The nationalist council member Babu Bhagwat Sahai Bedar noted that the *Imperial Gazetteer* described Sultanpur as "dreary" and "bleak," only "occasionally relieved by mango groves."[131] It was a district prone to heavy rainfall and flooding. Yet the *Gazetteer* also described Sultanpur as "mild and healthy."[132] Many of the council members took exception to this conclusion, noting that Sultanpur's climate was no better than anywhere else, and undoubtedly much worse.

Those who were present for the debate largely agreed that a prison was no place to seek cure.[133] A well-known freedom fighter himself, Pandit Badri Dutt Pande was the delegate from Almora, a hill station known for its salubrious climate and sanatoria. He described his own experience of imprisonment in a jail in Lucknow during the noncooperation movement. The temperatures in the prison, he recounted, rose to 117 degrees Fahrenheit. "For a hill-man, it

130. T. H. Symons, Director-General of the Indian Medical Service, in despatch to Earl Birkenhead, His Majesty's Secretary of State for India, Enclosure no. 1, Subject: "Overcrowding and Tuberculosis in Indian Jails," June 17, 1926, L/P/J/6/1927, British Library.

131. Legislative Council, "Supplementary Estimates," April 2, 1927, p. 1212, L/P/J/6/1927, British Library. The precise wording from the *Imperial Gazetteer* describes the district as "a dreary, bleak, and ravine-cut tract, occasionally relieved by mango trees." *Imperial Gazetteer of India*, vol. 23, 130. The *Imperial Gazetteer* was a multivolume geographic encyclopedia that contained information about economy, society, climate, and topography. It's worth mentioning that in the course of these debates, the delegate Baba Bhagwati Sahai Bedar insinuated that the jail-sanatorium had been built in Sultanpur only because of back-room dealings between the government and the delegate from Sultanpur, Surendra Pratap Sahi.

132. *Imperial Gazetteer of India*, vol. 23, 131.

133. In 1925, of the eighty-five tuberculosis patients who had been admitted to Sultanpur, only twenty had been "discharged as cured." Legislative Council, "Supplementary Estimates," April 2, 1927, p. 1209, L/P/J/6/1927, British Library.

was tremendously unbearable."[134] Spending so long in such a place, he feared, would make cure impossible, even in the hills.

What Sultanpur represented was the continuation of policies of relocation and segregation. But there was little to be found there in terms of cure. For this reason, many of the delegates insisted that tuberculous prisoners be released as soon as possible. Babu Bhagwati Sahai Bedar argued that if a prisoner had tuberculosis, they should be released or sent to the gallows: "In the Sultanpur jail, rest assured the poor man will naturally die."[135] The prison was a site of death; the sanatorium, life. Lala Nemi Saran, a Jain delegate from the Bijnor District near Delhi, argued that a hospital and a prison were entirely separate types of institutions.[136] A sanatorium-prison was still, ultimately, a prison. Architecturally and philosophically, the two could not be reconciled.

As bearers of civilization, and as rulers over a foreign people, the colonial state was thought to have a responsibility for its people, including its prisoners. Disease, and tuberculosis specifically, had exposed the tension between the colonial imperatives to control and to care. Anandi Prasad Dube, a Brahmin barrister from Allahabad, argued that it was the duty of "every enlightened State" to ensure "the proper care and welfare of the citizen from his birth up to his death."[137] To confine a tuberculous patient in a place like Sultanpur, Dube argued, was "nothing short of a crime."[138] If the prison generated "Indian crime," as the medical advisor J. B. Smith earlier noted, it was also emblematic of the crime of British colonialism.

Let's return to Usmani's would-be defender, Thakur Majit Sing Rathor. He too felt that cure was impossible in prison and insisted that tuberculous prisoners should be freed.[139] The colonial state had itself set a precedent for release back in 1921, when almost all the tuberculous prisoners being held in

134. Legislative Council, "Supplementary Estimates," April 2, 1927, p. 1209, British Library.

135. Legislative Council, "Supplementary Estimates," April 2, 1927, p. 1213, British Library.

136. Legislative Council, "Supplementary Estimates," April 2, 1927, p. 1214, British Library.

137. Legislative Council, "Supplementary Estimates," April 2, 1927, p. 1224, British Library.

138. Legislative Council, "Supplementary Estimates," April 2, 1927, p. 1224, British Library.

139. Legislative Council, "Supplementary Estimates," April 2, 1927, p. 1203, British Library.

Sultanpur were set free—not out of humanitarian concern but due to worries about overcrowding. And even more recently, Rathor noted, the freedom fighter Subhas Chandra Bose had been released from imprisonment in Mandalay, where he had also fallen ill with tuberculosis. The government had offered to send him for treatment in India or somewhere in Europe.[140] Such munificence should be extended to all tuberculous prisoners, Rathor insisted.

Yet for all his boldness, Rathor stopped short of advocating for release in Usmani's case. Ultimately, Rathor was a politician, and he feared that he would be painted as sympathetic to Bolshevism. Nevertheless, he insisted that as a general principle prison was not the place for those with tuberculosis. "Either such a prisoner should be set at liberty or else, if he is considered to be a danger to the society, he should be sent to Bhowali or Almora."[141] Rathor continued, "I insist that the considerations of humanity, the necessity of life require that patients suffering from tuberculosis, whether they are Indian or European ought to be set free. They ought to be allowed freedom of movement, and freedom of life, so that they might try to escape death by undergoing satisfactory treatment, and, if this cannot be done, they ought to be treated at the expense of the State in sanatoria and they should not be kept in jail so long as they suffer from this disease."[142] Openness was not simply about being outside, but about being free. Freedom was manifestly physical, in the sense that it required freedom from confinement by the colonial state (or, in the case of Indian women, freedom from confinement in the zenana).[143] But for these political prisoners, freedom was also more than physical, in that it required the removal of the imperial yoke. In this sense, the freedom required for cure was an intensely political matter.

140. After a brief stay in Calcutta, Bose traveled to Europe. He made a stop in Germany to visit Jawaharlal Nehru after his wife, Kamala, died while seeking treatment at a sanatorium, as described in chapter 2.

141. Legislative Council, "Supplementary Estimates," April 2, 1927, p. 1203, British Library.

142. Legislative Council, "Supplementary Estimates," April 2, 1927, p. 1204, British Library.

143. The analogy between prison and zenana was quite explicit, as parallel architectures of confinement and unfreedom marked by gendered differences. Inderpal Grewal puts it quite bluntly when she writes, "within European colonial discourse," the zenana "signified female incarceration." Grewal, *Home and Harem*, 200.

The Goldilocks Principle

Was the sanatorium a site of freedom? It was certainly a complicated meeting place where unusual friendships might develop—say, between a Sikh gentleman from Gwalior and a destitute Englishman—but sanatoria were never completely severed from the constraints of life outside.[144] Divisions of religion, caste, class, gender, and race found their way into the very design of sanatorium life in early twentieth-century India. In Almora, a hill station in the United Provinces, the Church of Scotland had established a sanatorium run by women missionaries exclusively for European and Anglo-Indian Christian women.[145] In the Madras Presidency, the Union Mission Tuberculosis Sanatorium in Madanapalle set aside beds exclusively for the use of European Christians.

This preference for Christian patients reflected the high level of investment in sanatoria by missionaries. We might look, for example, to a proposal for a sanatorium in Kashmir, developed by Dr. Arthur Neve of the Mission Hospital in Srinagar. A deeply religious man with a long mustache and a thin patch of hair on his balding crown, Neve was a medical missionary who, along with his brother Ernest, had devoted his life to providing healing alongside spiritual awakening. Neve was known for delivering sermons to his captive Hindu patients, bedridden and unable to escape his evangelism.

Neve was also recognized for his expertise on tuberculosis. He envisioned for Kashmir a sanatorium with separate blocks for Hindus and Muslims, subsidized beds for the poor, and more expensive beds for the wealthy. A Brahmin cook would be needed to provide food for high-caste Hindu patients. Like the maharaja of Patiala, he too advocated for the building of a separate "home for dying consumptives," which would house "advanced, and practically incurable cases."[146] When patients died in the sanatorium, he explained, it gave the entire

144. See the critiques of romantic visions of the sanatorium as enclosed social spaces in Bryder, *Below the Magic Mountain*; Condrau, "'Who Is the Captain of All These Men of Death'"; Condrau, "Beyond the Total Institution."

145. The sanatorium at Almora, in the United Provinces, originally began as the home of the London Missionary Society. It was established in 1908 for the treatment of European and Anglo-Indian Christian women.

146. Arthur Neve, "Tuberculosis in Kashmir," September 2, 1916, enclosed in letter from the Superintendent Surgeon, Jammu and Kashmir State Hospitals, Gulmarg, to the First Assistant to the Resident in Kashmir, no. 1529, Subject: Sanatorium for Tuberculosis, "Establishment of Sanatoria for Treatment of Patients Suffering from Tubercular Diseases," *Proceedings of the Home Department*, May 1912, no. 46, British Library.

institution "a bad name."[147] In this way, the sanatorium was porous to the social world outside its walls, staunchly upholding its religious and economic divisions.[148]

Neve penned his proposal for a sanatorium in Kashmir in response to a circular from the Home Department that wound its way around courtly *darbars* and government offices across the country. In the wake of the sanatorium experiment at Dharampur, the circular called for the building of sanatoria in each of the provinces. The circular referred specifically to incipient reports of an increase in tuberculosis in Indian cities as well as in the larger towns. Sanatorium treatment, it was thought, might offer the "only *hope of cure*."[149] The circular further suggested that provincial governments look to public charity or private philanthropy to fund their efforts.

In general, the responses from the provincial governments drew on five forms of excuse:

1. Tuberculosis was not a serious problem. Coorg, for example, had no large towns where tuberculosis might thrive.[150] In the Central Provinces, many civil surgeons had only a vague "impression" that tuberculosis was increasing, but they lacked any real "proof."[151]

147. Neve, "Tuberculosis in Kashmir," September 2, 1916, *Proceedings of the Home Department*, British Library.

148. This is a point made by numerous historians of tuberculosis, who have argued against the otherworldliness of the sanatorium envisioned by Thomas Mann in his iconic *Magic Mountain*, as well as in the total institution concept advocated by Goffman. If the sanatorium did manage to break down social norms, it was only always temporary, as the patient was expected to eventually return to society.

149. H. C. Woodman, Esq., Additional Deputy Secretary, Home Department, Government of India, "Prevalence of Tuberculous Diseases in India: Establishment of Well Equipped Sanatoria in Different Parts of India for the Treatment of Tuberculous Patients," in *Proceedings of the Home Department*, June 1910, British Library. According to Niels Brimnes, the circular was initiated by the director of the Indian Medical Services, Sir Pardey Lukis. See Brimnes, *Languished Hopes*, 35.

150. Major W. G. Grey, Secretary to the Chief Commissioner of Coorg, to the Secretary to the Government of India, Home Department, "Establishment of Sanatoria for Treatment of Patients Suffering from Tubercular Diseases," June 14, 1910, no. 1280, *Proceedings of the Home Department*, May 1912, no. 41, British Library.

151. Lieutenant-Colonel R. P. Colomb, Second Secretary to the Chief Commissioner, Central Provinces, to the Secretary to the Government of India, Home (Medical) Department, "Establishment of Sanatoria for Treatment of Patients Suffering from Tubercular Diseases," October 31, 1910, no. 1673-VI-23-3, *Proceedings of the Home Department*, May 1912, no. 47, British Library.

2. There was no money. In the Northwest Frontier, it was thought that funds could be better spent on education and sanitary reform. In Bengal, the hospitals were in desperate need of new equipment.[152] In Bombay, the public had already built two sanatoria for the poor and middle classes: one in Poona, for Hindus, and the other in Nasik, for Parsis.[153] In Burma, provincial funds had already been committed to laboratories, surgical equipment, operating theaters, a Pasteur Institute, a lunatic asylum, and a new general hospital.

3. Patients were unwilling to leave their homes and their families behind to live in a sanatorium.

4. The climate was largely unsuitable for effective sanatorium treatment. In Coorg, it was too damp.[154] In the Northwest Frontier, it was reported that Hazara District had a favorable climate during one season, but that patients would have to migrate elsewhere during the off-season.[155] In Punjab, the climate was thought to be so pleasant that sanatoria were unnecessary; people could simply live outside. The climate was either too salubrious or not salubrious enough.

5. Sanatoria didn't really work, so there was no reason to build them.

With few exceptions, the responses from the provincial governments drew from these five forms of excuse to explain their inaction. Even Neve balanced his ambitious proposal with his insistence that the people of Kashmir would

152. H. Wheeler, Secretary to the Government of Bengal, Municipal (Medical) Department, to the Secretary to the Government of India, Home Department, "Establishment of Sanatoria for Treatment of Patients Suffering from Tubercular Diseases," August 21, 1911, no. 1740-Medl., *Proceedings of the Home Department*, May 1912, no. 50, British Library.

153. L. Robertson, Secretary to the Government of Bombay, General Department, to the Secretary to the Government of India, Home Department, "Establishment of Sanatoria for Treatment of Patients Suffering from Tubercular Diseases," August 18, 1910, no. 3970, *Proceedings of the Home Department*, May 1912, no. 44, British Library.

154. Grey, "Establishment of Sanatoria for Treatment of Patients Suffering from Tubercular Diseases," June 14, 1910, British Library.

155. Mr. W. R. H. Merk, Chief Commissioner and Agent to the Governor-General, North-West Frontier Province, to the Deputy Secretary to the Government of India, Home (Medical) Department, Simla, includes letter forwarded from Lieutenant-Colonel A. L. Duke, I.M.S., Administrative Medical Officer, North-West Frontier Province, no. 559-C, September 3, 1910, "Establishment of Sanatoria for Treatment of Patients Suffering from Tubercular Diseases," September 15, 1910, Nathiagali, no. 1724-N, *Proceedings of the Home Department*, May 1912, no. 45, British Library.

Figure 1.4. Muthu's sanatorium at Tambaram, just south of the city of Madras (1939). From "Origins of Tambaram Sanatorium," *The Hindu*, December 20, 2014, https://www .thehindu.com/features/downtown/origins-of-tambaram-sanatorium/article6710929.ece.

never pay for a sanatorium. The higher-ups in the Kashmiri government politely concurred.[156]

The bottom line was clear: the colonial government wanted to avoid paying for sanatoria. Prior to the 1920s, leprosy and malaria were the diseases that received the greatest financial support and attention in the colonies, especially in India. Although the National Insurance Act of 1911 provided free sanatorium treatment for the working class in Britain, the Crown was loath to add tuberculosis to its colonial burden. Sanatorium treatment was an expensive affair, requiring the construction of new infrastructure and the support of patients over long periods of treatment. After the passage of the Montagu-Chelmsford reforms of 1919, which further devolved responsibility for public health measures and spending to the provincial level, the problem of tuberculosis among the native population was left in the hands of philanthropic organizations like

156. Superintendent Surgeon, Jammu and Kashmir State Hospitals, Gulmarg, to the First Assistant to the Resident in Kashmir, Subject: Sanatorium for Tuberculosis, "Establishment of Sanatoria for Treatment of Patients Suffering from Tubercular Diseases," September 2, 1916, no. 1529, *Proceedings of the Home Department*, May 1912, no. 46, British Library.

CHAPTER ONE

the Dufferin Fund, medical missionaries, and private individuals: for example, David Chowry Muthu.[157]

A Model Colony

In the early 1920s, Muthu traveled around India to assess the severity of the tuberculosis situation. After concluding his journeys, he, like Lankester before him, submitted a confidential report of his findings to the Government of India. Throughout the country, Muthu noted, there were no more than eighteen tuberculosis homes and sanatoria.[158] He urged the government to support the establishment of additional sanatoria.[159]

What Muthu envisioned for India was more radical than the sanatoria that he had operated in Britain, which combined elements from the German open-air sanatorium with the Swiss emphasis on high altitudes and the British focus on graduated exercise and occupational therapy. Traditional sanatorium therapies, he contended, were inadequate in the Indian context, unless they were part of a broader garden colony:

> In the garden settlement there would be a sanatorium for early cases. In another part, houses or bungalows would be reserved for those suspected or threatened with tuberculosis. Still in another part, children of tuberculous parents or those in the pretuberculous stage would be looked after and placed under the best hygienic conditions and provided with an open-air school. In another place, convalescent or ex-patients would be accommodated with their families and be kept under medical supervision, and, if necessary, trained in some outdoor occupation. A public hall would be found useful for propaganda work, for giving lectures on hygiene and health subjects, and as a place of recreation and entertainment. A dairy farm with cows kept under ideal sanitary conditions would complete the equipment

157. See Brimnes, *Languished Hopes*, 26. See also Harrison, *Public Health in British India*. The Dufferin Fund, formally known as the National Association for Supplying Female Medical Aid to the Women of India, was established in 1885 by Lady Dufferin, the wife of a viceroy of India. The fund provided tuition for British women to acquire medical education to serve as doctors, midwives, and nurses in India and was an important contributor to the spread of Western medicine in India.

158. Muthu, "The Problem of Tuberculosis in India," 192.

159. A reference to this report can be found here: Associations and Institutions, *British Journal of Tuberculosis*, 31. Unfortunately, I was unable to locate a copy of the actual report.

of the garden colony, whose grounds would be laid out with spacious walks and broad avenues, so as to give the picturesque appearance of a health resort.[160]

Muthu's vision laid bare the utopianism of his approach to tuberculosis treatment. In India, as well as in Britain, the garden had long been a space of elite pleasure and leisure, as well as botanical research. In eighteenth-century Britain, the emergence of urban gardens for the people was a response to the growing sense that rapid population growth in cities had led to a concomitant rise in disease, including tuberculosis. Urban gardens and parks were attuned both to sanitation and to "moral and political health," providing a recreational alternative to drinking and gambling, while simultaneously providing evidence of good governance.[161] Gardening, particularly in its relation to botanical and agricultural sciences, was central to imperial efforts in India. The quest for botanical knowledge "guided the exploitation of exotic environments and made conquest seem necessary, legitimate, and beneficial."[162] Underlying the movement of botanical specimens and ideas between metropole and colony was an "almost sacred" investment in improvement—not only the improvement of agricultural practices, but also the refinement of the aesthetic ideals of the masses.[163] Closer at hand, Muthu undoubtedly drew inspiration from the Theosophical Garden in nearby Adyar, which itself borrowed from the gardening practices of landed elites, both European and Indian.[164]

As he imagined it, the sanatorium was only one small part of the larger pedagogical and curative functions of the garden colony.[165] The sanatorium would be hooked into a network of institutions including urban dispensaries, rural health villages for ex-patients, and open-air schools. "Fresh air, food, and rest help to recuperate the patient's failing energies and strengthen the soil, so that Nature may begin her beneficent work," wrote Muthu.[166]

160. Muthu, "The Problem of Tuberculosis in India," 192.

161. Drayton, *Nature's Government*, 181.

162. Drayton, *Nature's Government*, 181.

163. In 1838, for example, Kew Gardens opened to the public in an effort to educate, refine, and increase the "rational pleasure" of the working class. See Drayton, *Nature's Government*, 156.

164. Srinivas, *A Place for Utopia*, 74.

165. Notably, gardens in South Asia have come in many forms: pleasure gardens, sacred gardens, shade gardens, fruit gardens, rock gardens, herb gardens, wild gardens, mazes, and more recently, zoological gardens, botanical gardens, and sports parks. See Srinivas, *A Place for Utopia*.

166. Muthu, "Some Points in the Treatment of Pulmonary Tuberculosis," 955.

Yet not all nature was therapeutic. Within the medical topography of colonial India, swamps were miasmatic, productive of disease rather than cure. Jungles could be sites of productive extraction, but were equally places of terror and adventure—of the safari—with the attendant dangers of wild animals. The agricultural field was a site of labor, and given its relationship to the countryside, potentially therapeutic as well.

But what the sanatorium garden represented was a form of ordered, controlled nature, one that could serve as a curative milieu for tuberculosis patients.[167] In contrast to the industrial city, the sanatorium and its bungalows were akin to a small, sparsely populated village that opened up onto nature. In its pedagogical role, the garden colony was a model for society as it should be, as well as an image of society as it once was, intimately tied to nature. The sanatorium and the broader garden colony were intended as a paradigm for a vitalizing form of living, a mode of architecture and social life to which the city could aspire.[168]

This valorization of nature in the philosophy of the sanatorium movement, particularly in Muthu's version of it, might be productively understood alongside the importance that Gandhi gave to villages, as well as the modernist vision of the Scottish biologist and urban planner Patrick Geddes, who arrived in India in 1914. Geddes had developed a vitalist, "bio-centric philosophy of the urban," one that was inspired in part by his experience of observing tuberculosis patients in India "sleeping on the verandah or sitting on the *chabutra* (raised platform) and not simply traveling to a faraway mountain resort."[169] Through the "reunion of town and country, man and nature," Geddes thought it was

167. The garden was similarly prominent in an important parallel institution to the sanatorium, the asylum. Critically, however, the asylum was organized around confinement rather than openness. See Ernst, "Asylum Provision and the East India Company in the Nineteenth Century"; Ernst, *Mad Tales from the Raj.* For an argument that the sanatorium shared more in common with asylums and health resorts than with hospitals, see Bates, *Bargaining for Life,* 5.

168. As Smriti Srinivas has argued, utopianism was central to city planning in early twentieth-century South Asia. "Utopias are realized . . . in attempts to renew or heal 'Life,' whether through gardens or public health, and in the revitalization of knowledge and practice." The garden colony in particular provided what she calls a design for "cultural alternatives and futures," as well as a "critique of British imperialism and its spatial formations." Srinivas, *A Place for Utopia,* 4, 6.

169. Srinivas, *A Place for Utopia,* 14, 29. On the influence of the sanatorium's curative architecture on modernism, see Campbell, "What Tuberculosis Did for Modernism."

possible to live life "more abundantly."[170] He drew inspiration from the botanical gardens of England and from Mughal gardens that had been preserved by their British inheritors.[171] As Smriti Srinivas has argued, Geddes understood that "pleasure and horticulture are seamlessly interwoven with the knowledge of disease and its treatment."[172]

In its curative role, Muthu's garden colony exhibited a "mimetic therapeutic logic," seeking to "reproduce the qualities of (an apparently disease-free) preindustrial and preurban existence—an existence therefore in accordance with Nature's law."[173] The logic of the sanatorium, and the garden colony more generally, was to bolster the vitality of the body so that it might move through a temporary state of disease and return to a healthy condition—a kind of autorestoration effected by nature. Within the garden colony, disease might once again be curative rather than pathological. Such an autorestoration itself was a kind of freedom—not a freedom from, for example, confinement, but rather a positive freedom, the freedom to live, and potentially to live without relapse, as the body's previously exhausted vital capacities could be restored.

Critically, sanatorium treatment was not simply a prescription for fresh air. Muthu claimed that the most successful treatment for tuberculosis was a highly structured, personalized regimen that removed the patient from the pestilence of the city and properly disciplined both body and mind, while increasing vital energies. Returning to the city could be dangerous. For Muthu, a few weeks in the cool, fresh air of a hill station—the favored retreat of British military men, governors, and missionaries—was not only inadequate but positively iatrogenic. A little bit of cure, without the supervision of a doctor, was much more dangerous than no cure at all. As Muthu explained, a visibly broken door is opened and closed much more gently than one that appears intact but has been haphazardly patched up.

Muthu claimed that the sanatorium superintendent should behave like the captain of a ship, "knowing that in his right steering lie the welfare and the safety of those who are slumbering under his care and protection."[174] In this sense, the superintendent was a kind of sovereign, directing the choreography

170. Srinivas, *A Place for Utopia*, 35.

171. Srinivas, *A Place for Utopia*, 59. On the British preservation of Mughal gardens, see Ali and Flatt, "Introduction."

172. Srinivas, *A Place for Utopia*, 40.

173. Gordon, *Literary Modernism, Bioscience, and Community*, 69.

174. Muthu, *Pulmonary Tuberculosis and Sanatorium Treatment*, 109.

of the garden colony so as to effect cure for its inhabitants.[175] Rather than a return to a pristine nature, the garden, with its bovine and picturesque views and broad walkways, required the production of a kind of tamed or artificial nature.[176]

Never short of metaphors, Muthu also argued that the sanatorium director should be like a teacher, ensuring "patients are educated in right thinking and right living."[177] This pedagogical function was one of the primary purposes of sanatorium treatment in the garden colony.[178] As a model for how life should

175. The choreography of the superintendent might be productively compared to the choreography of pre-Sultanate royal gardens. As Daud Ali has noted, such gardens were not meant to represent nature so much as society. It was a projection of the social order, and the dramas that unfolded in the garden mirrored broader social dramas in miniature. See Ali, *Courtly Culture and Political Life in Early Medieval India*, 231.

Daud Ali has also demonstrated how royal gardens could operate by a kind of mimetic efficacy, as the power of the king to cause flowers (via his gardener) to continue to bloom out of season (*akala*) exemplified his sovereign power over nature. Such a wonder or spectacle made the garden into the inverse of nature, a demonstration of the king's power to violate the natural order and produce his own law. See Ali, "Botanical Technology and Garden Culture in Somesvara's Manasollasa," 49.

In this sense, the garden was also a way for the sovereign to represent his power to himself. The garden was a projection of a properly ruled realm, a space where the realm could be reflected upon, a physical space that was at once a "mental and speculative domain." See Ali and Flatt, "Introduction"; Ali, "Gardens in Early Indian Court Life."

176. Such an approach to the garden has a long history in India. As Daud Ali has written, early Indian gardens "were not perceived as 'wild,' 'untamed' or 'pristine' nature, but instead, carefully constructed and highly supplemented places. This 'artificial' character of gardens suggests that the natural world, to the extent that it was embodied in the garden, was not seen *in opposition* to human manipulation and artifice.... [There was] no Romantic concept in the early sources of the garden as a 'respite' from society and city." Ali, "Gardens in Early Indian Court Life," 223. Such gardens were "highly manipulated and ornamented places," described in Gupta-era handbooks for poets as "constructed" and "artificial" (233).

177. Muthu, *Pulmonary Tuberculosis and Sanatorium Treatment*, 108–9.

178. According to Flurin Condrau, historians of tuberculosis have viewed this pedagogic mission in a cynical light, as evidence that the sanatorium was less about cure and more about discipline, control, and the reconstruction of subjectivity. The issue for me is that such a view allows historians to retroactively determine curative efficacy rather than understanding efficacy itself as a historical artifact. See Condrau, "Beyond the Total Institution," 73.

As Michael Worboys has pointed out in his essay in the same volume, similar debates took place in the first decade of the twentieth century among medical

be lived, the sanatorium and garden colony were also paradigms for how society should be reorganized.

In the early 1920s, there were only three sanatoria in the entirety of the Madras Presidency—an area with a population that was equivalent to the entirety of Great Britain and Ireland—located in Madanapalle, Conoor, and Mysore. Muthu looked to add to that number. In 1926, he acquired 250 acres of land from the Madras government, located on a slope of a hill just south of the city. He named his project Tambaram, after the *taluk* in which it was located.[179] The foundation stone for Tambaram Sanatorium was laid in 1927 by C. P. Ramaswami Iyer, a lawyer and prominent member of the Executive Council of the Governor of Madras.[180] In April of the following year, the twelve-bed sanatorium (out of which four had already been filled) was properly inaugurated by the Indian politician and ambassador V. S. Srinivasa Sastri.[181]

Along the lines of his utopian vision, Muthu attempted to craft his Tambaram estate into a comprehensive garden colony. The problem of tuberculosis would prove to be an incitement to his imagination of curative utopia, one that would ideally spread beyond the sanatorium to the cities, towns, and villages of India and provide a new template for living based on a kind of return to nature. His cure was, if nothing else, nostalgic: a return to an idealized Indian past made possible by his own return from Britain. About halfway into

———

experts, some of whom argued that the sanatorium's role was as much educational as it was curative. It's important to consider, however, whether the curative function of the sanatorium could be so easily separated from its pedagogic function. For Muthu, pedagogy was clearly an aspect of curative intervention. See Worboys, "Before McKeown," 157. On the importance given to the pedagogical mission of the sanatorium, see also Worboys, "The Sanatorium Treatment for Consumption in Britain."

179. A taluk is a geographic unit of administration in India, smaller than a district but larger than a village.

180. A cross-section of Madras notables witnessed the laying of the foundation stone, including the businessman Muthiah Chettiar, the former minister Aneppu Parsuramdas Patro, High Court justices M. David Devadoss and Tiruvenkatachariar, and A. Rangaswami Iyengar, the editor of the *Hindu*.

181. Those present at the inauguration included Minister for Development Dewan Bahadur R. N. Arogyaswami Mudaliar, Dr. P. Subbaroyan, Justice Party member O. Kandaswami Chetty, and Dr. A. Lakshmipathy, a key figure in the Ayurvedic revival in south India, who in 1926 founded a "health village" outside Madras named Arogya Ashram. Muthu asked Gandhi to compose a note for the occasion, but Gandhi politely declined, explaining that if he indulged such requests he would never have time for anything else. Muthu, "The Problem of Tuberculosis in India," 193.

the Tambaram project, however, Muthu ran out of money.[182] He turned to the Madras government as well as to the Indian public for additional funds.[183] But as we already know, sanatoria in India were a difficult sell. Muthu came up empty-handed. His model of Indian society as it could be—rather, as it should be, and perhaps, as it once was—remained a dream unrealized.

182. His original plans were more ambitious: "six wards for men and six wards for women, besides administration offices, quarters for visitors, for post-graduate courses, etc." He only managed to complete about "half the sanatorium, with three wards on each side of the administrative building," "verandahs for two patients," and "quarters for medical officers and nurses." Muthu, "The Problem of Tuberculosis in India," 193.

183. Muthu, "A General Survey of Tuberculosis in India," 24.

Chapter Two

"Even mangoes can be got in England now,"
put in Fielding. "They ship them in ice-cold
rooms. You can make India in England
apparently, just as you can make England
in India."

"Frightfully expensive in both cases,"
said the girl.

—E. M. Forster, *A Passage to India*

In the late colonial world, a time before antibiotics, curative measures were frequently tethered to specific places. What mattered as much as therapeutic substance and modality—the *what* and *how* of cure—was the *where* of cure. A certain place could be curative for one person and pathogenic for another. British soldiers, for example, did their best to avoid being diagnosed with tuberculosis, a diagnosis that could end their careers and exile them from India, where permanent cure—understood in terms of the capacity for labor—was thought impossible. By contrast, an Indian man living in London petitioned the British government for return passage to India, which his doctor said was his only hope of cure. At first glance, it would appear that the possibility of cure was limited by the demands of a racialized biology, one that had a proper place in the world. But when we encounter an Irish schoolteacher desperate for passage to the Himalayas, or Kamala Nehru, the wife of India's first prime minister, sailing off to the Black Forest of Germany, the neat alignment of race and place comes unmoored from curative potential. As bodies, diseases, microbes, and materials traveled both to and away from India, a racialized geography became intimately linked to determinations of cause (What made you ill?) and responsibility (Who should shoulder the cost of treatment?). For some, travel itself could be curative—but it could also be pathogenic, as in the case of Indian coolie laborers who developed tuberculosis on their long journey to South Africa. In the continuing search for a better alchemy between bodies and their surroundings, one often finds that Cure Is Elsewhere.

Before Sunrise

In a world of myth, where cosmology takes precedence over physics, neither time nor space obey regular laws. When cure is elsewhere, time and space must be bent, folded, extended, or snipped so that it can be brought here and now (or if not now, then soon).

Let's begin again, far removed from the late colonial imagination of dusky zenanas and utopian garden colonies. The scene that greets us is the battlefield. The prevailing emotion is chaos, teetering into despair. In their war against the forces of King Ravana of Lanka, the cobbled-together army of the exiled Prince Rama of Ayodhya faces a turning point. Rama's half-brother, Lakshmana, has been downed by a magically enhanced spear through the heart. Blood pours from his body "like snakes down a mountain," we are told.[1]

By the time the physician Sushena arrives on the scene, Lakshmana's life hangs by the most fragile of threads. The medicine of the battlefield is made of tourniquets and triage, surgical amputations and stop-gap measures. But what Lakshmana needs is a rare herb with the power to bring even the dead back to life. This herb, *sanjivini*, grows on a distant mountain. Sushena warns that Lakshmana won't last past daybreak, and the cure that he so desperately requires is too far away to be retrieved in time, at least, by ordinary means.

Luckily, Rama's devoted comrade, a monkey named Hanuman with the power to cover great distances like an epic bullet train—he is, after all, the son of the wind—volunteers to fetch the herb. Ravana learns of Hanuman's mission and immediately orders his minister, the sorcerer Kalanemi, to divert him from his quest. Through his powers of illusion, Kalanemi materializes an attractive lake, conveniently located along Hanuman's route to the mountain. Tired and thirsty, Hanuman eyes the lake and predictably stops at the hermitage that Kalanemi has constructed at the water's edge. Under the guise of hospitality, the sorcerer offers the exhausted Hanuman a poisoned refreshment and encourages him to take a dip in the crocodile-infested lake.

When Hanuman evades these traps, Kalanemi insists on performing a mantra over him, one that will grant him the power to discover the curative herb from among the dense flora that grows on the mountain top. But there's a small catch: the recitation of the mantra will take all night. And of course, the only hope of reviving Lakshmana lies in recovering the herb before sunrise. The encounter between Kalanemi and Hanuman hinges on the manipulation

---

1. Valmiki, *Rama the Steadfast*, 337.

Figure 2.1. "Hanuman with the Sun in His Tail Carrying the Mountain of Healing Herbs," gouache drawing, Iconographic Collections, Library reference no. ICV no. 45553, V0044940, Wellcome Library, London, https://catalogue.wellcomelibrary.org/record=b1183804. Copyrighted work available under Creative Commons attribution-only license CC BY 4.0.

of time.[2] Since Kalanemi can't quite seem to kill Hanuman, he decides instead to keep him occupied. In either case, the result will be Lakshmana's death.

Hanuman finally recognizes that he has been ensnared in a potentially fatal illusion. Faced with magic and cunning, Hanuman responds with brute force, strangling the sorcerer with his powerful tail. He returns to his quest, but when he arrives at the faraway mountain, he sees that Kalanemi, despite his proclivity to deception, was telling the truth. The mountain is verdant and lush, and Hanuman is neither botanist nor physician. Discerning which of the plants is the life-giving sanjivini is an impossible task, so he decides instead to take the entire mountain. Growing to massive proportions, he flies back toward Rama and his army carrying the mountain in the palm of his hand.

Through his vast and watchful network of spies, Ravana keeps an eye on Hanuman's progress. Knowing that Lakshmana will only last until dawn, Ravana attempts to subjugate time to his own ends. He commands the sun, whom he had previously vanquished and who is therefore subject to his orders, to rise early. By the time Hanuman arrives with the herb, it will be too late.

While flying back to Rama's encampment, Hanuman spies the faint outline of the morning glow on the horizon. Without giving it a second thought, he wrenches the sun from the sky before it can complete its awakening and tucks it safely under his armpit, effectively delaying the dawn. Hanuman succeeds in delivering the mountain to Sushena, Lakshmana is resuscitated, and Hanuman returns the sun to its rightful perch.[3]

In the late twentieth and early twenty-first centuries, campaigns to acquire access to medicine for the poor and the marginalized have frequently operated through this mythic logic: humanitarian-minded doctors can fly in, or local physicians can be trained with knowledge from abroad; drugs and technologies can be imported or the technical means of their manufacture can be reverse engineered and reproduced.[4] The underlying presumption is that

2. Kalanemi's name refers to the time (*kala*) leading to sunset, or the increasing darkness (kala) as night approaches. See Hudson, *The Body of God*, 282.

3. On the many variants of this story, see Lutgendorf, *Hanuman's Tale*.

4. Although not technically a cure, it is instructive to think about the challenges of importing smallpox vaccine, shipped to Indian ports from Britain from the beginning of the nineteenth century. The challenge was to transport the vaccine across the watery expanse separating metropole from colony while preserving its efficacy (the vaccine itself was notoriously susceptible to the effects of both heat and time). One solution was to transport the vaccine in the bodies of European children. These children were inoculated with vaccinia, a virus closely related to smallpox that conferred immunity to smallpox, but with infinitely milder symptoms. A sample of vaccinia could

time and space can be somehow managed. In other words: if cure is elsewhere, it is only a matter of time before it arrives here too. If cure is elsewhere, it can—it must—somehow be brought here. This was of course the case with the mid-twentieth-century migration of the antibiotic streptomycin from Rutgers University to London and finally to Madras.[5]

The difficulty inherent to this line of thinking is that it keeps Indians trapped in the waiting room, not only of history, but of biology, frozen in anticipation of a treatment from elsewhere.[6] How then might we respond when faced with a cure that is not portable—in which the treatment is not materia medica that can be relocated and reproduced, technology that can be transported, knowledge and technique that can be shared across space and time? Not all cures can be extracted, decontextualized, bioprospected, or otherwise translocated.[7] How might we conceive of a cure that depends on its emplacement for its curative power? Put simply, what happens if the mountain won't come to Lakshmana?

---

then, at least in theory, be extracted from these children's bodies on arrival and passed onto other bodies, to maintain the chain of transmission (although willing participants were hard to come by). This means of transport was not without its complications: "Early efforts at using European children traveling to India as carriers of the vaccine proved problematic, not least because parents opposed such a move. This, in turn, caused the authorities to look elsewhere for carriers. Although reports suggest that it was relatively easier to win the assent of orphans' guardians in this regard, this did not prove to be a lasting solution either, because of the rarity of such travelers." Bhattacharya, Harrison, and Worboys, *Fractured States*, 34.

Later in the nineteenth century, smallpox vaccine was transported from Britain in tubes of calf and humanized lymph, but it would often become denatured during the journey, or while entangled in the bureaucracy of the customs office. Eventually, the vaccine would be produced domestically, effectively sidestepping the question of international transport.

5. See chapter 3 on the early trials of the antibiotic streptomycin.

6. On the idea of the waiting room of history, see Chakrabarty, *Provincializing Europe*.

7. Such nonportable cures can be found in Amit Prasad's work on medical tourists who travel to India in pursuit of forms of "miraculous" (and experimental) stem cell therapy. Such forms of therapy are made possible by India's weaker regulatory environment, which has led to strident criticism of both the state and the practitioners of these new forms of healing. Prasad, "Ambivalent Journeys of Hope"; Prasad, "Resituating Overseas Stem Cell Therapy."

Breakdown

There is an ancient solution to this question, as old as the tale of Hanuman, wrought in the itineraries of pilgrims traveling to holy places etched into the landscape: sites of healing, the dwelling places of saints and gods, where you might receive therapeutic benefaction. If cure could not come to you, you had to go to it.

It was entirely possible to articulate a similar solution in more secular terms and in more modern times, such as the one proposed in the first decade of the twentieth century by a man named William Taylor. An old India hand, Taylor arrived in India in 1873 as a medical officer in the British Army. For the better part of eighteen years, he served in a series of extraordinarily violent punitive expeditions across Burma and the Northwest Frontier, burning villages, seizing property, and capturing and killing rebel sympathizers. For his efforts, he was made the principal medical officer of the British Army in India in 1898.

Taylor shot up the ranks, returning to Britain just three years later to assume the highest medical position in the military, that of director-general of the Army Medical Services. From his new post, Taylor kept watch over the health of British soldiers stationed across the far-flung reaches of the empire.[8] In South Africa, for example, he noted that "numerous instances have come under observation, both among men who have been invalided and among men who have been discharged time-expired, in which latent tubercular disease has apparently been called into activity by the hardships and exposure incidental to active service."[9] This failure of cure to endure among British soldiers in South Africa made Taylor skeptical about whether such a cure was possible in Britain's other colonial holdings.

In 1904, he wrote a memo to his successor in India, T. J. Gallwey, expressing serious doubts about admitting tuberculous soldiers back into the British Indian army, even after treatment: "in the present state of our knowledge *apparent cures cannot be depended on as permanent for service purposes*. If returned to duty such men would almost certainly break down under unsuitable conditions of

---

8. As the historian David Arnold has argued, British understandings of landscapes and the environment shaped the ways in which they observed and produced knowledge about the tropics and, in particular, India. In Taylor's case, knowledge of one colonial holding (South Africa) became central to his understanding of another (India). See Arnold, *The Tropics and the Traveling Gaze.*

9. Director-General, Army Medical Service, to the Principle Medical Officer, His Majesty's Forces in India, memo, August 13, 1903, no. 53-Curragh-630—(A. M. D. 2.), M 1219 1904, British Library.

climate or through exposure on service."[10] For Taylor, cure involved more than the temporary cessation of symptoms. Rather, a real, permanent cure was tied to the capacity to labor.[11] For soldiers, such a cure was one that allowed for the resumption of military service. What Taylor feared was that British soldiers in India were experiencing the kind of cyclical cure evident in South Africa, the kind that built soldiers up only to have them suffer repeated breakdowns when they returned to duty.[12]

Taylor was not the first to connect cure to labor. A similar conception of cure had been described by Alexander Crombie, a highly respected physician and researcher in the Indian Medical Service.[13] In May 1899, Crombie had attended an international conference on tuberculosis in the chambers of the Reichstag, the legislative body of the German empire. He sent a report about what he had learned back to the Home Office, noting that the "curability of phthisis is now regarded much more favourably than formerly. Many cases attain cure in the clinical sense, *i.e.* the local symptoms pass away, the bacilli disappear from the sputum, and the general condition improves so that there is *complete ability to resume work*."[14]

10. Director-General, Army Medical Service, to the Principle Medical Officer, His Majesty's Forces in India, memo, August 13, 1903, British Library, emphasis added.

11. A similar point has been made by Gianna Pomata in her analysis of therapeutic contracts in early modern Italy between patients and healers that made payment dependent on the achievement of cure within a particular period and for a specific fee. Patients who felt that their healer had failed to cure them could refuse to pay or reclaim payments made in advance. For many patients, the judgment that they had been cured depended in part on their ability to return to work. Pomata, *Contracting a Cure*. My thanks to Jaipreet Virdi for pointing out the relevance of this work.

12. On the relationship between tuberculosis, race, and labor in South Africa, see Packard, *White Plague, Black Labor*. The fear of recurrent breakdown and the possibility of returning to duty foreshadows conversations that would take place around shell shock and trauma during World War I. See Leese, "'Why Are They Not Cured?'"; see also Geroulanos and Meyers, *The Human Body in the Age of Catastrophe*. For a literary rendering of treatment for shell shock during World War I, see Barker's *Regeneration* trilogy (*Regeneration*, *The Eye in the Door*, and *The Ghost Road*). On the racialized history of the determination of shell shock among Indians, see Buxton, "Imperial Amnesia."

13. Notably, Crombie had worked closely with Ronald Ross on his inquiries into the cause of malaria. Crombie would eventually run afoul of Ross in a speech in which he denigrated the diagnostic value of microscopy. Given Crombie's prominent standing in the medical service, this speech was crushing for Ross.

14. Alexander Crombie, "Report on the Recent Congress on Tuberculosis at Berlin, with special reference to the Prevalence and Prevention of the Disease in India,"

Alongside its optimism, Crombie's report conveyed the sense that cure was about more than disappearing bacteria and passing symptoms. Cure was also, and perhaps primarily, about the ability to work. Crombie cited the example of a German sanatorium established for tuberculous workers at a soda manufactory in the municipality of Danenfels. The possible treatment outcomes for its workers were not described in relation to the recession of symptoms or the eradication of bacteria, but rather, in terms of fitness for work:

- Cured so as to resume work in the factory
- Much improved, nearly cured, able to resume work in factory
- Improved, but hardly fit for work
- Improved, fit for work till a second admission at the sanatorium
- Absconded before completion of cure
- Not improved, died shortly after discharge
- Died in the sanatorium
- Still in sanatorium[15]

Given that the sanatorium in Danenfels had been built by a company for its workforce, it should come as no surprise that cure was focused on transforming the patient back into a productive laborer. Without a return on investment, what would be the point of such an extensive and expensive treatment?[16]

Taylor, and perhaps Gallwey as well, would have been aware of Crombie's report, copies of which were sent to the Government of India. While they too associated cure with the capacity to work, they felt less optimistic than Crombie about the possibility of a lasting cure—at least in a colonial setting. According to Taylor, the conditions of service in India—both the environment ("exposure") and the work itself ("hardships")—posed a limit to the endurance of cure, for British soldiers anyway. He ordered that British soldiers in India be

---

September 21, 1899, enclosed in letter from George Francis Hamilton, Secretary of State for India, to Governor General of India in Council, no. 198 (Revenue), *Proceedings of the Home Department*, October 1899, no. 95, British Library, emphasis added.

15. Crombie, "Report on the Recent Congress on Tuberculosis at Berlin," September 21, 1899, British Library.

16. As Flurin Condrau put it, the "underlying economic principle suggested that any treatment was viable provided it restored a patient sufficiently to permit participation in the labour market again." Condrau, "Beyond the Total Institution," 86. Such analyses of cost and benefit in relation to health and disease have their roots, at least in part, in the quasi-utilitarian political economic calculations of the lawyer and reformer Edwin Chadwick. See Hamlin, *Public Health and Social Justice in the Age of Chadwick*.

invalided and discharged as soon as the diagnosis of tuberculosis was "unmistakably established."[17]

Neither Taylor nor Gallwey expressed much concern about Indian soldiers, who made up the majority of the empire's forces on the subcontinent. By and large, Indians were understood to enjoy a relative immunity to tuberculosis, one that was often explained in terms of a combination of racial, environmental, and civilizational factors. As discussed in chapter 1, Indian bodies were thought to be better suited to Indian climates than their British counterparts. The misfit between British bodies and Indian environments was thought to render British bodies all the more vulnerable to disease, and specifically to tuberculosis. The biology of British bodies, developed over generations of exposure to the British environment, was maladapted for long-term survival in India.[18] Under such conditions, the British soldier had little hope of cure.

Reservoirs of Infection

Back in India, Gallwey began implementing Taylor's instructions. Tuberculous British soldiers were to be transported on troop ships that regularly plied the waters between England and India during the cooler months stretching from September to January. But what about those soldiers who fell ill during the hotter months between February and August? Gallwey worried that having them wait around in India was a dangerous proposition—not only for the other troops they might infect but also for themselves.[19]

Despite India's climatic heterogeneity, the region as a whole was nevertheless taken to be unsuitable for achieving cure among British soldiers.[20] "As the disease is communicable and that as cases do not do well in a hot climate, it will be best to get the men out of India as soon as possible," Gallwey wrote. "Seeing that the non-trooping season is the hot season it is certain that the men should not be kept back during that period to await passage in a Transport."[21] To quickly return

17. Director-General, Army Medical Service, to the Principle Medical Officer, His Majesty's Forces in India, memo, August 13, 1903, British Library.

18. For an earlier history of the adaptation of bodies to geographies and climates, and the idea of "seasoning" in particular, see Seth, *Difference and Disease.*

19. Curzon et al. to John Brodrick, Secretary of State for India, January 7, 1904, writing from Fort William in Calcutta, Lord Curzon, the Viceroy of India, M 1219 1904, British Library.

20. See Harrison, *Climates and Constitutions.*

21. T. J. Gallwey, "Despatch to England by private steamers of men suffering from tuberculosis," February 11, 1904, M 1219 1904, British Library. See also John Brodrick,

these soldiers to England, he suggested that passage for soldiers who fell sick outside of those cooler months be booked on packet boats—regularly scheduled ships, often private, used to transport mail, freight, and civilian passengers. "In view of these measures," Gallwey added, "it will not now be essential to establish a tuberculosis sanatorium in this country."[22]

The new policy was put into place almost immediately.[23] In the fall of 1904, twenty-one tuberculous soldiers arrived in Bombay and were quarantined in the neighborhood of Colaba while awaiting passage back to England aboard the troopship *Plassy*.[24] A handful of soldiers too acutely ill to await the *Plassy*'s arrival were instead embarked on the *Soudan*, a private ship owned and operated by the Peninsular and Oriental Steam Navigation Company.

The accommodation of these soldiers required elaborate planning. Concerns were expressed about the "possibility of the *propagation* of the disease amongst healthy troops, and of the vessels getting *impregnated* with infection."[25] The language of propagation and impregnation resonated with the previously discussed metaphor of seed and soil. Here, the metaphor of (fertile) soil was extended beyond the human body to encompass other things. Tuberculous passengers threatened to communicate their disease not only to their fellow passengers but to the ship itself, transforming it into a floating reservoir that contained and passed along infection to others. The proposed solution was to isolate such soldiers on the main deck, away from

----

India Office, to Governor-General of India in Council, February 19, 1904, Military no. 33, M 1219, British Library, which affirms the need to use private shipping companies during the nontrooping season.

22. Surgeon-General Sir T. J. Gallwey, Principal Medical Officer, His Majesty's Forces in India, to the Secretary of the Government of India, Military Department, memo, January 7, 1904, M 1219 1904, British Library.

23. For example, in August 1904, the Peninsular and Oriental Steam Navigation Company (P & O) carried about eleven tuberculosis patients from Bombay on the ss *Arabia*, due to arrive in London by the middle of September. Viceroy to London Office, telegram, August 29, 1904, M 11571 1904, British Library. See also F. Whitmore Smith, Assistant Military Secretary, draft letter, September 2, 1904, M 11681 1904, British Library.

24. Colonel R.A.M.C., Principal Medical Officer Bombay and Nagpur districts, to the Deputy Assistant Adjutant General, telegram, no. 6294, M 2318 1905, British Library.

25. Major Walter Campbell, Director of Movements & Quartering, War Office, to the Director of Transports, Admiralty, S.W., December 3, 1904, M 16388 1904, British Library, emphasis added.

other passengers. There, they would live with minimal shelter to "secure the benefits of the open-air treatment on the way home."[26] The sea voyage was not simply a means of arriving at cure elsewhere, but potentially curative in its own right.[27]

The plan was for the tuberculous soldiers aboard the *Soudan* to be accommodated on the starboard side of the ship, where the awnings and side curtains could shield them from the wind and rain. And as the weather shifted throughout the voyage, they could be relocated along with these curtains and awnings.[28] These patients would eat at mess tables in the men's hospital, located directly under their accommodations on the upper deck. They would be provided with separate baths, toilets, and washing basins in the men's hospital for their exclusive use.[29] In sleeping, eating, defecating, and washing, these soldiers would be limited in their peregrinations aboard the ship.

Everything was carefully planned. And as with most good plans, things went awry. According to the commanding officer onboard the *Soudan*, the space provided for these patients aboard the main deck, screened off from the harsher elements, "was found suitable in warm weather, but in cold and inclement weather [patients were forced to] sleep in the Armoury and in the hatches" to keep them apart from the others aboard the ship. This arrangement, as the officer put it, was "not satisfactory."[30]

26. Colonel R.A.M.C. to the Deputy Assistant Adjutant General, telegram, British Library. However, the accommodation of the sick would require the displacement of third-class passengers, which would reduce revenues for the ship owners. Here, the solution was to dispatch tuberculous patients exclusively from Bombay in numbers large enough to fill an entire cabin. Military Department to Secretary of State for India, "Despatch by private steamer of men suffering from tuberculosis," confidential dispatch, June 2, 1904, Enclosure of Despatch no. 75, M 8091 1904, British Library.

27. See, for example, Weber, "Remarks on Climate and Sea Voyages." In the nineteenth century in particular, sea voyages were in and of themselves thought to be therapeutic for those with tuberculosis.

28. General Officer Commanding, Bombay Brigade, to the Quarter-Master General in India, January 17, 1905, M 3656 1905, British Library.

29. G. J. Baugh, Director, Royal Indian Marine, to General Officer Commanding, Bombay District, telegram, October 18, 1904, no. 3421, M 2318 1905, British Library.

30. Colonel J. Cameron, Royal Engineers, Officer Commanding the Troops on board the I.T.S.T. "Soudan," "Copy of remarks by the Commanding Officer on Voyage Report of Transport 'Soudan' from Bombay to Southampton. 21st October to 14th November 1904," November 14, 1904, M 16388 1904, British Library.

The *Soudan* arrived in Southampton after a three-week journey.[31] The director of movements and quartering at the War Office, Major Walter Campbell, was deeply concerned about the hygienic condition of the ship. "Nothing short of disinfecting all parts of the ship to which troops have access would be effective."[32] Yet, as the commanding officer on the ship had indicated in his report, the sick troops had not been confined to a single area. As they moved about the ship, to eat, to use the bathroom, and to escape the elements, they had dragged the illness along with them, potentially "impregnating" the ship and its parts with their infection.

Over the next few months, more elaborate procedures were developed for minimizing the spread of disease. Spittoons were to be provided to prevent expectoration on the ship itself. Along with handkerchiefs and underclothing, they were to be thoroughly disinfected upon arrival. The deck, furniture, and hammocks would also require disinfection, not only upon arrival but at least once during the voyage, with a solution composed of either chlorinated lime or a branded disinfecting agent known as Izal.[33] The ship's owners were also required to fumigate cabins occupied by tuberculous patients.[34] Clearly, disinfection was no small undertaking.[35]

An additional complication was posed by the fact that health examinations were not required for officers before embarking on ships, neither in India nor in Britain. Passengers were often diagnosed with a variety of illnesses over the course of the journey—not only tuberculosis but venereal disease or measles—producing a constantly shifting epidemiological landscape onboard. Such shifts made it difficult to segregate the sick from the healthy, as well as to separate those with different forms of illness—each of which was understood to

31. Walter Campbell, Director of Movements & Quartering, War Office London, to the Military Secretary, India Office, February 15, 1905, 120/India/5517 (G.M.G.2.), M 3656 1905, British Library.

32. Walter Campbell, Director of Movements & Quartering, War Office London, to the Director of Transports, Admiralty, December 22, 1904, India 5517 (Q.M.G.2.), M 17257 1904, British Library.

33. Quartermaster-General in India to the Secretary to the Government of India, Military Department, March 9, 1905, M 4010 1905, British Library; Walter Campbell, Director of Movements & Quartering, War Office London, to the Military Secretary, India Office, May 2, 1905, M 5756 1905, British Library.

34. Military Department, "Despatch of men suffering from tuberculosis by private steamers," June 20, 1904, M 8091 1094, British Library.

35. G. T. H. Boyes, Director of Transports, to the Director of Movements & Quartering, War Office, January 4, 1905, 6977/1904, M 242 1905, British Library.

pose different kinds of risks and to require different forms of care—from each other.[36]

A prime example is that of Major F. V. L. Pritchard of the Ninety-Sixth Berar Infantry, who in October 1911 was diagnosed with a bronchial catarrh, a kind of irritation in the lungs, while stationed in Bombay. Eight days later, he was pronounced "recovered."[37] But just two days after that, his catarrh seemed to have returned. A brief recovery, indeed, and certainly no cure.

In the nineteenth and early twentieth centuries, the overlap between a wide variety of diagnoses that were either related to tuberculosis or could develop into tuberculosis—not only bronchial catarrh, consumption, and phthisis but even malaria—produced a useful ambiguity for sympathetic medical boards, physicians, and soldiers resisting forced retirement. If Pritchard had been diagnosed with tuberculosis, he would have been—according to the policy established by Taylor in 1904—invalided and permanently sent back to Britain, with no hope of return. But the diagnosis of bronchial catarrh (rather than tuberculosis) made it possible for him to salvage his career.[38]

Pritchard was granted a year's leave to recover, which he began with a trip to Mount Abu, a hill station in Rajasthan, before returning to Bombay. There, he embarked on the *Plassy* for the journey to England. What we know from the voyage report was that Pritchard was "accommodated in the first saloon and under no segregation of any kind as he was an ordinary passenger and appeared totally unaware of the danger he was to saloon passengers near him."[39] When he arrived in Southampton three weeks later, he was found to be "suffering from advanced tuberculosis."[40] Over the journey, his diagnosis had shifted from bronchial catarrh to tuberculosis. Pritchard's reprieve had been short-lived.

36. As an example, venereal patients were thought to require separate bathrooms and washing areas. They were also thought to need greater privacy than other patients, so much so that they could not be cared for by women nurses.

37. C. V. Kemball, Director of Movements & Quartering, to the Quarter-Master-General in India, June 21, 1912, General Number 7318 (Q.M.G.2.), M 12012 1912, British Library.

38. For a parallel use of bronchial catarrh as a deliberate alternative to the more stigmatizing and undesirable diagnosis of tuberculosis in the early twentieth century, see Johnston, *The Modern Epidemic*, 55, 129.

39. Major J. B. Anderson, Embarkation Office, Southampton, to Director of Movements & Quartering, War Office, London, August 15, 1912, no. 555/12, M 12012 1912, British Library.

40. C. V. Kemball, Director of Movements & Quartering, to the Quarter-Master-General in India, June 21, 1912, British Library.

While his initial diagnosis had preserved the possibility of his return to active duty, it had also made it possible for him to infect his fellow passengers, and the ship itself.

The Coolie Problem

Concerns about shipboard infection had been raised even earlier, sparked by the voyage of the SS *Umzinto* from the South African province of Natal to Calcutta in 1903. The *Umzinto* bore five passengers who were found to harbor advanced cases of pulmonary tuberculosis. One died during the journey, "while the rest landed at Calcutta in a very pitiable condition."[41] The passengers on board the *Umzinto* were not, however, British soldiers, but rather Indian coolies.

The history of Indian labor migration across the British Empire has its roots in the abolition of the slave trade across Britain's colonial holdings in 1807, followed by the abolition of the ownership and use of slaves in 1833.[42] With the decline of the institution of slavery over the course of the nineteenth century, the various European empires sought other sources of cheap, mobile labor. Chief among them were poor Chinese and Indians, known as *coolies*, who were recruited by force and inducement to replace this lost labor on sugar and cotton plantations, as well as in mines and on railways. This system of labor recruitment, control, and exploitation was known as indenture.

Between 1830 and 1917, Indians impoverished by colonial trade and manufacturing policies arrived at the crowded ports of Madras and Calcutta. Despite the requirement of medical examination prior to embarkation, sick Indians were often filed onto ships packed beyond capacity, setting sail for other colonies within the empire: Natal, Mauritius, Jamaica, British Guiana, Trinidad, and Fiji. As indentured laborers, these Indian migrants agreed to work for a fixed period of time—usually five years—in return for which their employers were obligated to provide them with wages and medical care. At the end of this period of indenture, coolies could—in theory—choose either to return to India or to renew their contracts. Despite the legal abolition of slavery and the specific

41. Government of India, Department of Revenue and Agriculture, Calcutta, to John Brodrick, Secretary of State for India, December 8, 1904, J & P 3077 1904, British Library.

42. Notably, the earlier act did not entirely stem the traffic in enslaved persons, and the latter act did not result in full emancipation.

terms of indenture, Indian coolies frequently worked under conditions of deprivation and violence, leading to frequent conflicts between coolies, their employers, local populations, and British colonialists. Serious concerns about the living and working conditions of coolies were expressed by both Evangelicals in Britain and the colonial government in India.

The conditions of the coolie laborers aboard the *Umzinto* led to the modification of the Indian Emigration Act of 1883. Ship intake forms were amended to include tuberculosis as a separate category. Consequently, laboring populations, as targets of close surveillance, were among the first Indians to be recognized as vulnerable to the disease. In addition, the category of "chest diseases" was adjusted to read "other chest diseases"—in other words, chest diseases other than tuberculosis. That tuberculosis warranted a separate category suggests the extent of the disease among coolies as well as fears of its infectivity. The amendment to the act contained further stipulations:

- Patients with symptoms of pulmonary tuberculosis (cough and expectoration) should be isolated onboard the ship, preferably on the upper decks so as to be exposed to the open air.
- They should have minimal furniture.
- They should not be allowed to spit on floors or walls.
- They should be provided with lint handkerchiefs that could be burned.
- They should be taught to cover their mouths while coughing.
- They should use spittoons or iron buckets for coughing, three-quarters full with disinfectant or water.
- They should also have separate vessels for vomit and bodily excretions. The contents of these receptacles should be thrown overboard each day and the receptacles sanitized.
- They should have special dishes, utensils, bedding, and clothing, all of which must be kept separate and disinfected after use.
- Clothes and bedding should be burned or disinfected through a combination of boiling, soap and water, and a disinfecting solution including either carbolic acid or mercuric chloride.
- Patients' quarters must be washed every day with a disinfecting solution.
- Attendants should be fully warned of the dangers of infection. They should wash their hands with soap and water before eating and spend as much time as possible in the open air.

- All woodwork, walls, and floors should be scrubbed with soap and hot water or disinfectant.[43]

Ships, and all the people and things that they carried—from coolies and crew to furniture, spittoons, handkerchiefs, buckets, utensils, and bedding—were now understood to be critical reservoirs of infection.[44] Despite these new regulations, organized around sanitation and disinfection, passage onboard these ships continued to be treacherous. Disease affected Indians at all stages of their journeys to and from India.[45]

In 1904, for example, 7,692 Indians departed from India to Natal, almost 80 percent of whom came from Madras.[46] Eight were recorded to have died during the difficult passage.[47] The rest survived to face what were perhaps even

43. Government of India Department of Revenue and Agriculture, Calcutta, notification on "Emigration," December 6, 1904, no. 1258-47-8, J & P 3077 1904, British Library; see also Government of India Department of Revenue and Agriculture, Calcutta, notification on "Emigration," October 24, 1904, no. 1135-47-2, J & P 3077 1904, British Library. For details about the distribution of the amendments to the Indian Emigration Act to the colonies of Natal, Mauritius, Jamaica, British Guiana, Trinidad, and Fiji, see Graham to Under Secretary of State, India Office, September 5, 1905, J & P 2765 1905, British Library.

44. This focus on "reservoirs of infection" echoes the figuration of the prison and the zenana in chapter 1, while foreshadowing the focus of the Bhore Committee Report in 1946: "The importance of measures to improve living conditions has been amply demonstrated in other countries where, even before anti-tuberculosis measures were instituted, the mortality from the disease began to fall as the result of a rise in the general standard of living. While such measures are no doubt important, a direct attack on the *reservoirs of infection* is equally necessary. Without it any marked fall in the incidence of the disease cannot be expected." See Health Survey and Development Committee, *Report of the Health Survey and Development Committee*, 133, emphasis added.

45. In 1860, the first coolie ships set sail from India to Natal, a voyage that took about sixty days. The introduction of steam power dramatically reduced the duration of the journey, although coolies still fell ill during the journey.

46. In the same year, 1,672 Indians made the journey back from Natal, bringing with them just over 20,000 pounds in savings. By my calculations, this amount would be worth over 2 million pounds in 2017, or about 1,300 pounds per person on average earned over the course of at least five years. See C.O. to Public Department, "Natal Immigration Report for the Year 1902," August 31, 1905, no. 29870, J & P 2703/05, British Library.

47. Yet even coolie ships could be therapeutic for some. In the 1870s, a frail medical student named Nabinchandra Datta found work aboard a coolie ship headed to Mauritius, a journey that apparently rejuvenated him and allowed him

more challenging conditions in South Africa.[48] Of the almost 90,000 Indians living in Natal, composed of a mixture of free subjects and indentured laborers, 1,602 were reported to have died that same year. Official records indicated that 269 of these deaths were due to "phthisis" and 266 were the result of "pneumonia and other lung complaints."[49] As with diagnosis, the determination of cause of death was a complicated and often imprecise matter, due to the difficulties involved in discerning between conditions with overlapping presentations. The distinction, for example, between "tuberculosis" and "other chest diseases," or between "phthisis" and "other lung complaints," could be almost impossible to ascertain in practice, either diagnostically or as a cause of death. Yet the very fact that these distinctions were made, at least as categories, suggests a recognition on the part of officials that tuberculosis (or phthisis) was a serious problem for its labor force—and as such, for the reproduction of capital and colonial power more generally.

This fear of losing labor—and losing money—led to the establishment in 1905 of a series of coercive rules in South Africa requiring the "disinfection or destruction of the huts of Indians who have been notified as suffering from phthisis."[50] The employers of indentured workers were required to conduct daily inspection of coolie barracks, as it had been observed that Indian laborers were often hesitant to report illnesses, especially when it involved their children. Such inspections were ostensibly a means of preserving the health of Indians in South Africa. But they were also a means of disciplining a racialized labor pool. Compelled to travel across the ocean by economic pressures and promises of reward, Indian laborers now found themselves subject to localization and surveillance. Here too, the health of a population came to matter not simply because they were subjects of the British crown, but because they were workers. If Indian laborers fell ill and died, if infection spread across the coolie barracks, British investments in South Africa would be eroded as a new pool of laborers would need to be brought in from elsewhere.

---

to return to Calcutta and reapply to the Medical Board, which had previously deemed him physically unfit to become a doctor. See Mukharji, *Nationalizing the Body*, 49–50.

48. Mukharji, *Nationalizing the Body*, 49–50.

49. Mukharji, *Nationalizing the Body*, 49–50. Others have estimated that the percentage of tuberculosis-related deaths among Indians was closer to 25 percent. Govinden, "The Indentured Experience," 64.

50. C.O. to Public Department, "Natal Immigration Report for the Year 1902," August 31, 1905, British Library.

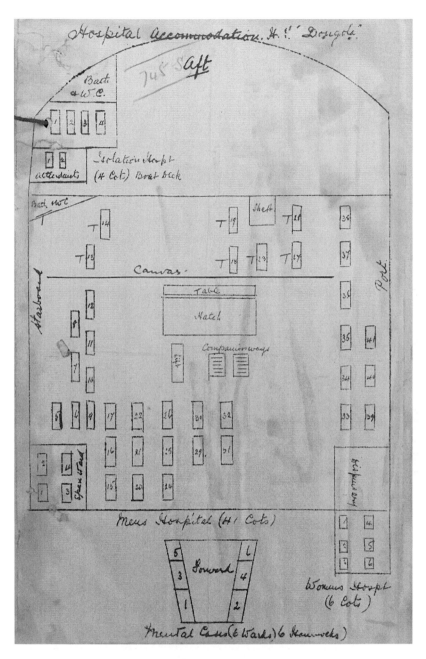

Figure 2.2. Diagram of accommodations aboard the HT *Dongola*. Rectangles marked with the letter *T* were reserved for tubercular cases. These patients were also provided with separate latrines and bathing facilities. Embarking Medical Officer, Karachi Brigade, to the Principal Medical Officer, Karachi Brigade, memo on "Plans of H.T. Dongola," June 25, 1910, IOR: L/MIL/7/4781, M 11445 1910, British Library.

Strikethrough

While British soldiers and Indian indentured laborers traversed the oceans in pursuit of health, wealth, and work by moving away from India, a handful of British civilians traveled to India, hoping that the change of climate would have a therapeutic effect. However, the arrangements made aboard trooping ships for the passage of tuberculous soldiers and officers were exclusively for adult British men. Arrangements for nonsoldiers, especially for women and children, were rather more complicated. Many of those who went to India to pursue cure had familial connections in the colonies. A striking example was Miss C. Fox, a schoolteacher living in the village of Rathmullan, on the Irish seaside.[51] Debilitated by tuberculosis, she gave up her position as a schoolteacher and was forced to live on the charity of her brother-in-law, Sub-conductor J. C. Rosser of the British Army.

Rosser and his wife lived in the Indian hill station of Simla, where he attended to his duties in the office of the quartermaster general of India, a critical post in charge of ensuring the regular supply of weapons and provisions for the British Army throughout India. Rosser was well respected, and his words carried some weight. In December 1910, he wrote to the quartermaster general formally requesting passage for Miss Fox to travel to India.[52] According to his sister-in-law's doctors, he explained, "her only chance of recovery is residence in a warmer climate. As it would be far more beneficial to the health of Miss Fox and more advantageous to myself pecuniarily," he added, "my wife and myself are prepared to give her a home in India."[53]

In cases like this, the relationship between climate, race, and health was far from straightforward. British soldiers were ordered to leave India to escape an environment that was thought to make cure impossible. Paradoxically, Miss Fox was attempting to travel to that very same climate to achieve cure. The

51. On the cost of tuberculosis treatment and the availability of sanatorium beds in early twentieth-century Ireland, see Jones, *"Captain of All These Men of Death."*

52. Through this history of petitioning, we see the emergence of a different kind of genealogy for the welfare state, one in which the subject makes claims based on ties of kinship and labor, while drawing on older traditions, both British and Indian, of noblesse oblige and sovereignly duty. See Siddiqi, *The British Historical Context and Petitioning in Colonial India.* On the colonial and postcolonial states as political systems built up around the petition, see also De and Travers, "Petitioning and Political Cultures in South Asia."

53. Sub-conductor J. C. Rosser, India Miscellaneous List, to the Quarter Master-General in India, Simla, December 8, 1910, M 1993 1911, British Library.

tight relationship between a racialized biology and its natural environment was not so tight after all.

Fox's prescription was not unique; the idea that the Indian hill stations—and Simla in particular—could cure tuberculosis was much in vogue in the late nineteenth century. In 1887, for example, Rudyard Kipling published "A Bank Fraud," a short story that appeared in the pages of the *Civil and Military Gazette*. In the story, an ill-tempered accountant named Riley is transferred from his posting in a large London bank to a provincial branch located in, of course, Simla. Riley doesn't know it—in fact, he never finds out—but his transfer was bartered as a favor to his influential father, who believes that the warmer climate will cure his son's consumption. Riley proves to be an insufferable man with an exceedingly high opinion of himself and a decided lack of imagination. He believes that he has been sent to India to set things right at a local bank branch. His self-righteousness and lack of experience in India win him no friends. As he continues to sicken, his work suffers and he is terminated by the bank. His livelihood, and his life, lies in the hands of a reviled yet compassionate coworker who maintains the charade that Riley remains both employed and appreciated by the bank. In Kipling's story, cure is tied to climate and geography, as well as to the possibility of movement opened up by financial influence. Critically, India—or at least a certain part of India—was figured as a site of healing. At least some white bodies might be cured in India, or so it seemed.[54]

We might ask what specifically money had to do with the kinds of cure that were prescribed, and to whom. Fox might have instead traveled to the continent, where she could have basked in the salubrious (and costly) climates of Switzerland or Germany, like many of her wealthier peers. But given her familial connections, India might well have been the cheaper option—if only she could get there. Unable to shoulder the cost of passage to India via private steamer, Rosser requested that Fox be allotted a second-class passage by a ship leaving England during the trooping season, when soldiers were regularly ferried between India and Britain.[55]

54. Despite the prescription of a "warmer climate," there seems to have been some recognition that certain parts of India were in fact too warm. Thus, the frequent resort to Simla, which, as a hill station in northern India, enjoyed a much cooler climate than many other parts of the country.

55. Sub-conductor J. C. Rosser, to the Quarter Master-General in India, Simla, December 8, 1910, British Library.

Assistant Military Secretary J. H. Seabrooke of the India Office responded directly to Miss Fox. He noted that high-priority passengers would have to be accommodated before she could be considered. She would also have to pay for her own food, and she'd need to provide a medical certificate indicating that she was fit for travel and "not in a state of health which would be injurious to other passengers."[56]

"The Doctor will certify that I am medically <u>fit for the journey</u>," Fox replied, "but as I am suffering from a slight <u>lung trouble</u>, he cannot undertake to say that my state of health <u>would not</u> be injurious to other passengers. Will a passage be granted under above circumstances?"[57] Despite the brevity of her notes, Fox was rather fond of underlining what I think she might have taken to be the important bits.

Fox's "slight lung trouble" and potential infectiousness created a problem for the India Office. Seabrooke explained to Fox that they would need to find her an accommodation in an isolation hospital onboard an India-bound ship.[58] A series of exchanges followed between various offices of the government, clarifying Fox's condition and searching for accommodation onboard three ships headed to India: the *Rewa*, the *Dongola*, and the *Plassy*.[59] Seabrooke further suggested that an onboard women's hospital might be partitioned to create an isolated accommodation for Miss Fox.[60]

Throughout these conversations, the case of a Mrs. Jackson was repeatedly invoked as a kind of precedent for Miss Fox's situation. Jackson's husband, a sergeant in the army, was set to return to India. Given her tuberculous condition, she preferred to join him rather than stay alone in Britain. The existence of an immediate familial tie meant that she was entitled to her passage. Nevertheless, Mrs. Jackson's situation was quite challenging. As the officer in charge of troops traveling aboard the *Plassy* wrote in his Voyage Report: "We embarked at Southampton one woman [Mrs. Jackson] suffering from tuberculosis, which rendered the Isolation Hospital unavailable, and when a case of measles broke

56. J. H. Seabrooke, Assistant Military Secretary, to Miss Fox, January 5, 1911, M 15483 1900, British Library.

57. C. Fox to the Under Secretary of State for India, January 7, 1911, M 367 1911, British Library.

58. J. H. Seabrooke, Assistant Military Secretary, to Miss Fox, January 12, 1911, M 367 1911, British Library.

59. Lieutenant-General Beauchamp Duff, Military Secretary, to the Admiralty, January 12, 1911, M 367 1911, British Library.

60. R. Ritchie, Military Department, to the War Office, February 3, 1911, M 1093 191, British Library.

out, this was much to be regretted; further inconvenience arose when a case of whooping cough and one of Erisipelas [*sic*] followed. In fact, in the opinion of both the Medical Officer and myself, this matter was of grave moment."[61]

Clearly unhappy with Rosser's request, the director of transports underscored the officer's findings: "The Isolation Ward on Transports is almost always required for cases of Infectious Disease contracted on the voyage."[62] Mrs. Jackson, he noted, was a "special case and should not be taken as a precedent."[63] As Rosser's sister-in-law—in other words, not a member of his immediate family—the rules did not oblige the government to provide Fox with passage. Nevertheless, the director of transports relented: given that Rosser himself would be entitled to second-class accommodation by virtue of his posting in the British Army, he suggested that Miss Fox might travel aboard the *Dongola* in a second-class cabin appropriated solely for her use.[64]

Seabrooke quickly responded that it was "impossible to appropriate a whole second class cabin for Miss Fox's use." The right hand, it seemed, was operating quite independently of the left. He asked instead whether she might be accommodated in one of the hospitals aboard the *Plassy*, setting sail in early February.[65]

At this point, the director of movements and quartering, G. V. Kimball, entered the fray. Evidently, curative expeditions required the intervention of many parts of the bureaucratic machine. Kimball asserted that Miss Fox "could not be accommodated under any circumstances in the Hospital for Women and Children in any of the Transports, and that the Isolation Hospital, should be reserved, as originally arranged, for infectious cases which may occur during the voyage.... If your Department is desirous of providing an Indulgence passage for Miss Fox, special accommodation should be provided which will not interfere with existing arrangements."[66]

61. Officer Commanding Troops on Board in the Voyage Report, comment, February 15, 1911, letter from the Admiralty to the Military Secretary, M 2032 1911, British Library. Erysipelas is an infection of the upper layers of skin whose most prominent symptom is a red, swollen rash.

62. Director of Transports to the Admiralty, January 14, 1911, M 616 1911, British Library.

63. Director of Transports to the Admiralty, January 14, 1911, British Library.

64. Director of Transports to the Admiralty, January 14, 1911, British Library.

65. J. H. Seabrooke, Assistant Military Secretary, to the War Office, January 16, 1911, M 616 1911, British Library.

66. E. Kemball, Director of Movements & Quartering, to the Military Secretary, India Office, January 24, 1911, M 1093 1911, British Library.

There was a clear sense that the India Office wanted to grant Rosser's request on behalf of his sister-in-law. But it was equally clear that other offices of the government perceived the granting of such an accommodation as an indulgence rather than as an obligation, and a complicated one at that. The granting of such an indulgence threatened to upset the regular movement of troops and other prioritized passengers between Britain and India.

The various offices involved in the cases of Fox and Jackson began to sense that such passages might become increasingly common. A letter from the Military Department addressed to both the Admiralty and the War Office noted that "it is likely that cases will again arise of persons suffering from tubercular disease, ~~who have been recommended to proceed to a warmer climate and~~, for whom it will be impossible to refuse to provide passages to India."[67]

In reading through the letters that traveled between government offices, the care taken by colonial bureaucrats in their writing shines through. A stray phrase might set an unfortunate precedent. Unforeseen consequences could be costly. Overly generous declarations could launch a thousand ships full of Foxes and Jacksons. Each strikethrough represented foresight on the part of a government bureaucrat, an effort to limit the effects of a potentially infelicitous turn of phrase.

Eventually, the Military Department recommended that one or two berths be set aside for such cases, both on ships headed to India and on those returning. It was further requested that arrangements be made for Fox onboard the *Rewa*, to sail in early March 1911, "without endangering the health of other passengers on board, and without decreasing the number of passengers that can be carried in that vessel."[68]

In the face of this request, Kimball, the aforementioned director of movements and quartering, backed down but noted that it would be "unwise and unreasonable to subject other individuals to the risk of tubercular infection at a time when their own health is obviously below par, and under the conditions of such crowded quarters as a hospital for women and children on board a Transport must necessarily be."[69] He agreed to the special accommodation

67. R. Ritchie, Military Department, to the Admiralty, February 3, 1911, M 1093 1911, British Library.

68. R. Ritchie, Military Department, to the Admiralty, February 3, 1911, M 1093 1911, British Library.

69. E. Kemball, Director of Movements & Quartering, to the War Office, February 14, 1911, India/7692 (Q.M.G.2), British Library.

provided for Miss Fox. But he made it clear that she could not be accommodated in the Isolation Hospital, citing again the case of Mrs. Jackson.

The small window opened by Kimball was shut firmly by a letter from the Admiralty. Once more citing the previously mentioned report from the voyage of Mrs. Jackson, the letter stated that "it would be impossible to provide accommodation for Miss Fox in the 'REWA' . . . without making some arrangement as would decrease the number of passengers that could be carried in this vessel."[70]

Seabrooke regretfully conveyed the bad news to Fox. "No other transport," he wrote, "sails for India until the Autumn."[71]

After learning this news, Fox's letters became more insistent. "Will a passage be granted in a transport sailing <u>early</u> in the Autumn?"[72] Why the rush? Was she worried that she might never be granted passage? Was her condition worsening without the tropical warmth? Or was she running out of money? In the letters between tuberculous supplicants and government bureaucrats, it was often difficult to read between the lines. Bureaucrats were careful not to promise too much. But supplicants in need of passage, treatment, or financial support were equally careful, afraid to reveal too much about their conditions. The trepidation evident in these letters created a space for imagination. Not only ours, reading these letters over a century after they were written, but for those on the receiving end. The government bureaucrats who read these messages obviously had their own ideas about tuberculosis, but they also had to navigate within the labyrinthine confines of rules, regulations, and political realities.

In Seabrooke's letters, we can sense his sympathy. But his responses were frequently rendered noncommittal through the act of revision. In response to Miss Fox's plaintive plea, he originally wrote, "passage to India will if pos-sible be provided for you some time next trooping season." After revision, this became: *"your application for* passage to India *during* next trooping season *will be considered."* The original version of Seabrooke's letter further noted, "As no arrangements have yet been made for the engagement of the vessels, it cannot yet be stated definitely whether the requisite accommodation is likely to be available." A further revision displaced the burden onto Miss Fox, making it about her health: *"And as your state of health causes an exceptional difficulty* [in

<hr />

70. Military Secretary, India Office, February 16, 1911, M 2032 1911, British Library.
71. J. H. Seabrooke to Miss Fox, February 17, 1911, M 2032 1911, British Library.
72. Letter from C. Fox, February 28, 1911, M 2668 1911, British Library.

margins] and it cannot yet be stated that passage will be granted you."[73] If Fox became sicker, she might no longer be fit to travel, and she might also pose a contagious threat to others onboard. Under the force of these revisions, the promise was no longer to accommodate her if possible but rather to consider her case if her health—or rather, her illness—remained stable. The appearance of stability became, for Fox, a precondition for the possibility of gaining passage to India and, by extension, for the possibility of cure. Seabrooke promised to write to her again in the early autumn with further details.

Undeterred and perhaps anxious that her pleas would be lost in the machinations of government, Fox wrote back to confirm receipt and once again expressed her hopes that she'd be granted passage in early autumn.[74] When she didn't hear back, she wrote again in August asking about passage.[75] Her persistence finally reaped dividends. Fox was granted passage in one of ten berths allotted for tuberculosis patients on the upper deck of the *Plassy*: the very same ship that had been inconvenienced by the passage of Mrs. Jackson.[76]

Fox finally sailed to Bombay in mid-October, from where we might imagine she set off to Simla to meet her sister and brother-in-law. Her trail runs cold in the archives, as do those of many such petitioners whose business with the government had been concluded. We're left to wonder what happened to Miss Fox. Did she recover her health in Simla? Was she cured by the therapeutic power of the hill station, ministered to by her doting sister and dutiful brother-in-law? For me—and I imagine, for you—there is no satisfying resolution. Neither death nor cure. But for bureaucrats like Seabrooke and Kimball, the problem of Miss Fox had been resolved, their responsibilities to her, and to her brother-in-law Sub-conductor Rosser, fulfilled.

Enemy Subjects

Miss Fox's case raises the critical question of the state's responsibility for its subjects. We encountered a version of this question in chapter 1, in relation to the colonial state's relationship to imprisoned Indian subjects. Here, responsibility

73. Assistant Military Secretary J. H. Seabrooke to Miss C. Fox, April 13, 1911, M 2668 1911, British Library, emphasis added.

74. Letter from C. Fox, April 19, 1911, M 4475 1911, British Library.

75. J. H. Seabrooke and C. Fox, correspondences dated August 12, 1911, and August 16, 1911, M 9751 1911, British Library.

76. R. Groome, Director of Transports, to the Director of Movements & Quartering, War Office, October 25, 1911, M 13717 1911, British Library.

was refigured as largesse. When it came to travel and treatment, who would foot the bill? This was true not only for civilians like Miss Fox but also for soldiers and other employees of the state. Ascertaining when and where a soldier had fallen ill, and whether it was a result of their duties, determined whether the government would foot the bill for their treatment—and if they didn't get better, for their disability pension or next-of-kin benefits. The problem of curing tuberculosis became, in this sense, a problem of movement and location.

Determining the reasons why a soldier became tuberculous was no simple task. Symptoms waxed and waned, diffused across time. The challenge was to distinguish between cases that could be attributed to military service, those that were preexisting, and situations in which a soldier might simply be malingering.

Such discernment was often an iterative process, as evidenced by the production of hefty files containing extensive conversations between various government offices—as we've seen in the case of Miss Fox. One remarkably thick file belonged to a fellow Irishman named John Montgomery Fiddes, only seventeen years of age when he enlisted in the British Army in 1901. Fiddes remained unattached to a unit for several years, before he was finally assigned to the Ninety-Third Infantry in Burma in August 1907. Originally established as a South Indian battalion to quell rebellion, this regiment had been relocated, restaffed, and repurposed to put down insurrections in the Burmese hills and consolidate control over British-held territories.

In the six years leading up to his posting in Burma, Fiddes had taken only a single month of leave. Yet, after spending less than a year in Burma, he was sent back to Europe for six months of sick leave on account of what was diagnosed under the vague category of *debility*. Across the British Empire, the category of debility operated in an ambiguous relationship with tuberculosis. Sometimes, tuberculosis was distinct from debility, and at other times, tuberculosis itself could be debilitating. What was clear was that debility was frequently tied to ideas of able-bodiedness and the capacity for labor.[77] Such a diagnosis meant that Fiddes might still return to active duty if his condition were to improve. Like Major Pritchard, whom we met earlier, Fiddes had been saved from a diagnosis of tuberculosis and the premature termination of his military career.

In September 1908, Fiddes appeared before the Medical Board of the India Office in London. His examiners noted that it was "too early to say whether the

77. See Livingston, *Debility and the Moral Imagination in Botswana*, 261.

disease [had] been completely arrested."[78] For the moment, they ruled that he was "unfit to return to India."[79] Fiddes was granted an additional ten months of leave on top of the original six. Just as these sixteen months of leave were coming to an end, Fiddes was (finally) diagnosed with pulmonary tuberculosis. He was given yet another six months to recuperate at the Queen Alexandra Sanatorium in Davos-Platz, Switzerland. Yet, by the time of his next review in May 1910, after a total of twenty-two months of leave, he had yet to show significant signs of improvement.

Like many other long-term sufferers in the Indian Army, Fiddes was proving to be more trouble than he was worth. There was no doubt that Fiddes was truly ill; the questions that concerned the Medical Board were when and where he had contracted this disease. Ascertaining who had financial responsibility for cure depended in large part on determining the circumstances of his illness: how had Fiddes fallen ill? As Fiddes had originally been diagnosed with debility rather than tuberculosis, the board determined that his current condition was not the result of his time in Burma. Fiddes's original diagnosis of debility had left open the possibility of his return. Now, that same diagnosis was closing down his chances for remuneration.

The board's decision had grave consequences for Fiddes's pocketbook, as well as for his possibilities of promotion. Unable to return to duty in India, he was placed on half pay near the end of 1910. Fiddes wrote several letters in protest, insisting that he had in fact contracted the disease during his brief service in Burma. He gathered letters of support from the many physicians and medical examiners with whom he had consulted. Among them was Dr. Alfred Thomas Tucker Wise, who ran a respected sanatorium practice in Switzerland.[80] Wise

78. Military Collection regarding Captain J. M. Fiddes, no. 269, file 118, British Library.

79. Military Collection regarding Captain J. M. Fiddes, British Library.

80. Wise was a well-known sanatorium director and the author of numerous books on the therapeutic effects of high altitude and the alpine climate on phthisis. Drawing on the work of a Dr. Francis of the Bengal Army, Wise argued that the curative effect of cold climates was related in part to the fact that the lungs were forced to work harder, resulting in greater blood flow in the pulmonary tissues. In hot climates, by contrast, there was less blood flow, and therefore a greater incidence of phthisis that proceeded more swiftly toward death. See Wise, *Alpine Winter in Its Medical Aspects*, 44–46. On Wise's belief in the "bactericidal power" of blood, see Burke, *Building Resistance*, 292. Although I have been unable to confirm this, it's possible that Dr. Wise was related to Dr. T. A. Wise, a medical orientalist who wrote a treatise on Hindu medicine and his son, Dr. James Wise, a civil surgeon based in Dhaka. If this

maintained that Fiddes had been "contaminated" during his service in Burma: "I am of the opinion that the attack originated from a nasal catarrh [an obstruction] acquired in the early part of 1908. His obstructed nasal passages compelled mouth-breathing during active exercise. . . . During maneuvers and long marches, contaminated dust . . . entered the lungs."[81] Wise's support of a Burmese etiology drew upon a theory of contagion, but more importantly for Fiddes's case, it also implicated the grueling conditions of military labor in an unwelcoming environment.

Fiddes wasn't scheduled to face the London Medical Board again until February 1912. Impatient and unwilling to spend the money to travel back to London, he obtained certificates from two Swiss physicians declaring that he was cured and traveled directly to India to resume his duties with the Sixty-Ninth Punjabis Infantry. To the best of my knowledge, this was a rather irregular thing to do. Fiddes had clearly taken matters into his own hands. And as his diagnosis of tuberculosis had been made in Europe rather than in India, he seems to have been able to evade the rule requiring the discharge of tuberculous soldiers in India—at least, for the time being.

On his arrival in India, the declaration of cure certified by his Swiss doctors did not match up with the assessment made by the infantry's medical officer, Captain W. M. Jack of the Indian Medical Service. After inspecting Fiddes, Captain Jack noted that he was "rather anemic and did not look at all well."[82] However, Jack was unable to find any specific markers of "active disease."[83] As in Burma, Fiddes's symptoms were indeterminate. Nevertheless, his condition continued to deteriorate. In November 1912, after the regiment was deployed to Malakand on the Northwest Frontier, Fiddes suffered from what was diagnosed as an acute case of bronchitis and admitted to a hospital in Lahore. Well aware of Fiddes's medical history, Captain Jack remained vigilant but could find no definitive signs of tuberculosis.

Fiddes soon returned to duty, but within a month, his symptoms again reappeared. Captain Jack wrote that Fiddes appeared "anemic and rather wasted," with a slight spike in his evening temperature and a crackling sound in the lungs.[84]

----

is the case, then Fiddes's support from Wise suggests a possible reliance on colonial networks of old Indian hands.

81. Military Collection regarding Captain J. M. Fiddes, British Library.
82. Military Collection regarding Captain J. M. Fiddes, British Library.
83. Military Collection regarding Captain J. M. Fiddes, British Library.
84. Military Collection regarding Captain J. M. Fiddes, British Library.

But he also remarked that Fiddes had "no sweats, and very little cough."[85] Significantly, Fiddes had never coughed up blood, the paradigmatic sign of tuberculosis. Confronted by this unruly battalion of nondefinitive signs and symptoms, Captain Jack sent a sample of Fiddes's sputum to the divisional laboratory.[86] Under the microscope, the sample was made to reveal the presence of rod-shaped tubercle bacilli. Fiddes's temporary escape from a diagnosis of tuberculosis, and his claims to cure, had come undone.

Undoubtedly aware of the repercussions for Fiddes, Jack was careful to situate his case notes in geographic terms: "I consider that the original attack was brought on by service *in Burma*, and the present attack . . . induced by the severity of the climate *at Malakand*."[87] Military service, geography, climate, and bacteria were once again folded into a determining etiology for Fiddes's condition.

Captain Jack recommended that Fiddes once again be granted six months' leave from his duties: "A change of air is absolutely necessary for his recovery."[88] Notably, these words were not written in Captain Jack's hand, but rather pre-printed on the medical report. A "change of air"—in other words, a change in geography—was a standardized prescription. This was medicine operating according to rules, rather than the idiosyncratic therapeutic experiment of a rogue physician. For Fiddes, the Indian environment was pathogenic. Cure could only be found elsewhere.

The medical board acquiesced to Captain Jack's assessment down to the word and granted Fiddes additional leave. Rather than returning to Switzerland, however, Fiddes asked to be sent instead to Australia.[89] The board raised no objections, declaring only that he should by no means return to the soggy climate of England, unsuited to therapeutic success. But even after six months in Australia, Fiddes had yet to fully recover. Conscious of the trickling away of his career ambitions and the dwindling of his finances, he went to great pains

85. Military Collection regarding Captain J. M. Fiddes, British Library.

86. Sputum consists of mucous ideally coughed up from the lower portions of the respiratory system, to be examined under the microscope for bacteria.

87. Military Collection regarding Captain J. M. Fiddes, British Library, emphasis added.

88. Military Collection regarding Captain J. M. Fiddes, British Library.

89. On the desirability of southern Australia as a therapeutic environment for British tuberculous patients, see Anderson, *The Cultivation of Whiteness*. See also Alison Bashford on the Australian government's push, from 1912, to limit the entry of British consumptives, through the strategic redeployment of earlier measures used to exclude Chinese immigrants. Bashford, "The Great White Plague Turns Alien."

to reassure the India Office that he was on the mend. He wanted to make it clear that he would return to service, as both his salary and his promotion were at stake.

As Fiddes flitted between England, Switzerland, Burma, India, and Australia, the costs began to add up. His uncle, a retired brigade surgeon in Ireland who had been footing much of the bill, wrote in September 1913 to the undersecretary of state of India asking for clarification as to the terms of his nephew's leave. This set off another flurry of exchanges between medical boards and bureaucratic officers across Australia, India, and Britain. Fiddes contributed to the debates, insisting that his extensive treatment and travel expenses should be covered by the India Office. He pointed out that his doctors had all agreed that he had contracted tuberculosis during his original service in Burma.

In December 1913, Fiddes's Australian physicians reported that Fiddes had—once again—been cured of tuberculosis. He returned to India in February 1914. Just three months later, while being assessed for a new posting in China, it was found that Fiddes's condition had—once again—deteriorated. A medical board composed of three Indian Medical Service officers determined that his tuberculosis had returned and he was therefore "unfit for hard work."

"I broke down owing to tuberculosis for the third time," Fiddes wrote in despair.[90] "It was quite evident that I would never be fit for service in the Indian Army again." In January 1915, Fiddes was officially invalided out of the army, retiring on half pay. For the next two years, he shuttled back and forth between Switzerland and Britain. Having racked up considerable debt, he urged the undersecretary of state of India to provide him with a disability pension. "I beg to state that I am totally incapacitated owing to consumption contracted in Burma. My doctor, having examined my blood, is of the opinion that the tuberculosis was agravated [sic] by, if not caused by malaria."[91] As was the case with the Rajput police inspector whom we met in chapter 1, diseases were serial. Malaria and tuberculosis were not separate and distinct; one could quite seriously be taken as a cause for the other.[92]

Fiddes reminded the undersecretary that the government owed a pension to any soldier who had contracted tuberculosis while in service. His condition,

90. Military Collection regarding Captain J. M. Fiddes, British Library.

91. Military Collection regarding Captain J. M. Fiddes, British Library. Fiddes's demands on the state bordered between petition and complaint, the former constituting a request for a favor and the latter a demand for redress. On this distinction, see Gupta, *Red Tape*, 167.

92. On malaria as a cause for other illnesses, see Roy, *Malarial Subjects*, 252.

CHAPTER TWO

he explained, necessitated heavy expenditures: "I am in receipt of permanent half pay of seven shillings per day. I have no private means. I have been ordered to winter in Davos Platz, Switzerland, and to undergo an expensive treatment with tuberculin. I will be unable to do this if I am not entitled to a wound pension."[93] The response was swift: disability pension would only be given to those who were injured in the present war, what would come to be known as World War I.[94] Even if he had contracted his illness while serving in Burma, his repeated sick leaves had led him to miss the war entirely. As such, he had forfeited the right to compensation.

Ironically, at the same time, other factions of the government were making precisely the opposite argument, that Fiddes had been actively engaged in the war efforts—but for the other side. In late 1916, while undergoing sanatorium treatment, Fiddes was surprised to learn that he had been accused of "consorting with enemy subjects" by the acting British counsel at Davos.[95] Fiddes was astounded, and furious. He wrote a brazen response, insisting that this accusation was the result of a personal feud between himself and the wife of a Major Dickinson, with whom he had quarreled.

The British counsel in Berne read his letter as a confession, reporting to London that Fiddes had been observed "in the company of Austrians and Germans on New Year's Eve."[96] In spite of the narrowing of allegiances during wartime, the Swiss sanatorium had offered the possibility of international sociability, a place in which friendship and small kindnesses might flourish. A German man had regularly visited Fiddes when he was bedridden. A young Hungarian girl had tutored him in French. Much to the chagrin of the British ambassador, Switzerland's impartial stance in the war made it possible for enemies to fraternize.[97]

93. Military Collection regarding Captain J. M. Fiddes, British Library. Tuberculin, a substance used for both diagnostic and treatment purposes, is discussed at length in chapter 3.

94. The question of who would be granted a pension in the wake of war extended far beyond the British Empire. For a discussion of the distribution of pension benefits along the lines of race and disability, see Linker, *War's Waste*. War-related disability pensions were also distributed on the basis of gender. For a discussion of the difficulties faced by disabled women in gaining access to pension benefits, see in particular Anderson, *War, Disability and Rehabilitation in Britain*.

95. Military Collection regarding Captain J. M. Fiddes, British Library.

96. Military Collection regarding Captain J. M. Fiddes, British Library.

97. During and after World War I, tuberculosis patients, especially soldiers, could all too easily find themselves subject to allegations of treason. The impartiality of

Putting an end to the matter, the India Office made it clear that Fiddes had retired from service and, as such, was no longer subject to military discipline. The espionage accusation behind him, Fiddes continued to pursue payment from the British government for his mounting treatment expenses. The India Office in London decided to transfer Fiddes's case to government officials in India, where, as with the case of Miss Fox, its trail runs cold. With a palpable sense of relief, an overburdened bureaucrat declared, "Now that we have left further dealings with Lt. Fiddes to the people in India, I presume that this [file] can be put away without any action?"[98] With this transfer, Fiddes's file came to a close, and we find ourselves left with this rather untidy conclusion to a decade of curative efforts.

The Repatriation of a Distressed Native

There are many other such cases in the military archives—cases that required both legal and medical discernment—but Fiddes's story is perhaps the most detailed, and the most colorful. The financial burden associated with Fiddes's case led the India Office to carefully consider the *where* and *when* of his diagnosis, rather than simply concerning themselves with the *what*—a daunting task considering the lack of diagnostic precision and multiplicity of acceptable etiological factors.

In the middle of 1919—three years after Fiddes's case had been closed—the British government circulated an official policy regarding their financial support for tuberculous officers and nurses. For nurses and officers receiving full or half pay, if the "disability" had been caused in and by military service, the army would provide 4 pounds 14 shillings 6 pence per week. If the disability had been merely aggravated by military service, the army would provide two-thirds of the cost of sanatorium treatment, up to 3 pounds 3 shillings per week. There would be no additional allowance for rations or lodging.

Yet the state's assumption of responsibility for its (British) soldiers did not easily extend to others: not to British women, as we have seen in the case of

----

Switzerland, and of the sanatorium more generally, rendered it suspect in political terms, as a site for the violation of norms and allegiances. In the wake of World War I, for example, rumors circulated that Indian prisoners of war, many of whom contracted tuberculosis while in confinement, had been the target of German propaganda efforts and were liable to foment disturbance if returned to India. See Jarboe, "The Long Road Home."

98. Military Collection regarding Captain J. M. Fiddes, British Library.

Miss Fox, nor to its colonial subjects. At stake were the very grounds of responsibility: what kinds of ties make a government responsible for a person? An instructive case was that of a Bengali living in London named Bimal Gangooly. He had arrived in Britain aboard the packet boat *Goorkha* in the early 1910s. In London, he wanted to study to be a railway traffic engineer. But his life took other turns. From 1914 to 1915, he served as a member of the Indian Voluntary Ambulance Corps. And in January 1915, Gangooly was operated on at the Netley Hospital in London for what was described as a case of "tubercular glands." By the end of that year, he was deemed "unfit" and discharged from the Ambulance Corps. Nevertheless, Gangooly continued to work through his illness. He dedicated the next five years of his life to the Paddington Train Station in London, where he served in the Superintendent's Department.[99] With time, he hoped to qualify as an assistant traffic superintendent for the Indian Railways.[100]

Through all of this, Gangooly's condition worsened. In December 1920, he traveled to Leysin, a sanatorium town in Switzerland, with the support of friends like the wealthy industrialist and business scion Dorab Tata. He received additional support for subsistence and treatment from the India Office through a grant arranged by the Countess of Dudley, who had spent the previous twenty years working on behalf of disabled and convalescing officers. Despite his best efforts, when Gangooly returned to London in early 1921, his symptoms came with him.

It was in London that Nirmal Chandra Sen learned about the severity of Gangooly's situation and agreed to serve as his intermediary to Joseph Bhore, the secretary to the High Commission of India.[101] Sen was from a well-to-do Bengali family, the son of the controversial Brahmo Samaj reformer and mystic Keshub Chandra Sen, who had worked to establish the Nababidhan or "New Dispensation," a "universal" religion that threaded together elements of Vaishnavism and Christianity to find theological support for British rule in India.

Sen had moved to London in 1913, around the same time as Gangooly, with his wife Mrinalini, a lauded Bengali poet and prominent activist in the fight

99. C. B. Gangooly to Joseph Bhore, May 10, 1921, J & P 3147: 1921, British Library.
100. Report on Gangooly, "Mr. B.C. Gangooly, a distressed native of India suffering from tuberculosis," J & P 3094 1921, British Library.
101. Bhore would play a major role in the shaping of health care in India, as the chair of what came to be known as the Bhore Committee, a group of experts who assessed the health situation in India between 1943 and 1946, culminating in a report that virtually defined public health in independent India.

for voting rights for Indian women.[102] Mrinalini had formerly been the wife of the minor prince Indra Chandra Sinha of Paikpara, whose death made her into a prominent symbol of widow remarriage when she climbed over a wall to elope with Nirmal.[103] In London, the couple maintained a commitment to social service and activism. Mrinalini, for example, would actively protest Katherine Mayo's book *Mother India* for its diminishment of Indian women, while Nirmal worked as the educational advisor to the India Office.

The day after Sen's meeting with Bhore, Gangooly followed with a typewritten letter:

> I am very ill—so ill that I cannot sit up nor can I stand on my legs for long in comfort. I have become very weak and I am unable to hold the pen to write letters.
>
> A mass of tubercular glands have appeared on the appendix but nothing can be done to relieve my pain until the glands burst when there may have to be an operation. The doctor tells me that the general tendency of my complaint is that I would get gradually worse and there is nothing he can do for me. I have exhausted what little money I have saved and at the present moment but for my friends I would be unable to have the bare necessaries of life leave alone the question of special diet and proper medical attention. I cannot pay my doctor and it is a kindness of the part of Dr. I. DeZilva . . . to treat me free.
>
> Had I been in the regular forces I would have been entitled to a pension, but having belonged to a Volunteer Unit, i.e., The Indian Volunteers Ambulance Corps, formed by the India Office, I had no legal claim for a pension although my present plight is the *direct result of my active service during the war*.
>
> Serious though my case is even now I do not wish to become a burden on the Indian revenue. I am not asking for any monetary grant from the authorities. *But as my doctor tells me that a sea voyage and a return to the sunny clime of India may yet save my life, I am compelled to apply to you for my repatriation.* I feel confident that later on my relations and friends will be too willing to refund whatever expenses are incurred by the Government for my repatriation. But there is no time to inform them of my position now and if I have to wait indefinitely the last and only hope for my recovery will disappear.

102. See Sinha, *Specters of Mother India*.
103. Southard, *The Women's Movement and Colonial Politics in Bengal*.

I have already taken up [a] good deal of your time with the recital of my tale of suffering. Broken in health and spirit I am making this last appeal to you for my repatriation.[104]

The pathos evoked by Gangooly's letter, and his situation, is undeniable. A stranger in a strange land, his health and his aspirations taken from him by disease, Gangooly survived only on the kindness of others—namely, other Indians like Tata, Sen, and DeZilva. In other words, he depended for his survival on ties of kinship and community. His letter called for Bhore, on behalf of the British state, to contribute to those efforts, not out of obligation, but rather out of generosity.

Bhore passed on Gangooly's plea to the Judicial and Public Department of the Indian Office, which had become the coordinating body for the repatriation of distressed colonial subjects living in Britain in the wake of a parliamentary inquiry in 1910.[105] Ironically, the department agreed with Gangooly that they held no responsibility for his condition. Service in the voluntary ambulance unit was not equivalent to service in the military. In addition, there was some uncertainty as to whether Gangooly hadn't already been ill when he joined the Ambulance Corps, in which case his condition would not have been caused (although it was perhaps aggravated) by his service. Finally, it was noted that Gangooly had in fact been offered free passage to India after his discharge in 1915, but that he had declined the offer.[106]

G. E. Shepherd from the Judicial and Public Department further explained that, as a "general rule," the department did not actually return Indians to India. Despite the scope of their responsibilities, no funds had been set aside for repatriation for fear it would encourage colonial subjects to enter Britain irresponsibly. There had, he noted, been exceptions, particularly before the war when cheap passage could be had for about £16. Now, it would cost "nearly £60 for a 2nd class passage."[107] Moreover, Shepherd argued that "the Shipping Companies would likely object if they knew that he was tuberculous, and the

104. C. B. Gangooly to Joseph Bhore, May 10, 1921, British Library, emphases added. "Dr. I. DeZilva" most likely refers to Dr. Irving C. De Zilva, an Indian doctor who in 1930 proposed the establishment of a separate hospital for Indians living in London. See "Indian Hospital in London," *Indian Review* 31 (1930): 863.

105. As Shompa Lahiri notes, many of these "distressed" Indians were students sent to Britain to study by families whose finances ran dry or who underestimated the costs of supporting a child in Britain. Lahiri, *Indians in Britain*.

106. S. D. Stewart to the J & P Secretary, May 17, 1921, ME 10302/8, British Library.

107. G. C. Shepherd, minute paper, n.d., J & P 3094 1921, British Library.

cost would be much greater."[108] Although Gangooly had promised that family and friends would reimburse the government for his trip, it was noted that there was "no means of compelling him to refund" the money.[109]

Nevertheless, Gangooly's letter had pulled on some heartstrings. It was recommended that Gangooly might be granted free passage onboard one of the captured prize ships headed to India, and that he should wait until such a ship became available.[110] But there was also the fear that he might be unable to wait that long.[111] "Every day that I have to stop in London will make it more difficult for me to undertake the journey. Even now I can look after myself without the assistance of any nurse but I do not know what may happen if I am compelled to prolong my stay in England indefinitely," Gangooly wrote. As one officer put it, it was a matter of "Mr. Ganguli's [sic] life."[112] If he were to remain in London, the officer noted, he would likely have to be admitted to a Poor Law Infirmary. "From the nature of his complaint, it is not likely that he would recover."[113]

Given the severity of his condition, it was proposed that Gangooly be taken aboard the *Rheinfels*, sailing at the end of June. Yet, despite the broad sympathy for his condition among the various bureaucrats involved in his case, concerns about public health made it difficult to arrange his passage. "Putting Mr. Ganguly [sic] into a cabin with another passenger will create difficulties."[114] It was thought that Gangooly might be accommodated in a deck berth rather than in a cabin, to minimize his contact with the other passengers.

Despite this flurry of correspondence, Gangooly's case was never resolved, at least not in a fashion visible through the archives. In August 1921, over three months after Gangooly wrote his letter to Bhore, there had been no progress on the matter. Uncertainty about when he fell ill, as well as the voluntary nature of his service, allowed the colonial government to disclaim responsibility for Gangooly's predicament. Like Fiddes and Fox, he too disappears from the record. The archival trail comes to an end. In his case, I fear, that end was likely death.

If we step back for a moment, we might ask: why was Gangooly advised to go back to India in the first place? As with Miss Fox, this prescription might

---

108. G. C. Shepherd, minute paper, n.d., British Library.
109. G. C. Shepherd, minute paper, n.d., British Library.
110. A prize referred to a ship captured from enemy forces.
111. C. B. Gangooly to Joseph Bhore, May 10, 1921, British Library.
112. Letter from India Office, May 23, 1921, J & P 3094 1921, British Library.
113. Letter from India Office, May 23, 1921, British Library.
114. Letter from India Office, May 23, 1921, British Library.

have had more to do with finances than with biology. Gangooly was clearly too ill to work in London and had pushed the limits of charity from friends and acquaintances. On the other hand, it might have been the case that his doctor truly believed India to be curative because it was warm. However, as we well know, climatic cures were closely linked to ideas about race and geography. Displaced as he was, as a colonial subject stuck in the metropole, Gangooly remained Indian. Returned to his proper place in the world, returned to an environment suited to his biology (despite the rapid changes to that environment), he might have achieved his cure—or so hoped his doctor. But perhaps Dr. DeZilva secretly agreed with the official who wrote that Gangooly would likely not recover. Perhaps he was unconvinced about the therapeutic alchemy produced by returning racialized bodies to their proper places. Perhaps what he hoped was that sending Gangooly elsewhere would simply give him a chance, and give him hope, by deferring his cure to another place and time. Looking back at the early twentieth century from a moment in which specific cures are preferred over general remedies, it's tempting to search for singular reasons: why was India meant to be curative for Gangooly? In his particular case, however, the constitution of cure could not be separated from matters of money, labor, race, climate, and geography, and all at the same time.

The Indian Sun

When it came to healing, race, place, gender, and geography congealed in curious ways. We've met many travelers in search of cure: British soldiers leaving India for Britain, an Irish soldier seeking cure in Switzerland and Australia, an Irish woman banking on the therapeutic power of the Indian climate, an Indian man in London counseled that his only hope for survival was to return to India. When it came to cure, place mattered, but not always in a way one might expect. Cure was not always the therapeutic alchemy produced by racialized biologies restored to their equally racialized "natural" environments. Cure was not always the panacean herb on a faraway mountain (although sometimes it was). Cure might not be static, always in the same place, but remain, resolutely, elsewhere.

Let me offer one last tale of cure sought after elsewhere, that of Kamala Nehru, the wife of India's first prime minister, who for years endured periods of relative health punctuated by nausea and vomiting. She had visited doctors and tuberculosis sanatoria in Bombay and Calcutta, but no one could provide her with lasting relief. In 1935, her condition took a significant turn for the worse. She was already an Indian body in India. Where else was there for her to go? Where else might cure be found? Or rather, where might she go to find a cure that would endure?

In May of that year, while her husband Jawaharlal occupied a jail cell in Almora, Kamala set sail from Bombay. Her doctors had advised her that the German environment and therapeutic institutions would prove more beneficial for her health than anything in India.

Just prior to her departure, she asked Gandhi to visit her in Bombay. Remarking on the two days that he spent with Kamala in Bombay, Gandhi wrote to Jawaharlal that she seemed to have never experienced "so much peace of mind as she seemed to enjoy then. Her faith in the benevolence of God, she said, was never so bright as then. Her mental disturbance had vanished and she did not mind what happened to her. She went to Europe because you all wished it; it seemed to be her obvious duty to do so."[115] In a speech delivered at a Congress-run hospital renamed after Kamala, Gandhi noted, "During my last meeting with Kamala in Bombay while she was leaving for Europe for treatment, she told me that she might not come back and that I should see that the work of the hospital [at Allahabad] went on."[116] Despite Kamala's dire warnings, Gandhi expressed faith that she would recover. "When I said good-bye to her in Bombay," he wrote to Nehru, "I did not feel that we were parting for all time, and I naturally said: 'We are going to meet again in a year's time.' . . . I claim to have that hope still."[117]

Kamala took up residence at a sanatorium in the Black Forest of Germany, the birthplace of the open-air movement. Gandhi had written to Nehru six years earlier registering his disapproval of the idea that Kamala be removed from the Indian climate:

> I wish you will not listen to doctors when they object to the Indian sun. You have heard of Dr. Muthu. Revashankerbhai's son Dhiru was suffering from tuberculosis of the bone. After having tried sanatorium cure in Solon and all the doctors he could get hold of in Bombay, he sent for Dr. Muthu, paid him a fee of [a] thousand rupees per day. Dr. Muthu had no better advice to offer than to prescribe open air, light food and sun treatment. The affected bone was discharging some time one pound of pus per day. The affected bone had to be exposed to the sun every morning for a few hours and he had to lie in the open air the whole day long. He was not even sent

115. Gandhi, *The Collected Works*, vol. 68, 46.
116. Gandhi, *The Collected Works*, vol. 77, 116 (speech at Kamala Nehru Memorial Hospital, Allahabad, November 19, 1939).
117. Gandhi, *The Collected Works*, vol. 68, 106.

to a sanatorium. He is now completely cured. European sun may be better, but the Indian rival is by no means to be despised.[118]

When Kamala finally left for Germany, her husband, the future first prime minister of the future Indian nation, was serving one of his many prison terms at Almora. In August 1935, just a few months after Kamala had set sail, Gandhi received an express cable from Germany informing him that her health had deteriorated. The European sun had not proved to be so beneficial after all. Gandhi immediately sent a telegram to the viceroy and the governors of Bengal and the United Provinces apprising them of Kamala's situation: "'CONDITION SERIOUS OWING TO PERSISTENT NAUSEA AND VOMITING.' IN VIEW OF THIS SERIOUS NEWS MAY I APPEAL FOR PANDIT JAWAHARLAL NEHRU'S UNCONDITIONAL DISCHARGE ENABLING HIM IF AT ALL POSSIBLE TO CATCH DUTCH AIR MAIL FLYING NEXT TUESDAY?"[119] The colonial government granted Nehru a reprieve from prison on account of Kamala's worsening state. Nehru had been hesitant to accept special treatment during his prison stint, but Kamala's condition was serious enough to warrant an exception to his democratic morality. He left Almora on September 3, 1935, arriving in Allahabad via train and automobile the very next day. From there, he boarded a flight to Karachi, and then onward, through a series of stopovers, until he reached Kamala. In his *Discovery of India*, he describes how he raced to her side, crossing the distance between Almora and Badenweiler in just five days. He writes that Kamala's doctors gave him hope: "I imagined that she was improving and that if she could only survive that crisis she might get well."[120]

You can almost imagine Nehru in the Black Forest, trudging daily from his pension to the sanatorium, to sit at his wife's side, to speak with her gently, to read aloud to her from Pearl S. Buck's nostalgic vision in *The Good Earth*, and to reminisce about the past. Nehru, who was writing of this moment from another in the future, during yet another confinement in Ahmednagar Fort, drifts from the scene of the sanatorium to an even earlier moment, the time immediately following their marriage. Driven by nationalist passion, for love of liberty, he writes that he devoted the sum of his energies to the cause, the people around him merely "substantial shadows" in comparison to his Herculean task.

118. Gandhi, *The Collected Works*, vol. 44, 55 (this letter to Nehru was written on January 26, 1929). The Dr. Muthu referenced by Gandhi is the same one we met in chapter 1.

119. Gandhi, *The Collected Works*, vol. 67, 374 (telegram to viceroy sent on August 30, 1935).

120. Nehru, *The Discovery of India*, 28.

Yet he never forgot Kamala. He returned to her "again and again as a sure haven."[121] He drew strength from her, to be channeled through him into the making of the nation: "What indeed could I have done," he asked plaintively, "if she had not been there to comfort me and give me strength, and thus enable me to re-charge the exhausted battery of my mind and body?"[122] Nehru realized too late that Kamala was tragically finite, that her energy had its limits, as he sat alongside her sickbed.

As Nehru watched, Kamala went from crisis to crisis, but then would suddenly show signs of improvement, renewing hopes of recovery. Through a steady correspondence, Nehru updated Gandhi on Kamala's condition. Gandhi counseled Nehru to remain by her side, that his presence there was "an elixir of life to Kamala."[123]

"We have to be prepared for ups and downs in Kamala's health," he wrote to Nehru.[124] "I marvel at the resisting power Kamala is showing and so long as she has got this tremendous reserve of strength and will, we can hope for the best."[125]

At the same time, Gandhi encouraged Nehru to accept reelection to the post of president of the Indian National Congress. When he won the post in absentia, Gandhi asked him to return to India as soon as Kamala showed "distinct signs of improvement."[126] But Nehru was torn. Kamala and her doctor initially supported Nehru's decision to return, but then she began to show signs of uncertainty. "Kamala did not at all like the idea of my leaving her. And yet she would not ask me to change my plans."[127] To Nehru, it seemed that "those who are ill, and especially those who have the misfortune to stay in a sanatorium, seem to develop a sixth sense which tells them much that is sought to be hid from them."[128] But it was not just that the sanatorium-bound had knowledge of what was concealed from them. They also seemed to have knowledge that they hid from the healthy. Kamala did not need to be told of her fate, but Nehru did.

A few days before his impending flight, Kamala's doctor asked him to postpone his journey for about ten days. He wrote, "As these last days went by a

121. Nehru, *The Discovery of India*, 30.
122. Nehru, *The Discovery of India*, 30.
123. Gandhi, *The Collected Works*, vol. 67, 457 (written on September 22, 1935).
124. Gandhi, *The Collected Works*, vol. 68, 106.
125. Gandhi, *The Collected Works*, vol. 68, 106.
126. Gandhi, *The Collected Works*, vol. 68, 45.
127. Nehru, *The Discovery of India*, 36.
128. Nehru, *The Discovery of India*, 35.

subtle change seemed to come over Kamala. The physical condition was much the same, so far as we could see, but her mind appeared to pay less attention to her physical environment. She would tell me that someone was calling her, or that she saw some figure or shape enter the room where I saw none."[129] In late February 1936, Kamala succumbed to the call of this spectral presence. Her death made it possible for Nehru to heed the call of the Congress. After the cremation of Kamala's body, Nehru returned to India and, along with his daughter Indira, scattered Kamala's ashes in the Ganges.

Reflecting on Kamala's life and death, Nehru wrote that he held himself accountable for his failure to make good on Kamala's sacrifice. "I had taken from her what she gave me. What had I given her in exchange during these early years? I had failed evidently and, possibly, she carried the deep impress of those days upon her."[130] She gave her energies, and he took them. Nehru confessed to having drained Kamala of life, leaving her devitalized and near death.

As Gandhi put it, Kamala "was going to Europe in search of health." Her cure, she had hoped, could be found elsewhere.

"The visit," according to Gandhi, "proved to be a search of death."[131]

129. Nehru, *The Discovery of India*, 36.
130. Nehru, *The Discovery of India*, 30.
131. Gandhi, *The Collected Works*, vol. 77, 88 (first printed in *Harijan* on November 25, 1939).

Chapter Three

The truly great problems are set forth only
when they are solved.

—Henri Bergson, *The Creative Mind*

All manner of cures, From Ash to Antibiotic,

have had to prove their value. At the end of the nineteenth century, the bacteriologist Robert Koch proposed a cure for tuberculosis whose substance remained, for a time, a mystery. Nevertheless, his penchant for pageantry allowed him to gather support for his seemingly miraculous discovery. Koch's quite literal reliance on spectacle over substance opened the door to a broad questioning of what counted as evidence of cure, and how such evidence should be produced. With the development of antibiotics in the mid-twentieth century, the question of demonstrating cure's efficacy once again became a matter of serious concern. As a procedure for determining once and for all whether a cure worked, the randomized controlled trial proposed to do away with ambivalence, as well as with historical forms of cure and modes of evidentiary production. In 1950s Madras, an international team of researchers undertook India's first randomized controlled study, a test of antibiotics on working-class tuberculosis patients. Their aim was to determine whether these new medicines were a universal cure. If antibiotics could work in India, indifferent to the influences of poverty, geography, race, and environment, then they could work on anyone, anywhere—or so it was thought. Cure would no longer be elsewhere. Yet, even as sanatoria shuttered their doors, the antibiotic cure quickly stumbled onto its limits, in the form of relapse and resistance.

The Trial of the King

In the royal city of Madurai lived a hunchbacked king. He ruled over the Pandya kingdom, under the guidance of the Jain monks who occupied the hills just beyond the city. There were those close to the king who found this arrangement distressing, to say the least. The king's wife, for example, a former Chola princess named Mankaiyarkkaraci, as well as his minister, Kulaccirai. Both were devout followers of the god Shiva and were perturbed by their king's allegiance to another faith.

One day, Mankaiyarkkaraci and Kulaccirai heard news of a precocious child from the nearby town of Sirkazhi who spun beautiful verse and exhibited miraculous power. The child's name was Sambandar, and his reputation grew with each passing day. In Sambandar, the king's wife and minister sensed an opportunity. They invited him to Madurai to exorcise the Jain monks from the city and extract the king from their control.

What Sambandar lacked in years he more than made up for through the force of his commitments. His love for Shiva was overpowering, rivaled only by his enmity toward competing sects. The two feelings hummed symbiotically throughout Sambandar's devotional stanzas:

> Those Buddhists and mad Jains may slander speak.
> Such speech befits the wand'rers from the way.
> But He [Shiva] who comes to earth and begged for alms,
> He is the thief who stole my heart away.[1]

The antagonism was undoubtedly mutual. At the time—roughly the sixth century—varied sects vied for followers and political patronage. Buddhism and Jainism posed potent challenges to the Shiva-centered traditions of south India.

As the story goes—at least from the Saivite perspective—the Jain monks of Madurai feared that Sambandar would turn the king away from them, and from their faith. Casting aside their famed ethic of nonviolence, they torched the inn where Sambandar was staying. Caught in the flames, Sambandar cried out to Shiva for salvation (and a bit of retribution):

> False Jains have lit for me a fire:
> Oh, let it to the Pandyan ruler go,
> That he the torture of slow flame may know.[2]

---

1. Sambandar, "Stanza 18," 27.
2. Sambandar, "Stanza 23," 33.

Figure 3.1. Bronze statue of the Saivite poet-saint Sambandar. Collection of the Metropolitan Museum of Art, New York City, https://metmuseum.org/toah/works-of-art/2010
.230.

As he prayed, so it was: the fire metamorphosed into a ravenous fever that consumed the Pandya king. The Jain monks chanted over the king's febrile body their most potent mantras, but this was, after all, no ordinary illness. The king's fever refused to subside.

Capitalizing on this failure, Mankaiyarkkaraci and Kulaccirai whispered into their liege's ear about a recent arrival in the city who wielded tremendous spiritual powers. The stories they told the king were impressive. Sambandar, it was said, had cured a man of malaria, rid a woman of epilepsy, and reanimated the bones of the dead. For one who could cure death, what was a little fever?

Against the protests of the Jain monks, Sambandar was summoned to the royal bedside. He slathered the king's body in ash while reciting his own hymns:

> The sacred ash is our mantra,
> the ash covers the bodies of the gods;
> the sacred ash is all beautiful things,
> the ash is all that is praised.
> The sacred ash is the tantra text,
> the ash is the core of our faith.[3]

The sacred ash was also the cure, better than any mantra or tantra. Sambandar transformed the hunchbacked ruler into a beautiful, upstanding specimen of a man, his fever banished. Beauty, after all, was but an outward-facing sign of the king's newfound spirituality and restored health.[4]

The grateful king converted to Saivism. To be clear, this wasn't a kind of exchange at gunpoint, your life for your religion. If a Jain couldn't cure the king, and a Saivite could, what did that say about their respective faiths? The therapeutic dual between Sambandar and the monks was in effect a trial pitting Saivism against Jainism. Through his victory, Sambandar proved, at least to the king, that his faith was truer, stronger, better, and, most importantly, efficacious.[5] The defeated Jains, as some people like to tell the story, were impaled for their efforts.[6] Their cure had proven itself to be no cure at all. And with its

3. Peterson, "Campantar II.202 *Tirunirrup Patikam*," 277.
4. On Tamil visions of beauty and its relationship to power both royal and divine, see Wentworth, "Yearning for a Dreamed Real."
5. On the critical role of efficacy as a reason for worshipping one deity over another in Tamil-speaking south India, see Roberts, *To Be Cared For*.
6. The reality of the event of impalement is a matter of much popular and scholarly debate and has come to define a certain kind of Tamil Saivite hagiography.

failure, their spiritual authority was diminished, their political reach cut short, their very lives rendered forfeit.

The Savior of Guinea Pigs

In the earliest days of my research in India, I stood in the spare on-call room of Tambaram Sanatorium, the institution just beyond the city limits of Chennai that was founded by David Chowry Muthu in the late 1920s.[7] On the wall hung a framed image of Robert Koch, overseeing the quiet movements of government physicians during their breaks. Koch is widely regarded as the father of microbiology, the discoverer of the bacteria that causes tuberculosis, and the man who confirmed—along with Pasteur—that pathogenic microbes live among us. As with Sambandar, Koch's fame—and his reputation for producing something that bordered on the miraculous—traveled. His influence was such that his image found its way across an ocean and into many chest hospitals across India.

Koch himself had crossed that ocean twice.[8] After spending months in Egypt in pursuit of a microbiotic cause of cholera, the outbreak abruptly ended. Refusing to end his investigations, Koch packed up and headed to India in December 1883, which was thought to be the source of the disease. Within two months of arriving in Calcutta, Koch's team identified the same bacteria that they had found in an Egyptian water tank shared by many of those who had fallen ill. Koch concluded that this bacteria was the cause of the disease.

His findings were an irritant to sanitary policy in India, which operated largely through an environmental mode of understanding disease, relying on concepts like miasma or climate. Koch's contagion was also a threat to the reputation of health officials, including the sanitary commissioner for the colonial government of India, J. M. Cunningham, who spent years working to undermine or at least minimize Koch's findings by stressing the importance of local conditions. The fact that Koch was unable to replicate the disease in an animal model provided health officials with ammunition to argue that Koch's bacteria were either an insufficient cause for cholera, or that they were only a symptom of the disease.[9] As an editorial note in the Lahore *Tribune* put

7. On the founding of Tambaram Sanatorium, see the end of chapter 1.

8. On Koch in India, see Harrison, *Public Health in British India*; Chakrabarti, *Bacteriology in British India*.

9. For similar arguments about the place of bacteria in the etiology of tuberculosis, see chapter 1.

it, Koch's "discovery has not been accepted by members of the profession in England and India. One ardent scientist had the audacity to swallow the bacillus alive before a wondering audience!"[10] What counted as adequate evidence (and how you could demonstrate it) was a problem, it seemed, not only in matters of cure, but of cause as well.

Koch would return to India once more, in May 1897, this time to Bombay, where he worked to prove that rats were the vector for the bacteria that cause plague (although he attributed the spread of plague between rats to cannibalism). His investigations into the etiologies of cholera and plague, however, were bookended by a concern with tuberculosis. Just before his first trip to India, he had declared that microscopic bacteria were the cause of tuberculosis. His colleagues expected that a cure would naturally follow in the wake of his etiological investigations; knowledge of cure was understood to be immanent to knowledge of cause. Instead, Koch turned his attention to cholera and plague.

It was only in August 1890, eight years after that earlier declaration of cause, and after his two trips to India, that Koch announced that he had found something like a cure for tuberculosis. Nearly six thousand physicians had descended on the city of Berlin, including some of the most preeminent names in science and medicine, Joseph Lister, Paul Elrich, and Rudolph Virchow among them, to attend the Tenth International Medical Congress. Koch's announcement, delivered that day to his peers, was construed as the fulfillment of a long-awaited promise.[11] His words, carefully chosen as they were, nonetheless spread with the force of rumor on that sweltering August day.

To be clear: what Koch said was that he had identified a substance that halted the spread of tuberculosis in guinea pigs. What many heard was that he had finally found a cure for a dreaded disease that had plagued humanity since antiquity. "Koch's lymph," as this miraculous discovery was called, generated intense excitement among both physicians and the general public, garnering write-ups in medical journals and newspapers around the world. In the immediate wake of Koch's announcement, the American surgeon Nicholas Senn declared that "no other event in the world's history ever attracted so much attention, and no discovery in medicine or surgery ever found such ready introduction and

10. "Editorial Notes," 11.

11. Within other forms of bacteriological reason—for example, that of Pasteur and French bacteriology more generally—the identification of a microbial cause of disease might be understood to lead not to cure, but rather to vaccination. See Valmet, "The Making of a Pastorian Empire."

universal acceptation."[12] By November, English-language newspapers in India like the Allahabad *Pioneer* and the Lahore *Tribune* were carrying almost daily commentary and coverage of Koch's discovery and of its potential value for India:

> The general belief is that consumption is incurable. . . . In Punjab many more cases are met with now than was the case only 10 years ago. All *hakims, vaidyas,* and doctors are unanimous that consumption is on the increase. The Punjab was comparatively free from it a few years back. . . . Poor Guru Dutt, whose life was of such brilliant promise, and for whose untimely death the heart of the Punjab is still bleeding, was a victim of this disease. . . . The news that Dr. Koch, the well-known pathologist of Berlin, has well-nigh succeeded in discovering a cure for consumption, has been hailed with joy throughout the world. . . . The accounts of the results of Dr. Koch's experiments have been watched with breathless interest.[13]

In the absence of sectarian battles over spiritual power, the determination of curative efficacy in biomedicine remains tied to questions of authority (who claims to have the power to cure), substance (what precisely they claim is curative), and demonstration (how they articulate their claims to others). Cure is a procedure or process (to cure or to become cured); but it is also an established fact (this is a cure) marked by signs of efficacy produced through this process. In the case of the Pandya king, one such sign was beauty. But in biomedicine, how can a cure be established as curative? By turning to evidentiary logics every bit as tied to concerns about authority, substance, and demonstration as was the trial of the king.

On November 13, 1890, Koch published a much-anticipated summary of his findings in the *Deutsche Medizinische Wochenschrift,* a preeminent German medical journal. Koch was quite circumspect, almost coy, about his miraculous discovery. He explained that he had meant to keep his research quiet until he had gained "sufficient experience regarding the application of the remedy in practice and its production on a large scale."[14] Forced now to counter the "many accounts [that had] reached the public . . . in an exaggerated and distorted form," Koch had grudgingly agreed to set the record straight in the

---

12. Senn, *Away with Koch's Lymph!,* 3. The embrace of Koch's views was particularly enthusiastic in the United States, where the *New York Times* ran a front-page story under the heading "Koch's Great Triumph." See Feldberg, *Disease and Class,* 57.

13. "A Cure for Consumption," 11.

14. Koch, "A Further Communication on a Remedy for Tuberculosis," 1193.

Figure 3.2. Koch portrayed as St. George, warrior, martyr, and healing saint. Image reprinted in Stead, "Dr. Koch," 547. In a study on the folklore of pulmonary tuberculosis, Rolleston notes that the cure of tuberculosis was frequently associated with the Holy Trinity, Mary, and St. Pantaleon. Rolleston, "The Folk-Lore of Pulmonary Tuberculosis."

pages of the journal.[15] Nevertheless, he refused to reveal the composition of his cure until he had completed his research, offering only that it was a "brownish transparent liquid."[16]

Koch was deeply concerned with managing the forms of publicity around his cure. In the absence of a singular standard for evidentiary production, witnessing and other forms of publicity remained critical to the acceptance of a scientific discovery as truth. Scientific truth required dissemination and enactment, either on the stage or on the page.[17] Undoubtedly Koch's words held great weight. He had proven himself to be a credible witness to his own genius, so much so that many of his colleagues accepted his assertion of having found a cure despite his refusal to divulge its contents. According to the reformist journalist William Thomas Stead, Koch's secrecy represented a grievous breach of professional ethics. "All dealers in secret remedies are quacks," he wrote, questioning Koch's actions and the ready acceptance of many of his medical colleagues.[18]

Koch staunchly defended his secrecy. He feared that making the production process public would lead to the untrammeled manufacture of inferior serum injected into desperate patients.[19] Not only would patients be harmed, but the reputation of his cure would be tarnished. For Koch, concerns about the ethics of scientific secrecy were greatly overshadowed by the dangers posed by inappropriate variability in how his cure was produced and applied.

Despite his desire to manage the dissemination of information, Koch knew that he had to do more than simply claim that he had found a cure. Seeing was still believing. In order to gather together witnesses of the highest scientific renown, Koch arranged for a demonstration of his cure in Berlin. News of Koch's discovery, and of his demonstration, traveled swiftly across the waters.[20] And as it traveled, it attracted ever-larger audiences to witness his miracle firsthand. Many observers of the chaos in Berlin—of the lay and

15. Koch, "A Further Communication on a Remedy for Tuberculosis," 1193.

16. Koch, "A Further Communication on a Remedy for Tuberculosis," 1193.

17. On the historical relationship between stagecraft and truth, see Sennett, *The Fall of Public Man.*

18. Stead, "Dr. Koch," 547.

19. Concerns about reputation, trust, and patient desperation have persisted into the era of randomized clinical trials. See, for example, Lowy, "Trustworthy Knowledge and Desperate Patients," 49–81.

20. Both direct witnessing and virtual witnessing (made possible by the circulation of descriptions of scientific spectacle) were central to the making of scientific truth in the seventeenth century. Such practices remained important to establishing the validity of claims to cure until the development of the randomized controlled trial

professional crowds, of the intense excitement, of the hopes sufferers and their families pinned to Koch's discovery—were reminded of the journeys undertaken by pilgrims to sacred places of healing.[21] The pilgrim hoped for a vision of the divine on earth, and for an end to their suffering. Koch's demonstration promised just that: the miracle of the cure on display, and the faint possibility that the spectator might also be healed. The mysterious substance—Koch's lymph—was even named in the same fashion as a saint's relic. Koch's demonstration succeeded in bringing together elements of theater, scientific witnessing, and religious pilgrimage.

For those who could not make it to Berlin, other demonstrations would soon follow, through the select distribution of his cure across Europe and the United States. In carefully distributing his cure, Koch also distributed the possibility of direct witnessing across a range of sites. Proof of cure was a question not only of epistemology, but of aesthetics.[22] Science had to be made available to the senses and, in Koch's case, to the sense of vision—which also meant that the spectacle had to be bound by time and space.

But what precisely had these crowds come to see? Although Koch refused to reveal the composition of his miraculous substance, he was quite forthcoming about its purported effects. Unlike the more tepid remarks he had made in August, Koch boldly claimed in his article that early-stage phthisis, or pulmonary tuberculosis, "can be *cured with certainty* by this remedy."[23] The duration of treatment was also appealingly brief: "Within four to six weeks," he reported,

---

in the mid-twentieth century, as discussed below. Shapin and Schaffer, *Leviathan and the Air-Pump*.

21. Here too, cure was in a sense elsewhere. Yet the dissemination of Koch's substance through both spectacle and reportage brought cure closer to home for many.

22. Aesthetic concerns remain central to arguments about therapeutic efficacy, particularly in contemporary forms of investment and marketing related to pharmaceutical production and sales. See, for example, Kaushik Sunder Rajan's work on the forms of speculation that bridge the life sciences and the market. Sunder Rajan, *Biocapital*, 281. See also Lochlann Jain's work on the aesthetics of enforced optimism built into advertising related to cures for cancer in the United States. Jain notes that "cancer fills the core of so many economies," such that "if a cure were to be found, the economy might just crash." Jain, *Malignant*, 8. See also Joseph Dumit's reflections on the persuasive power of pharmaceutical advertising as dependent upon a relation to the would-be patient that resembles a religious form of witnessing that leads to conversion. Dumit, *Drugs for Life*, 66–67.

23. Koch, "A Further Communication on a Remedy for Tuberculosis," 1195, emphasis added.

CHAPTER THREE

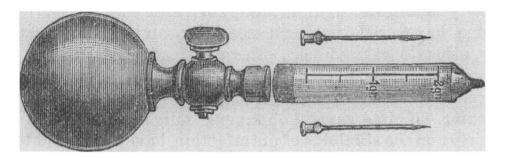

Figure 3.3. Electrotype of Koch's syringe, used to inoculate patients. Koch, "A Further Communication on a Remedy for Tuberculosis," 1197.

"patients under treatment for the first stage of phthisis were all free from every symptom of disease, and might be pronounced cured."[24] In his article, Koch conceptualized cure in terms of the recession of clinical symptoms over a period of time, rather than relying on a more bacteriologically based definition as would have been expected from a founding figure in microbiology. This choice would come to haunt him.

Of Twisted Joints and Rotting Bones

Two days after its German publication, Koch's report was translated into English as a special supplement to the *British Medical Journal*, a copy of which found its way to the home of the writer and physician Arthur Conan Doyle. The creator of Sherlock Holmes was captivated by Koch's words, despite his admission that he had no particular interest in tuberculosis. Nevertheless, the broad fascination with Koch's cure for a nineteenth-century Britain plagued by tuberculosis cannot be overstated.[25]

Although a great admirer of Koch, Doyle was exceedingly skeptical of much that went under the umbrella of scientific advancement. Even so, Koch's

24. Koch, "A Further Communication on a Remedy for Tuberculosis," 1195.

25. The fascination extended beyond Britain to its Indian colony: "The youth of its victims, the general hopelessness the disease inspires in every one but the patient, and its wide prevalence, all contribute to invest consumption, of all the ills which flesh is heir to, with the most mournful interest; and if Dr. Koch's treatment is all it claims to be, his latest will also be the most signal and reputable of all his triumphs in the field of bacteriology. . . . Should it prove successful, [it] will be one of the greatest discoveries of modern medical science." Correspondent, "Latest Foreign Intelligence," 1.

report made quite an impression: "A great urge came upon me suddenly that I should go to Berlin. . . . It was an irresistible impulse and I at once determined to go."[26] Within a few hours, Doyle was aboard a train to London. After pausing there to see the aforementioned journalist William Thomas Stead, for whom he agreed to write a character sketch of Koch, Doyle continued on to Berlin.

Doyle arrived a day before one of the demonstrations, desperate to lay his hands on a ticket for this monumental piece of medical theater. He approached the British ambassador and a journalist from the *Times*, to no avail. "Tickets were simply not to be had and neither money nor interest could procure them," he wrote.[27] With no other avenues available to him, Doyle went to Koch's home hoping to meet the great scientist in person. To his great disappointment, he was turned away by Koch's butler. In a last-ditch attempt, Doyle bribed his way into the hall outside of the auditorium and threw himself in front of Koch's colleague, Dr. Ernst von Bergmann, who was to lead the demonstration (Koch himself would be absent, unwilling "to be present when his name would be so frequently mentioned").[28] Von Bergmann mocked Doyle's earnest plea and refused him entry.

Fortunately for Doyle, a sympathetic onlooker, a visiting physician from Detroit named Henry Hartz, witnessed this less than collegial behavior. He met with Doyle later that afternoon and shared his notes on von Bergmann's demonstration. Doyle had missed a grand display of medical pageantry. Over forty patients were exhibited, many of whom had been wheeled into the auditorium in their hospital beds. Some were inoculated in front of the assembled physicians, a small amount of Koch's substance subcutaneously injected into their backs by a uniformed Eduard Pfühl, an army surgeon and Koch's son-in-law. The majority of the patients suffered extreme reactions to the inoculation: fever, rigors, vomiting, swelling, and inflammation. Despite these symptoms, a correspondent from the *Lancet* reported that most of the patients who had already received the treatment "were now regarded as practically cured."[29]

The day after the demonstration, Hartz secured Doyle's entrance into von Bergmann's clinic so that he could examine these same patients for himself. As part of his character sketch on Koch, Doyle described the scene in the clinic:

26. Doyle, *Memories and Adventures*, 87–88.

27. Doyle, *Memories and Adventures*, 89.

28. *Lancet* Correspondent, "Demonstrations of Cases Treated by Koch's Antitubercular Liquid," 1120.

29. *Lancet* Correspondent, "Demonstrations of Cases Treated by Koch's Antitubercular Liquid," 1120.

A long and grim array they were of twisted joints, rotting bones, and foul ulcers of the skin, all more or less under the benign influence of the inoculation. . . . Here and there I saw a patient, bright-eyed, flushed, and breathing heavily, who was in the stage of reaction after the adminis-tration of the injection: for it cannot be too clearly understood that the first effect of the [inoculation] is to intensify the symptoms, to raise the tempera-ture to an almost dangerous degree, and in every way to make the patient worse instead of better.[30]

Doyle witnessed a similar state of affairs at the clinic of Dr. Levy and at the Charité Hospital run by Dr. Bardeleben, where patients were also being treated with Koch's lymph. But contrary to Koch, he did not interpret these clinical observations as signs of cure. Instead, Doyle concluded that "the whole thing was experimental and premature."[31] The miracle substance, he conjectured, very likely left bacteria hidden "deep in the invaded country."[32] Doyle was quite possibly the first to criticize Koch's cure in such a public fashion, and on the grounds of Koch's own science, bacteriology.

Koch's camp had, up to a point, been able to "harmonize" contradictory research results to align with their expectations.[33] Adverse reactions to Koch's lymph—renamed tuberculin—were partially explained away as cases in which the disease had progressed too far. Koch himself had freely admitted that treat-ing more advanced cases was difficult, especially when the lungs contained numerous large cavities, excessive necrotic tissue, or other microorganisms.

Koch also made a point of laying out the specific action of his treatment. His lymph did not "kill the tubercle bacilli," he explained, but rather destroyed infected living tissue.[34] Koch acknowledged that bacteria might continue to survive in already-dead tissue and that uninfected living tissue must be pro-tected at all costs from infection. For this reason, he advocated the use of sur-gery to remove necrotic tissue, as well as the repeated administration of his treatment at gradually higher dosages.

The fact that his cure had no direct effect on bacteria might explain why Koch made use of a nonbacteriological, symptom-based conception of cure. Despite this disclaimer, critics of Koch's cure formulated their argu-ments in terms of both bacterial survival and clinically observable symptoms.

30. Doyle, "Dr. Koch and His Cure," 556.
31. Doyle, *Memories and Adventures*, 87–88, 90.
32. Doyle, "Dr. Koch and His Cure," 556.
33. Gradmann, "A Harmony of Illusions."
34. Koch, "A Further Communication on a Remedy for Tuberculosis," 1194.

Dr. Fraentzel of Berlin warned of the possibility of relapse without long-term treatment. Dr. Feilchenfeld, an assistant at Dr. Levy's clinic, cautioned that bacilli might reappear in sputum samples after having seemed to disappear. On both bacteriological and symptomological grounds, Koch's cure was threatened by the future. As other scientists conducted their own inquiries into Koch's cure, they came to similar conclusions.

Proving Grounds

The debate around tuberculin was not simply about the efficacy of a particular substance. Equally crucial was the question of what constituted proper evidence of cure, as well as of its failure. Arguments against Koch arrived primarily from pathology and clinical medicine, rather than from experimental or laboratory-based research.[35] The highly esteemed pathologist Rudolph Virchow drew on autopsy findings to point out that the infection only spread as cells died. Against Koch, he corralled this evidence to interpret the death of infected tissue as a sign of spreading disease rather than cure. Likewise, the physician Ottomar Rosenbach demanded to know why certain clinically observable reactions to tuberculin, like fever, should be interpreted as signs of cure rather than as iatrogenic side effects.

The grounds for proving and refuting cure were unstable, which allowed for the admission of multiple methods for producing evidence and contradictory interpretations of such evidence. Put simply, there was no universal standard by which to judge the efficacy of the cure or its failure. Neither Koch's reputation nor his demonstrations proved capable of withstanding these critiques. Tuberculin would be shown to have some diagnostic value, and although it would continue to be used as a therapeutic option (even in India), it would never achieve broad acceptance as the ultimate cure for the dreaded white plague.[36]

A host of therapeutic options rushed to fill the vacuum left by Koch's failure. Gold treatment, heliotherapy, collapse therapy, travel, and confinement were all on offer to those who suffered from tuberculosis.[37] However, it was

35. See Gradmann, "A Harmony of Illusions."

36. On the use of tuberculin for therapeutic purposes in India into the 1920s, see Brimnes, *Languished Hopes*, 51.

37. Collapse therapy refers to a procedure that quite literally collapses a patient's lung to afford it time for caseous structures to sequester the offending bacteria, and for the lung to rest.

sanatorium-based treatment that took the lead. In the years following the tuberculin scandal, sanatorium therapy thrived despite its inability to offer a specific treatment that targeted bacteria.[38] With Koch's failure to make good on a cure, "sanatorium doctors made the case that their institutions should now be seen as the only credible alternative left to provide large-scale treatment."[39] Nevertheless, the heavy cost of sanatorium treatment, the difficulties involved in treating large numbers of patients, and skepticism about its efficacy meant that it remained an imperfect alternative.

The story of tuberculin is not only about the failure of a cure. It is also a story about the kinds of expectations that are made of science and medicine, about a charismatic scientist and the forms of publicity in which he engaged in order to gather support for his discoveries. For a few months, Koch's announcement raised hopes in Berlin, and around the world, that the end of tuberculosis was near.

The warm embrace of Koch's discovery was short-lived. Within the year, researchers and clinicians had scrutinized Koch's findings and raised serious objections on a variety of evidential grounds. This would be the scene of Koch's greatest failure. As criticism of Koch mounted, he would eventually reveal that his cure was in fact a denatured form of *Mycobacterium tuberculosis*. His hope had been that the bacterium would prove itself to be a *pharmakon*, threatening illness in one form while promising cure in another. Yet in the years to come, his reliance on denatured bacteria only offered further fodder to his critics, especially British medical officers in India who protested against the expanding authority of bacteriological reasoning. As Dr. Edward Berdoe put it in a rather colorful letter published in the pages of the Lahore *Tribune*: "it is quack-nostrum mongering and nothing paying like quackery. . . . I hope the Indian people will not be exploited to further the business but that such a strong opposition will be excited that the Indian Government will be forced to stay its hand."[40] Berdoe continued, "Dr. Koch's tuberculin was announced with a great flourish of trumpets and as we all remember proved a ghastly failure."[41] The status of Koch's discovery was downgraded from a triumph of bacteriological reason to an embarrassing footnote in an otherwise illustrious career.[42]

38. For more on the curative logic of the sanatorium, see chapter 1.
39. Condrau, "Beyond the Total Institution," 79.
40. Berdoe, "Plague, Pestilence and Quackery," 5.
41. Berdoe, "Plague, Pestilence and Quackery," 5.
42. Gradmann, "Robert Koch and the Pressures of Scientific Research."

But what if we instead ushered Koch's failure back into the limelight? Might it form the basis for a genealogy of cure, or at least of its limits? Might Koch's discovery—and its subsequent failure—also help us to grasp how we come to know whether a cure is, in fact, curative? The tuberculin episode is also a story about the many forms of evidence and interpretations that could be marshaled in the name of contending truths. This all changed in the 1940s and '50s, with the emergence of a new form of treatment—antibiotics—and a new evidentiary standard that was touted as universal: the randomized controlled trial.

Scarcity Is the Mother of Experimentation

In 1943, just over fifty years after Koch's failure, a laboratory at Rutgers University succeeded in isolating the first effective antibiotic against tuberculosis, streptomycin. Like Koch, the team led by the microbiologist Selman Waksman initially demonstrated the efficacy of this new substance in guinea pigs.[43] Another team of researchers, led by William Feldman and H. Corwin Hinshaw at the Mayo Clinic, extended these studies to human subjects. Within four years of beginning their research, the Mayo Clinic team discovered the existence of streptomycin-resistant strains of tuberculosis. The team reported that resistance developed within "weeks or months" of beginning treatment.[44] The newest hope of curing tuberculosis had met its limit, and quickly.

In spite of this limit, the story of streptomycin did not end there. The British government had imported a small supply of the drug in 1946.[45] The British Medical Research Council (MRC) took control over this supply, establishing a trials oversight committee and a separate tuberculosis research team. The MRC Tuberculosis Research Unit was composed of its director, a clinician named Philip D'Arcy Hart, a clinic coordinator named Marc Daniels, and Austin Bradford Hill, the head of the MRC Statistical Research Unit.

43. Streptomycin was first isolated in the lab by one of Waksman's graduate students, Albert Schatz, although Waksman would receive much of the credit.

44. Hinshaw, Pyle, and Feldman, "Streptomycin in Tuberculosis," 434. Although clinical resistance would become an issue from the 1940s, an earlier history of lab-induced resistance as a model for research purposes stretches back to at least 1905 (although in relationship to trypanosomiasis rather than tuberculosis). See Gradmann, "Magic Bullets and Moving Targets."

45. In the same year, the pharmaceutical company Merck began the mass manufacture of streptomycin in the United States.

For over a decade, Hill had been advocating for the use of randomization and control groups in clinical trials.[46] The British supply of streptomycin provided Hill with an opportunity to put his methods into practice. Hart was similarly eager to test out Hill's methods, frustrated with the many contradictory studies of gold treatment that lacked a standardized measure of efficacy. Although elements of the randomized controlled trial had been previously used in agricultural experiments and vaccine trials, the MRC study is widely recognized as the first to bring the pieces together.

The motivations behind the use of this new methodology have been a subject of much debate among research scientists and historians of medicine.[47] At the time, there was no domestic production of streptomycin in Britain. As Hill noted, "It was just after the Second World War . . . and Britain literally had no currency. We had exhausted all our supply of dollars in the war and our Treasury was adamant that we could have only a very small amount of streptomycin."[48] The MRC had access to about 50 kilograms of the drug, which was only enough to treat between 150 and 200 patients. The streptomycin shortage provided Hill a convenient alibi in his pursuit of a randomized clinical trial.

Approval for the trial hinged on the surmounting of a major ethical quandary: What was the proper way to distribute limited, experimental drugs for a life-threatening disease? Was randomization—basically, leaving it to chance—ethical given the exceedingly high stakes? In this moment, the grounds of ethical scrutiny had shifted from secrecy to chance, from the dissemination of knowledge to the distribution of therapy. It was no longer about the contents of the curative substance, but rather a matter of who would get it (and who would not). In the face of enormous public demand, randomization allowed for the allocation of scarce resources in a purportedly unbiased fashion.

Hill approached Geoffrey Marshall, the head of the oversight committee, arguing that "it would not be immoral to make a trial—it would be immoral *not* to make a trial since the opportunity would never rise again."[49] As with Koch's attempt to displace the ethical question of secrecy by focusing instead on the integrity of his cure, Hill attempted to refocus attention from the ethical question of distribution to what he took to be the more pressing ethical

46. On Hill's efforts, see Porter, *Trust in Numbers*, 204–5.
47. Doll, "Controlled Trials"; Teira, "On the Impartiality of Early British Clinical Trials."
48. Hill, "Memories of the British Streptomycin Trial," 78.
49. Hill, "Memories of the British Streptomycin Trial," 78.

concern around the possibility of knowledge production. Once streptomycin was manufactured in bulk, Hill feared that there would no longer be any external justification for attempting randomization. Ironically, scarcity of the drug allowed for a kind of ethical distribution that might have been impossible had the drug been more readily available. Scarcity produced its own ethical quandary, one that found its solution in the form of the randomized trial. In retrospect, he wondered whether the oversight committee would have approved the trial if not for the shortage: "I rather doubt it, but I shall never know."[50] As Hart noted, "The small amount of streptomycin available made it ethically permissible for the control subjects to be untreated by the drug—a statistician's dream."[51]

To further limit the number of patients eligible for the study, as well as to minimize the impact of confounding factors, the research team restricted participation in the study to subjects between the ages of fifteen and thirty with "acute progressive bilateral pulmonary tuberculosis of presumably recent origin, bacteriologically proved, unsuitable for collapse therapy."[52] Potential subjects were initially identified by referring physicians across Britain. The narrow parameters defining who counted as a desirable subject undoubtedly left many more severely ill patients untreated. Yet the epistemological validity of the results of any such study depended upon testing the drugs on a subset of patients whose conditions were somehow similar. How similarity was defined was of course not given in advance, but in this case, the focus on "recent origin" suggests a desire for favorable results (which might not have been as forthcoming with subjects suffering from more advanced stages of the disease). Subjects who fit the criteria were admitted into the nearest participating hospital or sanatorium with an available bed.

Every facility was provided with two series of randomly numbered envelopes, for men and for women. Each envelope contained a card inscribed with the letter S (for streptomycin) or C (for control). On admission, an envelope was opened and the subject was assigned to one of the two groups. Of the 109 subjects accepted into the trial, two died during the first week of preliminary investigations. The remaining 107 subjects were divided into two groups: fifty-five in the experimental group and fifty-two in the control group. A team of experts without knowledge of the subjects' grouping conducted monthly

50. Hill, "Memories of the British Streptomycin Trial," 78.
51. Hart, "A Change in Scientific Approach," 573.
52. Medical Research Council, "Streptomycin Treatment of Pulmonary Tuberculosis," 770.

assessments based on chest X-rays, sputum samples, and cultures.[53] Importantly, patients from both groups were admitted into a hospital or sanatorium and put on bed rest, which until that point had been the standard for treatment. As I discuss below, the value of bed rest would soon become a critical concern for tuberculosis researchers.

The MRC team worked hard to establish the randomized controlled trial as the new standard for evidentiary production. Other evidentiary procedures, such as those that commanded attention in the controversy surrounding Koch's lymph, were at best only weak indicators. The form of evidentiary demonstration was no longer spectacular, contained in space and time and therefore visible to the eye; rather, this novel form of inquiry was distributed across space and time.[54] At best, it could be described, but not easily visualized. Even the earlier Mayo Clinic studies of streptomycin were described by the MRC team as "encouraging but inconclusive."[55] The MRC study further argued that "evidence of improvement or cure following the use of a new drug in a few cases cannot be accepted as proof of the effect of that drug."[56] The anecdotal or

53. This ignorance about which subjects were allocated into which group allowed for "blind," and therefore "truer," assessments. Such trials are exemplary of a paradigmatically modern mode of evidentiary production, one in which facts are deemed credible only if they "appear innocent of human intention." Daston, "Marvelous Facts and Miraculous Evidence," 94. It is only after a fact is produced that it can be rightfully conscripted as evidence for a particular claim. But as Thomas Kuhn famously argued, such claims are admissible only if they fit within an existing or emergent paradigm. Kuhn, *The Structure of Scientific Revolutions*. Read in one direction, the triad of paradigm-claim-fact produces a sociologically deterministic understanding of scientific research and knowledge production. Read in the other direction, the triad of fact-claim-paradigm comes off as a naively optimistic understanding of how science progresses.

54. To be clear, the place of spectacle in science did not entirely disappear after Koch. Halfdan Mahler, who would later lead the WHO, underscored the importance of overcoming resistance in India to the BCG antituberculosis vaccination by emphasizing that it was the "biggest show on earth." Halfdan Mahler in McMillen, *Discovering Tuberculosis*, 100. Such a spectacle operated less like a public performance on stage, as with Koch, and more through the assertion of scale, distributed across space and time: not directly visible to the eye, but still impressive. This same assertion of scale would occur in the randomized controlled trial, which was similarly unavailable to witnessing.

55. Medical Research Council, "Streptomycin Treatment of Pulmonary Tuberculosis," 769.

56. Medical Research Council, "Streptomycin Treatment of Pulmonary Tuberculosis," 769.

idiosyncratic (the results of a "few cases") could guide the shaping of research programs and the kinds of questions that might be asked, but Hill and Hart were adamant that such forms of inquiry could never hope to generate definitive answers.

More than a shift in what was true, the MRC study enacted a dramatic shift in how something came to be counted as true. When it came to determining whether a cure was a cure, truth was becoming a question of proper methodology. In the glaring light of this new procedure, the authors of the MRC study recast the preceding history of medical research as a series of ad hoc and potentially dangerous experiments lacking both ethical and epistemological grounding.[57] Their goal was to replace the variability of evidentiary forms with a single procedure that would produce reliable evidence through randomization, control, and statistical extrapolation—and through this, establish their own study as the paradigm for a new era of medical research.[58]

To a Certain Degree

If the form of the randomized controlled trial was meant to lend universality and credibility to truth claims, the use of statistical measures narrowed the range of claims that were possible. After six months of treatment, the MRC team cautiously noted that "no clinical 'cures' were affected, and that only 15% of subjects [treated with streptomycin] were bacteriologically negative."[59] These kinds of statistical figures provided a numerical representation of the limited efficacy of streptomycin. The form of the trial enabled the MRC team to claim that streptomycin with bed rest was effective in comparison to bed

---

57. Flurin Condrau makes a related observation: "Modern bio-scientifically informed judgments on historical treatments are of limited value. This is evident in the history of antibiotic treatment against tuberculosis. Here, the close link between antibiotic effectiveness and the regime for randomised clinical control studies has dramatically restructured the evaluation of medical success." Condrau, "Beyond the Total Institution," 76.

58. Things would change dramatically in subsequent decades, with the strategic use of the randomized controlled trial as a means of justifying, regulating, and profiting from the sales of particular substances. A telling example involves the assessment of Tibetan medicine via randomized controlled trials. See Adams, "Randomized Controlled Crime."

59. Medical Research Council, "Streptomycin Treatment of Pulmonary Tuberculosis," 781.

rest alone, but they could not claim that streptomycin was curative in and of itself, bereft of bed rest.

What statistics offered was a means of measuring the relative efficacy of one treatment in comparison to another in a manner that might be touted as "objective."[60] Objectivity, in this sense, was also a kind of aesthetic, one that lent authority to particular kinds of claims by providing them with what might appear to be an unassailable numerical basis.[61] The use of statistical figures also made it more difficult to make absolute claims. The question was no longer "Is it a cure?" or even "Is it a cure for me?" With the development of the randomized controlled trial and the use of statistics, it became necessary to ask about degrees of efficacy. Treatments were increasingly understood as partial, potentially promises of cure but never guarantees.

The MRC team described the partial efficacy of streptomycin through the twinned concepts of relapse and resistance. Although no pathogenic bacteria could be detected in 15 percent of subjects after six months of treatment, there was a risk that these subjects might harbor bacteria in quantities below the threshold of detection. Sputum cultures had limited sensitivity, allowing bacteria to escape notice only to repopulate later. The MRC team admitted to this possibility of relapse after improvement, especially in subjects with greater cavitation in their lungs, where bacteria could effectively hide. While they felt confident declaring that a subject was bacteriologically negative at a particular point in time (at least as far as the sensitivity of their techniques would allow), they knew that the future posed a threat to any claim of cure.[62]

Along with posttreatment relapse, the MRC team was deeply concerned about drug resistance. Of the fifty-five subjects enrolled in the experimental group, almost two-thirds developed resistance to streptomycin during the course of the study. The MRC team monitored when each of these subjects first produced a sputum sample that was drug resistant in vitro, concluding

60. As the historian of science Georges Canguilhem put it, "The statistical calculation of therapeutic performances introduced into the understanding of the cure an objective measure of its reality." Canguilhem, "Is a Pedagogy of Healing Possible?," 57.

61. On the varying, historically specific aesthetics of different forms of objectivity, see Daston and Galison, "The Image of Objectivity." See also their book-length examination of these ideas, *Objectivity*.

62. The idea that statistics might be used to determine differential cure rates was debated at least as far back as the nineteenth century. Opponents of this idea argued against what they perceived to be the evacuation of clinical judgment. See Porter, *Trust in Numbers*, 203.

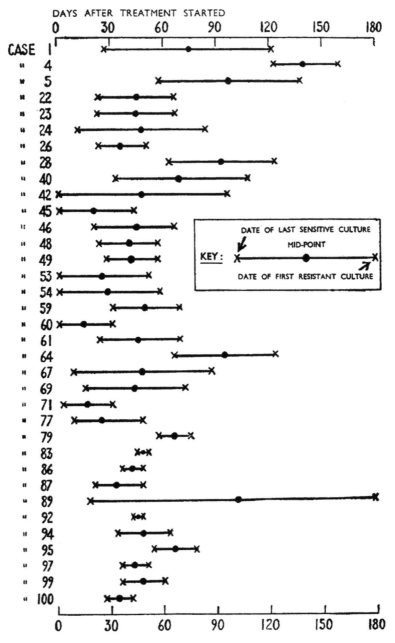

Figure 3.4. Diagram depicting time until emergence of drug resistance. Medical Research Council, "Streptomycin Treatment of Pulmonary Tuberculosis," 779.

that resistance emerged on average fifty-three days after starting treatment.[63] Because subjects improved primarily during the first three to four months of treatment, the MRC researchers speculated that "resistance is responsible for much of the deterioration seen in [streptomycin-treated] cases after first improvement."[64] Streptomycin induced resistance in subjects, producing the limits of its own efficacy. As resistance occurred in the majority of subjects treated with streptomycin, resistance was not idiosyncratic but expected and highly measurable.

The identification of other antibiotics that were effective against tuberculosis raised hopes that resistance could be overcome. After streptomycin, the first potential candidate was para-aminosalicylic acid (PAS). Initially, studies of the efficacy of PAS resulted in contradictory results. To resolve the question of efficacy, the MRC was asked to conduct its own inquiries into the matter: "As a decisive answer had been reached for streptomycin by the method of controlled clinical trial, it was agreed by clinicians in doubt about the value of PAS that the method should be applied to trial of this drug."[65]

The MRC study on PAS, published in 1950, consisted of three groups: streptomycin alone, PAS alone, and streptomycin with PAS. During the six months of this study, each of these groups also received bed rest. As in the streptomycin study, the MRC report on PAS avoided the use of the word *cure* in favor of enumerating bacteriologically negative cases. The MRC team reported that the combination of streptomycin and PAS was more effective than either drug administered alone, providing the first proof of the efficacy of combination therapy within this new evidentiary model. What researchers found even more striking was the significantly decreased levels of streptomycin resistance in the group treated with the combination: resistance was detected in thirty-three of the forty-nine streptomycin-only subjects (about 67 percent), compared to only five out of the forty-eight subjects treated with combination therapy (around 10 percent). Combination therapy was found to be both more effective and less productive of resistance.

In the following years, many of the antibiotics currently used to treat tuberculosis arrived on the scene. The MRC conducted numerous trials to test

63. Medical Research Council, "Streptomycin Treatment of Pulmonary Tuberculosis," 779–80.

64. Medical Research Council, "Streptomycin Treatment of Pulmonary Tuberculosis," 782.

65. Medical Research Council, "Treatment of Pulmonary Tuberculosis with Streptomycin and Para-amino-salicylic Acid," 1073.

the efficacy and relative drug resistance of various combinations of these drugs. Nonetheless, it was hard to say whether antibiotics worked, at least by themselves, because they had always been offered with another form of treatment: bed rest. At the time, bed rest stood in for the entire complex of diet, exercise, rest, and discipline associated with the sanatorium, a combination whose strictness was impossible to achieve at home. The subjects involved in the MRC antibiotic studies had always been admitted to hospitals or sanatoria. As one of the early reports on streptomycin out of the Mayo Clinic declared: "It must always be emphasized that treatment with streptomycin is not a substitute for rest in bed and sanatorium care, which are still fundamental in the treatment of tuberculosis."[66] This was a view held across the United States and Europe, as evidenced by the words of a Swiss sanatorium superintendent who wrote that streptomycin would "never replace therapy by collapse measures or sanatorium treatment."[67] The advent of combination therapy provided an opportunity to change the equation. If bed rest could be eliminated entirely—if drugs were found to be effective on their own—then many more patients could be treated at a much lower cost. Treatment for tuberculosis could be brought to the masses. At least, that was the dream.

No Rest for the Consumptive

In 1956, the vexed question of bed rest was answered in the south Indian city of Madras. The 1950s and '60s were clearly a heady time for science in India. Under the influence of India's first prime minister, Jawaharlal Nehru, and in the wake of independence, science was imagined to be science for the people and the nation, as opposed to a universal or Western science that just as often worked against or at the expense of the people.

The Madras Study, as it has been described, was the first randomized controlled trial in India, designed to measure differences in outcome between subjects treated in a sanatorium with antibiotics, and those given antibiotics at home.[68] At the time, there were estimated to be about 2.5 million active cases

66. Hinshaw, Pyle, and Feldman, "Streptomycin in Tuberculosis," 433.
67. Mordasini, "Streptomycin and Tuberculosis," 52.
68. Notably, an earlier series of studies in Delhi had already tested home-based antibiotic therapy, but without the rigorous methodological control of the randomized controlled trial. See Brimnes, *Languished Hopes*, 185. See also Brimnes's chapter titled "Post-colonial Hopes II: Domiciliary Therapy" for a longer discussion of the Madras Study in the context of the institutional history of Indian antituberculosis efforts.

of tuberculosis in India, but only 23,000 available beds.[69] If admission and bed rest in a hospital or sanatorium were necessary for curing tuberculosis, then this mismatch presented a serious problem. Combination therapy raised hopes that tuberculosis treatment could be extended beyond institutional confines.[70]

The director of the Madras Study was the British Dr. Wallace Fox, a global expert on tuberculosis. Fox had been involved in many of the early MRC antibiotic trials. Prior to coming to India, he had worked for the MRC in Kampala, studying the efficacy of antibiotics on East African tuberculosis patients and comparing the results to a similarly treated British group.[71] In East Africa, where socioeconomic conditions were ostensibly worse than in Britain, were antibiotics still as effective? The Kampala studies demonstrated that the difference in outcomes was statistically insignificant. Antibiotics, like disease, were not racially or geographically specific, decisively countering a long history of mapping pathologies onto specific peoples and places.[72]

In all of these trials, subjects in both control and experimental groups were admitted to hospitals or sanatoria. As the MRC streptomycin study had noted,

69. The estimate of 2.5 million active cases was calculated by P. V. Benjamin, the director of Madanapalle Sanatorium, in 1943. He based this calculation on an estimated annual mortality of at least 500,000. This number continued to be cited as the official estimate for at least fifteen years. See Brimnes, *Languished Hopes*, 44.

70. The Madras Study prefigured the 1978 Declaration of Alma-Ata, in its aim of "Health for All," by focusing on developing a form of treatment that did not, in theory, require movement. In this formation, cure was not elsewhere (in the sanatorium, for example) but at home. The proper cure for the masses depended on immobility or stasis. Immobility became central to such a utopian dream of health, one that was simultaneously tied to economic concerns. If mobility was an elite privilege, then cure had to be here—localized, static, immobile—in order to be democratic, and therefore affordable. This was a medicine organized around people in place, a sedentary medicine, one that reflected the vision of the Bhore Committee.

71. Fox et al., "A Comparison of Acute Extensive Pulmonary Tuberculosis and Its Response to Chemotherapy"; Hutton et al., "Acute Pulmonary Tuberculosis in East Africans."

72. The use of India as a living laboratory for experimentation by the WHO was a matter of great concern for Indian critics, who objected in particular to the roll-out of the BCG antituberculosis vaccine. See McMillen, *Discovering Tuberculosis*, 94, 108. Yet, as Helen Valier points out, the decision to study antibiotic efficacy in India might have had less to do with the availability of Indian subjects for experimental treatments and more to do with British physicians' resistance to doing away with bed rest and extended therapy. Valier, "At Home in the Colonies," 226.

bed rest was until that time "considered the only suitable form of treatment."[73] In that sense, the Madras Study inverted the therapeutic logic of the previous MRC studies; all study subjects would receive antibiotics, but only some would receive bed rest.

This study was also a critical extension of a postwar and postcolonial internationalism in health, as a joint effort of the MRC, the World Health Organization (WHO), and the Indian government. For such a collaboration to work, Indians needed to be included not only as subjects, but also as researchers. One of the first Indian scientists to join the project was S. Radhakrishna, who had recently graduated from Madras Presidency College with a master's degree in statistics, just months before the start of the study. His was one of the first cohorts to which a degree course in statistics had been offered. Disinclined toward a career in agricultural science or government administration— the "IAS craze," as he called it—he applied for a job with the new research center being established by Fox in Madras.[74]

A few days after submitting his application, Radhakrishna was called in for an interview at Rajaji Hall, in the Madras neighborhood of Triplicane. There, he was confronted by an interview committee including the globe-trotting Dr. Fox. At the interview, Radhakrishna was asked about his education and presented with a few statistical problems to solve. Then, Fox turned to him and asked a series of rather different questions:

What do you know about TB? (Nothing.)
Would you be scared to work with coughing patients? (No.)
Are you married? (Not yet.)

"Suppose you get married next year, and your wife objects [to you working with TB patients]?" Fox asked. Radhakrishna recalled answering this last question by explaining to Fox that "in India, marriage is all arranged. Only those [women] prepared to accept [this job] will come [for marriage]." His interview completed, Dr. Radhakrishna joined as one of the first Indian employees of the newly established Tuberculosis Chemotherapy Centre in October 1956. During the next five years, the two men worked together with a dedicated team including two medical officers, an assistant medical officer, two bacteriologists,

73. Medical Research Council, "Streptomycin Treatment of Pulmonary Tuberculosis," 770.
74. By IAS, Dr. Radhakrishna was referring to the Indian Administrative Service. Such jobs continue to be highly desirable, in particular for their stability.

an assistant bacteriologist, a laboratory technician, and a laboratory research assistant.

For the Madras-based research team, the question of relapse was of critical importance. Although the reduction of clinical symptoms and the improvement in radiological results were important measures in the Madras Study, the most important sign of therapeutic success was bacteriological. In the fallout of the scandal surrounding Koch's lymph back in 1890, no cure for tuberculosis could be worthy of the name unless it eradicated the cause of the disease. If bacteria survived the treatment, even in minute quantities below the threshold of detection, there was a danger that they could repopulate. This was a threat on the level of the individual, but there was an even greater risk at the level of the population. In discussing those patients who developed drug-resistant strains during the initial trials, the 1959 Madras Study report repeatedly described them as a "source of danger to the public health" and a "serious public health risk."[75]

Flip of a Coin

To learn more about the Madras Study, I met Dr. Radhakrishna in his familial home in the Egmore neighborhood of Chennai, on a January morning in 2012. His home was located on a dead-end street adjacent to the site of the old Hotel Dasaprakash, an art deco building erected in 1954 (only two years before the start of the Madras Study) and just recently torn down to the ground. After a good deal of wandering around in search of this phantasmic landmark, I finally found Radhakrishna's home. Through a set of double doors and up a rickety spiral staircase, I was welcomed into a sparsely furnished but comfortable sitting room, introduced to Radhakrishna's brother, and offered a cup of freshly brewed filter coffee. A black-and-white photograph of a graduation day hung on the wall alongside portraits of deceased parents and grandparents. Radhakrishna's family was from Andhra Pradesh, but like all of his siblings, he had been born in this house, he explained to me, pointing through a side door to indicate exactly where the event had taken place.

Radhakrishna related the story of his life as a fortuitous combination of epiphany and serendipity. Born in 1935, he described to me idyllic scenes of a pre-Independence Madras, a time without the ill-advised flyovers and rampant corruption that characterizes the city today, at least according to its critics.

75. Tuberculosis Chemotherapy Centre, "A Concurrent Comparison of Home and Sanatorium Treatment," 91, 52.

He told me of family friends, once honest and hard-working people, who had descended into the murky and criminal world of Tamil Nadu politics.

No surprise then, that for Radhakrishna, the era of the Madras Study represented better, more hopeful times. In his view, the historical gleam of the study came from it having been the first randomized controlled trial in India. Through a "flip of a coin," as he put it, subjects were divided into the home-based and sanatorium-based arms of the study. The coin was a metaphor; treatment had in fact been allocated using sealed envelopes with cards denoting whether a subject belonged to the control or experimental group (the same method developed by Hill for the original MRC streptomycin study).

According to Gaye Fox, the wife of Wallace Fox, the Madras Study had been accomplished under "very difficult conditions."[76] Having accompanied her husband to Madras, she had witnessed the study firsthand: "It was said that the Indians might not be cooperative, but with a dedicated team the patients were persuaded to cooperate and the studies had very few absconders. The climate was also notoriously hostile, and yet many of the staff worked long hours, and Wallace usually worked an 18-hour day, often bringing colleagues back to chew over the problems in the evening."[77] In my meeting with Radhakrishna, he too stressed to me the difficulties of cooperation. It had been a challenge to instill the "concept of a randomized controlled trial" in both patients and the research staff, he explained. "Everyone wanted sanatorium treatment." He noted that it was particularly "hard to sell this concept to patients," that their fate would be decided arbitrarily. Patronage networks, gifts, status, clout: none of these mattered in the face of randomization. He suggested to me that the presence of foreign medical professionals helped to smooth over the arbitrariness of the coin: "People felt that this place was very superior, as there were foreigners here, that something special was being given here."

It was not only patients, but doctors as well, who objected to randomization. "[Doctors] said you can't do trials on human beings—it's unethical. The doctor knows best; you can't experiment [on people]," Radhakrishna told me. But in the absence of tested and validated protocol, "every time a doctor gives medicine to a patient, he is experimenting," he argued. Radhakrishna himself admitted that randomization would be "extremely unethical" in the course of regular medical practice. Deciding a patient's fate randomly was only

76. Cited in Christie and Tansey, *Short-Course Chemotherapy for Tuberculosis*, 46.
77. Christie and Tansey, *Short-Course Chemotherapy for Tuberculosis*, 46.

CHAPTER THREE

acceptable, and in fact mandatory, within the context of the randomized controlled trial. Modern medical trials are rarely about curing any one person. While a clinician might work to cure the patient standing before them, a researcher is generally tasked with discovering a cure for a condition shared by many.

For Radhakrishna, such a trial was an exceptional event through which the normally unethical became imperative, as a means of establishing the ethical and epistemological grounding for everyday clinical practice. Like Hill—and like Koch before him—Radhakrishna displaced the grounds of ethics: the locus of concern should not be the trial, he maintained, but rather the clinic. From the vantage point of the present, it's difficult to say whether Radhakrishna was simply reading contemporary understandings of evidence-based medicine into the past. In the absence of trials to produce such evidence, medical treatment is figured as idiosyncratic and variable, vulnerable to the whims of individual physicians. Without the backing of this new form of evidence, Radhakrishna argued that all clinical practice would be rife with epistemological and ethical uncertainty. In other words, it was not the randomized controlled trial that was ethically dubious, but rather those everyday practices of clinical medicine unsupported by evidence from such trials.[78]

Unscientific Feelings

The subjects for the Madras Study were recruited primarily from poor neighborhoods adjacent to the Tuberculosis Chemotherapy Centre. In total, 193 subjects were admitted into the study: ninety-six in the home-based group and ninety-seven in the sanatorium-based group. Both sets of subjects received isoniazid and PAS for twelve months. During the study, home-based patients attended the clinic on a weekly basis to collect their medications. In addition, research staff regularly visited homes to retain patients in the study, and to urge them to adhere to the strict therapeutic regime. Surprise urine tests were administered, as drug levels were taken to be a more reliable index of adherence than

78. Ethnographic studies of randomized controlled trials have shown how a presumably standardized evidentiary procedure has nevertheless been deployed in variable ways to take advantage of what are framed as local ethical and regulatory norms. Standardization, then, is not at odds with variation. See in particular Petryna, "Ethical Variability." Moreover, such variability can be a feature, rather than a bug, producing more successful and cost-effective results that meet the demands of capital. See Sunder Rajan, *Biocapital.*

patient testimony. The research team's involvement in the lives of the home-based study participants suggests that a quality of sanatorium treatment—the supervision of a physician or superintendent—had become decentralized and mobile, extending to the home.

Considerable effort was also exerted to keep subjects in the sanatorium. The Madras government had made about one hundred beds available for the study at Tambaram Sanatorium.[79] "Nobody wanted to go to the sanatorium for twelve months," Radhakrishna explained, except when they were experiencing symptoms. A year was a long time, and symptoms often receded after a few months. To stem the desire to leave, Fox, Radhakrishna, and a public health nurse visited subjects at Tambaram every Saturday. Special accommodations were made to maintain enrollment in the study—for example, subjects were permitted to take a few days leave to attend family weddings, like "prisoners on parole," as Radhakrishna put it. Milk powder was also given to the children of patients, as a way of supplementing their food supplies in the absence of a parent.[80] The research team also established a fund to provide financial assistance to families when it was deemed "essential."[81] Some home-based subjects also received funds to subsidize transportation to the clinic.

These retention strategies did not go unnoticed. Fox was heavily criticized by his Danish colleague at the nearby Madanapalle Sanatorium, Dr. Johannes Frimodt-Moller, for allowing the scientificity of his results to be endangered by humanitarian sentiments. A similar critique was issued to Fox by Johannes Holm of the WHO: "You wish to do everything possible for each one of your patients . . . including those who, for the purposes of the trial, can be described as failures and thereafter can be of little or no scientific interest. I realize that this is from humanitarian, or if you prefer it, clinical considerations and feelings."[82]

79. This was in fact the same sanatorium founded by Dr. Muthu in the 1920s, where I found myself looking at a framed image of Koch near the beginning of this chapter.

80. Ramah McKay has written about the ways in which investments in global health tied "therapeutic food" to medical aid while simultaneously making food unavailable to those without medical conditions. Within such a formulation, food is not a government-provisioned good distributed to the poor, but rather a form of humanitarian aid. In the Madras Study, the provision of food was also a kind of incentive to keep subjects in the study. McKay, *Medicine in the Meantime.*

81. Tuberculosis Chemotherapy Centre, "A Concurrent Comparison of Home and Sanatorium Treatment," 53.

82. This source has also been cited in two earlier studies that were foundational to my research, by Sunil Amrith and Helen Valier. Amrith, "In Search of a 'Magic Bullet' for Tuberculosis," 124; Valier, "At Home in the Colonies," 223.

"Failures," for Holm, were those subjects who proved resistant to cure by the standardized experimental regimen.[83] In theory, such failures provided important data about the limitations of cure. But in describing these subjects as failures, Holm revealed his own agenda: not simply to test whether antibiotics alone worked as well as antibiotics with sanatorium admission, but to produce powerful evidence that it was so. Historians have interpreted Holm's irritation with Fox as indicative of a fundamental divide between the aims of the WHO and the MRC. Whereas the WHO was interested in halting the spread of infection, the MRC, at least as represented by Fox, was focused on curing patients.[84] A divide, in other words, between an epidemiologically focused public health and an almost social work–style clinical science.[85] Whereas the WHO cared about developing cost-effective public health interventions, the MRC's investment was in individual cures.[86]

However, the criticisms levied by both Frimodt-Moller and Holm suggest to me that their concerns ran deeper. The extension of supervision and incentives outside of the sanatorium and into the home threatened to muddy the difference between the two wings of the trial. If a randomized controlled trial was the ultimate arbiter of the curative power of a drug, Fox's ad hoc modifications threatened to diminish the validity of the results.[87] The tension between standardization and adaptation to local conditions was palpable: while

83. That Holm describes experimental subjects or participants as "patients" reveals the conceptual difficulties inherent in separating research from clinical medicine.

84. Valier, "At Home in the Colonies," 223.

85. Brimnes, *Languished Hopes*, 189.

86. On the centrality of economism, and in particular cost effectiveness, to tuberculosis research in post-Independence India, see Amrith, "In Search of a 'Magic Bullet' for Tuberculosis."

87. In an essay on the uses of standards and standardization, Stefan Timmermans and Steven Epstein argue that "the uniformity achieved through standardization necessarily carries traces of the local settings." Timmermans and Epstein, "A World of Standards but Not a Standard World," 83. The suggestion is that standardization does not only and always arrive at absolute uniformity but rather creates a space within which certain variations are permitted without necessarily detracting from the standard. However, as Marcia Meldrum has pointed out in her assessment of a polio vaccine trial conducted just two years before the start of the Madras Study, concessions to local needs, such as those made by Fox, raised questions about the validity of the study procedure and the universality of its results. Meldrum, "'A Calculated Risk,'" 1233–36. Such concerns were more deeply felt in the early years of randomized controlled trials, when such variability could throw into question the validity of the very form of the randomized controlled trial.

researchers understood that there were limits to portability, there remained a desire that both cure and the methods for demonstrating cure could be used elsewhere.[88]

Despite these criticisms, the Madras Study generally succeeded in producing the kind of data many researchers and government officials hoped for. In both wings of the study, 90 percent of men were bacteriologically negative at the end of the treatment period. The gap between women in the two groups, however, was quite significant. In the sanatorium wing of the study, 97 percent of women were bacteriologically negative, compared to only 76 percent in the home-based group. The published report contains no serious discussion of the gendered characteristics of home life that might have contributed to the discrepancy between the two groups, other than a brief comment on increased marital infidelity and pretreatment differences.[89]

The Madras Study was lauded as providing the first evidence from a randomized controlled trial that sanatorium treatment was unnecessary and that it would be "appropriate to treat the majority of patients at home."[90] In what was conceived of as the worst of conditions—abject poverty, tiny dwellings with limited air circulation, little rest, hard labor, and perennial malnutrition— the majority of home-based subjects not only became clear of the pathogenic bacteria but remained clear, according to follow-up studies performed by the research team.

In subjects with no detectable bacteria at the end of the trial, follow-up studies were conducted in order to determine whether the cure was truly a cure. Were these patients really bacteriologically negative, or were the bacteria

88. Tuberculosis researchers working across India and East Africa were aware of the specificity of local conditions. To treat nomadic communities, for example, was something quite different than treating sedentary populations with stable homes. It's notable that a similar problem has emerged around the treatment of migratory laborers in contemporary India, who might move throughout the year in relation to work-related opportunities. See McMillen, *Discovering Tuberculosis*, 63–64. Nevertheless, Fox and others were committed to the idea that a treatment that works under what were perceived to be the worst of conditions should be applicable to the rest of the world. On this, see Valier, "At Home in the Colonies," 227.

89. According to Dr. Radhakrishna, one of the nurses involved in the trial had been working on a study of male subjects whose wives purportedly ran away with other men while they were away in the sanatorium. These "other men" were, for some reason, often suspected to be milkmen. I'm not sure that this study ever saw the light of day, and I've unfortunately been unable to locate a copy.

90. Tuberculosis Chemotherapy Centre, "A Concurrent Comparison of Home and Sanatorium Treatment," 128.

in hiding? Of the 130 study subjects who showed no bacteria at the end of the first year, 90 percent remained clear throughout the four years of follow-up. The relapse rate was about equal between subjects from both wings of the study. The majority of these relapses occurred in the first year following treatment. As such, the passage of time increased certainty that the treatment had been effective. A bacteriologically negative result four years after the end of treatment was stronger evidence of efficacy than the same result immediately after treatment, when the bacteria could simply be in hiding.

Initially, Fox was cautious about how he discussed his findings. In the Madras Study and in the studies that followed, patient improvement was neatly delineated in terms of clinical, radiological, and bacteriological measures. Throughout the 1960s and early '70s, a series of further studies across Asia and East Africa were undertaken to determine the most effective and efficient combinations and schedules of treatment.[91] The method of these studies was to test various combination therapies provided intermittently and for shorter durations. By 1971, Fox had the confidence to declare that "standard regimens given for 18 months or more . . . should *cure nearly all patients*."[92] Here, cure was understood as the cessation of all clinical, radiological, and bacteriological signs over an extended period of time. If relapse was proof of failure, nonrelapse stood as a kind of negative proof of cure—but a shaky one. The possibility of relapse would always haunt the security of the cure, particularly in the first year following treatment. However, this possibility diminished significantly over time. In this sense, time lent assurance that relapse might no longer pose a threat.

The specter of relapse forms a kind of limit, one that is not necessarily insurmountable, but nevertheless remains at the heart of cure. Within a bacteriological imagination, where microbes lurk in shadowy corners of the body, cure is always haunted by the possibility of this limit. Such a limit is organized not only around bacteria, but around time. The evidence of this limit is, in fact, sturdier than the evidence of cure itself. Cure can only be defined negatively, as an absence of symptoms and signs, which raises the question—is it a real absence, or merely a perceived one? Against relapse, there is no insurance,

91. As Joseph Dumit has argued, contemporary clinical trials are oriented against both cure and short-duration treatments, focusing instead on the increased profits that come from medicalizing ever larger populations for chronic conditions that require extended treatment. In this earlier moment, however, before the marketization of the randomized controlled trial, the aims were precisely the opposite. See Dumit, *Drugs for Life*.

92. Fox, "The Scope of the Controlled Clinical Trial," 569, emphasis added.

neither in the literal nor figural sense—no way of knowing whether cure will be maintained or fade away.[93]

The possibility of resistance and the ever-present specter of relapse offer a limit to claims to a cure for tuberculosis. Such cures might be thought of less as endings tout court, and more precisely as endings lacking finality. Rather than a permanent rupture with illness, the temporal structure of such a cure might be usefully modeled as a promise that, like all promises, could be broken. Despite advances in chemotherapy, such as that represented by the Madras Study, the global treatment of tuberculosis remained on shaky ground.[94] Antibiotics have never been able to cure everyone suffering from tuberculosis, and even a cured subject might not be cured forever.

Many of the ethical and epistemological questions related to demonstrating treatment efficacy in biomedicine first emerged through investigations into tuberculosis treatment. In this sense, tuberculosis might be understood as a kind of model organism, one that helped to fashion certain habits of thought that have come to inflect how we understand other conditions, such as cancer or schizophrenia. The point, however, is not that problems of cure related to tuberculosis apply equally to all conditions but rather that this history of research opened up and provided (at least provisional) answers to ethical and evidential questions that continue to be grappled with in contemporary biomedical research.[95] Throughout this history, concerns about authority, substance, and demonstration remained central to proving cure. Yet, even as what counted as a proper procedure for producing evidence narrowed, and procedure itself became critical to confirming the efficacy of cure, there remains a sense in which cure itself becomes evidence of authority—as in the story of Sambandar and the king.[96] Even when cure is fragile, incomplete, or partial—and

93. On insurance in India and the idea that one's life is something in which to invest, see Patel, "Risky Subjects."

94. Even in the 1950s and '60s, researchers and international bodies like the International Union against Tuberculosis had reservations about the possibility of properly controlling, much less eradicating, tuberculosis. These concerns were often framed in terms of socioeconomic problems. See McMillen, *Discovering Tuberculosis*, 166.

95. For a discussion of how clinical trials for HIV drugs were opened to nonscientists, thereby continuing debates about the appropriate means of proving therapeutic efficacy, see Epstein, "The Construction of Lay Expertise"; Epstein, *Impure Science*.

96. An important example can be found in debates beginning in the 1970s concerning the necessity of randomized controlled trials (RCTs) for demonstrating the curative efficacy of coronary artery bypass grafting (CABG) in the face of techniques of

even when this is openly admitted, through the language of relapse, resistance, and rates—the fact of cure nevertheless serves as assurance of the authoritativeness of the procedure through which it is certified.

Superimpositions

The Madras Study aimed to refigure the scientific imagination, establishing new parameters for what counted as rigorous research and ethical clinical practice. No longer was it enough to cure the king with sacred ash. Nor could you stand on your gleaming reputation as a prominent scientist. And the results of treatment on a few guinea pigs, or humans, were only suggestive. When the story of the Madras Study is told, it is often recounted with a triumphalist conclusion: randomized controlled trials became the new gold standard for determining whether a treatment was effective; tuberculosis became curable; and the era of sanatorium treatment was over.[97]

But to what extent did this vision of science, and of curative research more specifically, echo beyond the protocols of the Madras Study? In 1961, in the wake of the first phase of the study, a film was released in Madras and across Tamil-speaking south India called *Paalum Pazhamum*, or *Milk and Fruit*.[98] In the film, science becomes articulated with questions of love, duty, and domesticity.

————

visualization like angiography. "The controversy over RCTs for CABG was also a battle for professional authority and financial resources." Jones, "Visions of a Cure," 505-6.

97. The number of sanatoria in Europe and the United States was already declining prior to the Madras Study, due to the general decrease in tuberculosis-related morbidity. See Valier, "At Home in the Colonies," 218. Although trials like the one in Madras influenced clinical practice, the evidence they produced was not uniformly and passively adopted into treatment. Bed rest, for example, remained critical to many physicians' view of tuberculosis treatment even after the results of the Madras Study had been publicized. See Valier and Timmermann, "Clinical Trials and the Reorganization of Medical Research."

98. The turn to film allows for an understanding of how the aesthetics of science and medicine, and in particular the cure for tuberculosis, travel far beyond the laboratory or clinic. Given the centrality of cinema to Indian public culture, examining film allows us to come closer to lay understandings of tuberculosis and its cures, as well as of the process of scientific research. Moreover, film allows us to understand something about what Tim Boon describes as the "*cultural* presence, the variety of beliefs—held not only by those suffering [from] or treating the disease but by the whole of society—in the culture of particular periods." See Boon, "Lay Disease Narratives, Tuberculosis, and Health Education Films," 24. In other words, according to

Figure 3.5. Shanti washing dishes and coughing as superimposed lab equipment floats across the screen in the Tamil film *Paalam Pazhamam*. Screenshot from *Paalam Pazhamam* (1961), directed by A. Bhimsingh.

The actor Sivaji Ganesan played the role of Ravi, a medical researcher who lands a prestigious job at a hospital in Madras. Ravi is both caring and ambitious. He immediately announces to his new colleagues that he will not rest until he has found a cure—not for tuberculosis, but rather, for cancer. The nonspecific symptomology of both conditions allows for their frequent intersubstitution, not only in film but in clinical practice as well. Moreover, the cure for cancer remains—even more than tuberculosis—a kind of high-status pursuit, the ultimate challenge for medicine. From the very beginning, cure is at the center of the film, a powerful motor for plot development, and perhaps more importantly for romance. Ravi falls in love with and marries Shanti, a nurse at the hospital who doubles as his lab assistant, played by the actress Saroja Devi.

One sequence in the film is particularly crucial, both for the narrative push that it provides, but also for the way in which it depicts the relationship

---

Boon, we move beyond the patient's account to the forms of narrative that circulated among those who might not (or not yet) be sick (24).

between science and health. The sequence begins with Ravi and Shanti happily mixing chemicals in the lab, side-by-side as researcher and assistant, husband and wife. But their happiness is short-lived. In the very next scene, Shanti is washing glassware when a superimposed array of lab equipment suddenly begins to float across the screen. Noxious fumes pour out of the beakers and flasks. Shanti begins to feel ill, but she ignores the feeling and moves to the kitchen, where she prepares a meal for Ravi. The superimposed gases return, reminding the viewer of the previous scene. Shanti begins coughing violently. Hearing her cough, Ravi wakes from a nap and races to her side. As he embraces her, she coughs up blood onto his shirt. There is no need for words. In the tradition of Indian melodramatic cinema, her body has already expressed the truth of its condition. X-rays only confirm what Ravi, and the viewing public, already know: Shanti has tuberculosis. The bloody cough, coupled with the X-ray, provide a definitive means of visualizing tuberculosis, and of distinguishing it from cancer.[99]

In a film otherwise unremarkable for its editing, the use of superimposition produces a specific vision of science. It is, after all, lab equipment that floats across the screen. This superimposition signals a scientific imaginary that runs counter to the triumphalism of the Madras Study. Rather than science leading to cure, the gendered labor of scientific research instead leads to illness. In diagnosing Shanti, Ravi declares, "The *vyathi* [disease] has gone inside of her, making us all fools." Quite literally, the chemical fumes have made her ill by entering her body, and shown us that we are foolish for failing to see the iatrogenic aspect of science, of domestic love, and of duty.

In the wake of Shanti's diagnosis, cancer is pushed aside in favor of tuberculosis, and Ravi turns away from cure and toward care. He takes on the labor of nursing, brushing Shanti's hair, spooning soup into her mouth, and applying vermillion to her forehead. Shanti is clearly upset by all of this—not by his love, but by his misplaced priorities. She forces him to return to the hospital to continue his research. Unbeknownst to her, when Ravi arrives at the hospital, he finds a small box from Switzerland, labeled simply *TB Medicine*.

99. Notably, in V. Sridhar's 1968 Hindi remake of the film, *Saathi*, Shanti's disease actually shifts from tuberculosis to heart disease, while Ravi remains a cancer researcher. For a reading of *Saathi* in terms of female sacrifice—in particular, the sacrifice of conjugality for science—see Banerjee, *Enduring Cancer*.

Ravi is overjoyed. But when he returns home with the box, he finds that Shanti has departed. She leaves him a note explaining that she left so that he could focus exclusively on his research. In the only other use of superimposition in the film, Shanti's face appears above the note, reading its contents: "If I stay here, you won't reach your goal. . . . My soul will only achieve peace if you go about your business."

The film cuts to Shanti sitting on a train, coughing and staring out the window. By chance, the man sitting next to her is a former patient whom she had nursed back to health in the hospital, a Muslim businessman. He's shocked by her appearance. "Elenja pettiye! [You've become thin!] Unga ud-ambukku enna acche? [What's happened to your body?]" he asks. "TB," she responds. "TB!" he exclaims.

Her former patient puffs on a cigarette, distraught. "Where are you going with this body?" he asks, as if the idea of traveling in such a condition were incomprehensible. She responds that she doesn't know. Unfortunately, the decision seems to be taken out of her hands. The following sequence alternates between shots of two trains edited together to give the impression of an impending collision. The trains are shown colliding. The newspapers and radios report the accident and announce the death of Shanti, the wife of a Madras-based cancer researcher.

Ravi throws himself back into his work, distraught but determined to honor Shanti's final wishes. His family is not so sanguine about the matter. They insist that he marry Nalini, the daughter of a family friend whom they had wanted him to marry before he had decided upon Shanti.

"I know nothing about love, only about curing cancer," he explains to them. "That's why I married Shanti. She understood that. Only afterwards did love emerge." He tries saying all of this to Nalini. "I have to pursue a cure so that her soul can achieve peace," he tells her.

But Nalini insists. "I too will help you in your lab work." And with that, they get hitched.

Little do they know that Shanti did not, in fact, die in the train crash. Her former patient, the Muslim businessman, finds her lying in the wreckage. "Let me be as if dead," she tells him. On the brink of death, Shanti exiles herself from life. Like Kamala Nehru (as we have seen), and like Kasturba Gandhi (as we will see), Shanti's death would allow her husband to continue to serve others.[100]

100. On Kamala Nehru, see chapter 2. On Kasturba Gandhi, see chapter 5.

But the Muslim businessman has other ideas. "I'm going to Switzerland for some work," he says to her. "Listen to what I'm saying: if you come to that country, *that* nature itself will cure you, okay?" (notably, the curative nature in question is specifically Swiss).[101]

Shanti and the businessman discover, of all things, a Tamil doctor in Switzerland. A pair of wide establishing shots of the pristine waters and magnificent hills of Switzerland sets the scene. The camera moves in closer to reveal the interior of a chalet, bathed in sunlight from a window in the back.

"I never thought I would come this far to meet a Tamil doctor," the businessman exclaims in delight. Discussing Shanti's condition, the Tamil doctor remarks rather poetically, "The one who was thought to be unable to walk can now walk. The cure," he says, using the English word, "is now complete." He then repeats himself in Tamil, "Udambu gunamaaku aayitru." The body has been cured or restored.

When Shanti thanks him, the doctor replies that her cure wasn't caused by medicine or pills. Rather, the curative agent was nature itself.[102] As we will see, cure is intimately tied to the act of its enunciation—yet the Tamil doctor disclaims any therapeutic power of his own. His poetic words, unlike the words of the poet-saint Sambandar with whom we began this chapter, carry no sovereign force, no divine sanction. His proclamation of cure, then, is merely descriptive, not a performative act but a statement that nature has completed its therapeutic task.[103] Although Shanti is cured, the doctor insists that she remain resting in bed to avoid the possibility of relapse. Whatever the Madras

---

101. In the 1989 Hindi film *Chandni* (directed by Yash Chopra), we have a similarly romantic triad, although in this case, it is a disabled man who pursues his cure in Switzerland, and it is his wife who is on the verge of marrying another man. In both films, the original couple is separated by illness, their romantic restoration made possible only by a prior physical restoration in Switzerland. And in both films, the intervening third party is easily dispensed with. On the development of Switzerland as a site in the Tamil filmic imaginary, see Pandian, "Landscapes of Expression." On the place of Switzerland in Bollywood, see Schneider, *Bollywood*.

102. On the therapeutic power of nature, see chapter 1.

103. Whether the declaration of cure constitutes merely a description or a performative kind of statement, it finds a particularly apt parallel in the juridical verdict, which both confirms and produces the truth of guilt. On scenes of enforced waiting in Hindi cinema, particularly in relation to the hospital and the courtroom, see Cohen, "Foreign Operations."

Study might have demonstrated, the sanatorium and its vocabulary remained alive in the imagination of 1960s Tamil cinema.

Back in Madras, Ravi's new wife, Nalini, has proven to be more interested in going on excursions in town than doing lab research. "Don't you have any other thought than this research?" she cries. In a fit of rage, she grabs a beaker of *vesham* (poison) that she intends to drink, but Ravi knocks it from her hand. The ensuing chemical fog robs him of his eyesight, this time, without superimposition.

When the fully recovered Shanti finally returns to Madras, she learns that Ravi has remarried and lost his vision. She pretends to be a nurse and offers her services to Ravi's family. None of them had met her before her "death," so no one suspects a thing—except for Ravi, that is. When Ravi meets Shanti, he immediately thinks that she's the ghost of his dead wife. She insists that she is not. He grudgingly accepts that his mind is playing tricks on him.

In a dramatic twist, Ravi's older brother Shekhar returns from Harvard University, where he had performed many eye surgeries. He restores Ravi's vision. In gratitude, Ravi offers to arrange a marriage between Shekhar and his nurse, whom he has yet to see. On the morning of the wedding, he comes to learn from a suspicious relative, played by the actor M. K. Radha, that his nurse is actually his first wife. He runs to the marriage hall, where he learns that the marriage has already been halted. It seems that the Muslim businessman had come to the house to check on Shanti and, in the process, divulged her secret. Ravi's family decided not to worry him before his eyes had fully healed, so they kept the truth from him.

The romantic triad is resolved and, in fact, turns out to be a pentad: Ravi and Shanti are reunited; Nalini files for divorce and sets off to (of all places) Switzerland to join the Red Cross, and Shankar is married to Shanti's sister, who happens to be visiting from Ceylon. The film ends on a happy note, with the exception of poor Nalini, who speeds away on a bus, sunglasses covering her tears.

There are many fascinating twists and turns in the film. Yet I'm left wondering: what was in the box that Ravi received in the hospital? Certainly, we are meant to imagine cure—but when we imagine cure, what precisely is it that we are imagining? *Paalam Pazhamum* did not simply attempt to displace the brave new world established by the Madras Study. Lab equipment floated above noxious fumes, medicine in boxes arrived too late, and cure was discovered elsewhere, in a Swiss sanatorium operated by a Tamil physician. Juxtaposition is taken to an extreme as images—and imaginations—are overlaid and yet remain visible. The scientific imagination of *Paalam Pazhamum* represents a superimposition upon the Nehruvian rationalism of the time, which might leave us wondering: which image is the more real?[104]

104. For an important discussion of the greater degree of reality ascribed to the imagination over what might be thought of as material reality in the Tamil tradition, see Shulman, *More Than Real*.

Chapter Four

The way in which we historicize time
is determined to a great extent by the point
in time in which we are living.

—Romila Thapar, *Talking History*

Cures, we might think, should be endings: the end of suffering, of treatment, and of illness more generally. What happens when cures instead come and go, when you can be cured and then cured again? In the transition from sanatorium-based therapy to antibiotics in mid-twentieth-century India, physicians and patients grappled with questions of procedure and prognosis. How long would it take to cure a patient, and who had the authority to say that they were cured? Moreover, just what did it mean to be cured if you could be cured repeatedly? Toward the end of the twentieth century, the use of standardized records made successful antibiotic treatment a matter of consistency and duration. Alongside X-rays and microscopes, documents filled with neat rows of checkmarks became a critical technology for tracking progress. In a literal sense, effective treatment became conceptualized as a problem of marking time. Yet cure could be a fragile accomplishment, one equally endangered by the passage of time. Even as patients

Wax and Wane

through the potential endlessness of treatment, they also seem to experience no end of cures, of endings that follow endings. The further entanglement of tuberculosis with HIV in India throws into relief the ways in which tuberculosis could be figured as almost chronic, and yet curable—and somehow both at the same time. Rather than an ending, such a cure can be interminable.

So far, our explorations of cure have been decidedly earthbound. Now, let's climb: beyond the highest hill stations with their rarefied air, until we arrive in the celestial abode of the gods. A word of caution: such beings are not to be trifled with. You would do well to behave yourself. The gods are all light and heat and emotion, easy to anger. Which means that the stakes are always high.

Perhaps you've heard about what happened to Chandran, the great Moon King.[1] He didn't always look like that, you know. Once he was perennially full, brimming with luminosity. But that was before his marriage to the twenty-seven daughters of Daksha Prajapati, the lord of all creatures.[2] Each of his brides had her special qualities, but Chandran only had eyes for one: Rohini. His desire for her was unquenchable, his cosmic lust burning like fever. Bathed in Rohini's brilliance, he soon forgot about her sisters, his other wives, who waited for him in their lunar mansions.

These other wives, the *nakshatras* or divine constellations, felt his neglect deeply, not just as hurt sentiment but as a failure to perform his husbandly duties. Chandran had been expected to dispense his masculine virility in a more or less equitable fashion as he circulated through the sky. That was the way the sky held together, divine bodies in perfect synchrony. Disproportional lust had introduced a disturbance into the system.[3]

The nakshatras complained to their father, Daksha. It was he who had married them off so cavalierly to a husband with no sense of moderation. As we know, the anger of a divine being is a dangerous thing, burning perhaps even hotter than lust until it has spent itself. How much more dangerous might be the anger of the lord of all creatures? As Daksha exhaled, his fury escaped his parted lips and possessed Chandran. Like a ravenous beast, Daksha's fury

---

1. The moon is also referred to as Soma, Sasin, Amsuman, or Indu. See Cerulli, *Somatic Lessons*, 106.

2. The number of Daksha's daughters that marry Chandran vary across tellings; in some, there are twenty-eight daughters.

3. In his reading of the story of the moon alongside the story of King Agnivarna's affliction from the *Raghuvamsa*, Daud Ali frames the central issue as a "problem of attachment," which "was not about the morality of the sexual relationship itself, and did not take the form of a body of consistent interdictions against particular acts, behaviours or liaisons. It instead concerned the disposition that the self was to have with the external world as a whole. The senses posed the danger of a loss of self-mastery." According to Ali, disorder or disequilibrium was not produced by lust or attachment per se, but rather by excessive attachment that could lead to one's undoing. Ali, "Anxieties of Attachment," 117.

consumed the moon. His brilliance, which he had already depleted through his dalliances with Rohini, would soon fade to black.

As Chandran's luminescence retreated from the night sky, the creatures of earth who depended on his light and his sovereignty over rain for sustenance began to wither. Touched by their plight, the other gods pleaded with Daksha to relent. In some tellings of the story, Daksha instructs the *aswins*, celestial twin physicians, to provide Chandran with *soma*, an ambrosia that substitutes for his spent semen and delivers immortality to the drinker (and in fact, the Moon King is often called Soma). In another telling, Chandran undertakes *tapasya* (severe penance) that he devotes to Shiva, in a bid to regain his lost heat.

Whatever the means, Chandran is cured. But what happened to him is more than a simple cautionary tale, a warning for those earthly kings who would let their lust get the better of them and forgo their duties. There are consequences for Chandran's actions. Bad behavior and excessive attachment on a cosmic level bears fruit on the terrestrial plane: first, in that Chandran's waning deprived life on earth of his brilliant sustenance and, second, in that Chandran's illness has now descended to earth, a fury that afflicts fragile mortals.

It is this last detail that transforms the story into an origin myth. Chandran is not simply the primordial victim of tuberculosis; he is patient zero.[4] This claim to origination explains why the story of the moon continues to be invoked to this day, even if many of the more salacious details are left out.[5] A medical textbook published by a pair of doctors in the state of Odisha in 2015 includes a rather informative chapter on the history of tuberculosis that proceeds like a whirlwind through Neolithic remains, Egyptian mummies, Romantic poets, the Old Testament, Hippocrates, Herodotus, Robert Koch, and the Chinese *Huangdi Neijing*, before presenting about three pages of what might be termed Indian history, which begins as follows: "TB is an ancient disease in

---

4. As David Barnes puts it, the figure of patient zero is a "stock character in an oft-repeated drama of transgression, calamity, and (eventually) punishment." More broadly, the figure of patient zero grounds a narrative of disease spread that provides it not only with a beginning, but with a beginning that arrives from elsewhere: as an epidemic (descending upon the people) rather than endemic (which is always already among the people). Barnes, "Targeting Patient Zero," 65.

5. See also Andrew McDowell's powerful discussion of a Rajasthani woman haunted by a kind of tuberculous ghost, one he aptly describes as a "literary revenant" that draws from the embodied description of rajayakshma in the *Kalika Purana*. McDowell, "Chunnilal's Hauntology."

India. 'It is also said that the Moon-God was the first to become a victim of this disease, which is as a result also known as Rajayakshma, or king's disease.'[6]

Myth and history are words we use to describe what are usually taken to be two distinct ways of approaching the past. Here, the moon's affliction is rather seamlessly integrated into a history of tuberculosis, which is also a history of rajayakshma: the king of diseases, frequently translated as the king's disease or the royal disease, in honor of its first victim, the moon, who governed not only the constellations, but was also the "king of plants, of heavenly bodies and of the Brahmins."[7]

If we wanted to be strictly historical, we might point to the fact that, in the fifth century, the Sanskrit lexicographer Amarasimha located the term *yaksma* as belonging to the same semantic universe as other conditions that manifest through *sosa* (emaciation) and *ksays* (wasting) of the body's vital fluids and tissues.[8] By the eighteenth century, wasting had in fact become the primary sign of yaksma.[9] It wasn't, however, until the nineteenth and twentieth centuries that yaksma became linked to the lungs.[10] By the early twentieth century, rajayakshma itself had become distinctively identified with what was known in English as consumption, phthisis, or tuberculosis.

This is history by way of philology, the study of how a language has developed. But when it comes to disease and its cures, time can flow in straight lines or in grand loops and cycles, and sometimes both ways at once. The story of the moon illustrates that our ideas of cure depend on how we think about and experience time—and that our concepts of time are shaped by our sense of cure.

Embedded in the story of the moon's cure is a problem. Take a look at the night sky. The moon continues to wane. If the moon has been cured, how can this be? Lest anyone think I'm unfairly subjecting myth to the steely vision of empiricism, this is a concern that has struck many commentators and retellers of the story. Some versions of the story suggest that this waning is due to the fact that the moon is a habitual offender: he can't help but be drawn back to

---

6. Tripathy and Tripathy, *Tuberculosis Manual for Obstetricians and Gynecologists*, 5. It is unclear to me what is being quoted, as no reference is provided.

7. Filliozat, *The Classical Doctrine of Indian Medicine*, 100. On the multiple meanings of rajayakshma, see also Zimmerman, *The Jungle and the Aroma of Meats*, 77.

8. Cerulli, *Somatic Lessons*, 106.

9. Cerulli, *Somatic Lessons*, 166. Filliozat takes this up as well, and argues that it is not at all an imposition to understand rajayakshma as a general kind of wasting disease or form of cachexia, some of which are generalized and others of which affect particular parts of the body. Filliozat, *The Classical Doctrine of Indian Medicine*.

10. Cerulli, *Somatic Lessons*, 106.

Rohini, so he is continuously punished—in which case the regularity of the cyclical time of the moon is the product of a repeated disturbance, an aberration that has become part of the cycle.

But there are other solutions to the problem. Take, for example, this version of Chandran's story, from a mid-twentieth-century Ayurvedic manual on the treatment of tuberculosis, written in Tamil: "On seeing that Chandran, the king of the nakshatras and the Brahmans, was exceedingly fond of/in love with his wife Rohini, his other wives complained to Daksha. He cursed Chandran to come down with this disease. After Chandran repented, the *aswini devas* gave him treatment. They gave him medicines to promote his *ojas* [vitality] and he was cured/recovered/returned to health. Finally, Daksha sent this disease to be caught by the inhabitants of the world."[11] Certain elements of the story remain the same: Chandran disturbs the cosmic order, provokes his wives, and incurs Daksha's wrath. The aswins once again provide their celestial treatment. But the primary cause of rajayakshma/tuberculosis is a curse. In such stories, it is more than a metaphor to say that language shapes the world. Pragmatics literally overcomes physics. Curses contort the world in an overpowering fashion. They have an irresistible gravity. The Sanskritist Alf Hiltebeitel goes so far as to refer to curses as fatalities: performative declarations that set into motion a set of circumstances in which a specific form of death becomes inevitable.[12] A curse, once uttered, becomes like an arrow released

---

11. Serfoji, *Carapēntira vaitya muṟaikaḷ: Kṣayarōka, uḷamāntai rōka cikitsai*, 11th ed., ed. S. Venkatarajan (Thanjavur: Mankalingam Pavar Press, 1956), translation mine, acc. no. 000154, Chennai, Roja Muthiah Research Library. The precise contents of the cure provided by the aswins remains obscured—unless you count the details provided in the recipes that follow. There are instructions on how to make various "medicated *ghritas*," or preparations made of ghee (clarified butter), that counter the effects of *sosam*, "that which dries up the system." The manual also contains various recipes for treating specific symptoms of tuberculosis, including fever and cough. Everyday substances found in most kitchens, like *miligai* (black pepper), feature prominently among the materia medica, as do more precious substances like *thangam* (gold). G. Jan Meulenbeld provides us with a thicker description of ojas, drawn from the *Charaka Samhita*: "When ojas has diminished, one is afraid, weak, and constantly worried, the organs of sense do not function normally, one's complexion is not healthy, nor are the mental faculties, dryness and slimming prevail. The ojas, which resides in the heart in a (human) body, is considered to be pure and of a reddish and yellowish colour; its loss leads to death." Ojas has been variously translated as a vital force or subtle energy, a force of the gods given to humans, or a fluid system necessary for life. Meulenbeld, "The Woes of Ojas in the Modern World," 160.

12. Hiltebeitel, *The Ritual of Battle*.

from its quiver: it cannot be taken back. Put simply, curses are efficacious, and curses are binding.

Luckily, there's a workaround. Not the withdrawal of the curse, but an additive operation: the moon will continue to wane, yet the administration of cure means that he will also wax. Chandran's curse remains in place, posing an insurmountable limit to the efficacy of cure. The disturbance to the system has become a permanent feature, the speck of sand at the heart of a pearl. The past is preserved at the level of celestial biology; there is no reset button.[13] Chandran's illness, and the curse that unleashed it, have not been overcome so much as dialectically subsumed. And in the process, he has been irrevocably transformed into the moon you see waxing and waning in the sky above you. For the moon, to wax and wane is precisely what it means to be cured.[14]

Two Kinds of Cure

The problem with repeated waxing is that it presupposes repeated waning. Well after the antibiotic revolution had commenced, this ambivalence continued to bother "very well educated and well informed people" in India, who wondered whether a cure for tuberculosis was possible.[15] To assuage their concerns, a Madras-based doctor named Mathuram Santosham wrote a cheaply priced book titled *What Everyone Should Know about Tuberculosis*.[16]

13. Such a conception of cure might be productively compared, on one hand, to the idea that cure is simply about restoration or return and, on the other, to the rather different idea that cure is unidirectional. This latter idea suggests that after you are cured, there is no going back to how you were before you fell ill, no return to what Georges Canguilhem describes as a state of "biological innocence." Canguilhem, *On the Normal and the Pathological*, 137.

14. Looking to the moon as inspiration for his moving ethnographic meditation on poverty in rural Rajasthan, Bhrigupati Singh, in *Poverty and the Quest for Life*, explicitly calls for an attentiveness to "waxing and waning movements, the interrelation of varying thresholds of life," what he describes as a "lunar sense of enlightenment" (117). Singh's critical move is to turn away from an "unblemished" model of ampleness or totality (such as the sun) in favor of a model of "waxing and waning intensities" (223). In writing of the gods as "partially mortal" (55), he offers an imagination of vitality premised on varying thresholds, ebbs and flows, rather than the overly simple binaries of life and death, plentitude and poverty. In this sense, my reading of the circumstances of the moon, and my analytic attention to the waxing and waning of cure throughout this chapter, resonates deeply with his project.

15. Santosham, *What Everyone Should Know about Tuberculosis*, 3.

16. Santosham, *What Everyone Should Know about Tuberculosis*, 3.

Having treated well over one thousand tuberculosis patients over almost four decades, Santosham had witnessed firsthand the effects of generations of therapies, from sanatorium treatment and gold therapy to thoracoplasty and antibiotics.[17] After graduating from Madras Medical College, Santosham was appointed in 1937 to what he would later describe as a "dustbin posting" in the tuberculosis ward at the government hospital in the neighborhood of Royapettah. It was, he suspected, a punishment for his proindependence activism as a member of the student wing of the Congress Party.[18]

Much to his surprise, Santosham found in tuberculosis a calling and a career, establishing a tiny pulmonary clinic in the Egmore neighborhood of Madras in 1938. Nine years later, he built a much larger sanatorium outside of Madras, which he named Santoshapuram, after his father, who had served as a *tehsildar*, or revenue collector, for the colonial government.

In his writings, Santosham's optimism about the curability of tuberculosis is striking: "To such who are in a mood to give themselves or their dear ones as living preys and voluntary victims to tuberculosis, this will be the answer of this book: 'fear not, dejected friends, for tuberculosis is curable.'"[19] What he meant by *curable* was a far cry from the waxing and waning of the moon. Cure, he explained, was "getting over the existing evil effects of the disease and being free from the fear of it in the future."[20] He meant not only freedom from disease but freedom from the fear caused by the potential for future incarnations of the disease. Whereas the freedom required for the sanatorium cure was figured in spatialized and even existential-political terms, the form of freedom envisioned by Santosham was configured in terms of time.[21] Such an idea of cure, as an ending that endures, might sound far more appealing than the perpetual waxing and waning of the moon.

Yet, as we turn the pages of Santosham's book, this idea of a definitive end is belied by figures of cure that multiply. Cure, it seems, could follow cure. As he pointed out, those of his patients who were truly cured were cured at least twice.

---

17. Thoracoplasty is a surgical intervention that entails the removal of ribs to collapse the lung, allow it to rest, and give the body time to seal over bacteria with caseous materials.

18. In the years to follow, Santosham's reputation grew as a member of the legislative assembly, closely tied to the prominent Tamil politician Rajaji and his Swatantra party.

19. Santosham, *What Everyone Should Know about Tuberculosis*, 6.

20. Santosham, *What Everyone Should Know about Tuberculosis*, 10.

21. On freedom and the sanatorium cure, see chapter 1.

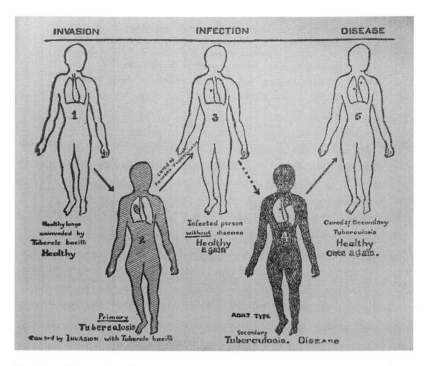

Figure 4.1. Diagram from Santosham's book illustrating the progression of disease. Santosham, *What Everyone Should Know about Tuberculosis*, 10.

A diagram from his book, most likely drawn by Santosham himself, shows the progression of tuberculosis as well as its cure. Initially, the patient's body is merely invaded with bacteria in what Santosham described as "primary tuberculosis." If the bacteria in the lungs are then successfully walled off by tubercles, "fortresses" within which the tuberculous tissues are rendered "sealed and innocent," then the patient would become asymptomatic.[22] The body of the patient would remain "infected," and yet *without* disease" and "healthy again."[23] According to Santosham, this sealing-off process most frequently occurred without therapeutic attention, and often without the patient even noticing. This, he explained, was the first cure. For many, the curative process ended here.

In some cases, the fortress walls collapsed. Bacteria escaped, multiplied, and colonized other parts of the lungs before entering the bloodstream. Santosham

22. Santosham, *What Everyone Should Know about Tuberculosis*, 75.
23. Santosham, *What Everyone Should Know about Tuberculosis*, 75.

called this "secondary tuberculosis," a condition that was not, generally speaking, self-healing. Such a patient required sanatorium care, antibiotics, and possibly surgery. This was the second cure.

This second cure, however, was far from uniform. Some patients were only partially cured while others were completely cured. Santosham attributed cases of partial cure to the ignorance that led a patient to depend more on their own "feeling of well being than on the doctor's doubts regarding the partly cured disease."[24] "I know a woman who was getting treated for tuberculosis for many years and yet would not believe that she was suffering from a serious malady. She laughed away the doctor's advice of 'bed rest' saying that she did not feel ill to that extent. She got married one fine evening against her doctor's orders, danced all night and died the next morning."[25] Santosham had encountered many such cases in his sanatorium practice. An eighteen-year-old boy who interrupted treatment to take the entrance test for medical school and died of tuberculous meningitis on the last day of his exams. A married woman who returned home for Diwali, became pregnant, and once again fell ill (women's bodies were thought to be particularly susceptible to incurability). An engineering supervisor who returned to his job for fear of losing a promotion, only for the disease to spread throughout his body. "Even temporary disobedience to the rigid rules imposed often ends in the recurrence of the disease and even in untimely death," Santosham warned. "Repentance may be too late."[26]

Yet Santosham did not simply blame his wayward patients. He also blamed antibiotics. Santosham recalled the formal arrival of streptomycin in India in 1948, prior to the Madras Study, and he reflected on the immense effect it had produced on the forty patients he had residing at his sanatorium at that time.[27] The drug remained exorbitantly expensive (Rs. 30 per vial, with a treatment course consisting of one hundred vials), and its import required permissions from the state and central governments, as well as from the Reserve Bank of India. Nevertheless, for Santosham, the antibiotic was a "boon," one that, he wrote, "salvaged out many from the gate way to the grave."[28] But it was also, he warned, "like a fairy with a certain reservation: she will grant only one

---

24. Santosham, *What Everyone Should Know about Tuberculosis*, 12–13.
25. Santosham, *What Everyone Should Know about Tuberculosis*, 4.
26. Santosham, *What Everyone Should Know about Tuberculosis*, 11–12.
27. On the Madras Study, see chapter 3.
28. Santosham, *What Everyone Should Know about Tuberculosis*, 48, 49.

request and that only once."[29] Compounding metaphors, he further likened streptomycin to a "pistol with only one round to fire."[30]

Antibiotics were to be blamed not because they failed to effect an enduring cure, or because their powers were limited, but rather because the speed of their perceived efficacy discouraged patients from continuing treatment: "Any drug that promptly relieves the distressing symptoms of the disease, creates a state of mind whereby the individual who had suffered hitherto, refuse[s] to undergo any further treatment and, on the other hand, prefers to go to work to stabilise the financial position of himself and his family."[31] By contrast, the "declaration" of what Santosham called a complete cure depended not on the "state of mind" of the patient but rather on the "final say" of the doctor.[32] "The final bugle of victory can only be blown by the doctor."[33] Internal sensations and feelings could not be trusted. To make this point clear, Santosham displays in his book a series of X-ray images of the lungs of a patient with tuberculosis. Such images made it possible to track the progression of disease (and cure) over time. These X-rays reveal the objective correlate underlying (and possibly belying) the subjective feeling harbored by the patient, the body rendered transparent and available to the clinician's expert eye.

The first image in figure 4.2, in the top left-hand corner, shows a patient's lungs before treatment. The second image shows the "disease cleared" shortly after treatment with streptomycin. Tellingly, Santosham does not refer to this as cure. The third image, taken two months after streptomycin treatment, reveals some minor activity in the lungs. The final image reveals that, four months after completing streptomycin treatment, the disease has been definitely and visibly reestablished in the lungs. At once, these images reveal the limitations of subjective feeling as well as the limited curative power of streptomycin.

If My Body Allows

In contemporary India, tuberculosis is almost always said to be a curable condition, one for which there is presumed to be a definitive end point. Yet antibiotics like streptomycin never quite succeeded in smoothing over the temporal

29. Santosham, *What Everyone Should Know about Tuberculosis*, 140.
30. Santosham, *What Everyone Should Know about Tuberculosis*, 142.
31. Santosham, *What Everyone Should Know about Tuberculosis*, 236.
32. Santosham, *What Everyone Should Know about Tuberculosis*, 2.
33. Santosham, *What Everyone Should Know about Tuberculosis*, 147.

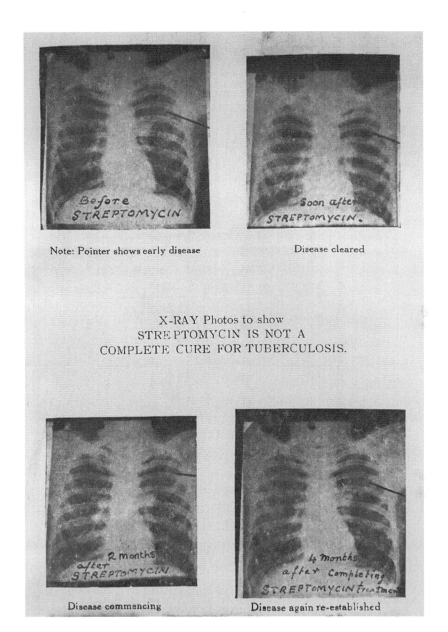

Figure 4.2. X-ray images depicting the effects of streptomycin on the lungs. Santosham, *What Everyone Should Know about Tuberculosis*, 75.

complexities of cure. Far from it. In the course of my fieldwork, it was not uncommon for me to meet patients like Santosham's, who had been cured, and then cured again.

In the summer of 2015, I visited various tuberculosis treatment centers operated by the Damian Foundation, a Belgian organization founded in 1954 to treat leprosy in India. As the number of new leprosy infections dwindled in the decades that followed, the Damian Foundation expanded their ambit to include tuberculosis. At one of their treatment centers on the edge of Delhi, I met Nilam, a former schoolteacher who had been diagnosed with a form of tuberculosis resistant to many of the currently available drugs used to treat the condition.

Nilam was in her late twenties, unmarried, and without children. This was a matter of great concern for her and her family. The reason she hadn't married was that, for seven years, on and off, Nilam had been ill. It all started back in 2008, when she came down with a fever. As was the case with many of the patients whom I met, her first recourse was a visit to a neighborhood doctor, who diagnosed her with tuberculosis.[34]

For almost a year, Nilam stayed in her parents' home and swallowed pills. Her parents told their inquisitive neighbors that she had a bad case of typhoid, which, it seemed, was a better thing to have than tuberculosis. Both were contagious, but what made tuberculosis worse, especially for women, was that it was thought to sap their reproductive capacity. Women with tuberculosis often feared that they would be deemed unmarriageable if others learned of their condition.

That the greater burden of stigma from tuberculosis is placed on women has been well established by studies among urban populations in India.[35] Even after being declared cured, women who have suffered from tuberculosis are less likely to be seen as suitable marriage partners.[36] Having been afflicted

34. On the availability of antituberculosis drugs in India, especially through the market, see Ecks and Harper, "Public-Private Mixes."

35. See, for example, Ganapathy et al., "Perceptions of Gender and Tuberculosis."

36. The particular ways in which the burden of tuberculosis is borne by women are not new. In the 1964 Tamil film *Navarathri* (Nine nights), the male lead, played by Sivaji Ganesan (who also played the role of Ravi in the film *Milk and Fruit*, discussed in chapter 3), visits a brothel to find satisfaction. There, he meets the heroine of the film (played by the magnificent Savithri), who is being held there against her will. In an effort to escape the brothel and the sexual advances of the drunken hero, she turns him into her Scheherazade and induces him to talk. He confesses that he had been tricked into marrying a woman with tuberculosis. Her condition was revealed to him only after their marriage. His wife believes that they shouldn't have sexual relations, and

with the condition, they are also seen as less capable of having children and are thought to run the risk of passing on their condition to their children, despite the fact that tuberculosis is no longer conceived of as inheritable by medical professionals. And yet, something like inheritance is presumed in the calculation of marriageability and reproduction, if not as illness, then in the form of the passing on of frailty.

Eventually, Nilam's doctor told her that she was cured. She made it clear to me that she did not discontinue treatment of her own volition. But she trusted in the declaration of the doctor and felt better. Just two years later, her symptoms returned. This time, her family encouraged her to go to a well-known surgeon from a government hospital, who, like many public-sector doctors, operated his own (illicit) private practice after hours. Under the government surgeon's supervision, her family was certain that she would receive better treatment. The higher price tag reflected their faith in his competence. Nilam completed yet another year of antibiotics and, like her previous doctor, he also told her she was cured.

The declarations of cure began to pile up. "Each time I was treated," she told me, "I thought at the end that I was fine. But it came back."

At the end of 2013, Nilam again began treatment. Six days a week, she would wake early and travel with her mother to the government treatment center, a greenwashed concrete building in an area known as Jivan Park, on the dusty outskirts of Delhi. There, the treatment attendant would open up a box with her name written on it and hand her a blister pack of pills. Such boxes were an important managerial technology, meant to ensure that a patient had supervised, standardized doses available for the entire course of their treatment. The box ensured both the proper dosage and duration of the curative process.

When Nilam was done swallowing these pills, she would wait patiently for her turn to duck behind a curtain, where she would receive an injection of the antibiotic kanamycin. Like many whom I met, she believed that injections were more efficacious than pills. And in fact, when I met her in 2015, she was feeling better. Before her illness began, Nilam had worked as a Hindi teacher in a local school. After this treatment was completed, she told me, she wanted to start teaching again. That is, she added, if her body allowed.

---

that she will soon die. We're led to believe that he has her blessing to seek his pleasure elsewhere—thus, the brothel—although his escapades grind to a halt after a severe tongue lashing from our heroine.

But feeling cured is not the same as being cured. Declarations of cure were products of authority. Although Dr. Santosham had described cure as "being free from the fear of [the effects of disease] in the future," he nevertheless insisted that the patient's subjective experience of their own condition was inherently unreliable.[37] Such freedom from fear should be heteronomous in its origins, emerging from the doctor's declaration rather than from the patient's self-originating sense of certainty. For Santosham, the "final say" when it came to cure rested with the doctor.

Such an approach parallels similar divisions between sign and symptom, disease and illness, the objective and the subjective. On the side of the doctor, knowledge. On the side of the patient, mere feeling. In other words, they cannot know whether they are sick or well; their body is in a sense beyond their knowledge. One of the primary tasks of the healer, then, is to persuade the patient to align their feeling with the healer's knowledge. As Georges Canguilhem put it, "A doctor will not understand a patient, at the end of a prescribed cure that has been executed and has eliminated an infection or a dysfunction, who refuses *to call himself cured* and does not behave as someone who feels better."[38] Here is cure figured as a performative speech act. From the doctor: a guarantee that the treatment was in fact efficacious, and a directive to believe and behave as one who is cured. From the patient: a confirmation of trust in the treatment, in the doctor, and in the underlying systems, biomedical and bureaucratic.

Critics of medicine have argued that such an approach subordinates feeling, renders it suspect as a form of knowledge, often to the detriment of patients—in particular women and those from marginalized groups—whose complaints are not taken seriously.[39] In accepting this division between knowledge and feeling, the authority that medicine enjoys over our bodies—and our lives—runs the risk of becoming absolute. What such critiques tend to leave unquestioned is how a doctor comes to know cure and declare it as such. Such a declaration relies on a combination of clinical experience and acumen, bureaucratic rule following and technological availability, all of which compose a particular kind of culture of objectivity.[40] Crucially, the declaration of cure also hinges on the relationship between language, body, and time.

37. Santosham, *What Everyone Should Know about Tuberculosis*, 10.

38. Canguilhem, "Is a Pedagogy of Healing Possible?," 13.

39. For historical and ethnographic work on the ways in which the suffering of certain kinds of bodies has been subordinated to the authority of medicine, see in particular Murphy, *Sick Building Syndrome*; Rouse, *Uncertain Suffering*.

40. On the history of cultures of objectivity, see Daston and Galison, *Objectivity*.

In a chest hospital in the Chetpet neighborhood of Chennai, I met tuberculosis patients who struggled with the ambiguity that seemed to inhere at the heart of cure. Up the spiral staircase that cuts through the center of the building, an atrium housed a few small offices and an enclave of bats clinging to the high ceiling. The ground floor of the hospital was heavily trafficked during the mornings, as an outpatient clinic for patients with tuberculosis. An auto rickshaw driver dressed in a cotton button-up peered in through the doorway, fearful of missing his turn to consult with a doctor. Other patients leaned against trees just outside in an attempt to escape the uncomfortable May heat, waving recently developed X-ray images like yesteryear Polaroids.

Established in 1917 with support from the King Edward Hospital Fund, the hospital once known as the King Edward VII Memorial Tuberculosis Institute was a large domed building that had faded with time. The construction of the hospital in Chetpet spurred the denizens of Spur Tank Road, the major street that ran along the entrance to the hospital, to protest that carting in sick patients from around the city would endanger their own health.[41] Their concerns were summarily overridden by the Madras Legislative Assembly, and the Tuberculosis Institute was erected with the blessings of Lord Pentland, the then governor of Madras.

The neighbors, however, had been correct to worry. Patients poured in from all over the city, and some even traveled from other parts of the state and from the nearby state of Andhra Pradesh. Murugesan, a poor man who professed to run his own bicycle repair business, hadn't traveled all that far. He arrived one morning in the chest hospital, complaining of an inescapable cough that had been bothering him for the past month. Ten years earlier, he explained, he had been diagnosed with tuberculosis. But he insisted that he had completed his treatment and that the doctor had declared him cured. Now, he was worried that it had come back.

When Murugesan claimed that he had been cured ten years earlier, his physician at the Chetpet clinic, Dr. Amutha, had her doubts. She directed him to get an X-ray and a sputum analysis. What was at stake in her diagnosis was not simply whether Murugesan had previously suffered from tuberculosis but rather whether he still had tuberculosis, or perhaps had it again. The distinction between an old infection and a new one was impossible to make without DNA sequencing technology, unavailable at the clinic. The presence of certain

41. Rao, "Tuberculosis and Public Health Policies."

forms of technology makes possible the asking of new questions.[42] Its absence produces limits, which necessitate other lines of questioning.

In this case, Murugesan's exam results coming back positive would throw into question his previous declaration of cure. Dr. Amutha could argue that Murugesan had not in fact been cured but had only been declared cured (say, by his previous doctor, who had perhaps given Murugesan the wrong type or amount of medication, or for an inadequate duration). In this case, the declaration of cure operates like a kind of true/false statement—but one that can never be fully confirmed as true. One can never know with certainty that tuberculosis will not return, that it is truly gone. Falsifiable only with the passage of time and a future diagnosis, the declaration of cure might be more precisely described as a theory: it is a proposed description of the body, one that is tested repeatedly and acquires adherents and critics over time. Rather than a theory of cure, then, we are left with cure as theory.

On the face of it, this sounds a great deal like cancer treatment, in which the term *cure* is often avoided in favor of the paired concepts of remission and relapse. To speak of remission is to openly admit to an uncertainty about the actual state of things (Are there still cancer cells lurking in the body somewhere?) and about the state of things to come (Will they metastasize?). To speak of remission is to anticipate this possibility of relapse.

By contrast, to be cured, as we often think of it, is to have illness behind you. Certainly, Nilam had thought that her days of treatment were over each time she was cured. Yet, curiously, patients like Nilam and also Murugesan were often referred to as relapse cases. Neither had ever been declared to be in remission, because this is a term that is never, to my knowledge, used to refer to tuberculosis patients. To pair relapse with cure is to admit to the fragility of cure, to the ever-present possibility that illness might return. Yet, crucially, this fragility is never admitted in advance. This, to my mind, is the key difference between cure and remission. Cure deliberately disregards the possibility of return, while remission actively anticipates it.

Checkmarks

Procedure itself offered another approach to declaring cure. In 1992, the Indian government's then thirty-five-year-old tuberculosis treatment program came under intense criticism for a host of reasons, including its inconsistent

---

42. The use of such technology required more than availability, but also training and infrastructure (such as a dependable source of electricity).

and overlong treatment procedures and an astounding lack of data regarding how many patients had actually been cured by the program.[43] In response, the government transitioned to the internationally recognized DOTS protocol, an acronym that stands for "directly observed treatment, short-course." As much a treatment program as a management strategy, DOTS provides a one-size-fits-all model that aims at cost effectiveness and assumes that people in places like India are unreliable and must be physically observed consuming each dose of their treatment. The DOTS strategy, as it is often described, is organized, in theory if not in practice, around six pillars: direct observation, a standardized short-duration treatment, quality diagnosis via sputum microscopy, a reliable supply of effective drugs, political buy-in, and careful monitoring and evaluation.[44]

For each patient enrolled in the government program, a treatment card was created as an accounting measure, introduced as part of this move toward greater standardization. For each dose of antibiotics a patient received under supervision, a checkmark was placed in a box. If a patient was unable to come to the clinic but had received a dosage in advance to take with them, a circle was drawn around the checkmark. If a patient missed a dose entirely, the treatment provider simply drew an empty circle.

Once a patient had produced a long enough string of checkmarks—representing the fact that they had taken all of the doses in the standardized treatment regimen—they were not, formally speaking, cured, but rather placed in the category of "treatment completed." Technically, to declare someone cured, the national program required negative sputum samples acquired from patients during and at the end of treatment to confirm that the bacteria that cause tuberculosis were no longer present. In the official reporting, however, the Indian government lumped together both "treatment completed" and "cured" cases into a metacategory: "treatment success."

43. The antituberculosis program in India had been subject to regular scrutiny from 1968, including via a series of critical reports issued in 1975 and 1988. Along with concerns about the treatment protocols and the reporting of cure rates, these reports noted problems related to unconfirmed diagnoses, lack of case finding and follow-up, lack of infrastructure and staff, and issues of governance. See Brimnes, *Languished Hopes*, 263–66.

44. The Madras Study, discussed in chapter 3, was an important precursor to DOTS, as were the pilot programs of short-durée therapy pioneered by Karel Syblo, which caught the attention of global financial and health institutions in their turn toward cost effectiveness. See McMillen, *Discovering Tuberculosis*, 189–91, 204.

On occasion, I would see treatment cards on which the patient's physician had written the word "cured" at the end of a long stream of checkmarks. But after the word "cured," I would see further checkmarks, and the words "cured again." Cure was meant to signal the end of illness, but here again was a kind of second cure. For public hospitals networked into the systems of audit in the wake of the post-1992 reform of the Indian antituberculosis program, checking boxes was a means of demonstrating the efficacy not only of the antibiotic cure but of the hospital itself. The need for a second cure could pose a potential problem, undercutting both cure and clinic.[45] When I asked Dr. Amutha why she might attempt to cure a patient who had already been declared cured, she explained that a patient could be "declared cured, but still have TB."

In this instance, Amutha was not claiming that another doctor had made a mistake. Rather, she meant that a patient could become asymptomatic and noninfectious but continue to carry reservoirs of bacteria. In fact, it is estimated that over half of all Indians are asymptomatic carriers of the bacteria that cause tuberculosis. In this light, it becomes possible to say that Murugesan's former doctor was correct to declare him cured. He had been cured, at the level of the symptom, and no longer required treatment—at least for the following ten years. In other contexts, this form of cure has been described as a functional cure, one that allows you to live symptom-free without medication—as opposed to a sterilizing cure, which requires the eradication of the microbes that cause a particular condition.[46]

These multiple ways of understanding cure were rarely formalized and distinguished in the clinics where I worked. Counting checkmarks and counting bacteria were not mutually exclusive. Similarly, doubts about the veracity of another doctor's pronouncement of cure seemed to elicit no hesitation in one's own way of doing things. Notably, understandings of cure were closely related to the forms of diagnostic technology that were at hand. In 1995, for example, the ex-director of the Tuberculosis Research Centre in Chennai, Dr. R. Prabhakar,

45. Veena Das has described how a woman she calls Meena was denied treatment when she required this second cure, in part because the clinic did not want to report treatment failure, which could become refigured as a failure of the clinic. Das, *Affliction*.

46. Recently, this language has been used to describe the result of treating HIV patients with hematopoietic stem cells obtained from a donor carrying a mutation that makes it difficult for HIV to enter into cells. When successful, such patients no longer require antiretroviral treatment, and thus, they are functionally cured. What remains unclear is whether the retrovirus has been entirely eliminated from their bodies, required for a "sanitizing cure."

lamented that a century-old technology remained central to diagnosing tuberculosis: "A great deal of emphasis (sometimes unduly) is laid on imaging and important clinical decisions are made on the basis of 'shadows.'"[47] X-ray images, he argued, "can never be considered as substitutes for eliciting signs and symptoms of the disease."[48]

Later that day, a pair of gray-bearded men came to our table. The older man was missing most of his teeth, so he had difficulty making himself understood. The younger man did most of the talking, speaking with Dr. Prabha about the older man's condition. He handed her a standard-size X-ray of the older man's chest, quite a bit larger than the three-by-three-inch images that were the standard in the hospital. Prabha took the X-ray hesitantly and held it to the light, peering at it intently. After about a minute, she let out a sigh of frustration and handed the image to Dr. Amutha, asking for her opinion. Amutha made an attempt at examining the image, before passing it back with a shrug. Prabha turned to the younger man.

"It's hard," she began to explain. "The X-ray is too big. It's hard to see on the big X-rays after you get used to the small ones." She instructed the younger man to take his companion to get a smaller X-ray—an MMR—from the hospital lab. The image would be processed in two days, she explained. They would have to come back then to receive a diagnosis.[49]

47. Prabhakar, Letter.

48. Prabhakar, Letter.

49. The gray-bearded men were clearly concerned about Dr. Prabha's instructions to return. The two of them worked in Kanchipuram, about seventy-five kilometers from the hospital. To cover the distance and arrive during clinic hours, the men had taken the day off work. When confronted with deferral or referral, patients often spoke anxiously about missing work. Patients feared that taking time off to visit the clinic would put their employment in jeopardy. Many of the patients were migratory laborers, coming from the neighboring state of Andhra Pradesh to find temporary employment in Tamil Nadu. Employment was difficult to come by and often intermittent—to take time off was to risk losing already precarious employment opportunities. Patients also feared that coworkers or employers would become suspicious. With or without a sound basis, rumors of illness could also lead to losing a job. Practices of deferral and referral forced patients into a dicey calculus—continue going back to this clinic, or another, in the hope of diagnosis and treatment, and risk unemployment; or continue to work without treatment and risk even greater illness and possibly death. As McDowell, Engel, and Daftary have pointed out, this practice of asking patients to come back later contributes to patients not coming back at all, resulting in cases that are described as "lost to follow-up." See McDowell, Engel, and Daftary, "In the Eye of the Multiple Beholders."

Developed in 1935 and used as a screening tool for tuberculosis across the world, the mass miniature radiogram, or MMR, is a smaller, cheaper version of a normal-sized X-ray. Although I had seen regular-sized X-rays used in private hospitals, the staff at the Chetpet hospital largely depended upon MMR images. Prabha and Amutha had received much of their tuberculosis-specific training at the government hospital. Having learned to read radiographic images of the chest at a particular size, they found it difficult to transpose their fluency across scale. Patients would often show up with different-sized X-rays, at different exposures, usually from private clinics or diagnostic centers. For the doctors who were trained with and accustomed to the MMR images, these larger images posed a serious problem of interpretation.

In the Chetpet hospital, diagnosing tuberculosis was an affair that extended across multiple spaces and many days. In another hospital located across town, the private HIV hospital where I worked in 2011, time and space were more compressed. The HIV hospital had made use of regular-sized X-rays, pressed against wall-mounted light boxes to be exposed to the interpretative powers of the clinician.

I remember Dr. Vijay in particular, who would quite confidently profess the existence of lesions after looking at an X-ray. He would point them out to me, tracing his finger along the image where the shadows swerved and the darkness congealed to indicate a pathological formation. Oftentimes, treatment began before the results of a sputum exam, on the basis of what was called a presumptive diagnosis. But even when the bacteriological results came back negative—when the laboratory technician was unable to find bacteria in the sputum—Vijay would begin what he called empirical treatment, arguing that the X-ray image suggested tuberculosis even if the bacteriological result showed otherwise.[50]

The analysis of both X-ray images and sputum results elicited a great deal of uncertainty among clinicians. In those quiet moments in the clinic, when the rush of patients receded, I heard clinicians express these doubts. When I asked Dr. Shanta, Vijay's wife, to reexamine an X-ray image that Vijay had already pronounced as tuberculous, she frowned. "I just don't see it," she said. Numerous

---

50. As McDowell and Pai point out, empirical treatment is widespread in the private sector in urban India, which they explain in part as grounded in a mistrust of the utility of diagnostic tests ranging from sputum microscopy to X-ray imaging and even DNA-based tests like Gene Xpert. Proceeding with treatment after a negative sputum test, for example, is not uncommon. McDowell and Pai, "Treatment as Diagnosis and Diagnosis as Treatment."

studies have demonstrated the high rates of inter- and intrarater variation in the reading of X-rays. These inconstancies are often framed in terms of observer bias, a problem of the observing subject who expects to see certain kinds of things and not others.[51] A suggestive image could all too easily turn out to be a play of shadow and light.

In spite of the very many doubts about the utility of interpreting shadows, X-ray imaging endures as a ubiquitous technology in India and enjoys a critical role in the Government of India's tuberculosis diagnostic protocol. X-rays persist as an imperfect means of seeing into the body, of diagnosing illness and gauging progress, of correlating external signs to internal physiological variations. Roadside diagnostic laboratories across Chennai prominently advertise X-ray services, available for a relatively small fee. Many smaller clinics without X-ray equipment referred their patients to laboratories with which they had established a relationship premised on trust and financial incentive. In many of the doctors' offices that I visited, calendars were branded with the name of particular diagnostic laboratories.[52]

Sputum microscopy—counting bacteria under a microscope—is not terribly sensitive, and yet it remains, along with X-rays, a primary means of diagnosing tuberculosis in India. The fact that sputum microscopy is a technique dating back over a century was frequently remarked upon during the course of my fieldwork as a sign of the lack of progress in tuberculosis diagnostics. At the same time, microscopy has its defenders as well. In 1995, Dr. N. K. Shah, the WHO representative to India, reflected on the utility of sputum microscopy: "True to the simplicity of the common man, what is relevant in the health for all context, is not always high technology and high cost diagnostics, but tests that are simple, sure and easy. For instance, in our revised National Tuberculosis

51. The difference between what Vijay and Shanta saw, and in their certainty about what they saw, might also be understood as a form of gendered difference: Vijay was more confident that he could interpret the X-ray with certainty, while Shanta (and Amutha and Prabha as well) was less certain.

52. In its ubiquity, the X-ray has also been denigrated. Through her research in the state of Kerala, Caroline Wilson describes how new medical imaging technologies became exceedingly popular in the 1990s, particularly in what are termed superspeciality hospitals. The Keralan doctors with whom she worked took X-ray imaging to be part of any basic investigation, and X-ray images to be legible to any clinician. The services of a radiologist were only required for the newer imaging technologies, which were not only more expensive but enjoyed a heightened technological aura. Wilson, "Thinking through CT Scanners."

Program . . . the age old, simple, cheap, sputum smear microscopy, is the surest bet both for diagnosis as well as for prognosis."[53]

Shah's argument in favor of sputum microscopy was based on criteria of efficacy, simplicity, and cost effectiveness. Despite its age, sputum microscopy remained for Shah the best means of providing diagnosis to the masses. He drew a line between high technology, which had its place, "especially when the disease appears vague or complicated, clandestine or deceptive and when localization and research needs are paramount," and "age old" technology like sputum microscopy.[54] The very simplicity and affordability of sputum microscopy made it perfect for a situation in which price was an issue but the goal remained "health for all."[55]

As a lab technician at the Chetpet hospital explained to me, the examination of a sputum sample from a patient deemed cured should reveal no bacilli for a period of six months after completion of treatment. This is what transformed a "treatment completed" case—in which a patient had taken each dose, as signaled by the string of checkmarks—into a "cured" case. If bacilli were discovered within that six-month window, then the patient would be classified as a relapse case, although in theory the patient might have been reinfected by a different strain of bacteria altogether. If bacilli were discovered after that six-month window, only then would the patient be classified as a case of reinfection—although, here too, there remained the possibility that the patient had never been cleared of the original tuberculosis-causing bacteria in the first place.

Sputum microscopy, like X-rays and checkmarks, were rough heuristics. If, for example, DNA-based tests had been readily available, the clinicians and lab technicians with whom I worked might have been able to say with greater certainty whether a patient previously declared cured was suffering from the same strain of bacteria or a new one.[56] The act of declaring someone cured is shaped, but not wholly determined, by the availability of both diagnostic and therapeutic technologies. Although the introduction of antibiotics in India certainly promoted a conception of cure as final, the optimism surrounding cure has always harbored a skeptical underbelly.

53. Shah, "Letter on Diagnostics."
54. Shah, "Letter on Diagnostics."
55. Shah, "Letter on Diagnostics." Shah's insistence on "health for all" through the use of basic technologies echoes the language of the Declaration of Alma-Ata in 1978 and its emphasis on primary health care.
56. On the early use of DNA fingerprinting to distinguish new infections or reinfections from relapse in San Francisco, see Barnes, "Targeting Patient Zero," 56–57.

Moving, Loving, Praying, and Praising

Back in the mid-twentieth century, Santosham admitted that certain forms of tuberculosis were recalcitrant to the best efforts of medicine. He categorized the disease into sixty-five varieties, based on its location in the body, duration, and rate of progression. Four of these, he explained, "may be called *incurable*."[57] Another four he described as "*probably incurable*."[58] Despite this strong disclaimer, Santosham warned his colleagues against refusing to treat a patient on categorical grounds.[59] "Before submitting a patient to a period of treatment, it is wrong to declare his disease *definitely incurable*, because a period of treatment can reverse the speed or progress."[60] The body under treatment was capable of many things. Nevertheless, treatment did not always turn out as one hoped. In a long passage from his book, Santosham reflected on one of his earliest patients, whose illness endured across generations of therapeutic ambition:

> I remember a lady in the early 1940s when I found her to be suffering from tuberculosis in one lung, with sputum positive for tubercle bacilli. She was a newly married bride at that time. First she was treated with A.P. [artificial pneumothorax, a form of collapse therapy]. And later she was treated with Streptomycin, I.N.H. [isoniazid], and P.A.S. [para-aminosalicylic acid] when those drugs became available.
>
> She went on giving birth to children during her treatment. All were healthy children.
>
> Her disease was never controlled by any drug. She regularly took treatment and took all the new drugs that became available one after the other. When she was about 50 years of age and all her children were grown up she was still under full course of treatment for tuberculosis.
>
> All these years she was doing her domestic duties to the husband and children and was attending all the Church and social functions. I met her in such functions many a time. She was the centre of a group of merry making guests in all parties and she was the best dressed also.

57. Santosham, *What Everyone Should Know about Tuberculosis*, 22, emphasis added.

58. Santosham, *What Everyone Should Know about Tuberculosis*, 22, emphasis added.

59. By contrast, the philosopher, theologian, and social critic Ivan Illich would argue that it was precisely when a patient seemed incurable that the physician should step away, allowing the patient an autonomy from the forces of medical authority—even if this meant death. Death, for Illich, was an eminently human experience that had increasingly been expropriated by medicine from the sphere of meaningfulness. Illich, "Death Undefeated."

60. Santosham, *What Everyone Should Know about Tuberculosis*, 23, emphasis added.

On and off she will get admitted in Sanatorium for a fort-night or a month and went back to her home.

At this stage her husband was run over by a transport bus. He was about 60 at the time. "He was a very loving husband" she said. "Everyday he will give my medicines before going to office and come back again and give the medicines all these thirty years."

By this time she had taken all the anti tuberculosis drugs in all permutations and combinations always more than 3 potent drugs. I had sent her often to other tuberculosis specialists, Sanatoria with year and year record of treatment and whole series of X-rays. She lived up to 52 years of which about 30 years with tuberculosis in a small house in Royapettah. The picture is of a person who lived with often repeating stormy episodes of tuberculosis religiously taking her treatment without a single day's default all her days. All the drugs did not give her full deliverance but they kept her well enough to do her duties to the husband and children for thirty years.[61]

Santosham's patient persisted through three decades of treatments. But eventually, her condition took a permanent turn for the worse. When she passed away, Santosham attended her funeral. In a second book published in 1985, he thinks back to the day of the funeral, and in particular to a prayer of gratitude offered by his patient's son. In recollecting his words, Santosham remembers being overwhelmed by memories of fortitude and failure:

I was recalling to my mind the host of drugs costing thousands she had swallowed, through which according to science [she] should have got well 30 times in her life. A great disappointment to the doctor and the patient, a failure of science. But looking at the other side of the picture except for the restraining influence of these drugs she should have died about a year after her first child birth. The drugs kept her moving, loving, praying and praising for 30 long years as a patient of tuberculosis gifted with a patience that survived 30 years to give to the home, a mother, wife and the world. She was a sermon on the subject of the benefits of patience and discipline, never despairing, ever hoping.[62]

Although she was never cured, Santosham had insisted on treating her. For three decades, she had been one of those "probably incurable" cases, but the cold hard reality of her incurability could only be ascertained from the perspective of

61. Santosham, *Tuberculosis at a Glance*, 68–69.
62. Santosham, *Tuberculosis at a Glance*, 70.

the grave. Despite such failures, Santosham insisted that tuberculosis was in general "very curable." His unblemished optimism survived alongside a sense that cure was never guaranteed, fragmented by *probablies* and undercut by cases like that of the woman who lived for thirty years with her condition.

In between the "very curable" and the "probably incurable," we find a kind of tuberculosis that looks like a chronic condition. As Santosham put it, tuberculosis was "a *chronic disease* that often slowly progresses and always takes long to recover from."[63] Chronic, and yet curable—the two terms were not in tension, although we often think of them as referring to opposed conditions. The chronic, we might imagine, is incurable and potentially terminal. It has no end, except for perhaps death. The curable, on the other hand, should end, once and for all, long before death.

For Santosham's patient, time was carved out over three decades of treatment into something that resembled (but was not quite identical to) the waxing and waning of the moon; moments in which things were better, when she could care for her family and attend church, and moments when things went awry. But the difference, for Santosham, was that her waxing and waning was not cure. Her condition was chronic and only potentially curable, until it wasn't.

In the early days of the antibiotic era, Santosham's patient underwent three decades of treatment for tuberculosis. Forty years after her death, tuberculosis remains strangely chronic, even if nobody describes it that way. The thing to keep in mind is that Santosham's patient was never declared cured. Over the course of seven long years, Nilam, on the other hand, had repeatedly been declared cured. In her life, cure had not been the end of illness, but rather an end: a temporary stopping point before the resumption of therapy. Nevertheless, Nilam continued to express to me the hope that she would be cured again, but this time, once and for all.

Platonic Cure

So much is at stake in the declaration of cure. We might treat such a declaration as the simple reporting of an observable fact: Nilam's doctors saw that she was cured, and they said so (again and again). As Santosham emphasized, the authority to declare someone cured belongs to the supervising physician. A patient might declare themselves cured, giving precedence to their experience of their own bodies over the credentials, expertise, and experience of the doctor.

63. Santosham, *What Everyone Should Know about Tuberculosis*, 236, emphasis added.

But in so doing, Santosham warned, they risked a partial cure, one that might unravel as they moved back into their everyday life. Nilam had not usurped authority from her doctors—she placed her faith in them, repeatedly, allowed them to declare her cured. Yet even a declaration of cure from an anointed authority could come undone.

The nature of such authoritative declarations became clearer to me in 2015, when I was invited to the Tuberculosis Research Centre in Chennai for the celebration of World TB Day, one of many annual commemorations inaugurated by the World Health Organization to spread awareness of certain diseases and their cures.[64] As part of the celebration, a former tuberculosis patient who had been declared cured, Mrs. Ramasami, had been asked to share the story of her treatment with a large room filled to capacity with minor politicians, journalists, physicians, students, and a handful of academics. Her hair pulled neatly back, she began speaking into the microphone, primarily in Tamil, her left hand tapping out the fluid rhythm of her words.

"My first TB attack [English] happened in 2003," she explained. This attack had come as something of a surprise to Mrs. Ramasami. "I had thought there was no chance that I could get TB." She was, in her own words, "a housewife" who didn't "live in a slum." But then she had fallen ill. Her disbelief led her to resist not only the diagnosis, but also the treatment: "I fought with the doctors. After the Mantoux test, and some other tests, the doctor said: You definitely need to take these medicines. But they were such big medicines! At first, I wouldn't take them. I threw them out the window. And when I was taking them, I had a lot of problems. Nausea and vomiting. The doctor asked for sputum. I refused to give it. I was acting very childish. I suffered relentlessly from a severe fever."[65] Over the course of seven long years, Mrs. Ramasami's condition had waxed and waned, punctuated by bouts of antibiotic therapy. "They

64. Back in 1982, to commemorate the centennial of Robert Koch's proclamation in Berlin of a bacterial etiology for the disease, the International Union against Tuberculosis and Lung Disease proposed an annual day of awareness, as part of a year of events coordinated under the theme "Defeat TB: Now and Forever," for which the Tuberculosis Association of India printed a pair of seals, as part of their regular annual sale of tuberculosis seals.

65. The Mantoux test, first developed in 1907 and further refined in the 1930s, involves the intradermal injection of a protein derived from Koch's tuberculin into the forearm. In theory, if the test is positive, the injection site will produce a raised, hardened bump forty-eight to seventy-two hours later. But the results can be difficult to interpret; false positives induced by previous exposure to tuberculosis or to the BCG vaccine are common.

started giving me injections. Injections and pills. Pills, so many pills! Twelve or fifteen pills, they gave me so many! . . . In the morning, a packet of pills, in the evening, a packet of pills, I was taking so many medicines! . . . I didn't have *awareness* [English]. I hadn't realized that these medicines would bring with them their own problems, like vomiting, constant vomiting." Mrs. Ramasami described the difficulties involved in the supervised treatment regimen. "For about three or four years, it controlled my life. . . . I'd arrive in the hospital at nine in the morning. Until twelve o'clock I would take the pills one at a time, waiting to vomit. After a while I'd take another pill. Then I'd wait and see. And again, I'd vomit. At the same time, I was still getting injections, for twenty-four months." The intense physical reactions produced by the drugs led Mrs. Ramasami to skip doses, stop her treatments early, and refuse some of the drugs.

> The main problem was that I wasn't taking the medications properly . . . I'd go back to the doctor with half of the medicines. I can't do it, I'd tell him. I can't take the pills. If I take this pill it itches, I'd say. If I take this other pill, I vomit. If I take this other one, I get nauseous. I said something like this for each and every medicine. . . .
>
> How should I put it—in truth I thought TB was a game and I didn't take it seriously.

The long duration of Mrs. Ramasami's treatment suggests a repeated failure to achieve cure, or perhaps to remain cured. If tuberculosis and its treatment is in fact a game, as she put it, it is one that is meant to be finite, with a clear end point. In such a finite game, there are rules to be followed, requiring a certain kind of seriousness that Mrs. Ramasami, by her own admission, lacked. She was, in this sense, a player of what we might think of as an infinite game— one in which winning and losing are far less important than simply remaining in play.[66] Of course, this had not been her intention.

If the antibiotic treatment of tuberculosis is a game, it is one that is explicitly rule-bound, serious, and, above all, finite. Patients should take their medications, regularly and dutifully, until they have completed their course of treatment and been declared cured by their doctor. Yet the finite game of treatment is one that frequently threatens to devolve into an infinite game. Rules are broken, supervision rebuffed, and it becomes entirely unclear whether it's even possible to win—or if the best you can hope to do is keep on playing.

66. My discussion of games is inspired by the work of Vinay Lal, who in turn borrows the idea of finite and infinite games from James Carse. See Lal, "Gandhi"; see also Carse, *Finite and Infinite Games*.

Like Nilam, Mrs. Ramasami had also undergone treatment for seven years. Under the government's standardized treatment protocols for tuberculosis, she should have been cured in no more than two to three years. Yet Mrs. Ramasami had never been declared cured over these seven years. This failure to be cured was one that Mrs. Ramasami took upon herself, as a recalcitrant patient, one that doctors would describe in jargon as nonadherent, noncompliant, or simply a default case.[67] While Mrs. Ramasami and her doctors seemed to accept that her cure had been postponed through personal failing, others were less willing to do so.

For example, Nilam. Although she had fallen ill again and again, she inoculated herself against accusations of personal failure. Nilam had told me that she was "not a defaulter," that she had always taken her medicine.[68] Instead, she blamed the host of private and government doctors who, in her words, "only cared about money." Blame was fungible, moving across and between groups to assert claims of responsibility: the patient for herself, or the doctor for the patient, or the patient's family for her. Blame also indexed what was thought to be an inappropriate orientation toward wealth generation, rather than, for example, toward proper care.[69]

What unites their stories is that neither Nilam nor Mrs. Ramasami attributed blame to the pills and injections, the very stuff of cure. To blame cure—to point to the failures of antibiotic treatment—would be to sacrifice their own hopes for a cure that was final, and to risk lapsing into a discourse of incurability. Instead, cure had to remain ideal, perfect, almost sacred,

67. The category of noncompliant patient emerged after World War II, as new treatments (like antibiotics) became available for a host of conditions requiring extensive treatment (like tuberculosis). As Jeremy Greene points out, the use of the category has been understood simultaneously as a means of extending medical authority and as a critique of that authority. See Greene, "Therapeutic Infidelities."

68. On the category of the defaulter in tuberculosis treatment in India, see Seeberg, "The Event of DOTS."

69. On the question of blame, see Farmer, *AIDS and Accusation*. Farmer discusses how race, class, gender, and geography come to configure the pathways through which blame flows, specifically in relation to the spread of HIV. As Niels Brimnes point out, the practice of treating the Indian patient as responsible for their own failure was crystallized through an emphasis on behavior and character. More sociologically oriented studies in the 1960s, and even the Madras Study of the 1950s (see chapter 3), turned attention away from individual responsibility to the state in its organization and administration of antituberculosis programs. See Brimnes, *Languished Hopes*, 192–94.

its efficaciousness unsullied by its earthly approximations.[70] For that reason, blame had to be attributed elsewhere: to the patient, to the family, or to the doctors.

At some point, Mrs. Ramasami's condition began to deteriorate. Before beginning another course of antibiotic treatment, she was admitted to a nearby private hospital where her right lung was surgically collapsed to stymie the spread of infection. After her hospitalization, Mrs. Ramasami was placed on a grueling regimen involving daily pills and biweekly injections. Like the Christian woman treated by Dr. Santosham, Mrs. Ramasami endured a range of treatments. Not only antibiotics, but hospital admission, bed rest, and collapse therapy. The treatments of the past continued to be conscripted as a means of bolstering the efficacy of antibiotics in the present.

After about two years, her treatment finally came to an end. Since then, Mrs. Ramasami hadn't experienced another attack. In Mrs. Ramasami's words, her seven years of therapeutic purgatory reflected nothing about the medical system, any doctor or nurse, her family, or even the relentless barrage of pills and injections. The failure to be cured, it seems, is never the failure of cure. In the treatment of tuberculosis, antibiotics are Platonic: a particular curative intervention might fail, but cure itself can never fail.[71] For that reason, cure can always be deferred to other times (the future) and other places (other clinics). The finite game can become infinite.

"Since 2010," Mrs. Ramasami concluded, "I haven't had any problems. Here, I was cured."

The audience burst into applause. As she moved to sit down, one of the doctors at the hospital took the microphone. "Thank you very much. . . . Just hold on. . . . Thank you very much and it's so nice that you somehow took all those tablets, and now you can proudly say that you're cured." For the doctor, if Mrs. Ramasami could finally say that she was cured, it was not simply because her problems had come to an end, but because her doctors had declared her cured—and this is why she had been invited to share her story

---

70. As Todd Meyers remarks, "Even in cases where the patient's expectations are not met (medical practice has failed to cure or to reestablish an earlier order), somehow the absence of cure does not necessarily induce doubt in medicine's potential to do so." Meyers, *The Clinic and Elsewhere*, 10.

71. Jaipreet Virdi makes a strikingly similar observation in relation to cures for deafness: "It makes possible all that was impossible and unfathomable, delivers on demands but doesn't always distinguish between the real and the fake. It only matters that it exists, this cure, and that it can deliver. If it fails to do so, then it's not the cure's fault. It's yours." Virdi, *Hearing Happiness*, 34.

Figure 4.3. Logo and slogan, in Tamil, for India's tuberculosis treatment program. Screen capture, Central TB Division, http://www.tbcindia.gov.in /index1.php?lang=1&level =3&sublinkid=4668&lid=3241.

டிபி–
பூரண குணமடைய
முழு உத்தரவாதம். டாட்ஸ்.

that day, as a model of penitence who had finally accepted the authority of her doctors. She had learned, it seems, to play a finite game.

Bad Publicity

In the five years since she had been declared cured, Mrs. Ramasami had been free from any further *attacks*, as she called them. Her cure had been completed. This was the way in which cure was frequently spoken about in the clinic and in everyday life, as an end point. Advertisements encouraging treatment appear on television screens across India. Posters are pasted on walls, replete with the language of cure. Similar promotional materials are distributed throughout India, featuring athletes, chess champions, and actors from the many regional film industries in the country. During a conversation with a doctor from the northeast of the country, who had previously worked with the government program, I asked him about those patients whom I had met, like Nilam and Murugesan, who had been cured and cured again, as well as those who remained (or became) uncured. I asked him about these ad campaigns, which called upon the Indian public to place their faith in a cure that is certain.

In the English-language version, supervised, standardized antibiotic treatment is described as a "sure cure for TB." In Hindi, the expression used is *pura course, pakka ilaaj*, which roughly translates as "a full or finished course [of therapy] for proper cure."[72] As with the English word *cure*, *ilaaj*—which comes out of Persian and Arabic and is used in Urdu, Hindi, Punjabi, and Gujrati—has a

72. The Hindi/Urdu word *pakka* has a broader semantic range beyond certainty and appropriateness that includes ideas of solidity, authenticity, completeness, absoluteness, and even ripeness. My thanks to Andrew McDowell for raising this point.

broad metaphoric range, useful to describe cures physical, spiritual, and even political. *Ilaaj* might also be rendered as "treatment," which places emphasis less on cure-as-end and more on the process and substance of cure, the actual medicine and its administration. In which case, "pura course, pakka ilaaj" might be rendered as "full or finished course [of therapy] for proper treatment"—as opposed to, say, an iatrogenic treatment that could lead to drug resistance. Similarly, in Tamil the slogan reads: *purana gunamadaia muzhu utthuravaadham*, which translates to "full guarantee to reach complete recovery or cure."[73]

The former government doctor admitted that many patients were not properly cured, at least not with the kind of certainty professed by these slogans. But he added, somewhat cynically, that to describe antibiotics as only a possible cure was not terribly catchy.[74] What became clear to me was that "pura course, pakka ilaaj" indexed a widely shared investment—financial, material, libidinal—in a specific vision of cure as final. This is a vision in which we are all at one time or another enrolled, both for ourselves and for others.[75] After all, shouldn't cure be a once-and-done kind of thing? A one-way street from sickness to health?

Such a conception of cure might be thought of, in the words of the historian of religion Mircea Eliade, as radical. Eliade described the "radical cure" as one

73. In her work on the translation of AIDS in Nepal, Stacey Leigh Pigg documents the contortions undertaken by health outreach workers attempting to explain or impart knowledge of the condition. Such contortions are induced in part by the historical formation of knowledge about a disease, local norms around what can be spoken about (and what cannot), and the often-elite register required to undertake technical translation. As Pigg points out, for example, AIDS was transliterated into Nepali, but an emphasis on the meaning of each roman letter as critical for proper understanding rendered the question of what AIDS means better suited to quiz games than health outreach. In India, tuberculosis has been largely rendered as TB despite the availability of vernacular-language options that might be proffered as translations. On the question of translation in health outreach, see Pigg, "Languages of Sex and AIDS in Nepal."

74. This offhanded comment reflects something about the formation of a "sphere of communicability" that situates the lay public as incapable, intellectually and emotionally, of grasping the nuanced range of possible therapeutic outcomes, a public that only responds to slogans. See Briggs, "Communicability, Racial Discourse, and Disease."

75. Cure is rarely ever one's own. Spending time in an Indian hospital reveals the ways in which disease control, broadly understood, is figured as the responsibility of not only the patient, but the family, medical practitioners and the state. See Venkat, "Scenes of Commitment."

that would offer us relief from the often-wrathful transformations produced by both illness and its treatment. Such a cure would operate through the "abolition of profane time."[76] Without the passage of time, there could be no illness, no treatment, no suffering. According to Eliade, such a radical cure required a return to a time before time, before the beginning of our troubles, before even the "beginning of the World."[77] In such a time, there are no relapses or reinfections, no side effects, neither grievances nor regrets, and, above all, no uncertainties.[78] Such a radical cure might culminate in the end of a cycle (death) or the beginning of a new one (rebirth). But at its foundation, the radical cure makes cure itself unnecessary, perhaps even unthinkable.[79]

Eliade identified strains of radical cure in premodern healing traditions (as well as within psychoanalysis). However, such a conception of cure is not alien to the history of what might be loosely termed biomedicine, which has at times proposed a vision of the body as a kind of thermodynamically closed system, one in which each part served a specific function in relation to every other part, as well as in relation to the integrated whole.[80] Such a vision of the body operates by reading biology through physics, the history of medicine as the history of science.[81] Nothing new from the outside could enter to disrupt

76. Eliade, *Myths, Dreams, and Mysteries*, 51.

77. Eliade, *Myth and Reality*, 88.

78. For a critique of Eliade and those who followed him on this point, see Thapar, *Time as a Metaphor of History*, 5–8.

79. It's worth noting that the radical cure as conceived by Eliade bears little resemblance to the radical cure described in the first chapter, which involved the building of more prisons to disperse the crowded prison population. This should give us pause about what precisely constitutes radicality in a given situation. Eliade himself has been the subject of much critique, for his romantic vision of premodern religious traditions and for the ways in which these views aligned with his support of fascism in Romania.

80. Within such a vision of the body and of illness, the historian and philosopher of medicine Georges Canguilhem identified what he described as a "tendency to conceive of a cure as the end to a disturbance and the return to a previously existing order, which is evidenced by all the terms with the prefix re- that serve to describe the healing process: restore, restitute, re-establish, reconstitute, recuperate, recover, etc. In this sense, a cure implies the reversibility of the phenomena whose succession constituted the illness; it is a variant of the principle of conservation or invariance that form the basis for classical mechanics and cosmology." Canguilhem, "Is a Pedagogy of Healing Possible?," 11.

81. I'm indebted here to the work of Georges Canguilhem. Michel Foucault, in his introduction to Canguilhem's *On the Normal and the Pathological*, would write that

CHAPTER FOUR

or disturb things. And as a closed system, the body could, at least in theory, be restored to its previous condition.

Illness might then be understood as a curative response, an almost deliberate deranging of the mechanism to set it right.[82] A fever, for example, was not necessarily pathological, but rather a means of reestablishing the normative order. Illness and cure were not invariably opposed forces, but rather one and the same.[83] Curative illness could turn back the clock (or more precisely, the body), from the pathological back to the normal.

If the alternative to this vision of cure is conceived of in terms of the incurable—which frequently takes the guise of further suffering, death, or interminable treatment—it might appear quite reasonable to invest in such a vision. If cure is an ending through restoration or return, then incurability is a prolongation of the infinite game of treatment (or perhaps an ending through death). That such a radical cure is unreachable, even for the gods, makes it all the more seductive as a site of investment.

Everyone's Opportunity

Rather than offering a rebuke of her doctors or an indictment of the toxicity of her medications, Mrs. Ramasami testified to her own failings. The world over, HIV patients give similar testimonies, as a means of bolstering treatment

------

Canguilhem's work was "intentionally and carefully limited to a particular domain in the history of science." Foucault, "Introduction," ix. He adds that "Canguilhem would undoubtedly allow one to say that the moment which must be considered strategically decisive in a history of physics is that of the formalization and constitution of the theory; but the moment that counts in a history of the biological sciences is that of the constitution of the object and the formation of the concept" (xvii). In this sense, Foucault reads Canguilhem's particular approach to the history of biology as one that emerges out of the history of science and, in particular, out of the history of physics.

82. Such a body might be thought of as a kind of romantic machine. See Tresch, *The Romantic Machine*. A similar idea has been proposed by Andrew McDowell in his discussion of the use of the idiom of "rotation" among Bengali doctors as a means of describing "a kind of mechanical pharmaceutical overlay on local, upanishadic, and ayurvedic views of the hydraulic or pneumatic body and its symptoms." McDowell, "Mohit's Pharmakon," 342.

83. We might think again of the distinction between curative and pathological disease described in chapter 1.

organizations and gaining access to goods and services.[84] I had, however, never heard such a testimony given by a former tuberculosis patient.

To the chagrin of many public health activists, tuberculosis patients have rarely identified with their illness. Like a cold or a broken leg, tuberculosis largely fails to infect personhood or sociality in an enduring way. In the overlapping idiom of public health experts and activists, there are "persons living with HIV," but there are only ever "TB cases."

A consequence of this was made clear to me by Dr. Nalini Krishnan, the director of what is perhaps the only NGO in the state of Tamil Nadu, and one of very few across all of India, that focuses on tuberculosis. Dr. Krishnan lamented the fact that tuberculosis was not HIV. Where were the tuberculosis patient advocacy groups, she asked? Groups that could push for newer treatments, greater government support, and more research?

Dr. Krishnan argued that having tuberculosis failed to mark patients in the same way as being HIV positive. In part, she speculated, this was because tuberculosis was curable, a transient condition. By contrast, HIV infection signaled a permanent ontological transformation due to its incurability—there was no moving on from HIV. The specter of curability seemed to preclude certain forms of both identity and community.[85]

I'm reminded of a night in 2011 when I found myself sitting in a police station. The night had begun rather differently. I was celebrating the birthday of a friend at an apartment located in a Chennai neighborhood facing onto the Bay of Bengal. My friend had taken a break from the festivities to get some air, only to discover that his motorcycle had gone missing. The watchman guarding the house across the street, half-asleep, gestured for us to approach the metal grate separating him from the road.

The police took it, he said.

We hoped that the police in question were those stationed nearby, at the tiny precinct next to the government wine shop that sold very little wine but quite a bit of beer and hard alcohol. My friend and I walked the short distance through the dark and quiet streets pierced only by the yelping of roving gangs of dogs.

---

84. The oratorical genre that might be described as therapeutic testimony is well documented in anthropological work on HIV in particular. Patient testimonies premised on repentance have become generic modes of raising awareness and funds and gaining access to much-needed medicines. See Biehl, *Will to Live*; Nguyen, *The Republic of Therapy*.

85. See Banerjee, "No Biosociality in India."

At the station, the bleary-eyed officer behind the desk admitted that, yes, they had taken my friend's motorcycle. But only to keep it safe, he explained. Why else? It had been locked improperly; anyone could have stolen it. Fortunate that they had gotten to it first.

He asked us to wait until the officer in charge returned. Only he had the authority to release the bike into our custody. As the rain poured down outside the station, the officer dispatched an underling into the elements to fetch tea and snacks. He began to ask us questions about our lives, our families, our work.

I began talking, perhaps too much. In those days, I hadn't yet turned my attention to tuberculosis. I spent my days in a small private HIV clinic in the city. Sitting with counselors as they delicately relayed the results of diagnostic tests. Rounding with nurses and doctors in the mornings as they checked on patients too ill to remain at home.

Like the hospital in Chetpet, the reputation of the HIV clinic drew patients from the farthest reaches of Chennai, as well as from surrounding parts of Tamil Nadu and the neighboring state of Andhra Pradesh. Some patients came regularly to collect medicines; others received their medicines from the government program and only came to the clinic when things took a turn for the worse and they required more intensive forms of care.

The officer expressed befuddlement at my line of research. "They're all going to die anyway, isn't it so?"

The question he was asking wasn't "Aren't they all going to die?"

He was asking, "They're all going to die, so what's the point?"

I'm reminded here of the words of Susan Sontag. "For purposes of invective," she wrote, "diseases are of only two types: the painful but curable, and the possibly fatal." That night at the police station, I offered the officer a third type. With the drugs that were now available to treat HIV, you could live a perfectly normal life. That was what the counselors told the patients each time they visited. Incurable, but not for that reason fatal.

Yet if I had been more honest, I would have had to admit that patients did die. The doctors at the clinic ascribed these deaths to a seemingly endless parade of multisyllabic opportunistic infections and related conditions like Kaposi's sarcoma, cytomegalovirus, immune reconstitution inflammatory syndrome, pneumocystis pneumonia, toxoplasmosis, and candidiasis.

But what I saw most often—the usual cause of death for many of those who spent their last days in the clinic—was tuberculosis.

At first, I was surprised by the number of tuberculosis cases I saw in the clinic. I had grown up in a middle-class American suburb in the 1980s and '90s, too late to know tuberculosis except by the vaccination marks on my parents' arms. In my family, I alone had been born in a country that thought itself removed from this plague.

Back in 2011, nobody at that clinic in Chennai seemed to worry too much about tuberculosis. After all, they told me, it was merely opportunistic, secondary, and curable at that. What really mattered was HIV, the underlying condition, the chronic seedbed from which tuberculosis sprouted. In the clinic, a once-fatal disease had become a chronic condition through the use of antiretroviral drugs. Here, critically, *chronic* signaled *incurable* but not *fatal*. Tuberculosis, on the other hand, was a curable disease that nevertheless turned out to be quite fatal. The juxtaposition of two conditions in one body made these temporal formulations all the more pronounced.

There was, however, at least one person at the clinic who seemed worried about tuberculosis. Pregnant with her first child, Dr. Shanta had been repeatedly cautioned not to see tuberculosis patients. Her pregnancy, she was warned, decreased her immunity and increased her risk of infection. That made it rather difficult for her to do her job, she explained, a hint of irritation creeping into her voice.

"Everyone has TB," she said with a shrug. "Either they've had TB, they have TB, or they will have TB." Shanta was not alone in her assessment. Forty years earlier, Dr. Santosham had argued that almost every Indian would be, at some point in their lives, invaded by the bacteria that cause tuberculosis: "No one can run away or hide himself from the all prevailing tubercle bacilli. It seems, sooner or later, we are sure to be caught by the bacilli that lurk unseen in the atmosphere."[86] Curable, incurable, chronic, fatal. And perhaps, above all else, inevitable?

She'll Never Recover

After giving birth, Shanta took an extended leave, and I spent more time with her husband, Vijay, also a doctor at the clinic. On a morning about six months after I began my research at the clinic, a man named Sendhil entered hesitantly through the sliding doors of Vijay's office. He was propped up on both sides by his brother and his elderly mother. Sendhil was in his mid-to-late twenties, clothes hanging loosely from his joints like a hastily constructed scarecrow.

Sendhil's mother and brother took turns explaining that he had not been sleeping, and that he had not taken his medications in two weeks. Sendhil

---

86. Santosham, *What Everyone Should Know about Tuberculosis*, 77.

slouched low in his chair, refusing to turn his head toward Vijay, fixing his gaze instead on the blank wall in front of him.

After listening to their worries, Vijay quietly asked Sendhil's mother to wait outside. He seemed concerned about what could be discussed in front of her. She acquiesced, gently closing the door behind her. As soon as she had exited, Vijay turned to Sendhil and began firing questions at him about what was wrong, and about why he had stopped taking his medications. Sendhil maintained his stoic silence. His brother Selvan answered in his place.

Sendhil would leave the house in the morning, as if going out to work. But just a few hours later, he would return home, drunk. The rest of the day would be spent sleeping. When he wasn't out drinking or asleep, he lingered around the house, not working, not doing much of anything. Worry creasing his face, Selvan also reported that Sendhil continued to experience what he called "fits," occasional seizures. In spite of these concerns, and in spite of Sendhil's silence, Vijay assured them that Sendhil was "almost normal" now. It was a miracle that he had survived at all, he added.

Later, after Sendhil and his family had left, Vijay filled me in on the backstory. About six months earlier, just prior to my own arrival at the clinic, Sendhil had been admitted to the inpatient ward. He was very ill and was eventually diagnosed with tuberculous meningitis.[87] The bacteria that cause tuberculosis had traveled to the protective membrane surrounding Sendhil's brain and spinal cord, resulting in severe inflammation. His immune system, weakened by HIV, had been unable to keep the infection in check.

Tuberculous meningitis is exceedingly difficult to diagnose and treat, particularly when specialists and certain kinds of medical equipment are in short supply. A few weeks earlier, I had observed a middle-aged man in a coma admitted into the inpatient ward. Vijay had performed a lumbar puncture to collect the man's cerebrospinal fluid. Even before receiving the results of the laboratory tests, he felt certain that the man was suffering from tuberculous meningitis.

Vijay had debated whether to invite a neurologist from a nearby hospital for a consultation. Many of the neurologists and other specialists whom he had previously called upon were extremely hesitant to work with HIV-positive patients. Knowing this, Vijay only asked for consultations when he thought that something might be done for the patient. In this case, Vijay sensed that

87. On anthropological and historical approaches to thinking about coinfection, see Livingston, *Improvising Medicine*; Engelmann and Kehr, "Double Trouble?"

the man was in a late stage of disease, and that it was too late. Almost as if to confirm the wisdom of his decision, the comatose man died the next morning.

But Sendhil's case was different. After a few weeks of intensive treatment and monitoring in the inpatient ward, he had been allowed to return home to continue both his tuberculosis and HIV treatments. Since this near-fatal episode, Sendhil's health had improved remarkably. In the months following his hospitalization, there had been no discernible trace of tuberculosis, and the viral levels in his body had been reduced to a fraction of their former level. The combined forces of these pathological microbes had been, at least momentarily, held at bay.

Confronted by Sendhil's silence, Vijay gestured toward the hefty patient file sitting on the desk in front of him, filled with admission and discharge records, counseling reports, drug regimens, clinical observations, laboratory results, and referrals. Sendhil's patient file was also a history of labor, of expensive drugs and scarce time devoted to the work of preserving a life.

Vijay turned toward Sendhil and repeatedly asked him why he was not taking his medications.

But it was his brother who responded over and over again, "He won't tell me why. He just drinks."

Taking a deep breath, Vijay launched into a kind of homily. "Your life is in your hands. We've put in all of this work for you," he said. "Now, you must do something. Keep yourself busy—play table tennis, badminton, get a job, anything at all. Keep yourself busy instead of lying around at home."

Although Sendhil had finally turned toward Vijay, he remained silent, his eyes glued to a spot somewhere between the doctor's chin and the clinic floor. It was impossible for me to say whether Vijay's admonitions had moved him.

But Vijay was not deterred by Sendhil's silence. "Listen: if something happens to you, your brother will be sad for some time, but he'll be okay again after a while. Your father will be sad too, but he will also be okay.

"Your mother," he continued—"and mothers are different from fathers," he added—"your mother will be heartbroken. *She'll never recover*. I've seen that your mother accompanies you on every visit to the hospital. Just think of how lucky you are. Listen: we all have problems. Some seem worse than others, but all are relative. We must learn to live with it."[88]

88. The generic trope of the dutiful and doting mother, while arguably pan-Indic, has a particularly strong hold in the state of Tamil Nadu, through such figures as Tamil Thai (Mother Tamil) and the former chief minister, Jayalalitha, commonly referred to as Amma, or mother. See Ramaswamy, *Passions of the Tongue*.

"Living with it" is a problem unique to chronic conditions. Ostensibly, when a condition is curable—especially if we think of cure as an ending—there is nothing to endure past that ending. One might merely live (as if merely living were ever so simple). And when a condition is fatal, endurance beyond a certain point is arguably beside the point. Dr. Vijay's ethical injunction to "live with it" only made sense in the context of a life that was figured as permanently altered over a stretch of time. The eruption of tuberculosis into that life, a condition that could be cured, only underscored the fact that HIV, an incurable but chronic condition, was something that had to be endured.

Despite her exile from the examination room, Sendhil's mother was re-incorporated as a critical figure in Vijay's address. She was the one who accompanied Sendhil to the hospital each time. She was the one who waited for him just outside. Although the physical presence of Sendhil's mother had been limited to the first minutes of the clinical encounter, her presumed desire for her son to live was very much present, articulated through the doctor's speech.

Here, Vijay had rendered explicit the generally unarticulated forms of care provided by Sendhil's mother in his argument. It was in the name of his mother that Vijay called on Sendhil to live: "She'll never recover." For Vijay, such a claim could not have been articulated from the position of just any kin relation. Vijay claimed that brothers and fathers could recover, but mothers would remain heartbroken, because "mothers are different from fathers." At the same time, Vijay invoked the singularity of Sendhil's mother; she was the one who accompanied him to the hospital every time. Sendhil's mother became a token of a general type: motherhood, Indian motherhood, or, perhaps more specifically, Tamil motherhood. At the same time, she was irrepressibly singular, as Sendhil's mother, as the one who accompanied him, as the one who would never recover.[89] In this sense, her condition was also chronic and incurable.

89. Indeed, such kin-based commitments might also be productively related to older Tamil ethical traditions frequently articulated in terms of concrete familial ties. For example, a particularly damning couplet from the sixth-century *Thirukkural* notes that a drunkard's glee brings suffering primarily to his mother. Vijay might not have consciously intended to invoke this stanza in singling out the relationship between Sendhil's nonadherence to therapy (which included his drinking) and his mother's suffering. Yet as Anand Pandian has convincingly argued, these older ethical traditions continue to suffuse Tamil life (and familial relations) in the present, albeit in fragmentary form, perhaps most often in the absence of explicit citation. Pandian, "Tradition in Fragments."

Although Vijay began by repeatedly asking Sendhil why he would not take his medication, Sendhil's silence forced him to adopt a different tactic. Rather than continuing to insist on the importance of committing to therapy, Vijay instead invoked another commitment structured by a form of maternal care that was both generic and yet painfully specific. For his mother, if not for himself, he had to live, and to live, he had to recommit himself to treatment, and to the minor customs that composed a life. Such commitments are rarely just one's own.

Having already spent more time with Sendhil and his family than he did with most of his patients, Vijay hastily scratched a list of drugs on his prescription pad. He tore out the page and handed it to Selvan. The two brothers left, Sendhil never having said a word.

Still No Cure

One morning in early 2011, I heard a patient telling Dr. Vijay that he had seen an article in the newspaper about a cure for HIV. The patient wondered whether the cure was available at that hospital. Vijay responded quite simply that there was currently no cure, but that the existing medications would keep the patient healthy. He later explained to me that there was in fact a cure. But he noted that the curative procedure was dangerous and unfeasible in an "Indian setting," as he put it.

What was this cure? In 2011, the journal *Blood* carried a report that a single subject, pseudonymously known as the Berlin Patient, had been cured of HIV. Since then, numerous reports have surfaced of HIV-positive patients who have been cured. At the time of writing, the Berlin Patient remains by all accounts cured. But in a recent case involving an infant who was also declared cured, the virus repopulated after an unexpectedly long period of dormancy, raising both cautions and hopes. Although resistance has been a critical term in HIV treatment since the inception of antiretroviral drugs, it has now become possible to speak of a (functional) cure, as well as of relapse.

To be clear, Vijay was not simply hiding information from his patient. To offer knowledge of cure raised hopes of its actualization. But in this case, cure remained resolutely elsewhere, for other people in other places. Vijay was trying to avoid making a promise that he could not keep. In his evasion, we can once again see how cures might operate like promises. Like promises, cures are not necessarily guarantees. Like promises, cures can be broken, microbes can repopulate in resistant forms, and patients can relapse.

Figure 4.4. A "safe sex" poster produced by the Ministry of Health and Welfare, New Delhi, in 1991. L0054327, Wellcome Library, London. Copyrighted work available under Creative Commons by-nc 4.0, https://creativecommons.org/licenses/by-nc/4.0.

The investment in a concept of cure as final threatens to foreclose recognition of the limits of cure, and in itself produces a limit to what we can know—what we are willing to know—when it comes to both our singular and collective fates. Part of this closure involves an unwillingness to conceive of other possibilities of cure, ones in which we are left without tidy endings. Ones in which, for example, our vitality waxes and wanes, but we are not necessarily marked as incurable or chronically ill.

Physiology is not reducible to psychology, but I can't help but think here of Sigmund Freud's 1937 essay "Analysis Terminable and Interminable," in which he describes the case of a prodigal Russian who arrives despondent in Vienna. After extensive therapy, Freud declares the man cured, only to have him return nine years later, neurotic and penniless. It seems that he is no longer cured.

How can this be so? Freud explains it in terms of the "residues of the transference"—what we might think of as the remnants of an incomplete therapeutic encounter. Freud's Russian patient requires intermittent treatment for the next fifteen years as pieces of his past continue to resurface. Pieces that peel away, Freud writes, "like sutures after an operation, or small fragments of necrotic bone."[90] For Freud, both therapy and illness seem interminable, an infinite game without end.

In the present moment, there are consequences to conceiving of tuberculosis as a chronic condition, quite different than those faced by Dr. Santosham and his patients in the mid-twentieth century. Chronicity has become an ever-expanding classification, justly critiqued for exposing increasing numbers of people to the predations of drug manufacturers, insurance companies, health care providers, and the state. To have a chronic illness is not only to become a patient for life, but also to become a patient (and consumer) before you ever begin to feel ill.[91]

As I thought further about Freud's Russian patient, and about Nilam, Murugesan, and Mrs. Ramasami, it occurred to me that, for each of them, there were endings. In fact, there was no end to endings. Each time Nilam was cured, there was an ending. Each time Mrs. Ramasami felt better and stopped her treatment, there was an ending. Perhaps illness and treatment are not interminable, as Freud suggested, but rather, infinitely terminable, always ending so that they may begin and end once more. Endings follow endings. In this sense, both illness and cure might be critical diagnostic signs of the waxing and waning of life.

90. Freud, "Analysis Terminable and Interminable," 218.

91. On the increasing medicalization of uncertainty and the associated extension of treatment over the course of a life, see Dumit, *Drugs for Life*; Jain, *Malignant*; Aronowitz, *Risky Medicine*.

Chapter Five

Everything ends, and describing what
is inevitable should not be viewed as a
form of pessimism. Take the example of
a romantic tale: "The lovers lived happily
ever after" would clearly be viewed
as an optimistic story. But if you add a
coda—"A hundred years later, they were
both dead"—does that turn the story
pessimistic?

—Cixin Liu

After a physician in Mumbai reported the first diagnosed cases of totally drug-resistant tuberculosis in India, many began to wonder whether the antibiotic era had finally come to an end.

After the Romance Is Over,

is cure still possible, or has tuberculosis become, once again, incurable? What kinds of therapeutic futures might be forged as the utopian dream of antibiotic therapy looks to be reaching its limits? After over five decades of antibiotic-based treatment in India, the spread of drug resistance has inspired a new accounting of biomedical forms of intervention. For those who refuse the pessimism of the moment, salvation is to be found in new therapeutic and technological marvels. Yet even with these novel possibilities, it's difficult to know how best to distribute such treatments to maximize their limited, nonrenewable efficacy. The question of who receives cure brings with it the question of who will be denied. Confronted by nightmarish visions of a postantibiotic future organized around widespread resistance and forms of triage, some have asked whether cure might require a return to those therapeutic forms that characterized the preantibiotic era: a return, for example, to early twentieth-century paradigms of sanatorium treatment and nature cure. Might an India at the dusk of the antibiotic dream begin to look like an India before antibiotics?

Gandhi's Refusal

In 1954, Prime Minister Jawaharlal Nehru traveled to Pimpri, on the outskirts of Pune, to inaugurate the penicillin factory of the newly established Hindustan Antibiotics Limited (HAL). As the first government-owned and -operated drug manufacturer, HAL was tasked with providing affordable antibiotics to the Indian masses. Although imported penicillin had been available in India since at least 1944, HAL promised to deliver locally produced antibiotics and on a grander scale. From the fledgling days of independence, it was clear that India needed to manufacture its own drugs if it was going to free itself from the import costs of the colonial era. Production ramped up quickly; between 1955 and 1957, the manufacture of penicillin by HAL almost tripled.[1]

The founding myth of HAL has to do in part with Kasturba Gandhi, the wife of the Mahatma. In February 1944, ten years before the construction of the penicillin factory, Kasturba Gandhi lay dying in the Aga Khan Palace in Pune after a cascade of heart attacks. She and her husband were being held there as political prisoners after Gandhi demanded that the British "Quit India" in a famous speech delivered in Mumbai in 1942. Throughout their imprisonment, Gandhi arranged for a caravan of healers to visit Kasturba, including practitioners of both Ayurveda and nature cure.[2] Through their ministrations, she seemed to recover her strength, but only for a time. Her condition returned, more severe.

Like a celestial physician, her youngest son, Devadas, appeared at the eleventh hour with imported penicillin. Despite Devadas's insistence, it is said that the Mahatma refused the treatment on his wife's behalf. The way the story is sometimes told, Devadas's appearance operates like a foiled deus ex machina. He arrived, he had the cure—all he had to do was administer it.

There are many renditions of this episode. Most include the saying of wise and serious things by both Kasturba and the Mahatma. They read like a cross between mythology and melodrama, by turns moralizing and nationalist.

Epigraph: Quoted in Rothman, "China's Arthur C. Clarke."

1. Throughout the 1950s, parliamentarians in the Rajya Sabha repeatedly inquired about whether the factory was churning out enough penicillin for the nation's needs, as well as when HAL might start to manufacture other antibiotics. They were also concerned about the price and quality of these swadeshi drugs in comparison to foreign imports, sending samples to laboratories in the United States and the United Kingdom for assessment.

2. Among the visitors were the Ayurvedic practitioner Pandit Shiv Sharma and the nature cure specialist Dinshaw Mehta.

Figure 5.1. Nehru looking through a microscope at the HAL penicillin factory in Pimpri, his daughter Indira standing behind him, on the occasion of the formal opening of the factory. "Jawaharlal Nehru at the Penicillin Factory, Pune, 1 August 1956," photograph, Wikimedia Commons, https://commons.wikimedia.org/wiki/File:Jawaharlal_Nehru_at _the_Penicillin_Factory,_Pune,_1956.jpg.

Curiously, their grandson Arun entirely omitted the incident from his devotional biography of Kasturba's life. But another grandson, Rajmohan, included it in his biography of the Mahatma.[3] This makes sense: the story of denial seems to say more about the Mahatma than about Kasturba.

Rajmohan's reading of the episode is essentially sympathetic: "Gandhi advised against using [penicillin] on Kasturba. The drug was untested; injections would be hard for her to bear; her agony should not be increased. The son yielded."[4] This is a benevolent (but paternalistic) Gandhi, one who refuses cure for another because he believes he knows best. After all, if the drug was truly proffered so late in the game, could it have made much of a difference? If not, then why prolong Kasturba's suffering?

But we might also ask why Gandhi had allowed nature cure and Ayurveda, but drew the line at penicillin. The answer might come down to his well-known critique of allopathic medicine and, more generally, of the poisoned fruit of modernity. Antibiotics are small things, but they are made by big things (factories) that stand for an even bigger thing (Western modernity). The accusation inherent in such a line of questioning is that Gandhi allowed his wife to die on principle. This is a vision of Gandhi as a dogmatic moralist.

In either case, the provision of this new therapeutic technology—the antibiotic—became closely tied to questions of distribution and denial across various scales of life, both temporal and geographic. The question of cure and its limits looks different when configured in relation to individual organisms or populations; across biographical life spans or generations; or at the level of the local, national, or global. In the last few decades, as HAL has faced a seemingly endless parade of financial woes, successive governments have responded by threatening to sell it off or close it down.[5] At these moments, someone always mentions that Nehru pushed for the penicillin factory in the wake of Kasturba's death—because if a supply of made-in-India penicillin had been available, she

---

3. Rajmohan Gandhi cites from his father's book. See Gandhi, *Ba, Bapu aur Bhai*.
4. Gandhi, *Mohandas*, 514.
5. In 1997, HAL was officially declared a "sick" public sector unit, one that was unable to keep itself afloat financially. Numerous plans for reconstruction and rehabilitation have been proposed, leading to government-provided aid and loans for the sake of revival. It appears that HAL is in a permanent condition of infirmity. Yet, as a critical manufacturer of drugs for the nation, it cannot be allowed to die. Nor, however, can it be cured. On the sickness and hoped-for revival of HAL, see Chandna, "India's Oldest Drug Maker Can't Help."

could have been treated in time.[6] Gandhi's refusal is conveniently left out of these invocations.

Too Many People

Tuberculosis enters the story through a partnership between HAL and the American pharmaceutical company Merck. With their technical assistance, HAL established a plant to begin the manufacture of streptomycin, the first antibiotic found to be effective against tuberculosis. The new plant was inaugurated in March 1962 and was predicted to produce forty tons of the drug each year.[7] Nehru was once again invited to the inauguration. If it's true that he had pushed for the penicillin factory in the wake of Kasturba's death, his investment in the streptomycin factory might seem even more personal. After all, his wife Kamala had died from tuberculosis about twenty-five years earlier, less than a lifetime before but already a part of another era.[8]

In addition to Nehru, the American biochemist Selman Waksman was also invited to attend.[9] Waksman's team had been the first to isolate and identify the antitubercular properties of streptomycin in their laboratory at Rutgers University in New Jersey. At the inauguration of the streptomycin plant, Waksman delivered a lecture in which he discussed the effects of antibiotics on various forms of life: bacteria, but also poultry and swine. Antibiotics—as the word itself suggests—could end certain forms of life, but they could just as well promote the growth of others. Waksman's speech was at turns hopeful and cautious.

"By learning to utilize antibiotics," he remarked, "man has simplified the problem of his survival on earth."[10] Yet Waksman warned that antibiotics, like "every other revolutionary discovery," had ushered in novel difficulties. With

6. Ironically, the image of Gandhi has been taken up by all manner of projects that harness nationalist sentiment to a capitalist program. His image can be found on everything from salt packaging and Apple computer advertisements to clothing, cigarettes, and currency. Much to his chagrin, Gandhi had in fact already begun to witness the promiscuous dissemination of his "brand" during his own lifetime. See Mazzarella, "Branding the Mahatma."

7. The establishment of HAL's streptomycin plant only partially remedied the problem of supply, as tuberculosis treatment from the 1960s ideally included three different drugs taken in combination. Frequently, however, patients were given only one or two drugs. On the problem of supply from the 1960s, see Brimnes, *Languished Hopes*, 255–57.

8. For a discussion of Kamala Nehru's death, see chapter 2.

9. For more on Waksman and the discovery of streptomycin in his lab, see chapter 3.

10. Waksman, *Hindustan Antibiotics Bulletin*, 142.

the increased control of infection through antibiotics, people were living longer, giving rise to "new public health problems."[11] Waksman was particularly concerned with resistance: not only the development of drug-resistant microbial strains, but the loss of "natural resistance," as he called it, in the bodies of both humans and nonhuman animals. This loss of resistance, he suggested rather ominously, had "dangerous potentialities."[12] Waksman's words suggest to me a sense of foreboding, a fear that the collective dream of mass antibiotics, inaugurated at a factory in Pimpri, might come crashing down in a catastrophe of its own making.

Or perhaps he was referring to something else entirely. Seven years later, at a conference of Nobel laureates in Lindau, Germany, Waksman spoke about meeting Nehru at the inauguration:

> Mr. Nehru said to me: "Why do you bring us such drugs? We have *too many people*. You bring us drugs to save many upon whose death we counted to keep our population under control."
>
> I said to him: "Mr. Nehru, that is your problem. My problem is to help save the lives that are already in this world."[13]

Would Nehru really have said such a thing? Or was Waksman simply speaking ill of the dead?

Nehru loved his big science: dams, mills, factories, rolled out through five-year plans. Although both Nehru and Gandhi were deeply invested in a politics of *swadeshi*, Nehru differed from Gandhi in his embrace of large-scale technologies in the service of the nation.[14] How then can we make sense of Nehru's purported denial of these drugs in the face of his well-known investment in a socialist scientific dreamworld?

Toward the end of his recounting before his fellow Nobel laureates, Waksman added that he was sure that India would resolve the problem of population "*sociologically* rather than prevent the progress of science."[15] In fact, such a solution had been in place in India for some time. Family planning policies

11. Waksman, *Hindustan Antibiotics Bulletin*, 142.

12. Waksman, *Hindustan Antibiotics Bulletin*, 142.

13. Waksman, "Successes and Failures in Search for Antibiotics."

14. *Swadeshi*, literally "one's own country," refers to a form of anticolonial nationalist protest that involved the making and purchase of goods within India rather than supporting British imports.

15. Waksman, "Successes and Failures in Search for Antibiotics."

came into place in India in the early 1950s, what have been described as the "world's first national policy to limit growth."[16] In R. K. Narayan's *The Painter of Signs*, the effects of such sociological measures play out in the failed romance between Daisy, a family planning campaigner, and Raman, whom she hires to paint propaganda. The signs that Raman paints are zealously dictated by Daisy, each message tailored to the conditions of the people who live in the fictitious town of Malgudi and its surrounds.[17] But eventually, sociology fails. Or rather, sociological knowledge reveals that something else, something more, is needed.

"No wall messages?"

"No. Not suitable for them. Literacy is only one per cent; direct talk is the only possible communication."

"Do you mean to say that you will speak to everyone [*sic*] of the one thousand two hundred?"

"Why not? I can, if I live in their midst. I am wiring to Delhi to send a medical team immediately. In all, the total population to be covered would be . . ." She hardly looked at him, completely absorbed in the statistics before her, drawing a pencil over a sheet of paper and adding up. "An average of—mind you it is only an average—four hundred adults in each village may have to be sterilized or fitted with contraceptives, and at least twelve villages in this lot."[18]

For the illiterate, writing is replaced by speech, but even this is not enough. The perceived inadequacies of such sociological measures, as Waksman put it, gave way to the implementation of forced sterilization during the mid-1970s, in a period of emergency rule declared by Nehru's daughter, Prime Minister Indira Gandhi.[19]

16. Connelly, *Fatal Misconception*, 90.

17. Narayan, *The Painter of Signs*, 58:

> She turned to Raman and said, "You know, here we should also have a pictorial medium rather than just words. A father and a mother and just one bright and healthy child with the caption, 'With just one, we will be happier.'"
>
> Raman could not help asking, "One? You have said two in other places. Why this reduction here?"
>
> "Oh, this village is different," she said. "With the monsoon and other things, the problems here are very peculiar."

18. Narayan, *The Painter of Signs*, 147.

19. On the history of forced sterilization, see Tarlo, *Unsettling Memories*.

If antibiotic medicine promised to prevent death in the 1950s and '60s, contraceptive and sterilizing interventions might be read as a response, an attempt to solve the problem of too many people in the decades to follow. Individual lives could be saved, but the reproduction of life had to be prevented. The perceived failure of a purely sociological solution, as Waksman had put it, paved the way for a medical one. The supposed weakness of the will, of the Indian peasant unable to sublimate his or her libidinal energies, made surgery a viable and seemingly necessary substitute.[20] Where writing and speech failed, surgery prevailed.

Nehru's words, if they were indeed Nehru's words, offer something like a logic of Malthusian sovereignty: let the sick die to keep the population down. But with the establishment of the HAL antibiotic plants, the inception of the national tuberculosis program in 1962, and the forced sterilization campaigns of the 1970s, another logic, equally Malthusian, emerged: cure the sick if you can, but keep the population down by stopping them from reproducing. At the level of the nation, the compensation for cure was the radical curtailment of the reproductive life of the poor.[21] Individual, biographical time, the time of a life span, might be extended, but in return, genealogical time, the time of generations, would be cut short.

Incurable Baldness

To be clear, these two forms of Malthusian logic were interwoven from the start.

On August 28, 1953, the Congress Party parliamentarian from Bombay State, Lilavathi Munshi, introduced a resolution into the Rajya Sabha calling for the forced sterilization of a specific group of people: "if our Government [is] interested in asking healthy people to exercise birth control, why not start with people who are suffering from *incurable* diseases and who are insane?"[22] According to Munshi, everyone from the prime minister down agreed that population growth placed an unmanageable burden on society. The incurable were low-hanging fruit.

Munshi's proposal provoked much debate in the Rajya Sabha. Some disagreed with her founding premise, insisting that advancements in agricultural science would render the problem of feeding the growing population irrelevant. Others insisted on the right of every Hindu to fulfill their dharma by

20. Cohen, "Making Peasants Protestant and Other Projects," 81.
21. For similar types of therapeutic compensation marked by the bodily sacrifice of the Indian poor, see Van Hollen, "Moving Targets"; Cohen, "The Other Kidney."
22. Rajya Sabha Official Debates, "Resolution Regarding Sterilisation of Adults," 535.

begetting offspring, in particular male children to conduct funerary rituals. One member raised the specter of Hitler's Germany, noting that there was but a small step between sterilizing the incurable and sterilizing political enemies.

The most notable opposition to Munshi's resolution came from Health Minister Amrit Kaur, the only woman in Nehru's first cabinet and the president of both the Tuberculosis Association of India and the All India Institute of Medical Sciences. "I opposed it with all the emphasis at my command because I looked upon it from the point of view of science as wholly unscientific, from the point of view of ethics as wholly unethical and from the point of view of practicability as wholly impracticable."[23] Kaur further criticized those who spoke in favor of the resolution as lacking any knowledge of the "science of eugenics."[24]

An important thread that ran throughout the parliamentary debate concerned the difference between the curable and the incurable. How might they be distinguished? And did all forms of incurability necessitate sterilization? Tuberculosis was central to this conversation. Munshi believed that it was a disease that was, for the most part, both incurable and hereditary:

> I have often heard responsible people say that such people may get cured, may be one in a thousand, but [that] it is cruel to deprive even this one person of the happiness of having children. On account of the progress made by science, I dare say that there may be some chance for one person out of a thousand or even out of a lakh to get cured of any disease which is supposed to be incurable, but it is equally true that on account of that mistaken notion of humanity we shall be inflicting misery on hundreds of children who will be allowed to come into this world through such parents. . . .
>
> Children born of advanced cases of [tuberculosis] are bound to catch the parental disease sooner or later. Would it not be desirable to restrain tubercular patients from bringing forth diseased children? You are starting many hospitals to cure patients but this will be dealing with that disease at the root and there will be fewer cases to deal with. Ultimately, we may

23. Rajya Sabha Official Debates, "Resolution Regarding Sterilisation of Adults," 634.

24. Rajya Sabha Official Debates, "Resolution Regarding Sterilisation of Adults," 634. This would not be the first time that Kaur had to intervene in debates regarding the science of tuberculosis. In 1952, for example, she attempted to assuage the mind of the chief minister of Madras, C. Rajagopalachari (popularly known as Rajaji), who was strongly opposed to the implementation of the BCG vaccine against tuberculosis in India. On the debate between Kaur and Rajaji, see McMillen, *Discovering Tuberculosis*, 104.

hope to root out that disease altogether if we can prevent such people from procreating. . . .

Even if people with such disease get cured they are never strong enough to do work and earn sufficient living which can enable them to fulfil their obligations to their children. . . .

Gradually we shall be able to eradicate the race of unfit and unhealthy people.[25]

Some in the assembly questioned Munshi's characterization of tuberculosis. Govinda Reddy from Mysore stressed that Munshi was behind the times: "Tuberculosis . . . was held to be incurable but now it is becoming a curable disease and they have now remedies for it."[26] Going even further, Rajagopal Naidu from Madras questioned the twin presumptions of incurability and inheritance:

Is tuberculosis incurable? Nothing is incurable in the world. Secondly, even assuming for a moment that it is incurable, there is absolutely no basis for the presumption that incurable diseases will be transmitted to the offspring. So, let us, for a moment, think of the fate of the person who is sterilised and who is suffering from tuberculosis. It may be that with these latest drugs, like streptomycin and other "mycins," they are able to cure tubercular patients. Suppose this law is enforced, that a tubercular patient is sterilised; and if he or she is cured after some time and wants to beget children what will be his or her fate?[27]

The categorical confusion between the curable and the incurable made the implementation of such a law practically difficult. T. V. Kamalaswamy, also from Madras, stressed that "unless there is widespread agreement as to which diseases are incurable and which not, we shall be creating hardships in the application of the sterilisation law that may be proposed."[28]

Although not opposed to sterilization in principle, Kamalaswamy pushed to introduce distinctions between potentially incurable conditions:

25. Rajya Sabha Official Debates, "Resolution Regarding Sterilisation of Adults," 536, 537, 541, 546.

26. Rajya Sabha Official Debates, "Resolution Regarding Sterilisation of Adults," 556.

27. Rajya Sabha Official Debates, "Resolution Regarding Sterilisation of Adults," 562.

28. Rajya Sabha Official Debates, "Resolution Regarding Sterilisation of Adults," 559.

T. V. KAMALASWAMY: For example, let us take night blindness—an extreme case like that. It is admitted by everybody that if a family is suffering from night blindness, rather if the mother has night blindness, her progeny is almost certain to have night blindness. On that ground, will it be fair to have sterilisation of the mother? So, incurable diseases should include only those diseases that are transmissible and which are hereditary.

AN HONORABLE MEMBER: And baldness too.

T. V. KAMALASWAMY: Yes, another extreme case is that of baldness. Baldness, they say, is an incurable disease.[29]

At stake in this debate was the relative distribution and denial of genealogical time. Who precisely might be allowed to reproduce? Where should the line be drawn? Notably, the use of the example of the woman (figured as a mother) with night blindness reveals a gendered imagination of hereditary illness as passing from mother to child—one that continues to haunt Indian women with tuberculosis to this day (as we saw in chapter 4). Moreover, what this curious exchange about night blindness and baldness made clear was that incurability was not only difficult to determine, but thought by some to be insufficient as a criterion for sterilization.[30] What is also evident from the debate is that the question of whether tuberculosis was curable or incurable remained unsettled.

The possibility of an antibiotic cure set the stage for a rebalancing of a fragile equation, in which population growth and individual, biological survival were on opposite sides. Genealogical time—a temporality of kinship and reproduction—was pitted against the biographical time of a singular life. The cure of the individual became in this sense a limit to the vitality of the new nation. When it comes to tuberculosis, eugenicist modes of reasoning have largely given way to logics of triage, in which anxieties about limited resources remain central. As we will see, questions of distribution and denial are critical to this conversation in light of growing attention to drug resistance in contemporary India.

29. Rajya Sabha Official Debates, "Resolution Regarding Sterilisation of Adults," 559.

30. The comparison of baldness, night blindness, and tuberculosis also suggests a broad sense of what properly constitutes disease in the first place, although this seems to be largely a rhetorical maneuver.

Gut Punch to the System

Back in 1953, members of the Rajya Sabha debated whether the incurable had become curable. Today the question is just the opposite: has the once curable become incurable? The possibility was raised in a letter addressed to the editor of the journal *Clinical Infectious Disease*.[31] In two pages of polite technical prose, Dr. Zarir Udwadia and his team at Mumbai's P. D. Hinduja Hospital announced that they had identified the first four cases of totally drug-resistant tuberculosis in India. Similar reports had been filed from Italy in 2007 and Iran in 2009, but the news from India seemed to elicit particularly feverish and frantic responses.[32]

In the summer of 2015, I seized the time between teaching terms to travel to India and meet Udwadia in person. A tall and slender man in his mid-fifties with thick black hair and dark-framed glasses, he appeared to tower over the desk in his small office. With crisp and compelling words, he spoke to me of his life and his clinical work.

Udwadia came from a family of prominent Parsi physicians, highly respected not only in Mumbai but across India. Tehemton Udwadia, his uncle, was a gastroenterologist who had pioneered laparoscopic surgery in India. Farokh Udwadia, his father, was a critical care specialist who had saved the life of the actor Amitabh Bachchan after he suffered a life-threatening punch to the gut on the set of the 1984 film *Coolie*.[33] But it was for his grandfather Erach Rustomji that Udwadia reserved his deepest admiration. Rustomji had been a general practitioner who ventured out in the midst of a smallpox outbreak to visit his ailing patients.

Udwadia himself studied medicine at Grant Medical College and the affiliated J. J. Hospital in Mumbai. His subsequent postgraduate training took place in Edinburgh, in the former tuberculosis unit of John Crofton, a well-known proponent of the viability of an antibiotic-based cure for tuberculosis.[34] Yet

31. Udwadia et al., "Totally Drug-Resistant Tuberculosis in India."

32. I would speculate that this has something to do with the fear that India's public health system lacked the means of controlling the spread of infection, as well as concerns about the quality of India's investment climate in light of a potential outbreak. The reports from Italy and Iran can be found here: Migliori et al., "First Tuberculosis Cases in Italy Resistant," 3194; Velayati et al., "Emergence of New Forms."

33. Bachchan's character, the titular coolie, would also recover from near death in the film, a condition induced by multiple gunshot wounds incurred in the final battle scene with the film's antagonist.

34. On Crofton, see Leeming-Latham, "Unravelling the 'Tangled Web.'"

he saw little of the disease during his time in what he described as the "sterile environments of Edinburgh."

Udwadia recounted to me that he first encountered drug resistance upon returning to India in 1991, at Mumbai's Parsee General Hospital. It was there that he met Zubin Irani, an eighteen-year-old man suffering from hemophilia, hepatitis B, and drug-resistant tuberculosis. "We threw everything possible at him," Udwadia told me. Despite his best efforts, Irani died coughing up blood. From *Aah* (1953, Hindi) to *Meghe Dhaka Tara* (1960, Bengali) and *Paalum Pazhamum* (1963, Tamil), and even as recently as *Amar Akbar Anthony* (1977, Hindi), the cough, often bloody, has provided a recognizable symbol of tuberculosis in Indian film. In the wake of resistance, a historical sign of the fatality of tuberculosis—albeit one that has been kept alive at the level of the imagination—seems to be returning. In both symptom and substance, an India after antibiotics might well begin to resemble an India before antibiotics.

"When you returned to India," I asked Udwadia, "did you find that others were already talking about drug resistance?"

"It wasn't seen as a big problem," he responded. "Which makes you wonder, doesn't it? Whether the treatment we've been getting today has in a sense contributed to this. It didn't suddenly just come out of nowhere. It was always there, but it was not recognized. A lot of good came from that simple two-page article: the government *woke up*. People began talking about drug resistance. . . . Maybe no other paper I could have written would have been more useful in terms of actually changing things. I began to believe in the redemptive power of the written word, something that you believe as people who write all the time."

What might it mean to awaken from a dream that has lasted for over five decades? A dream in which the incurable becomes curable and the mass manufacture of swadeshi drugs has seemingly brushed aside concerns about distribution and denial? To awaken is not simply to confront a reversal of fortunes, to find that the cure has come undone: it is to recognize that the romance between humans and antibiotics has been poisoned for some time.

The seed of this romance can be found in the mass manufacture and distribution of antibiotics during World War II.[35] Soldiers who had grown accustomed to dying on the battlefield or in the brothels from infectious diseases were suddenly salvageable, resuscitated and returned to war in an almost industrial fashion. Antibiotics have since become a necessary precondition for a range of

35. Although it is important to note that antibiotic substances have a deep macroevolutionary history in the soil that predates their concentration into clinically effective therapeutics by humans.

medical interventions that inadvertently increase the body's vulnerability to infection, ranging from surgery and chemotherapy to dialysis.

Yet the use of antibiotics in medicine pales in comparison to their much broader application beyond the hospital. Antibiotics have become "infrastructural to the production of many other things: more health, more meat, more fruit, more surgery, less death, more fertility, in everything from *in vitro* embryos cultured in antibiotics to fish farming."[36] If the Pasteurian revolution enacted a reconceptualization of society, one in which microbes became prominent "third parties in all relations," such microbes have increasingly become resistant to human efforts at attenuating their influence.[37]

Pornographic Nomenclature

"What I think really stirred things up is when we gave this moniker of TDR—total drug resistance—to four patients we saw rolling into this very room," Udwadia told me. Before receiving a diagnosis of TDR, these patients had on average been seen by four doctors and received ten different kinds of drugs, often over the course of many years. "These patients were resistant to all the drugs that our lab could test," Udwadia told me. "We just gave it the label."

Evidently rattled by Udwadia's letter, the Indian Ministry of Health dispatched a fact-finding mission to Mumbai. Udwadia told me about their visit, an account that was substantiated at least in part by other nongovernmental observers with whom I spoke. "The initial reaction of the government was less than kind. They actually said, you must retract this article, which, as you know, is the last refuge of a scoundrel," Udwadia said indignantly. "They were saying that we should have run this article through the government before we published it, which was crazy. Who runs a scientific article through the government?" The government, he added, had seized the original patient samples from the lab and threatened to revoke his medical license. "It was almost a Gestapo-type raid."

Were they accusing him of lying? I asked.

Not lying, he clarified. "Their initial claim," he explained, "was that the lab data was unsubstantiated."

The fact-finding team had in fact articulated a whole series of concerns on the grounds of procedure, nomenclature, and national interest. A brief schematic of their claims follows:

36. Landecker, "Antibiotic Resistance and the Biology of History," 20.
37. Latour, *The Pasteurization of France*, 38.

1. The lab at P. D. Hinduja hospital had not been accredited by the government's national tuberculosis program to conduct testing for second-line drug resistance. Therefore, its results were not credible.

2. Many antibiotics lack an accepted, standardized test for susceptibility. Without such tests, it would be technically impossible for anyone to claim that the cases in question were resistant to all first- and second-line drugs.

3. Udwadia's results were premised on drug susceptibility testing in vitro (in the lab) rather than in vivo (in the body of the patient). A drug might not work in a laboratory culture, but it might still work in a human body. The analogy between a microbial sample and the microbe-suffused human body was imprecise.

4. If and when new drugs appeared on the scene, the totality implied in "total drug resistance" would be rendered partial. Drug resistance was a moving target.[38]

5. The category of "total drug resistance" was not used by the WHO.[39] Rather, the WHO and the Government of India used a triumvirate of standardized and well-defined categories: multidrug resistance, extensive drug resistance, and extreme drug resistance.

Classifications of Drug Resistance

Multidrug-resistant (MDR) TB	Bacteria resistant to at least the first-line drugs isoniazid and rifampicin
Extensively drug-resistant (XDR) TB	Bacteria resistant to the first-line drugs isoniazid and rifampicin, as well as any fluoroquinolone and at least one of the injectable second-line drugs amikesan, kanamycin, and capreomycin
Extremely drug-resistant (XXDR) TB	Bacteria resistant to at least all first- and second-line drugs

38. Sullivan and Amor, "What's in a Name?"

39. As Erica Dwyer has argued, such a nomenclatural argument against the use of TDR TB as a term was prefigured by the similar objections of the South African government against the finding and naming of XDR TB in Tugela Ferry in 2006. See Dwyer, "The Making of a Global Health Crisis."

6. The use of the word *total* provokes fear and panic among the potentially sick, rather than promoting the message of testing and cure.

7. Spreading rumors about total drug resistance discourages foreign investment in India.

I asked Udwadia how he responded to such charges.

"People said: 'How can you use such a negative word? The patient has no hope when he's told that it's totally drug resistant.'" Udwadia admitted that, in general, the correlation between lab-based tests and in vivo resistance was not perfect. "But these are all patients that had been receiving these drugs over the years, and there was no doubt that they were truly resistant. We just said that this is the pattern of resistance exactly as we saw it."[40] And in fact, since Udwadia's detection of those first cases in late 2011, the pattern of drug resistance associated with TDR TB has been found in cities across India.

"Call it what you will," Udwadia said in exasperation. "If you don't like the name TDR because of negative connotations, call it extreme drug resistance—double XDR—which sounds pornographic to me."

Yet Udwadia was at pains to clarify that totally drug-resistant tuberculosis was not necessarily incurable. "We didn't say that TDR patients had *totally* no chance of getting cured. It's not that we then put up our hands and say, 'We're not going to treat you.' Some of them are cured"—he quickly corrected himself—"*declared* cured, with a combination of aggressive surgeries and experimental drugs. We will throw everything we have at these patients in a desperate attempt to cure them."

This was an everything-but-the-kitchen-sink approach to treatment: try everything—see what sticks. Udwadia described to me the use of injection ports to deliver the drug Augmentin to drug-resistant patients.[41] Augmentin amps up amoxicillin, an antibiotic developed in the 1960s, through the addition of potassium clavulanate, thereby increasing the drug's efficacy against resistant strains. Drugs like Augmentin are readily available at most pharmacies across India for the asking. Though not part of the standardized regimens used to treat tuberculosis, such drugs have been repackaged into what are referred to as salvage therapies. "If you inject a port into someone, if you chop off as much of their lung as you safely can, you know we've come full circle."

---

40. A resistance pattern is a description, usually in tabular form, of the various drugs to which a particular microbial specimen is found to be resistant.

41. An injection port is a device implanted in the body of a patient that allows for the repeated delivery of medication without multiple injections.

CHAPTER FIVE

The circle was potentially broken with the approval of a new antibiotic by the US Food and Drug Administration (FDA) in 2012. This novel compound was developed by a team of researchers headed by Koen Andries, a microbiologist who had started his career as a veterinarian interested in viruses before developing an interest in tuberculosis in humans. Andries and his team arduously combed through thousands of substances archived in the "compound library" of the Belgian pharmaceutical company Janssen, a subsidiary of the US-based Johnson & Johnson. With time, they came upon the quinolone molecule, the basis of the new drug, initially referred to by the researchers as R207910. The drug, eventually renamed bedaquiline, was the first antibiotic approved to treat tuberculosis since rifampicin in the late 1960s.

What is unique about bedaquiline is that it is unrelated to other antituberculosis drugs. While existing antibiotics used in the treatment of tuberculosis tend to target the cell walls or RNA of disease-causing bacteria to slow their rate of reproduction, bedaquiline cuts off the power supply to bacterial cells by inhibiting the work of ATP synthase, an enzyme involved in metabolic regulation. Bedaquiline not only seems to work faster but also avoids falling prey to the mutations developed in relation to these older drugs.

However, this new drug was immediately mired in controversy related to its fast-tracking through the FDA's approval process. Bedaquiline had been successfully put through only phase 1 and phase 2 trials. While phase 1 trials try to pinpoint the maximum safe dose by experimenting on a small number of research subjects, phase 2 trials focus on whether the drug actually produces the intended biological effect. In those trials, bedaquiline was potentially associated with heart and liver problems, as well as an increased likelihood of death. At the time of writing, phase 3 trials, in which a treatment is tested as part of a large randomized controlled study to see whether it improves on existing options, have yet to be completed for bedaquiline. Advocates of the rapid introduction of antibiotics into clinical use, especially for patients suffering from highly resistant forms of tuberculosis, have applauded the approval of the novel drug. But this fast-tracking has also led to increased vigilance and concern about the potential dangers of using the new antibiotic on a broader scale.

"We were the first in India to use bedaquiline," Udwadia told me. "With promising results." For the patients he saw in his free clinic, Udwadia received bedaquiline directly from the manufacturer. "We've applied for it purely on a compassionate basis. Sometimes they agree to give the drug, and sometimes they don't. But it's a huge ordeal: one of my residents literally fills up hundreds of forms in triplicate and sends them to Johnson & Johnson, the producer. Then, a group of wise men meets across a table somewhere in Europe and decides the fate of a patient who is dying here in India. Which seems a bit harsh to me," he added.

And how was the government incorporating bedaquiline into their national program? I asked Udwadia.

"They're completely at sea about how to introduce it," he told me. "How to responsibly have this drug introduced in the chaotic prevailing circumstances of India."

The Government of India's approach to bedaquiline was soon put to the test in a series of encounters with a girl from the city of Patna. I began to see news reports about the girl's case about a year and a half after meeting Udwadia. In what follows, I've tried to put together a bare framework of events.

The girl from Patna was first diagnosed with tuberculosis in 2011, at the age of thirteen. She started a course of antibiotics prescribed by a private-sector physician, but within a few months, her treatment began failing. In 2013, she went to Patna Medical College, where she was diagnosed with multidrug-resistant tuberculosis (MDR TB). She was put on a different treatment, which also began failing. In November 2014, her family brought her to Delhi's Vallabhbhai Patel Chest Institute. There, she was diagnosed with extensively drug-resistant tuberculosis (XDR TB) and put on yet another antibiotic course. By May 2015—scarcely six months later—this regimen had also proven ineffective.

"In the beginning of a new treatment, she feels better," her father, a civil servant, had explained to the journalist Menaka Rao. "Within a few months, she would start falling sick. She would start getting weak, would be breathless, and would not feel hungry. It was the same story each time."[42] In September 2015, her father took her to the National Institute of Tuberculosis and Respiratory Diseases, popularly known as the Lala Ram Swarup TB Hospital, also in Delhi. There, she was told that her case was incurable and that she should seek some manner of alternative therapy.

Someone eventually told her—it's not certain who—that her case should be reviewed for treatment with bedaquiline. Enough of the drug to treat three hundred patients had been gifted to the Indian Ministry of Health by the US Agency for International Development in 2016. In February of that same year, bedaquiline became available in India through what has been described by the

42. Rao, "A Domicile Rule Is Preventing."

government as a Conditional Access Program located at six hospitals across five Indian cities: Delhi, Mumbai, Chennai, Ahmedabad, and Guwahati.

The Ministry of Health insisted that, in order to be eligible for treatment with bedaquiline, patients needed to be domiciled in one of these cities. They argued that those who lived elsewhere could not be properly supervised. "Bedaquiline is administered for six months and follow-up of patients continue[s] for six more months," said Sunil Khaparde, the deputy director general of the Indian Central TB Division. "Thus, we have to be careful about patients' proximity to the hospitals."[43] To prove domicile, one must provide evidence of continuous residence in a state by presenting an electricity bill or other document. To be enrolled in the bedaquiline treatment program in Delhi, one had to prove domicile for three years.[44] Even though the girl and her father had agreed to stay in Delhi for the duration of the treatment, she was denied the drug.

With the support of an Indian nonprofit called Lawyers Collective, the girl's father went to court. On December 17, 2016, he filed a writ petition before the Delhi High Court demanding that the Ministry of Health disregard his daughter's domicile status and provide her with the drug. Anand Grover, the director of Lawyers Collective, argued that the girl enjoyed a constitutional right to treatment with bedaquiline, and that the hospital, as a public institution, had a constitutional obligation to provide treatment without discriminating on the basis of domicile.[45]

At the end of December 2016, under the direction of the Delhi High Court, a committee formed by doctors from the hospital insisted that the girl provide a sample of sputum for drug susceptibility testing to confirm her eligibility for bedaquiline. In fact, she had already provided a sputum sample in October 2016, which she was later informed had been somehow contaminated. Another sample provided in December 2016 resulted in a false negative result despite her obvious illness.

A new susceptibility test could take up to nine weeks, and her condition was deteriorating rapidly. Grover pointed out to the court that the Revised National TB Control Program's guidelines did not require such testing. On January 2, 2017, Dr. Jennifer Furin, a lecturer at Harvard and advocate for bedaquiline use in Africa and South Asia, offered her expert opinion that there

43. Singh, "Why Aren't More TB Patients Getting the New Life-Saving Drug?"
44. Rao, "Bedaquiline Debate."
45. A right to health has been frequently read into the Indian Constitution, in particular into the right to life enshrined in Article 21.

was no need for drug susceptibility testing, as the girl's medical history demonstrated that she clearly suffered from XDR TB.

As Grover put it, bureaucracy was standing in the way of the girl's constitutional "right to life and health."[46] The attorney for the government, as well as the doctors at the hospital, explained their reasoning in terms of compliance with standardized treatment protocols—but not simply for the sake of rule following.

"We have to follow strict protocols and guidelines in administering the medicine, otherwise it can be disastrous," said Saket Sekri, a lawyer for the National Institute of Tuberculosis and Respiratory Diseases in New Delhi. "If it is used incorrectly without the drug-susceptibility test, patients may develop a resistance to this drug, too." The government further noted that providing bedaquiline without pairing it with other drugs would risk the development of further resistance and waste her last chance at cure. Denial was posited as the basis of a safe and just distribution. Critics responded that not treating her quickly was not only threatening her life but further endangering others around her whom she might inadvertently infect.

On January 20, 2017, the Central TB Division reluctantly agreed to provide the girl with bedaquiline under the supervision of Dr. Udwadia, with whom she had been consulting. What was at stake, it seems, was no longer a eugenicist fear of reproducing frailty, but rather a worry about how best to utilize scarce resources: the question of triage.

Squandered Potential

One way in which to think about the relationship between distribution and triage is via the model of the commons. For many years, economist Ramanan Laxminarayan has been doing just that. Splitting his time between Princeton, New Jersey, Washington, DC, and New Delhi, where he ran his own research group as part of the Public Health Foundation of India, Laxminarayan seemed always on the move.

On a January morning in Princeton, I trudged through the snow and up to the mezzanine level of Guyot Hall to find Laxminarayan sitting in his office, snug in a warm sweater. I sat down across from him and told him about my work, handing him a copy of what would eventually become the third chapter of this book.

46. Lawyers Collective, "Government Agrees to Provide Bedaquiline to Young Girl Living with XDR-TB."

We began to talk about his work and how he had become interested in the question of antibiotic resistance. His training, he told me, had been in environmental economics and natural resources management. "I still think in a very environmental way," he explained. It began with hikes that he took with his PhD advisor. "He would tell me about how penicillin used to work in Vietnam. And how, after the war, it stopped working. It struck us both that penicillin resembled a natural resource."

Laxminarayan pursued this resemblance as part of his doctoral research. The way he thought about things, he explained, was that nonrenewable natural resources like coal had a "certain amount of effectiveness." This effectiveness could be augmented and stretched or quickly spent, but either way, it would eventually come to an end. What he wanted to figure out was how the human species might optimally distribute that effectiveness across time and space.

Laxminarayan thought about antibiotics—their distribution and triage— in terms of the tragedy of the commons. This idea was first articulated in the early nineteenth century by the British political economist William Forster Lloyd in his *Two Lectures on the Checks to Population*. Lloyd was a Malthusian who assumed that the relationship between mouths-to-feed and food-to-feed-them-with was unsustainable given their relative rates of growth. He conceived of this problem through the metaphor of the shared lands grazed by various cattle owners. Each cattle owner, in pursuing what they believed to be their own self-interest, might be tempted into overgrazing the commons, leading to a depletion that would affect not only their neighbors but themselves. Short term benefit for one would lead to long-term loss for all.

The tragedy of the commons was redeployed over a century later by the ecologist Garrett Hardin, who forcefully argued that individuals could not be relied upon to act in the interest of society, which was also in reality to act in their own self-interest. To avoid an inevitable depletion of common resources, Hardin called for greater government regulation.

In his own engagement with the idea of the commons, Laxminarayan takes from both thinkers by arguing that antibiotic efficacy constitutes a limited, nonrenewable resource.[47] As each individual, each country, draws on more for themselves, there remains less for others, and for themselves in the future. The problem of resistance, from his perspective, is even more pressing in countries like India, where disease burdens tend to be higher and newer drugs prohibitively expensive or difficult to access.[48] Laxminarayan was particularly concerned

47. Laxminarayan and Brown, "Economics of Antibiotic Resistance."
48. Okeke et al., "Antimicrobial Resistance in Developing Countries."

about the unregulated use of antibiotics in areas like livestock production, which greatly contributes to the speed at which this common resource is depleted.[49] Although the squandered potential of antibiotics affects some more than others, it nonetheless constitutes for Laxminarayan a tragedy of the commons with consequences for everyone. As is the case with climate change, he argues that an adequate response to antibiotic resistance requires coordinated action.[50] Resistance travels. Neither individuals nor single countries could produce an effective strategy without the involvement of others.

In its response to drug-resistant tuberculosis, Laxminarayan told me that India had only exacerbated this problem by ignoring it. "There's an unwillingness to spend twenty times more on patients. They feel like they could do more for drug-sensitive patients." The logic here—in its founding premises, similar to that put forth by Laxminarayan—was that antibiotics were a limited good. But what they ignore, he noted, was that each untreated drug-resistant patient would infect many more.

Forms of economic, epidemiological, and ecological reason converge in the conception of antibiotic efficacy as a limited natural resource, as potential that has been squandered. Bedaquiline has been vaunted as a miracle drug, potentially a step toward replenishing the antibiotic commons. Back in Mumbai, Udwadia acceded to this description, but only in part.

"We've seen dramatic results in patients who have received it," Udwadia told me. Yet he insisted that bedaquiline was not enough on its own. "When there's a complete no-hoper, with no chance, resistant to everything else except for this one drug, bedaquiline won't work and Johnson & Johnson won't provide it. And when we have tried to use it on such patients, they haven't responded. So it's not as if it's a wonder drug on its own. We need a whole new regime, and we are a long way off from that."

"So the drug in and of itself is not useful . . . ?" I began to ask.

"Any new drug on its own will be doomed to failure and will go the way of previous drugs. Any new drug."

"So for the very worst-off patients, who have such extensive resistance, it's not going to work . . ."

"On its own, no."

What might the future look like if the antibiotic commons cannot be adequately replenished with an entirely new therapeutic armamentarium? In the course of our conversation, Udwadia and I discussed the 1950s Madras Study.

49. Van Boeckel et al., "Global Trends in Antimicrobial Use in Food Animals."
50. Laxminarayan et al., "Antibiotic Resistance."

"One of the big findings," I noted, "was that you no longer need to have patients in a sanatorium, in a bed. The idea was to treat them at home."

"It's coming back to the hospital!" he exclaimed. "So one of my talks begins, 'Back to the Sanatorium Era,' with these patients laid out in a sanatorium in the cold of Switzerland. At times, it feels like that, that there are no drugs left."

"Do you think that we're going to start seeing those debates?" I asked. "About needing beds to treat tuberculosis?"

"It is actually being debated," he told me. "In Mumbai, we know that there is no place for them. There are no hospital beds. We'd need a sanatorium to house these patients."

In speaking of the sanatorium era, I took Udwadia to be referring less to a specific historical moment and more to the experience of life and illness without antibiotics. In this sense, Udwadia's vantage was relentlessly presentist. The past would be judged through the knowledge, tools, and questions of the present. What this left was a past composed of lacks and failures: a lack of drugs and a failure to recognize drug resistance. From the dusk of our romance with antibiotics, what Udwadia imagined—what he feared—was that India could return to such a past.

Final Stop on the Train

If such a past is indeed behind us, its physical remains nevertheless endure into the present. Many sanatoria in India have survived the end of the pre-antibiotic era. Elements of the earlier structure—for example, the open-air architecture—have endured, even if the broader therapeutic philosophy of which they were a part has not. For this reason, I have found that sanatoria are particularly valuable sites for understanding continuities and transitions in therapeutic form in India.

In North Delhi, there is a sanatorium that was built atop railroad tracks. Until 1910, the tracks only extended as far as the main railroad station in South Delhi. In anticipation of the coronation of King George V and Queen Mary as rulers of India, the tracks were built out to the north of the old city where the massive event would be held. The extension of the railroad was meant to facilitate the flow of Indian nobility and British aristocrats who had arrived to witness the spectacle of the Delhi Durbar of 1911.

The appearance of the British royals was marked by an unexpected announcement: in a move meant to capture something of the splendor and authority of the former Mughal rulers for the British monarchy, the capital of India would be shifting from Calcutta to the soon-to-be-constructed city of New Delhi. A foundation stone was laid at the site of the Durbar in an area known as Coronation Park. The site of the future capital was eventually shifted to the southern part of the city, and the newly built railroad station abandoned. It wasn't until twenty-five years later, ostensibly in honor of the Silver Jubilee of George V's coronation, that the station was repurposed into a tuberculosis sanatorium.

Given the colonial government's recalcitrance to spend money on sanatoria in India—at least for the native population—the construction of the Silver Jubilee Hospital was something special. Cottages were erected for patients along the sprawling sanatorium grounds, and vocational training was provided, following the model of the well-known Brompton Sanatorium in London.

After 1947, the sanatorium, like many other government institutions, was rechristened. For an independent India, a sanatorium in honor of colonial rulers would no longer do. The sanatorium was renamed after Rajendra Prasad, the first president of India, but is referred to as Rajan Babu, or RBTB for short. A larger-than-life stone bust of Prasad's head, sporting a pointy Gandhi cap, was installed at the front of the sanatorium, unblinking eyes fixed toward the front entrance.

The sanatorium—now a pulmonary hospital—has retained much of the breadth of its estate, nearly eighty acres of verdure with over one thousand beds, but the surrounding neighborhood has changed considerably. No longer is it a remote outpost, enlivened only by the comings and goings of royalty. The hospital has become accessible to the masses via the Delhi metro.

The metro and the hospital are held apart by one block of lurching traffic and half-finished facades that boast of air-conditioned luxuries in the offing. On a clammy afternoon in July 2015, I arrived at the front of the hospital, where hawker stands offered magazines and egg *paratas* and many other things. My eyes were drawn to a cart with a green plastic lighter hanging from a string, which men used to light cigarettes purchased loose from the man behind the cart.

The former sanatorium had become one of the largest tuberculosis treatment facilities in India, by some accounts the largest. Outside the walls of the hospital, all crunch and pack and traffic. Inside the walls, the formerly salubrious environment of the area had been preserved, a respite from the viscous grip of the city. Patients and their families milled around, many of whom had wrapped masks, *dupattas*, or handkerchiefs around their mouths to prevent the spread of infection.

I walked around the main structure of the hospital, which encircled a delicately manicured yet luxuriant courtyard. The walkway binding the courtyard was composed of interlaced gray and white tiles. On all sides were small rooms with beds, most occupied by patients, some with doors ajar. No one seemed interested in venturing into the scorching midday sun. One woman—a patient on the mend or a caretaker, I couldn't tell—sat in the shade of an awning covering the walkway, held up by sturdy white pillars, a few dogs relaxing next to her. Delhi had just experienced one of the worst heat waves in its history, and you could still feel it.

Trees of various kinds soared above the courtyard, lines of palms accompanying the pathway through the center. Living amid the verdure were life-size mesh creatures—I stopped to ponder the unlikely kangaroo gazing into the distance and a more probable deer grazing peacefully. The quiet was punctuated by birdsong, a high-pitched legato that brought to mind, perhaps a little too on the nose, the tuberculous swan songs of opera. This little piece of nature contained within the hospital walls revealed its inheritance from the therapeutic logic of the sanatorium—that open air, and nature itself, might be cure enough. The endurance of these architectural traces supported the resurrection of certain critical questions about therapy. "Old technologies do not simply wither away with the coming of the new," writes the historian David Arnold, "though materially as well as ideologically they might suffer sustained attack."[51] The sanatorium survives, even if it is no longer quite a sanatorium.

The serenity of the scene was cut short by the harsh whirring of an electric saw wielded by a construction worker laboring on one of the many building projects underway on the vast hospital grounds. These new wards bore less resemblance to the original sanatorium architecture and more to the blocky, compact structures of many contemporary hospitals.

Rajan Babu, I was told, was the final stop for tuberculosis patients across North India.[52] A tertiary care facility within the government system, devoted to particularly intractable cases. As the railway station had once been, so now the hospital greeted its visitors at the end. Final stop: when I first heard these words, I thought, *last resort*. This is where you go when everything else has failed you. But I realized that the final stop was also, often, the last place you go before you die.

51. Arnold, *Everyday Technology*, 6.
52. Udwadia had also described his clinic as the "final port of call" for many of his patients.

After my visit to Rajan Babu, I read the journalist Aman Sethi's account of life in Delhi, *A Free Man*. Early on, he writes of Satish, a man who was like a brother to Sethi's protagonist Ashraf. Satish was sick, and Sethi accompanied him to Rajan Babu for treatment.

At first, Satish seemed to have improved. "They said his TB was in recession, they said he would make it," Sethi tells us.[53]

Two days later, Satish was dead. Sethi learned of Satish's death after arriving at the hospital and finding someone else in Satish's bed.

> Now there is only Singh Sahib in Bed 56. Someone else has taken Satish's place—the same way he took someone else's. Satish's earthen water pot is gone from the bedside table, as is his spare underwear that used to hang on the headrest. His pink plastic bowl and steel tumbler have been replaced by plastic Pepsi bottles (now filled with water), a loaf of Harvest Gold bread, and a solitary boiled egg. The hospital authorities claim to change linen as often as possible but the sheets still bear unwashable traces of their many previous occupants. A man-sized sweat stain darkens the length of the bedsheet—a trailing after-image of countless coughing, sweating, retching bodies.[54]

Traces congeal into stains on bedsheets that might be replaced less often than the bodies that occupy the beds.

Curable disease, indeed.

The Return of a Question

Shortly before noon, I arrived at the antechamber preceding Dr. Anuj Bhatnagar's office, located in a shady corner of the courtyard at Rajan Babu. A group of people sat on a bench waiting patiently. A young man stood with someone who looked to be his father, insistently nudging open the door to Bhatnagar's office to peek in.

Bhatnagar was just finishing up with a patient. Four or five staff members, men and women, swarmed around the large office, answering the phone, updating patients, bringing various documents to Bhatnagar's heavy-looking desk for his signature. The constant motion facilitated an efficient synchrony, supported by the bass hum of the air conditioner.

---

53. Sethi, *A Free Man*, 155.
54. Sethi, *A Free Man*, 157.

This efficiency extended to Bhatnagar as well. He was wearing a blue-checked dress shirt, his sleeves meticulously folded into perfect rectangles that rested near his elbows, his hair neatly cut at right angles. A stethoscope balanced effortlessly around his neck.

In his final year of medical school, Bhatnagar told me, he had been struck by tuberculosis. Like many tuberculosis sufferers before him, he was pushed by this episode of illness toward the study of pulmonary afflictions. After finishing his medical degree, he was posted to Rajan Babu in 1995. Long before the Indian government incorporated treatment for drug-resistant cases into its program, difficult cases of what were described simply as "patient failure" were brought to the hospital, not only from across India but also from surrounding countries.

Starting in 2001, Bhatnagar continued, he began treating these patients himself. In the process, he developed a deep well of experience, as well as a set of questions about what it takes to treat drug-resistant tuberculosis. One such question had to do with whether drug-resistant patients need to be treated as inpatients. A year before we met, Bhatnagar had coauthored a paper in the *Indian Journal of Tuberculosis* that explored whether it was worth hospitalizing drug-resistant patients, or whether they might be treated at home like their nonresistant counterparts.[55] This study raised a question that had been asked—and powerfully answered—over fifty years earlier in the previously mentioned antibiotic study that took place in Madras, which purportedly signaled the death knell of sanatoria the world over.

The decades following the Madras Study have witnessed the consolidation of an outpatient-based antibiotic treatment protocol at a global level, or at least for those poorer parts of the globe. As discussed in chapter 4, the protocol known as DOTS refers to "directly observed treatment, short-course." To follow DOTS is to require patients to visit treatment providers—usually clinics, but in more rural areas a local nurse or other authorized individual—on a regular basis. At least in theory, patients are made to swallow tablets while being watched, so as to ensure that the regimen is strictly followed. The philosophy of DOTS stands on the observation that patients won't take their medications regularly and completely unless closely monitored. Such a view represents either an acute understanding of human psychology and behavior or a deep distrust of more often than not poor, nonwhite patients.[56] Fundamentally,

55. Bharty et al., "Initiation of MDR TB Treatment."
56. Harper, "Anthropology, DOTS, and Understanding Tuberculosis Control."

DOTS is intended to be a highly standardized, economized, and scalable mode of therapeutic distribution and denial.

The study coauthored by Bhatnagar seemed to resurrect precisely the same question that had been dealt with by the Madras Study: whether antibiotics were sufficient, or whether hospital admission was a necessary part of treating tuberculosis.

After the Madras Study, why was this question being reopened, I asked him.

"Despite the fact that the sanatorium era is over"—Bhatnagar corrected himself—"or *deemed* to be over, the fact is that a huge group of patients require admission, for a number of issues: for dietary issues, social issues, stigma. We find patients who are dumped here, and they have no place to go. Even after they are cured, they are still *dumped* by their families."

The lives of so-called dumped women are the subject of Sarah Pinto's ethnography of madness and psychiatry in North India. Nearly a half century after the formal deinstitutionalization of psychiatry in India, many women are still abandoned, it seems, to these very institutions. Their psychic conditions, but also their family situations, often make it difficult for them to receive care at home. Within a discourse organized around "dumping," these women are framed as crazy divorcées who represent burdens to their families, both natal and affinal. Yet, in the course of her fieldwork, Pinto found that this all-too-easy way of describing these women frequently covered over the complex interplay of their interests and desires, as well as the difficult legal and affective relations that structured and dissolved their family lives. To speak of dumping and abandonment is to, at least in part, miss the point.[57]

In Rajan Babu, admission (ideally) stands for a whole host of potentially therapeutic interventions—not simply medications but bed rest, nutrition, monitoring, and escape from the tension of everyday life. This is not quite the same as being dumped. "Once the patient started having a proper diet, they used to say, 'Let us stay here!'" Bhatnagar told me. The desire to stay, while likely overstated, nonetheless speaks to the potential desirability of inpatient life.

In recent years, Bhatnagar informed me, the admission rates had been quite high. "Patients are having complications from medicines, or from the more severe forms of tuberculosis." He had tried, he said, to warn government officials about the national program. "DOTS will either cure a TB patient or turn him into an MDR case." And that, he said, is "ultimately what has happened."

The Indian government, aligned with international protocols around DOTS, has tried to treat its way out of an epidemic. Many have been cured, some cured

57. Pinto, *Daughters of Parvati*.

repeatedly, and many have died after being cured. But according to a growing number of critics, the government's mode of distributing drugs had arguably succeeded in fortifying bacteria against those very drugs. Bhatnagar advocated for a movement away from DOTS, a program that he saw as having outlived its usefulness:

> If you ask me, DOTS is a very good *theoretical* program. But *practically*, on the ground, you're putting off a lot of patients by insisting that they have to come to a DOTS center for me to watch them swallow a dose. Suppose I am a daily wage earner. I work every day to earn. *Theoretically*, a DOTS center is walking distance from a patient's house. *Practically*, it is never so. I've heard a lot of patients saying, "Sir, I spend forty rupees going and forty rupees coming back. You say you're giving me medicines free of cost, but I'm spending eighty rupees in one day. When I only earn one hundred rupees, how will I feed my family?"

Bhatnagar's observations correlated well with what I had also heard from many patients—that treatment was an arduous, costly, and time-consuming affair. He instead advocated for treatment supervised by family members, neighbors, and others who lived within close proximity of the patient.

"I have written about MDR TB patients being hospitalized, and I've said that, yes, you hospitalize them for seven days, but don't force them to come to the DOTS center every day. They'll be spreading TB to the community. Make the patient's family member a [DOTS] provider, so that the patient is not traveling every day, and he's not coughing around."

Due to the side effects induced by these anti-TB drugs, Bhatnagar and his colleagues concluded that many drug-resistant patients would benefit from hospitalization, at least during the early days of their treatment. Yet, as the number of such cases rises, the economics and availability of hospital beds have once again become a concern, as was the case in the years leading up to the Madras Study. The transition from sanatorium care to home-based antibiotic treatment should have freed up beds, or rendered them redundant. But according to Bhatnagar, Rajan Babu continues to host over ten thousand inpatients each year.[58]

"Right now," Bhatnagar told me, "if you asked me how many XDR patients there are in the hospital—*confirmed* cases of XDR—I'd say around twenty-five. Unfortunately, with XDR, yes, we're back to the same question. For XDR, I

---

58. Not all of the patients at the hospital had been diagnosed with tuberculosis. Many suffered from a variety of other pulmonary conditions.

would recommend hospitalization. We have XDR patients whom we kept for two years, and now they're negative."

"Would you say that they're cured, then? Would you use the term *cure*?" I asked.

"I would use the term *cure*," he told me.

"But oftentimes," I insisted, "there's a hesitance to use the term *cure*, because there's a concern about relapse or reinfection. Even with the studies in Madras, it took researchers years after completing the study to confidently say that this is a cure."

"It's a standard policy at this institution, with any drug-resistant patient: say a patient completes the treatment today. You make sure that follow-up cultures are sent every three months for the next two years before we finally say that, yes, you are fine." For Bhatnagar, the curable had not quite yet become incurable.

Swiss Mantras

One future that Bhatnagar did not anticipate was eradication.

I asked him about what was then a recent draft document circulated by the international STOP TB initiative that spoke, once again, of the possibility of eradication—a hope that had been articulated in the 1950s in the wake of the development of the first generation of TB antibiotics.

Bhatnagar lightly chided me for my question. "Do you remember the history of the development of the BCG vaccine?" Developed in the early decades of the twentieth century and rolled out in one of the largest vaccination campaigns in history, the Bacillus Calmette-Guérin (BCG) vaccine has been found to offer minimal protection against tuberculosis.[59]

"Now I will develop a vaccine and TB will be eradicated," Bhatnagar said, playfully mocking his scientific forebears.

"BCG, antibiotics," I added.

"There's always been this talk," he responded. "BCG, streptomycin, then rifampicin, then fluoroquinolone," he said, rehearsing generations of therapeutic ambition. "This talk continues."

Historically, eradication campaigns have depended on the production and distribution of effective vaccines. Whereas cure has been understood to operate

---

59. The BCG vaccine played an important role in post–World War II development campaigns in India. See Brimnes, "Vikings against Tuberculosis"; Brimnes, "BCG Vaccination and WHO's Global Strategy."

at the level of the individual, eradication depends upon the aggregation of individual interventions in order to produce a population-level effect that is greater than the sum of its parts. In fact, eradication should render the question of cure irrelevant. Yet, through the promissory force of antibiotics, cure and eradication were sutured together in the therapeutic imagination.[60]

I continued to push. "But do you see an end point? Do you see something like eradication ever happening?"

"To be very frank," he said, "no.

"We are still," he reminded me, "a significant number of years away from developing a vaccine. We are still a significant time away from developing a prophylactic medicine. We are still unable to test a regimen that is short enough for compliance to improve. If someone says, 'This is a magic bullet,' I'm sorry, but I would not accept that."

Back in Mumbai, I posed the same question about eradication to Dr. Udwadia.

"I think eradication is a catchy global mantra that sounds good in Geneva," he said, "where they never see any TB anyway. It's a mantra that doesn't translate to the real world."

Yet dreams of eradication continue to circulate in India alongside the promise of cure. In December 2014, at a press event in Mumbai, the previously gut-punched actor Amitabh Bachchan revealed that he had been treated for tuberculosis during the filming of his popular quiz show, *Kaun Banega Crorepati*. "I used to wake up feeling weak," he said. "Today, I am standing in front of you completely cured."[61]

In his new role as brand ambassador for India's anti-TB campaign, Bachchan underscored the affinity between cure and eradication. Tuberculosis, he explained, is a "curable disease and we must spare no effort to take our country towards the target of zero TB deaths."

Bachchan went on to contrast what he perceived to be the therapeutic poverty of the pre-antibiotic past with the resplendent efficacy of the present. "Earlier, TB patients used to be sent to sanatoria," he explained. "Nowadays

60. On earlier prophecies that declared the eradication of tuberculosis inevitable with the development of antibiotics, see Bryder, Condrau, and Worboys, "Tuberculosis and Its Histories." See also McMillen's critique of what he describes as a "caricature of the era," one that emphasizes the optimistic discourse of eradication while underplaying the more sober and pragmatic concern with on-the-ground obstacles that made eradication appear to many tuberculosis workers as highly unlikely. McMillen, *Discovering Tuberculosis*, 69.

61. Debroy, "I Had TB in 2000."

there are good medicines. There is nothing more that you need to do apart from taking medicines on time. Today, modern diagnostic tools and advanced treatment regimens can diagnose and *cure patients completely.*" As the line between the pre-antibiotic era and the present blurs, Bachchan's speech represents a recommitment to the promise of cure.

Bachchan went on to star in two television advertisements produced by the marketing masters at Ogilvy & Mather, the communications firm behind the "Incredible India" campaign. In one ad, this former "angry young man" of Bollywood assumes the role of an auto driver who hijacks a man and woman on their way to the movies, taking them instead to the hospital. She has been coughing for over two weeks; she might have TB, he warns. But not to worry: with treatment, she too can be cured. These short clips conclude with the pithy tagline "TB harega, desh jeethega"—tuberculosis will lose; the country will win. At stake in the promise of cure, it seems, is nothing less than the fate of the Indian nation.

But, as Udwadia had put it, perhaps this is just another catchy mantra. Certainly, the slogan is meant to galvanize the nation and inspire faith in the promise of cure. Yet we might wonder whether the promise of cure threatens to restore us to our sleep, to a dreamworld in which sanatoria and bloody coughs remain artifacts of a long-forgotten past and antibiotics retain their efficacy.

The Angel Trapped in Stone

In the dusk of the antibiotic dream, what might it mean to return to the sanatorium era? Both Udwadia and Bhatnagar spoke to me about the awakening of slumbering potentialities, of forms of dying (coughing blood) and modes of therapeutic practice (sanatorium admission) that had by and large been consigned to the past with the development of antibiotics. At the end-of-days of the antibiotic era, remnants of the past are being revived in response to the threat of resistance.

In *The Writing of the Disaster*, Maurice Blanchot offers us a way of beginning to grasp this play of time and threat:

> It is impossible to say: the infiniteness of the threat has in some way broken every limit. We are on the edge of the disaster without being able to situate it in the future: it is rather always already past, and yet we are on the edge or under the threat, all formulations which would imply the future—that which is yet to come—if the disaster were not that which does not come,

that which has to put a stop to every arrival. To think the disaster (if this is possible, and it is not possible inasmuch as we suspect that the disaster is thought) is to have no longer any future in which to think it.[62]

In the most extreme of eschatological visions, a critical threshold has been transgressed, beyond which there is no return. There is no future to prepare for, because the disaster has already arrived, has already been with us.[63] Such visions diagnose a break with the techno-optimistic past inaugurated during the Nehruvian era of high science and antibiotic triumph, although not necessarily a break with technology itself. Although antibiotics might still have a role to play, they are no longer sufficient.[64]

For those who hew to a faith in reasoned collective human action, the near future still leaves room for recalibration. The relation between human and microbe might once again be set right. There are many in India, and elsewhere, who believe that the time of antibiotics has not come to an end. The limit may have been reached, but it has not (yet) been exceeded.

Those who hold optimistic visions of the near future call for the intensification of already-existing strategies: increased surveillance and self-governance of clinicians and patients, as well as the development of ever-newer antibiotics. But such visions also depend on the production and use of new technologies of governance that are intimately tied to the technocratic aspirations of contemporary India. Rather than a rupture with the past, these ways of looking to the future are suffused by an intensification of a techno-optimistic strain in Indian political thought that can be traced from Nehru to Modi.

62. Blanchot, *The Writing of the Disaster*, 2.

63. Such a relationship to time might be productively compared to what Andrew Lakoff has described in terms of preparedness: an approach to an uncertain future organized around diverse forms of threat to collective life. For Lakoff, the threat is always already inscribed into the material and cognitive conditions of the present. For those extreme eschatologists I describe, the threat has in a real sense already been realized. See Lakoff, "Techniques of Preparedness."

64. This might be understood as a kind of technological pessimism, although in a very different way than that described by David Arnold for late nineteenth- to early twentieth-century India. For Arnold, such pessimism contains within it two somewhat different perspectives. In the first, Indians, and especially poor, uneducated Indians, were unsuited for, incapable of, or uninterested in making use of modern technology nor in need of it. In the second, Indians had no need of such technologies, as they had developed their own ways of doing things that worked perfectly well and perhaps even better in light of local conditions. Arnold, *Everyday Technology*.

I encountered such optimism in a meeting with Sandeep Ahuja, a former officer in the Indian Administrative Service (IAS) whom I met in his Delhi office in late June 2015. In our conversation, he stressed the importance of conveying to the public that tuberculosis was not a death sentence.

"You mentioned that TB is treatable," I said to him. "That has been an important message since the seventies, maybe even earlier. The government has been saying TB is curable. Now, with drug resistance, even if it is treatable, is it curable? Are the drugs available? Like bedaquiline? Have you had to grapple with these kinds of things—?" I began to ask.

Ahuja stopped me. "With Operation ASHA, you're not seeing the way that TB treatment was historically delivered. You're probably seeing the way the future is going to be." He paused.

"Anyone for tea? Bharat? I'm tired of sitting. Allow me to stand. You don't mind, right?"

"No, I don't mind."

Sandeep Ahuja stood up and stretched his legs. An animated man with thinning hair parted neatly to the left and thick, double-bridged glasses, Ahuja looked every bit the former government officer that he was. For fifteen years, he had worked in the Indian Revenue Service and the Ministry of Finance.

But at the age of forty-two, Ahuja voluntarily retired from the IAS to pursue a master's degree in public policy at the University of Chicago's Harris School. On his return to India, Ahuja wanted to do something bigger. He teamed up with Dr. Shelly Batra, an OB-GYN, and searched for a cause.

"Polio was done. AIDS already had huge organizations. Malaria was more a sanitation problem," he told me. "TB, nobody bothered. Nobody cared." Ahuja and Batra founded Operation ASHA in order to figure out how to remedy what he perceived to be a shortcoming in the distribution of treatment for tuberculosis patients in India. Ahuja was careful not to blame the national tuberculosis treatment program. Nonetheless, he saw a limit to what the government was capable of when it came to the implementation of the DOTS protocol in India.

"There are gaps at every level," he told me. "It was a very senior officer from a donor agency that said, 'But DOTS is not done in India.' That's a fact. That's an unfiltered fact. DOTS may be a great regimen on paper. But in a country with 44 percent staff absenteeism, is DOTS the right regimen?"

"That's a very controversial claim, isn't it?" I asked. "Most people would say DOTS is the way to go."

"The World Health Organization has said it's the way to go. And every country has followed. But if DOTS was so good, there should be no cases of MDR. Forget about XDR and XXDR. Are we going to shut our eyes to the reality? We are only going to hurt ourselves by doing that. DOTS—as it has been envisaged—has failed in more ways than one. And one critical reason is: there's just not enough staff. And even staff that are posted find it impossible to attend office every time they're supposed to."[65]

I asked him, then, whether the solution was to find newer, more efficient drugs, or perhaps a vaccine.

"For TB, new drugs are definitely needed. But the fact remains, even after you have all that, why do millions of kids still die? You can develop all of this, and that's great. However, the world is blind to an important fact, something that even the drug companies have failed to do. Number one: develop the distribution network that Coke has. Go to the farthest hamlet and you'll find Coke. You will not find Tylenol."[66]

For Ahuja, the problem of distribution had to do with both the means and specificity of distribution. How could you make sure that the right person gets the right drugs throughout the course of their treatment?

"The poor do not—cannot—spell their names consistently. Mohinder, Mahinder, Mahindra: it's the same name. It's spelled differently. It's spelled in three different ways even by the educated in this country. Imagine in how many ways it will be spelled by people with low literacy levels. You cannot use names in this country or in most of Africa."[67]

Working with Microsoft Corporation, Operation ASHA developed a biometric-based software for tracking treatment, a system that they refer to as eCompliance. "There's no way to fudge a fingerprint," Ahuja told me. "Technology reduces time and mistakes." Mohinder, Mahinder, and Mahindra would become "de-duplicated."[68] Three names reduced to one fingerprint.

According to Ahuja, Operation ASHA did not replace DOTS, but rather augmented it. To think again in terms of Laxminarayan's model of the commons, the efficacy of antibiotics might be drawn out through a tinkering with their means of distribution. Each dose of medication delivered by Operation

---

65. According to a widely cited 2011 study by Muralidharan et al. based on direct observation of public clinics across nineteen states in India, health workers are absent, on average, 39 percent of the time. Doctors specifically are absent 43 percent of the time. Muralidharan et al., "Is There a Doctor in the House?"

66. This is likely hyperbole, given that Tylenol, or rather generic forms of paracetamol, are widely available across India. Ahuja's emphasis on distribution over novel drugs resonates with the capacious vision of innovation articulated by Nora Engel in her own work on tuberculosis control in India. See Engel, *Tuberculosis in India*.

67. See Das and Copeman, "Introduction."

68. Cohen, "Duplicate, Leak, Deity."

ASHA was verified through a time-stamped fingerprint scan. By this means, treatment could not be delivered all at once and adherence was confirmed.

This technology, for Ahuja, was neither new nor complicated. "It's intuitive," he explained. "It's developed from a low-literacy point of view. There's plenty of technology for the educated. This is technology for the poor." What Ahuja meant was not simply that the technology could help the poor, but that it could be used effectively by the poor, even those who are illiterate. Rather than hiring new staff to distribute these drugs, or depending upon existing clinics, Ahuja told me, Operation ASHA partnered with "local health workers or telephone booths, a pharmacy, a temple, a mosque, and there's one such center every five to ten kilometers, at key entrances to slums, so that patients routinely walk in front of them."

Ahuja's approach resonated with the perspective of the early twentieth-century Indian nationalist Margaret Noble, better known as Sister Nivedita. According to Nivedita, Indians needed to take control of the networks of distribution in the country in order for swadeshi articles to reach the rural poor. "The small shops—which are the real distributing centres in every city—have been so long in the hands of the foreign trade that they require to be captured now."[69]

Working with already existing institutions further bypassed the issue of absenteeism. "STD booths and phone booths open at six in the morning," Ahuja informed me. "The government will not possibly open their centers from six and find enough budget from that, and also ensure that the staff comes.

"Going back to Michelangelo: you know what he said?" Ahuja asked me suddenly. "He said, 'When I see a block of stone, I see the angel chained inside. And all I do is free that angel from the stone.' And that's all. So this model was always there. All these angels who were working in the field. All these shopkeepers, all these health workers, they were already there. They just needed to be *collected* in a certain way, and that's all we did. This is intuitive, and that is why it's going to succeed."

Ahuja's figuration of the future as already contained in the present allowed him to reject the idea that we had already transgressed the limit of the antibiotic era. In rejecting this limit, Ahuja also rejected a vision of the future that resembled the past, in the form of the sanatorium era. The future he instead imagined would be assembled from the peoples and technologies of the present. Here, we might turn to the historian of technology Carolyn Marvin. In her book about the historicity of technology, she writes, "People often imagine

69. Arnold, *Everyday Technology*, 100.

that, like Michelangelo chipping away at the block of marble, new technologies will make the world more nearly what it was meant to be all along."[70] There is a serious optimism underlying this vision, but one that differs from the technological optimism of figures like Rokeya Hussain and Megnad Saha in that it seems to leave social conditions untouched.[71] The poor would remain poor, the illiterate illiterate. To manage the problem of distribution, the poor would instead be reorganized—collected, to use Ahuja's word. Within such a vision, to cure tuberculosis would not be to cure the world's ills.[72]

70. Marvin, *When Old Technologies Were New*, 235.

71. Hussain is perhaps best known for writing *Sultana's Dream*, a work of science fiction set in a feminist utopia. Saha was an astrophysicist and a parliamentarian, a proponent of India's industrialization and the primary architect of river planning in the country. Arnold, *Everyday Technology*, 39.

72. It might be said, if somewhat cynically, that what Ahuja and others were advocating for was the further abandonment of the principles of social or political medicine, a form of intervention that addressed causal factors located in socioeconomic and political issues rather than simply attending to the narrow biological conditions of individual bodies. I suspect that Ahuja would more likely see himself as a techno-pragmatist.

India after Antibiotics

People have always been good at imagining the end of the world, which is much easier to picture than the strange sidelong paths of change in a world without end.

—Rebecca Solnit, *Hope in the Dark*

To Each Generation Its Miracle

As I was completing the revisions to this book, the US Food and Drug Administration (FDA) approved the use of pretomanid for the treatment of highly drug-resistant strains of tuberculosis in the lungs. This new anti-TB drug was the first to be developed by a not-for-profit organization, the Global Alliance for TB Drug Development. News of the drug's approval spread through the most grandiose of headlines: "Scientists Discover New Cure for the Deadliest Strains of Tuberculosis"; "One Small Drug, One Giant Leap for Tuberculosis Treatment"; "This Antibiotic Breakthrough Could Save Thousands of Lives a Year."

I couldn't help but think: we've been here before. When it comes to tuberculosis, it can seem as if each generation has its miracle cure, its particular romance with medicine, its specific ending. And each generation is condemned to witness its cure arrive at its limits, its romance wither. Pretomanid was the first antituberculosis drug to be approved by the FDA since bedaquiline in 2012, which was itself the first such drug to be approved in over forty years.[1] The

1. A third recently discovered drug, delamanid, has yet to receive FDA sanction, but has been approved for use in Japan, South Korea, and Europe.

approval of pretomanid was based on limited trials, small study sizes, and extremely short follow-up periods. This fast-tracking was made possible by the use of a special approval pathway for drugs that treat "serious or life-threatening infections in a limited population of patients with unmet need," a pathway created by the US Congress through its enactment of the 21st Century Cures Act in 2016.[2] As drug-resistant strains of tuberculosis spread, and as the existing pharmaceutical armamentarium proves increasingly ineffective, the urgent need for such drugs can seem painfully obvious.

Yet if each generation has had its miracle cure, they are miracles that have responded to different sets of problems. So in a sense, we have not been here before. The first wave of antituberculosis drugs like streptomycin promised to bring cure to the masses, solving the problems of scale, economy, and efficacy posed by the sanatorium. As we've seen, this particular solution was worked out (at least in part) in 1950s Madras, as an international team of scientists undertook a study seeking to demonstrate that antibiotics were just as effective when taken at home as when taken in a hospital or sanatorium. The fact that these drugs seemed to work among the poorest of the poor was taken as proof that they would work on anyone, anywhere, and that the drugs themselves were all you needed to produce cure. It was a cure almost panacean in its operation, one that was supposed to, at least in theory, cure everyone (at least everyone with tuberculosis)—regardless of race, class, geography, or gender.

Over half a century later, roughly one in four people on the planet carries the bacteria that cause tuberculosis. Pretomanid is but the latest cure for a condition that has witnessed no end of cures. The repetition of therapeutic promise is always a repetition with a difference; history is never so pendular as it might appear. A world of waning antibiotic efficacy presents different kinds of problems than a world before the development of clinically potent antibiotics. To paraphrase the words of Susan Buck-Morss, how might we come to terms with the mass dreamworld promised by antibiotic cure at the moment of its passing—at a moment when dreamworld potentially turns to catastrophe?[3]

Pretomanid is a response to a situation of deepening and widening drug resistance. Certainly, concerns about efficacy remain central, but they are no longer framed in relation to the sanatorium. Any new miracle cure must be effective against drug-resistant strains of tuberculosis, and must find new biological targets and therapeutic synergies to secure that efficacy. Taken alone, pretomanid is no cure, as it is thought to kill primarily actively replicating bacteria. Its

2. US Food and Drug Administration, "FDA Approves New Drug."
3. Buck-Morss, *Dreamworld and Catastrophe.*

efficacy comes from its combination with two other drugs—for now, beda-quiline and linezolid. On its own, the drug would more likely encourage drug resistance than overcome it.

Fear of resistance, alongside the high cost of new drugs, resurrects addi-tional concerns about scale and economy. To whom should the drug be distrib-uted, along what criteria, and by what channels? The license to manufacture the new drug has been granted to the commercial pharmaceutical manufac-turer Mylan. The estimated price for a six-month treatment course of the drug is $364, while the lowest global price for the combination treatment is esti-mated to be $1,040. Médecins Sans Frontières has called for Mylan and the Global Alliance for TB to bring the total price of treatment down below $500, arguing that anything higher would dramatically curtail treatment access for those who need it.[4] How the pragmatics of triage and the prerogatives of capi-tal might be reconciled with the ethic of access may never be answered once and for all. And in fact, such questions never remain quite the same questions. If the first generation of antibiotic cures was meant to overcome the limits imposed by the high cost and small scale of sanatorium therapy by providing mass treatment on the cheap, the latest generation of antibiotics counters the limits produced by this mass scale-up by instead scaling selectively. Treatment for some, but not the masses.

Moreover, the trials of the pretomanid-based combination exhibited a cure rate of 89 percent. The concept of "cure rate," as we've seen, conceals within it the tension between curability and incurability. This new cure is not necessarily a cure for everyone. Optimistically, we might interpret that un-cured 11 percent not as incurable but as not yet cured. This *yet* concatenates both the promise of cure and its eventual fulfillment. The allure of cure is orga-nized around its figuration as a definitive end point: the termination of illness, suffering, and treatment. This possibility of cure as ending underwrites both medical research and intervention, flickering in the distance as its ultimate aim and redemption. For most of us, cure is something that we want, or it is something that we are told that we should want.[5] This is critical to the power-ful discourse of cure, and to maintaining our deep investment in cure.

4. Médecins Sans Frontières, "Price Announced for New Lifesaving TB Drug."
5. This desire for cure extends far beyond tuberculosis, beyond infectious disease, and beyond potentially terminal conditions. Over the course of the twentieth century, for example, slouching became increasingly medicalized in the United States, in part due to the "unswerving belief that every condition—deadly or not—can and should be cured." This belief was tied to the rise of medical specialization and the proliferation

As we've seen, however, cure can unravel, repeatedly coming up against its limits. This is not a world at the end, nor a world without end, but a world with an infinity of ends. One can be cured, and then cured again. Ending follows ending. If we reject the promise of cure—of an ending that is final—then a cure that arrives at its limits has not failed. This is not a rejection of cure altogether, but rather an opening in which we might ask whether cure can be something other than a promise. In rejecting the promise of cure, we open a space for ethical and political reflection on a world not as it ends, once and for all, nor as it tirelessly persists, but rather as it comes crashing down around us again and again.

Rather than offering a definitive theory of cure, my aim in this book has been to demonstrate a method for approaching cure through the figure of the limit: a figure that turns our attention to how cure comes undone, how one might become uncured and require cure again, and how the curable might become, once again, incurable, but in an entirely different way than before. The problem of cure is not limited to tuberculosis, nor to infectious diseases. As we increasingly move beyond mass treatment and toward personalized, genomic, and regenerative medicines, it becomes all the more important to focus on limits. How, for example, might we think about cures that are made to order, organized around the biology of a singular body rather than a generic biological condition shared across many bodies—a cure that is unrepeatable, a cure for one? When a condition is so rare that a randomized controlled trial is impossible, how might its cure be tested, its efficacy determined? How might CRISPR and other forms of therapeutic technology recalibrate the relationship between inside and outside, body and environment? Regenerative medicine in particular, with its focus on the exhaustion and replenishment of the body, presents us with a form of cure that is honest about its limits: one that knows that the body will endlessly fail, will endlessly require cure after cure. New forms of therapeutic intervention, in other words, will not do away with the limits of cure but reveal them anew.

Crumbling Image, Misplaced Grave

Let me conclude, finally, where I began, by returning to a figure from the first chapter, who has haunted this project since its inception: David Chowry Muthu, the Indian doctor who made a career in England and returned to the country of his birth to establish a sanatorium. Unlike Koch, Muthu eluded me

---

of new medical technologies and surgeries, as well as to a desire for aesthetic normalization. Linker, "A Dangerous Curve," 607.

Figure E.1. David Chowry Muthu. Photo courtesy of Cyrus and Shelly Kapadia. Date unknown.

for some time. I finally found a photograph of him, not in his sanatorium, and not even in the city of his birth, but in a crumbling issue of the journal *National Review* housed in a library in Kolkata, over 1,700 kilometers away (some years later, with the help of his descendants scattered across the United States, Britain, and India, I would find many more, such as figure E.1).

For some time, the end of Muthu's story remained a mystery to me. The part that I knew was that, in July 1928, just a few months after he had inaugurated his sanatorium at Tambaram, Muthu's wife Margaret passed away back in England. He rushed back, effectively abandoning his work at the sanatorium. In 1930, Muthu requested that the Madras government purchase his sanatorium outright so that he could make his return to Britain permanent. Although the general weight of colonial government opinion was against involvement in the expensive affairs of sanatoria, the Madras government eventually took over the operation of Tambaram in 1937.[6]

6. Paul, "Co-operation," 480.

In the last decade of his life, Muthu began to more explicitly elaborate on the metaphysical underpinnings of his approach to medicine. Turning to matters more historical and spiritual in nature, he published a book on the antiquity of Indian medicine and penned an essay on the relationship between science and religion. These late writings seemed to have bought Muthu a measure of international spotlight. In 1930, his books had just gone into print in the United States. In September of that year, at the age of sixty-six, Muthu boarded the steamship *Berengaria* in Southampton headed to New York City for a speaking tour. He seems to have been something of a sensation among various quasi-esoteric organizations, such as the Threefold Group and the Charaka Club, delivering lectures on topics ranging from the history of surgery and medicine in ancient India to Gandhi's health, the freedom movement, and the status of Indian women.[7] Until his death, questions of spirituality and philosophy, history and biology remained for Muthu inseparable from his particular brand of vitalist thought. As his vision for the world reverberated through esoteric circles, his influence in the mainstream of medicine faded away.[8]

On returning from America to England, Muthu married his second wife, Winifred E. Cox. Cox was thirteen years his junior and had likely been employed as a nurse at one of his sanatoria. In October 1936, Muthu and Cox departed from Liverpool on the steamship *California*, headed to Bombay. At the time of his departure, Muthu was seventy-two years old. The ship's records indicate that he had intended to return to England, but I found no further trace of him.

Many years into the research for this book, a descendent of Muthu suggested to me that I look in Bangalore, where one of his daughters had lived. There, I came upon church records that revealed that Muthu had died from uremia at the age of seventy-five. On May 8, 1940, his body was buried in the cemetery of St. Andrew's in Bangalore.[9] I spent a day combing the cemetery grounds for his plot, hoping in part to learn something new from the grave

7. Founded in 1899 as the Medico-Historical Club by a group of five physicians interested in grappling with the aesthetics and history of medicine, the group renamed itself the Charaka Club in 1900. The Threefold Group was composed of anthroposophists who followed the teaching of Rudolph Steiner. Unfortunately, I was unable to locate transcriptions or notes related to Muthu's speeches in the United States.

8. As the historian Katherine Ott has argued, "Vitalist principles, if couched in theology and metaphysics, could not survive within medicine proper." Ott, *Fevered Lives*, 34.

9. Burial returns accessed by the generosity of St. Andrew's Church, Church of Scotland, Bangalore, India.

marker but mostly to finish what I had started so many years before. But the accumulation of bodies in the intervening years had led the groundskeepers to bury the newly dead in the space between existing plots, disordering their system for keeping track of bodies. Finding his gravestone proved an impossible task. A groundskeeper promised me that he'd locate the gravestone and contact me, but I never heard from him again. If there are endings, they are rarely so complete as we might like.

How do you end a story about the fantasy of endings? But maybe this is the wrong way to pose the question. After all, as with cures, there are always endings—there is no end to endings. In the absence of a grave marker, Tambaram Sanatorium remains the only physical remnant of Muthu's legacy in India. In 1993, it became the first public facility in India to admit HIV-positive patients. Separate wards have been dedicated to patients with HIV, as well to those harboring TB-HIV coinfections and various forms of multiple drug-resistant tuberculosis. In the turn to chemotherapeutics, the vitalist foundations of Tambaram have been decisively abandoned. It remains a sanatorium only in name. Nevertheless, Muthu's curative vision remains alive, if only as a potentiality, as we face the possibility of an India, and a world, after antibiotics.

ACKNOWLEDGMENTS

Writing a book like this one begins long before you actually begin the research. For me, it began with Liisa Malkki, the first person to teach me anthropology. She stunned me with the revelation that all that we take as given had first been made, and could therefore be made otherwise. Responsibility for my training was passed on to her former classmate, Lawrence Cohen, when I began my PhD at UC Berkeley. Lawrence taught me that curiosity demands its own rigor; his endless generosity is a gift I will never be able to repay. I also had the good fortune of learning from Stefania Pandolfo, whose irrepressibly singular approach to both anthropology and pedagogy inspired me to turn to other traditions not just as objects of analysis but as sources of insight. My thanks to Liu Xin and Pheng Cheah, who taught me to read the canon anew in ways that have proved enduringly generative for my work. While at Berkeley, I also had the honor to study with Saba Mahmood, who pushed me to articulate my ideas with a confidence I often lacked, while offering me kindness when I struggled (which was often)—her untimely death affected me more than I could have imagined.

While conceiving of this project and writing this book, I have been sustained at every turn by friendship and collegiality. In graduate school at Berkeley, I was fortunate to meet Emily Chua, Terra Edwards, Lyle Fearnley, Michele Friedner, Ruth Goldstein, Liz Kelly, Patricia Kubala, Janelle Lamoreaux, Theresa MacPhail, Jeremy Soh, Anthony Stavrianakis, Laurence Tessier, and Mareike Winchell. During a postdoctoral fellowship at Princeton, I had the joy of sharing ideas and space with João Biehl, Bridget Gurtler, Alecia McGregor, and Yi-Ching Ong, all of whom helped me to move away from the dissertation and toward the book. When I moved to the University of Oregon, I found an unexpected community in Mike Allen, Diane Baxter, Scott Blumenthal, Zach DuBois, Maria Escallón, Sangeeta Gopal, Lamia Karim, Gyoung-Ah Lee, Jennifer Presto, Kory Russell, Phil Scher, Bish Sen, Lynn Stephen, Kirstin Sterner, Arafaat Valiani, Jo Weaver, Frances White, and Kristin Yarris. And after moving to UCLA, I've been glad to find a home amidst such generous scholars as Patrick Allard, Hannah Appel, Shane Campbell-Staton, Soraya de Chadarevian, Nanibaa' Garrison, Akhil Gupta, Laurie Hart, Terence Keel, Chris Kelty, Hannah Landecker, Jessica Lynch, Purnima Mankekar, Megan McEvoy, Stella Nair,

Christina Palmer, Aaron Panofsky, Michelle Rensel, Nick Shapiro, and Hollian Wint. Other friendships that have sustained this project include those with Katie Bolbach, Moyukh Chatterjee, Maura Finkelstein, Dolly Kikon, Prakash Kumar, Lan Li, Shakthi Nataraj, Yujin Park, Sophia Powers, Amit Prasad, Jessica Ruffin, Aditi Saraf, Harris Solomon, Hamsa Subramaniam, Sharika Thiranagama, Margherita Trento, Anand Vaidya, Saiba Varma, Ani Vasudevan, and Greer Waldrop. Naisargi Dave believed that I had a future in academia long before I could believe it myself.

This book has benefited from the careful attention of many readers, who have done their best to save me from the worst of my intellectual and writerly habits. I received critical feedback from anthropologists and historians working around tuberculosis whose work I admire and build upon, including Niels Brimnes, Jean-Paul Gaudillière, Christoph Gradmann, Janina Kehr, Erin Koch, Andy McDowell, and Srirupa Prasad. Dwai Banerjee, Nick Bartlett, and Banu Subramaniam offered invaluable feedback on chapter 5. Mara Green read so many versions of so many words that eventually made it into this book, dropping her heavy editing pen when what I needed were words of encouragement. Lawrence Cohen, Alison Cool, Shamala Gallagher, Radhika Govindrajan, William Mazzarella, Projit Mukharji, and Sarah Pinto read drafts of the entire manuscript and offered not just feedback but an education in writing.

I have also benefited from a small battalion of editorial experts. Ken Wissoker and Josh Tranen shepherded this project into publication. The anonymous reviewers at Duke University Press, whom I wish I could thank by name, offered detailed commentary that helped me to refine both style and argument. Katie Van Heest's editorial eye transformed this book into a better version of itself. And at the last moment, Shreya Ramineni stepped in at my request and offered invaluable research assistance.

The research and writing for this book were supported, over many years, by the American Council for Learned Societies, the Social Science Research Council, the Charlotte W. Newcombe Foundation, the Wenner-Gren Foundation, UC Berkeley, Princeton University, the University of Oregon, and UCLA. Earlier versions of parts of the book appeared in *Public Culture*, *Cultural Anthropology*, *Technology and Culture*, and *Somatosphere*—my gratitude to the editors and reviewers at these venues. Finally, my thanks to the American Institute for Indian Studies for subsidizing this book and to the UCLA Library for facilitating the publication of an open-access edition.

Above all, this book would not exist without the generosity of the physicians, nurses, X-ray technicians, laboratory technicians, hospital administrators, NGO workers, patients, patients' family members, government officials, and researchers I met in India, most of whom must remain unnamed for reasons of confidentiality. I'd also like to mark the generosity of Madhu Pai, who made a series of crucial introductions. Likewise, my thanks to the archivists and other staff at the Roja Mutiah Library, the Tamil Nadu State Archives, the National Library in Kolkata, the British Library, the Wellcome Library, and the National Archives in London. The descendants of Dr. David Chowry Muthu provided invaluable information, documentation, and photographs that helped me understand his story.

My parents, Mythili and Venky, have made a habit of trusting and supporting my choices—including my decision to study anthropology—and for that I am grateful. My mother's sisters, Kala, Meena, and Sudha, have always been like second mothers to me. This book is dedicated to my mother's mother, my *patti*, Muthulakshmi Kesan, who protested wildly when I hugged her after she had taken a bath but before she had conducted her morning worship (and yet she let me do it time after time), and who proclaimed her disdain for the American need to express love verbally (and yet would often tell me that she loved me). She passed away after a difficult few years with cancer, during which time we all came to understand what it might mean to hope for cure in the face of pain. This book is also dedicated to my mother's father, my *thatha*, T. R. P. Kesan, whose love of knowledge led him to read the books I brought to his home in India, where I often stayed during my research, and to discuss with me their merits and shortcomings ("Bharat, why do anthropologists love talking about this Foucault character so much?" he once asked me), and whose love for me has led him to read every word I've written (and offer what must have been an exhausting amount of encouragement).

Finally, Jonathan Yamakami witnessed the making of this book from the earliest moments of fieldwork through to its publication. He endured my endless talk of tuberculosis and its cures for a decade. And he pushed me to become a clearer writer and a sharper thinker. I'm grateful for his relentlessness. Jonathan, this book would not be what it is without you.

BIBLIOGRAPHY

Archives

British Library India Office Records, London
National Archives, London
National Institute for Research in Tuberculosis Library, Chennai
National Library of India, Kolkata
Roja Muthiah Research Library, Chennai
Tamil Nadu State Archives, Chennai
Wellcome Library, London

Other Sources

Adams, Annemarie, Kevin Schwartzman, and David Theodore. "Collapse and Expand: Architecture and Tuberculosis Therapy in Montreal, 1909, 1933, 1954." *Technology and Culture* 49 (2008): 908–42.

Adams, Vincanne. "Randomized Controlled Crime: Postcolonial Sciences in Alternative Medicine Research." *Social Studies of Science* 32 (2002): 659–90.

Adams, Vincanne, Suellen Miller, Sienna Craig, Nyima Sonam, Phuoc V. Le Droyoung, and Michael Varner. "Informed Consent in Cross-Cultural Perspective: Clinical Research in the Tibetan Autonomous Region, PRC." *Culture, Medicine, and Psychiatry* 31 (2007): 445–72.

Ali, Daud. "Anxieties of Attachment: The Dynamics of Courtship in Medieval India." *Modern Asian Studies* 36 (2002): 103–39.

Ali, Daud. "Botanical Technology and Garden Culture in Somesvara's Manasollasa." In *Garden and Landscape Practices in Precolonial India: Histories from the Deccan*, edited by Daud Ali and Emma Flatt, 39–53. Delhi: Routledge, 2011.

Ali, Daud. *Courtly Culture and Political Life in Early Medieval India*. Cambridge: Cambridge University Press, 2004.

Ali, Daud. "Gardens in Early Indian Court Life." *Studies in History* 19 (2003): 221–52.

Ali, Daud, and Emma Flatt. "Introduction." In *Garden and Landscape Practices in Precolonial India: Histories from the Deccan*, edited by Daud Ali and Emma Flatt, 1–17. Delhi: Routledge, 2011.

Alter, Joseph. "Gandhi's Body, Gandhi's Truth: Nonviolence and the Biomoral Imperative of Public Health." *Journal of Asian Studies* 55 (1996): 301–22.

Alter, Joseph. *Gandhi's Body: Sex, Diet, and the Politics of Nationalism*. Philadelphia: University of Pennsylvania Press, 2000.

Alter, Joseph. "Heaps of Health, Metaphysical Fitness: Ayurveda and the Ontology of Good Health in Medical Anthropology." *Current Anthropology* 43 (1999): S43–S66.

Alter, Joseph. "Nature Cure and Ayurveda: Nationalism, Viscerality and Bioecology in India." *Body and Society* 21 (2015): 3–28.

Alter, Joseph. *Yoga in Modern India*. Princeton, NJ: Princeton University Press, 2004.

Amrith, Sunil. "In Search of a 'Magic Bullet' for Tuberculosis: South India and Beyond, 1955–1965." *Social History of Medicine* 17 (2004): 113–30.

Anderson, Julie. *War, Disability and Rehabilitation in Britain: "Soul of a Nation."* Manchester: Manchester University Press, 2011.

Anderson, Warwick. *The Cultivation of Whiteness: Science, Health, and Racial Destiny in Australia*. Durham, NC: Duke University Press, 2006.

Andrews, Bridie. "Tuberculosis and the Assimilation of Germ Theory in China, 1895–1937." *Journal of the History of Medicine and Allied Sciences* 52 (1997): 114–57.

Appadurai, Arjun. "Is Homo Hierarchicus?" *American Ethnologist* 13 (1986): 745–61.

Appadurai, Arjun. "Theory in Anthropology: Center and Periphery." *Comparative Studies in Society and History* 28 (1986): 356–61.

al-'Arabi, Ibn. *The Bezels of Wisdom*. Translated by R. W. Austin. Mahwah, NJ: Paulist Press, 1980.

Arnold, David. *Everyday Technology: Machines and the Making of India's Modernity*. Chicago: University of Chicago Press, 2013.

Arnold, David. "Hunger in the Garden of Plenty." In *Dreadful Visitations: Confronting Natural Catastrophe in the Age of Enlightenment*, edited by Alessa Johns, 81–111. New York: Routledge, 1999.

Arnold, David. *The Tropics and the Traveling Gaze: India, Landscape, and Science, 1800–1856*. Seattle: University of Washington Press, 2006.

Aronowitz, Robert. *Risky Medicine: Our Quest to Cure Fear and Uncertainty*. Chicago: University of Chicago Press, 2015.

Associations and Institutions. *British Journal of Tuberculosis* 21, no. 1 (1927): 31.

Banerjee, Dwaipayan. *Enduring Cancer: Life, Death, and Diagnosis in Delhi*. Durham, NC: Duke University Press, 2020.

Banerjee, Dwaipayan. "No Biosociality in India." *BioSocieties* 6 (2011): 488–92.

Barker, Pat. *The Eye in the Door*. New York: Viking, 1993.

Barker, Pat. *The Ghost Road*. New York: Viking, 1995.

Barker, Pat. *Regeneration*. New York: Viking, 1991.

Barnes, David. "Targeting Patient Zero." In *Tuberculosis Then and Now: Perspectives on the History of an Infectious Disease*, edited by Flurin Condrau and Michael Worboys, 49–71. Montreal: McGill-Queen's University Press, 2010.

Barth, Fredrik, Andre Gingrich, Robert Parkin, and Sydel Silverman. *One Discipline, Four Ways: British, German, French, and American Anthropology*. Chicago: University of Chicago Press, 2005.

Bashford, Alison. "The Great White Plague Turns Alien: Tuberculosis and Immigration in Australia, 1901–2001." In *Tuberculosis Then and Now: Perspectives on the History of an Infectious Disease*, edited by Flurin Condrau and Michael Worboys, 100–122. Montreal: McGill-Queen's University Press, 2010.

Bates, Barbara. *Bargaining for Life: A Social History of Tuberculosis, 1876–1938*. Philadelphia: University of Pennsylvania Press, 1992.

Bateson, Gregory. *Mind and Nature: A Necessary Unity*. New York: Dutton, 1979.

Benedict, Ruth. "Anthropology and the Abnormal." *Journal of General Psychology* 10 (1934): 59–82.

Benjamin, Ruha. "The New Jim Code." Presentation at UCLA Department of African American Studies, Los Angeles, 2019.

Berdoe, Edward. "Plague, Pestilence and Quackery." Letter dated June 18, 1897. *The Tribune* (Lahore), July 10, 1897, 5.

Bergson, Henri. *The Creative Mind: An Introduction to Metaphysics*. Mineola, NY: Dover, 2007.

Bharty, Sanjay, Brahma Prakash, Sweta Saraf, Rashmi Rai, Anuj Bhatnagar, and Uday Gupta. "Initiation of MDR TB Treatment: Is Hospitalization Worth?" *Indian Journal of Tuberculosis* 61 (2014): 57–64.

Bhatt, Gauri S. "Brahmo Samaj, Arya Samaj, and the Church-Sect Typology." *Review of Religious Research* 10 (1968): 23–32.

Bhattacharya, Sanjoy, Mark Harrison, and Michael Worboys. *Fractured States: Smallpox, Public Health and Vaccination Policy in British India, 1800-1947*. New Delhi: Orient Blackswan, 2005.

Bhimsingh, A., dir. *Paalum Pazhamum* [Milk and fruit]. Saravana Films, 1961.

Biehl, João. *Will to Live: AIDS Therapies and the Politics of Survival*. Princeton, NJ: Princeton University Press, 2007.

Blanchot, Maurice. *The Writing of the Disaster*. Translated by Ann Smock. Lincoln: University of Nebraska Press, 1995.

Bloch, Marc. *The Royal Touch: Sacred Monarchy and Scrofula in England and France*. Montreal: McGill-Queen's University Press, 1973.

Boddy, Janice. *Civilizing Women: British Crusades in Colonial Sudan*. Princeton, NJ: Princeton University Press, 2007.

Bonea, Amelia, Melissa Dickson, Sally Shuttleworth, and Jennifer Wallis. *Anxious Times: Medicine and Modernity in Nineteenth-Century Britain*. Pittsburgh: University of Pittsburgh Press, 2019.

Boon, Tim. "Lay Disease Narratives, Tuberculosis, and Health Education Films." In *Tuberculosis Then and Now: Perspectives on the History of an Infectious Disease*, edited by Flurin Condrau and Michael Worboys, 24-48. Montreal: McGill-Queen's University Press, 2010.

Briggs, Charles. "Communicability, Racial Discourse, and Disease." *Annual Review of Anthropology* 34 (2005): 269–91.

Brimnes, Niels. "BCG Vaccination and WHO's Global Strategy for Tuberculosis Control, 1948-1983." *Social Science and Medicine* 67 (2008): 863–73.

Brimnes, Niels. *Languished Hopes: Tuberculosis, the State and International Assistance in Twentieth-Century India*. New Delhi: Orient Blackswan, 2015.

Brimnes, Niels. "Vikings against Tuberculosis: The International Tuberculosis Campaign in India, 1948-1951." *Bulletin of the History of Medicine* 81 (2007): 407–30.

Bruns, Gerald. "Introduction: Toward a Random Theory of Prose." In *Theory of Prose*, by Viktor Shklovsky, ix–xiv. Normal, IL: Dalkey Archive Press, 1990.

Bryder, Linda. *Below the Magic Mountain: A Social History of Tuberculosis in Twentieth-Century Britain*. Oxford: Oxford University Press, 1988.

Bryder, Linda. "'Not Always One and the Same Thing': The Registration of Tuberculosis Deaths in Britain, 1900–1950." *Social History of Medicine* 9 (1996): 253–65.

Bryder, Linda, Flurin Condrau, and Michael Worboys. "Tuberculosis and Its Histories: Then and Now." In *Tuberculosis Then and Now: Perspectives on the History of an Infectious Disease*, edited by Flurin Condrau and Michael Worboys, 3–23. Montreal: McGill-Queen's University Press, 2010.

Buck-Morss, Susan. *Dreamworld and Catastrophe: The Passing of Mass Utopia in East and West*. Cambridge, MA: MIT Press, 2000.

Burke, Stacie. *Building Resistance: Children, Tuberculosis, and the Toronto Sanatorium*. Montreal: McGill-Queen's University Press, 2018.

Burton, Antoinette. "Contesting the Zenana: The Mission to Make 'Lady Doctors for India,' 1874–1885." *Journal of British Studies* 35 (1996): 368–97.

Buxton, Hilary. "Imperial Amnesia: Race, Trauma and Indian Troops in the First World War." *Past and Present* 241 (2018): 221–58.

Bynum, Helen. *Spitting Blood: The History of Tuberculosis*. Oxford: Oxford University Press, 2012.

Campbell, Margaret. "What Tuberculosis Did for Modernism: The Influence of a Curative Environment on Modernist Design and Architecture." *Medical History* 49 (2005): 463–88.

Canguilhem, Georges. "Disease, Cure, Health." In *On the Normal and the Pathological*, translated by Carolyn R. Fawcett, 105–18. Dordrecht: D. Reidel, 1978.

Canguilhem, Georges. "Is a Pedagogy of Healing Possible?" In *Writings on Medicine*, translated by Stefanos Geroulanos and Todd Meyers, 53–66. New York: Fordham University Press, 2012.

Canguilhem, Georges. "Is a Pedagogy of Healing Possible?" *UMBR(a): Incurable* 10 (2006): 9–21.

Canguilhem, Georges. *On the Normal and the Pathological*. Translated by Carolyn R. Fawcett. Dordrecht: D. Reidel, 1978.

Carse, James. *Finite and Infinite Games: A Vision of Life as Play and Possibility*. New York: Ballantine, 1987.

Catanach, I. J. "Plague and the Tensions of Empire: India, 1896–1918." In *Imperial Medicine and Indigenous Societies*, edited by David Arnold, 149–71. Manchester: Manchester University Press, 1988.

Cerulli, Anthony. *Somatic Lessons: Narrating Patienthood and Illness in Indian Medical Literature*. Albany: State University of New York Press, 2012.

Chakrabarti, Pratik. *Bacteriology in British India: Laboratory Medicine and the Tropics*. Rochester, NY: University of Rochester Press, 2012.

Chakrabarti, Pratik. *Western Science in Modern India: Metropolitan Methods, Colonial Practices*. New Delhi: Permanent Black, 2004.

Chakrabarty, Dipesh. *Provincializing Europe: Postcolonial Thought and Historical Difference*. Princeton, NJ: Princeton University Press, 2000.

Chandna, Himani. "India's Oldest Drug Maker Can't Help Modi Govt Revive Penicillin Production." *ThePrint.in*, October 7, 2019. https://theprint.in/economy/indias-drug-maker-help-modi-govt-revive-penicillin-production/302164/.

Christie, Daphne, and E. M. Tansey. *Short-Course Chemotherapy for Tuberculosis: Well-come Witnesses to Twentieth Century Medicine*. London: Wellcome Trust Centre for the History of Medicine at University College London, 2005.

Clare, Eli. *Brilliant Imperfection: Grappling with Cure*. Durham, NC: Duke University Press, 2017.

Clare, Eli. *Exile and Pride: Disability, Queerness, and Liberation*. Durham, NC: Duke University Press, 2015.

Cobbett, S. L. "The Resistance of Civilised Man to Tuberculosis: Is It Racial or Individual in Origin?" *Tubercle* 6 (1925): 577–90.

Cohen, Lawrence. "Duplicate, Leak, Deity." *Limn* 6 (2017). https://limn.it/duplicate-leak-deity/?doing_wp_cron=1503777434.3709189891815185546875.

Cohen, Lawrence. "Foreign Operations: Reflections of Clinical Mobility in Indian Film and Beyond." In *Critical Mobilities*, edited by Didier Ruedin, Francesco Panese, Gianni D'Amato, Shalini Randeria, and Ola Söderström, 213–34. Lausanne: EPFL, 2013.

Cohen, Lawrence. "Making Peasants Protestant and Other Projects: Medical Anthropology and Its Global Condition." In *Medical Anthropology at the Intersections: Histories, Activisms, and Futures*, edited by Marcia C. Inhorn and Emily A. Wentzell, 65–94. Durham, NC: Duke University Press, 2012.

Cohen, Lawrence. "The Other Kidney: Biopolitics beyond Recognition." *Body and Society* 7 (2001): 9–29.

Comaroff, John, and Jean Comaroff. *Of Revelation and Revolution*, vol. 1: *Christianity, Colonialism, and Consciousness in South Africa*. Chicago: University of Chicago Press, 1991.

Condrau, Flurin. "Beyond the Total Institution: Towards a Reinterpretation of the Tuberculosis Sanatorium." In *Tuberculosis Then and Now: Perspectives on the History of an Infectious Disease*, edited by Flurin Condrau and Michael Worboys, 72–99. Montreal: McGill-Queen's University Press, 2010.

Condrau, Flurin. "'Who Is the Captain of All These Men of Death': The Social Structure of a Tuberculosis Sanatorium in Postwar Germany." *Journal of Interdisciplinary History* 32 (2001): 243–62.

Connelly, Matthew. *Fatal Misconception: The Struggle to Control World Population*. Cambridge, MA: Harvard University Press, 2008.

Correspondent. "Latest Foreign Intelligence." *The Pioneer* (Allahabad), November 19, 1890.

Cummin, S. L. "Primitive Tribes and Tuberculosis." *Transactions of the Society of Tropical Medicine and Hygiene* 5 (1912): 245–55.

"A Cure for Consumption." *The Tribune* (Lahore), November 19, 1890.

Darwin, Charles. *The Descent of Man*, vol. 1. 1861. Reprint, New York: American Home Library, 1902.

Das, Veena. *Affliction: Health, Disease, Poverty*. New York: Fordham University Press, 2014.

Das, Veena, and Jacob Copeman. "Introduction: On Names in South Asia: Iteration, (Im)propriety and Dissimulation." *Samaj* 12 (2015). https://journals.openedition.org/samaj/4063.

Daston, Lorraine. "Marvelous Facts and Miraculous Evidence in Early Modern Europe."
   Critical Inquiry 18 (1991): 93–124.

Daston, Lorraine, and Peter Galison. "The Image of Objectivity." *Representations* 40
   (1992): 81–128.

Daston, Lorraine, and Peter Galison. *Objectivity*. New York: Zone, 2007.

Dave, Naisargi N. "On Contradiction: Humans, Animals, and 'The Way Things Are.'"
   Paper presented at the Boas Lecture, Columbia University, New York, February 21,
   2018.

De, Rohit, and Robert Travers. "Petitioning and Political Cultures in South Asia."
   Modern Asian Studies 53 (2019): 1–20.

Debroy, Sumitra. "I Had TB in 2000, but Now Completely Cured: Big B." *Times of
   India: Entertainment Times*, December 22, 2014. https://timesofindia.indiatimes.com
   /entertainment/hindi/bollywood/news/I-had-TB-in-2000-but-now-completely
   -cured-Big-B/articleshow/45597641.cms.

Delaney, Carol. *The Seed and the Soil: Gender and Cosmology in Turkish Village Society*.
   Berkeley: University of California Press, 1991.

Dirks, Nicholas. *Castes of Mind: Colonialism and the Making of Modern India*. Princeton,
   NJ: Princeton University Press, 2001.

Doll, Richard. "Controlled Trials: The 1948 Watershed." *British Medical Journal* 317
   (1998): 1217–20.

Doyle, Arthur C. "Dr. Koch and His Cure." *Review of Reviews* 2 (1890): 552–56.

Doyle, Arthur C. *Memories and Adventures*. New York: Cambridge University Press,
   2012.

Drayton, Richard. *Nature's Government: Science, Imperial Britain, and the "Improvement" of
   the World*. New Haven, CT: Yale University Press, 2000.

Dumit, Joseph. *Drugs for Life: How Pharmaceutical Companies Define Our Health*. Durham,
   NC: Duke University Press, 2012.

Dwyer, Erica. "The Making of a Global Health Crisis: Extensively Drug-Resistant
   Tuberculosis and Global Science in Rural South Africa." PhD diss., University of
   Pennsylvania, 2014.

Ecks, Stefan, and Ian Harper. "Public-Private Mixes: The Market for Anti-tuberculosis
   Drugs in India." In *When People Come First: Critical Studies in Global Health*, edited by
   Joao Biehl and Adriana Petryna, 252–75. Princeton, NJ: Princeton University Press,
   2013.

"Editorial Notes." *The Tribune* (Lahore), November 22, 1890, 11.

Eliade, Mircea. *Myth and Reality*. Translated by William R. Trask. New York: Harper
   and Row, 1963.

Eliade, Mircea. *Myths, Dreams, and Mysteries: The Encounter between Contemporary Faiths
   and Archaic Realities*. Translated by Philip Mairet. New York: Harper and Row, 1975.

Engel, Nora. *Tuberculosis in India: A Case of Innovation and Control*. New Delhi: Orient
   Blackswan, 2015.

Engelmann, Lukas, and Janina Kehr. "Double Trouble? Towards an Epistemology of
   Co-infection." *Medicine Anthropology Theory* 2, no. 1 (2015): 1–31. https://doi.org/10
   .17157/mat.2.1.212.

Epstein, Steven. "The Construction of Lay Expertise: AIDS Activism and the Forging of Credibility in the Reform of Clinical Trials." *Science, Technology and Human Values* 20 (1995): 408–37.

Epstein, Steven. *Impure Science: AIDS, Activism, and the Politics of Knowledge*. Berkeley: University of California Press, 1996.

Ernst, Waltraud. "Asylum Provision and the East India Company in the Nineteenth Century." *Medical History* 42 (1998): 476–502.

Ernst, Waltraud. *Mad Tales from the Raj: Colonial Psychiatry in South Asia, 1800–58*. London: Anthem, 2010.

Evans-Pritchard, E. E. *Witchcraft, Oracles and Magic among the Azande*. Oxford: Clarendon, 1937.

Fabian, Johannes. *Time and the Other: How Anthropology Makes Its Object*. New York: Columbia University Press, 1983.

Fanon, Frantz. "Colonial War and Mental Disorders." In *The Wretched of the Earth*, translated by Richard Philcox, 181–233. New York: Grove, 2004.

Farmer, Paul. *AIDS and Accusation: Haiti and the Geography of Blame*. Berkeley: University of California Press, 2006.

Favret-Saada, Jeanne. *Deadly Words: Witchcraft in the Bocage*. Cambridge: Cambridge University Press, 1980.

Feldberg, Georgina. *Disease and Class: Tuberculosis and the Shaping of Modern North American Society*. New Brunswick, NJ: Rutgers University Press, 1995.

Filliozat, Jean. *The Classical Doctrine of Indian Medicine: Its Origins and Its Greek Parallels*. Translated by Dev Raj Chanana. New Delhi: Munshiram Manoharlal, 1964.

Forster, E. M. *A Passage to India*. 1924. Reprint, Delhi: Pearson Longman, 2006.

Foucault, Michel. "Introduction." In *On the Normal and the Pathological*, by Georges Canguilhem, translated by Carolyn R. Fawcett, ix–xx. Dordrecht: D. Reidel, 1978.

Foucault, Michel. "What Is Enlightenment?" In *The Foucault Reader*, edited by Paul Rabinow, 32–50. New York: Pantheon, 1984.

Fox, Wallace. "The Scope of the Controlled Clinical Trial, Illustrated by Studies of Pulmonary Tuberculosis." *Bulletin of the World Health Organization* 45 (1971): 569.

Fox, Wallace, P. W. Hutton, Ian Sutherland, and A. W. Williams. "A Comparison of Acute Extensive Pulmonary Tuberculosis and Its Response to Chemotherapy in Britain and Uganda." *Tubercle* 37 (1956): 435–50.

Frazer, James G. *The Golden Bough: A Study in Magic and Religion*. London: Macmillan, 1926.

Freud, Sigmund. "Analysis Terminable and Interminable" (1937). In *The Standard Edition of the Complete Psychological Works of Sigmund Freud*, vol. 23: *"Moses and Monotheism," "An Outline of Psycho-Analysis" and Other Works*, edited by James Strachey in collaboration with Anna Freud, 216–53. London: Hogarth Press and the Institute of Psycho-Analysis, 1964.

Friedner, Michele. *Becoming Normal: Cochlear Implants and Sensory Infrastructures in India*. Minneapolis: University of Minnesota Press, forthcoming.

Ganapathy, Sudha, Beena E. Thomas, M. S. Jawahar, K. Josephine Arockia Selvi, Sivasubramaniam, and Mitchell Weiss. "Perceptions of Gender and Tuberculosis in a South Indian Urban Community." *Indian Journal of Tuberculosis* 55 (2008): 9–14.

Gandhi, Devadas. *Ba, Bapu aur Bhai*. New Delhi: Sasta Sahitya Mandal, 1956.

"Gandhi, Fortified by Goat's Milk, Fit for New Battles." *Reading Eagle*, October 12, 1930.

Gandhi, Mohandas. *The Collected Works of Mahatma Gandhi*. 100 vols. Delhi: Ministry of Information and Broadcasting, Government of India, 1960–94.

Gandhi, Rajmohan. *Mohandas: The True Story of a Man, His People, and an Empire*. New Delhi: Penguin, 2006.

Gandy, Matthew. "Life without Germs: Contested Episodes in the History of Tuberculosis." In *The Return of the White Plague: Global Poverty and the "New" Tuberculosis*, edited by Matthew Gandy and Allmuddin Zumla, 15–38. London: Verso, 2003.

Geddes, Patrick. *The Life and Work of Sir Jagadis C. Bose*. New York: Longmans, Green, 1920.

Geroulanos, Stefanos, and Todd Meyers. *The Human Body in the Age of Catastrophe: Brittleness, Integration, Science, and the Great War*. Chicago: University of Chicago Press, 2018.

Goodman, Kevis. "Romantic Poetry and the Science of Nostalgia." In *The Cambridge Companion to British Romantic Poetry*, edited by James Chandler and Maureen McLane, 195–216. Cambridge: Cambridge University Press, 2008.

Goodman, Kevis. "'Uncertain Disease': Nostalgia, Pathologies of Motion, Practices of Reading." *Studies in Romanticism* 49 (2010): 197–227.

Gordon, Craig. *Literary Modernism, Bioscience, and Community in Early 20th Century Britain*. New York: Palgrave Macmillan, 2007.

Gosling, F. G. *Before Freud: Neurasthenia and the American Medical Community, 1870–1910*. Urbana: University of Illinois Press, 1987.

Govinden, Devarakshanam. "The Indentured Experience: Indian Women in Colonial Natal." In *India in Africa, Africa in India: Indian Ocean Cosmopolitanisms*, edited by John C. Hawley, 55–76. Bloomington: Indiana University Press, 2008.

Gradmann, Christoph. "A Harmony of Illusions: Clinical and Experimental Testing of Robert Koch's Tuberculin, 1890–1900." *Studies in History and Philosophy of Science Part C* 35 (2004): 465–81.

Gradmann, Christoph. "Magic Bullets and Moving Targets: Antibiotic Resistance and Experimental Chemotherapy, 1900–1940." *Dynamis* 31 (2011): 305–21.

Gradmann, Christoph. "Robert Koch and the Pressures of Scientific Research: Tuberculosis and Tuberculin." *Medical History* 45 (2001): 1–32.

Graeber, David. "Remarks on Wittgenstein's Remarks on Frazer." September 24, 2019. https://davidgraeber.industries/paper/2019/9/24/remarks-on-wittgensteins-remarks-on-frazer.

Greene, Jeremy. "Therapeutic Infidelities: 'Noncompliance' Enters the Medical Literature, 1955–1975." *Social History of Medicine* 17 (2004): 327–43.

Grewal, Inderpal. *Home and Harem: Nation, Gender, Empire and the Cultures of Travel*. Durham, NC: Duke University Press, 1996.

Gupta, Akhil. *Red Tape: Bureaucracy, Structural Violence, and Poverty in India*. Durham, NC: Duke University Press, 2012.

Hamlin, Christopher. *Public Health and Social Justice in the Age of Chadwick: Britain, 1800–1854*. Cambridge: Cambridge University Press, 1998.

Hardiman, David, ed. *Healing Bodies, Saving Souls: Medical Missions in Asia and Africa.* New York: Editions Rodopi B.V., 2006.

Harper, Ian. "Anthropology, DOTS, and Understanding Tuberculosis Control in Nepal." *Journal of Biosocial Science* 38 (2006): 57–67.

Harrison, Mark. *Climates and Constitutions: Health, Race, Environment and British Imperialism in India, 1600–1850.* Delhi: Oxford University Press, 1999.

Harrison, Mark. *Public Health in British India: Anglo-Indian Preventive Medicine, 1859–1914.* Cambridge: Cambridge University Press, 1994.

Harrison, Mark, and Michael Worboys. "A Disease of Civilization: Tuberculosis in Britain, Africa and India, 1900–39." In *Migrants, Minorities and Health: Historical and Contemporary Studies*, edited by Lara Marks and Michael Worboys, 93–124. London: Routledge, 2002.

Hart, Philip D. "A Change in Scientific Approach: From Alternation to Randomised Allocation in Clinical Trials in the 1940s." *British Medical Journal* 319 (1990): 572–73.

Health Survey and Development Committee. *Report of the Health Survey and Development Committee*, vol. 2. Delhi: Manager of Publications, 1946. http://www .communityhealth.in/~commun26/wiki/images/e/ee/Bhore_Committee_report _1946_Vol_2.PDF.pdf.

Hegel, Georg W. F. *Lectures on the Philosophy of History.* Translated by J. Sibree. London: Henry J. Bohn, 1861.

Hegel, Georg W. F. *On the Episode of the Mahabharata Known by the Name Bhagavad-Gita by Wilhelm von Humboldt.* New Delhi: Indian Council of Philosophical Research, 1995.

Hill, Bradford A. "Memories of the British Streptomycin Trial in Tuberculosis: The First Randomized Clinical Trial." *Controlled Clinical Trials* 11 (1990): 77–79.

Hiltebeitel, Alf. *The Ritual of Battle: Krishna in the Mahabharata.* Albany: State University of New York Press, 1990.

Hinshaw, H. C., Marjorie Pyle, and William Feldman. "Streptomycin in Tuberculosis." *American Journal of Medicine* 2 (1947): 429–35.

Holton, Gerald. *The Scientific Imagination.* Cambridge, MA: Harvard University Press, 1998.

Homei, Aya, and Michael Worboys. *Fungal Disease in Britain and the United States, 1850–2000: Mycoses and Modernity.* New York: Palgrave Macmillan, 2013.

Hudson, D. D. *The Body of God: An Emperor's Palace for Krishna in Eighth-Century Kanchipuram.* Oxford: Oxford University Press, 2008.

Hutton, Paul W., Y. K. Lutalo, A. W. Williams, I. M. Tonkin, and W. Fox. "Acute Pulmonary Tuberculosis in East Africans: A Controlled Trial of Isoniazid in Combination with Streptomycin or PAS." *Tubercle* 37 (1956): 151–65.

Huyssen, Andreas. "Nostalgia for Ruins." *Grey Room* 23 (2006): 6–21.

Illich, Ivan. "Death Undefeated: From Medicine to Medicalisation to Systematisation." *British Medical Journal* 311 (1995): 1652–53.

Imperial Gazetteer of India, vol. 23. Oxford: Clarendon, 1908.

Inden, Ronald. *Imagining India.* Cambridge, MA: Blackwell, 1990.

Inden, Ronald. "Introduction: From Philological to Dialogical Texts." In *Querying the Medieval: Texts and the History of Practices in South Asia*, coauthored by Ronald Inden, Jonathan Walters, and Daud Ali, 3–28. Oxford: Oxford University Press, 2000.

"Indian Hospital in London." *Indian Review* 31 (1930): 863.

Jain, S. Lochlann. *Malignant: How Cancer Becomes Us*. Berkeley: University of California Press, 2013.

Jarboe, Andrew. "The Long Road Home: Britain, Germany and the Repatriation of Indian Prisoners of War after the First World War." In *Colonial Soldiers in Europe, 1914–1945: "Aliens in Uniform" in Wartime Societies*, edited by Eric Storm and Ali Al Tuma, 150–52. New York: Routledge, 2015.

Johnston, William. *The Modern Epidemic: A History of Tuberculosis in Japan*. Cambridge, MA: Harvard University Press, 1995.

Jones, David. "Visions of a Cure: Visualization, Clinical Trials, and Controversies in Cardiac Therapeutics, 1968–1998." *Isis* 91 (2000): 504–41.

Jones, Donna. *The Racial Discourses of Life Philosophy: Négritude, Vitalism, and Modernity*. New York: Columbia University Press, 2010.

Jones, Greta. *"Captain of All These Men of Death": The History of Tuberculosis in Nineteenth and Twentieth Century Ireland*. Amsterdam: Editions Rodopi, 2001.

Kathiresan, A. *Kasu Noi*. Thanjavur: Tamizh Palkalai Kazhagam. Mark 722. Roja Muthiah Research Library, Chennai, India, 1986.

Kehr, Janina. "Blind Spots and Adverse Conditions of Care: Screening Migrants for Tuberculosis in France and Germany." *Sociology of Health and Illness* 34 (2012): 251–65.

Kehr, Janina. "'Exotic No More': Tuberculosis, Public Debt and Global Health in Berlin." *Global Public Health* 13 (2019): 369–82.

Kehr, Janina. "The Precariousness of Public Health: On Tuberculosis Control in Contemporary France." *Medical Anthropology* 35 (2016): 377–89.

Kehr, Janina. "Une Maladie sans Avenir: Anthropologie de la Tuberculose en France et en Allemagne." *Bulletin Amades* 87 (2013). https://journals.openedition.org/amades/1526.

Kennedy, Dane. *The Magic Mountains: Hill Stations and the British Raj*. Berkeley: University of California Press, 1999.

Khandekar, Indrajit, B. H. Tirpude, and P. N. Murkey. "Right to Health Care." *Journal of Indian Academic Forensic Medicine* 34 (2012): 160–64.

Kim, Eunjung. *Curative Violence: Rehabilitating Disability, Gender, and Sexuality in Modern Korea*. Durham, NC: Duke University Press, 2017.

Kipling, Rudyard. "With the Night Mail." In *The Road to Science Fiction: From Gilgamesh to Wells*, edited by James E. Gunn, 318–35. Lanham, MD: Scarecrow, 2002. Originally published in *McClure's Magazine* (1905).

Kleinman, Arthur. *The Illness Narratives: Suffering, Healing, and the Human Condition*. New York: Basic Books, 1988.

Koch, Erin. *Free Market Tuberculosis: Managing Epidemics in Post-Soviet Georgia*. Nashville, TN: Vanderbilt University Press, 2013.

Koch, Robert. "A Further Communication on a Remedy for Tuberculosis." *British Medical Journal* 2 (1890): 1193–95.

Kuhn, Thomas. *The Structure of Scientific Revolutions*. Chicago: University of Chicago Press, 1962.

Kuklick, Henrika. *The Savage Within: The Social History of British Anthropology, 1885–1945*. Cambridge: Cambridge University Press, 1991.

Lahiri, Shompa. *Indians in Britain: Anglo-Indian Encounters, Race and Identity, 1880–1930.* London: Routledge, 1999.

Lakoff, Andrew. "Techniques of Preparedness." In *Surveillance and Security: Technological Politics and Power in Everyday Life*, edited by Torin Monahan, 265–74. New York: Routledge, 2006.

Lal, Vinay. "Gandhi: A Player of Infinite Games." *India Forum*, October 4, 2019. https://www.theindiaforum.in/article/gandhi-player-infinite-games.

Lancet Correspondent. "Demonstrations of Cases Treated by Koch's Anti-tubercular Liquid." *Lancet* 136 (1890): 1120.

Landecker, Hannah. "Antibiotic Resistance and the Biology of History." *Body and Society* 22 (2016): 19–52.

Lankester, Arthur. *Tuberculosis in India: Its Prevalence, Causation and Prevention.* Calcutta: Caledonian, 1920.

Latour, Bruno. "On the Partial Existence of Existing and Nonexisting Objects." In *Biographies of Scientific Objects*, edited by Lorraine Daston, 247–69. Chicago: University of Chicago Press, 1999.

Latour, Bruno. *The Pasteurization of France.* Cambridge, MA: Harvard University Press, 1988.

Lawyers Collective. "Government Agrees to Provide Bedaquiline to Young Girl Living with XDR-TB." Press release, January 23, 2017. https://lawyerscollective.org/2017/01/23/government-agrees-to-provide-bedaquiline-to-young-girl-living-with-xdr-tb/.

Laxminarayan, Ramanan, and Gardner Brown. "Economics of Antibiotic Resistance: A Theory of Optimal Use." *Journal of Environmental Economics and Management* 42 (2001): 183–206.

Laxminarayan, Ramanan, Adriano Duse, Chand Wattal, Anita K. M. Zaidi, Heiman F. L. Wertheim, Nithima Sumpradit, Erika Vlieghe, et al. "Antibiotic Resistance—the Need for Global Solutions." *Lancet Infectious Diseases Commission* 13 (2013): 1057–98. https://www.thelancet.com/journals/laninf/article/PIIS1473-3099(13)70318-9/fulltext.

Leeming-Latham, Clare. "Unravelling the 'Tangled Web': Chemotherapy for Tuberculosis in Britain, 1940–70." *Medical History* 59 (2015): 156–76.

Leese, Peter. "'Why Are They Not Cured?' British Shellshock Treatment during the Great War." In *Traumatic Pasts: History, Psychiatry, and Trauma in the Modern Age, 1870–1930*, edited by Mark Micale and Paul Lerner, 205–21. Cambridge: Cambridge University Press, 2001.

Lévi-Strauss, Claude. "The Effectiveness of Symbols." In *Structural Anthropology*, 198–204. New York: Basic Books, 1963.

Linker, Beth. "A Dangerous Curve: The Role of History in America's Scoliosis Screening Programs." *American Journal of Public Health* 102 (2012): 606–16.

Linker, Beth. *War's Waste: Rehabilitation in World War I America.* Chicago: University of Chicago Press, 2011.

Livingston, Julie. *Debility and the Moral Imagination in Botswana.* Bloomington: University of Indiana Press, 2005.

Livingston, Julie. *Improvising Medicine: An African Oncology Ward in an Emerging Cancer Epidemic.* Durham, NC: Duke University Press, 2012.

Logan, Peter. *Nerves and Narratives: A Cultural History of Hysteria in Nineteenth-Century British Prose.* Berkeley: University of California Press, 1997.

Lowy, Ilana. "Trustworthy Knowledge and Desperate Patients: Clinical Tests for New Drugs from Cancer to AIDS." In *Living and Working with the New Medical Technologies,* edited by Margaret Lock, Alan Young, and Albert Cambrosio, 49–81. New York: Cambridge University Press, 2000.

Lutgendorf, Philip. *Hanuman's Tale: The Messages of a Divine Monkey.* Oxford: Oxford University Press, 2007.

Mantena, Karuna. *Alibis of Empire: Henry Maine and the Ends of Liberal Imperialism.* Princeton, NJ: Princeton University Press, 2010.

Marriott, McKim. "Hindu Transactions." In *Transactions and Meaning: Directions in the Anthropology of Exchange and Symbolic Behavior,* edited by Bruce Kapferer, 109–42. Philadelphia: Institute for the Study of Human Issues, 1976.

Martin, Emily. *Flexible Bodies: Tracking Immunity in American Culture from the Days of Polio to the Age of AIDS.* Boston: Beacon, 1994.

Marvin, Carolyn. *When Old Technologies Were New: Thinking about Electric Communication in the Late Nineteenth Century.* Oxford: Oxford University Press, 1988.

Marx, Karl. "Economic and Philosophical Manuscripts." In *Early Writings,* translated by Rodney Livingston and Gregor Benton, 279–400. London: Penguin, 1992.

Mazzarella, William. "Branding the Mahatma: The Untimely Provocation of Gandhian Publicity." *Cultural Anthropology* 25 (2010): 1–39.

McDowell, Andrew. "Chunnilal's Hauntology: Rajasthan's Ghosts, Time Going Badly, and Anthropological Voice." *Ethos* 47 (2020): 501–18.

McDowell, Andrew. "Mohit's Pharmakon: Symptom, Rotational Bodies, and Pharmaceuticals in Rural Rajasthan." *Medical Anthropology Quarterly* 31 (2016): 332–48.

McDowell, Andrew, Nora Engel, and Amita Daftary. "In the Eye of the Multiple Beholders: Qualitative Research Perspectives on Studying and Encouraging Quality of TB Care in India." *Journal of Clinical Tuberculosis and Other Mycobacterial Diseases* 16 (2019). https://doi.org/10.1016/j.jctube.2019.100111.

McDowell, Andrew, and Madhukar Pai. "Treatment as Diagnosis and Diagnosis as Treatment: Empirical Management of Presumptive Tuberculosis in India." *International Journal of Tuberculosis and Lung Disease* 20 (2016): 536–43.

McKay, Ramah. *Medicine in the Meantime: The Work of Care in Mozambique.* Durham, NC: Duke University Press, 2017.

McMillen, Christian W. *Discovering Tuberculosis: A Global History, 1900 to the Present.* New Haven, CT: Yale University Press, 2015.

Medical Research Council. "Streptomycin Treatment of Pulmonary Tuberculosis." *British Medical Journal* 2 (1948): 769–82.

Medical Research Council. "Treatment of Pulmonary Tuberculosis with Streptomycin and Para-amino-salicylic Acid." *British Medical Journal* 2 (1950): 1073–85.

Médecins Sans Frontières. "Price Announced for New Lifesaving TB Drug Pretomanid Still Too High." Press release, October 29, 2019. http://msfaccess.org/price-announced-new-lifesaving-tb-drug-pretomanid-still-too-high.

Meldrum, Marcia. "'A Calculated Risk': The Salk Polio Vaccine Field Trials of 1954." *British Medical Journal* 317 (1998): 1233–36.

Meulenbeld, G. J. "The Woes of Ojas in the Modern World." In *Modern and Global Ayurveda: Pluralism and Paradigms*, edited by Dagmar Wujastyk and Frederick M. Smith, 157–76. Albany: State University of New York Press, 2008.

Meyers, Todd. *The Clinic and Elsewhere: Addiction, Adolescents, and the Afterlife of Therapy*. Seattle: University of Washington Press, 2013.

Migliori, G. B., G. De Iaco, G. Besozzi, R. Centis, and D. M. Cirillo. "First Tuberculosis Cases in Italy Resistant to All Tested Drugs." *Eurosurveilliance* 12, no. 5 (2007). https://www.eurosurveillance.org/content/10.2807/esw.12.20.03194-en.

Mills, J. P. Foreword to *Tribal Beliefs concerning Tuberculosis in the Hills and Frontier Tracts of Assam*, by Edward S. Phipson. Shillong: Assam Government Press, 1939. British Library: ORW 1989 A375.

Modell, Judith. *Ruth Benedict: Patterns of a Life*. Philadelphia: University of Pennsylvania Press, 1983.

Mordasini, Ernesto. "Streptomycin and Tuberculosis—a Short Review." *Tubercle* 29 (1948): 49–57.

Mukharji, Projit. *Doctoring Traditions: Ayurveda, Small Technologies and Braided Sciences*. Chicago: University of Chicago Press, 2016.

Mukharji, Projit. *Nationalizing the Body: The Medical Market, Print and Daktari Medicine*. London: Anthem, 2009.

Muralidharan, Karthik, Nazmul Chaudhury, Jeffrey Hammer, Michael Kremer, and Halsey Rogers. "Is There a Doctor in the House? Medical Worker Absence in India." April 12, 2011. https://scholar.harvard.edu/files/kremer/files/is_there_a_doctor_in_the_house_-_12_april_2011.pdf.

Murphy, Michelle. *Sick Building Syndrome and the Problem of Uncertainty: Environmental Politics, Technoscience, and Women Workers*. Durham, NC: Duke University Press, 2006.

Muthu, David C. "A Discussion on Poverty in Relation to Disease and Degeneration." *British Medical Journal* 2 (1905): 939–40.

Muthu, David C. "A General Survey of Tuberculosis in India." *British Journal of Tuberculosis* 21 (1927): 23–25.

Muthu, David C. "The Problem of Tuberculosis in India." *British Journal of Tuberculosis* 23 (1929): 190–93.

Muthu, David C. *Pulmonary Tuberculosis and Sanatorium Treatment: A Record of Ten Years' Observation and Work in Open-Air Sanatoria*. London: Baillière, Tindall and Cox, 1910.

Muthu, David C. *Pulmonary Tuberculosis: Its Etiology and Treatment, a Record of Twenty-Seven Years' Observation and Work in Open-Air Sanatoria*. London: Baillière, Tindall and Cox, 1927.

Muthu, David C. *Pulmonary Tuberculosis: Its Etiology and Treatment, a Record of Twenty-Two Years' Observation and Work in Open-Air Sanatoria*. London: Baillière, Tindall and Cox, 1922.

Muthu, David C. "Response to 'On the Social Aspects of Tuberculosis, with Special Reference to Its Infectivity.'" *British Medical Journal* 2 (1923): 518.

Muthu, David C. *A Short Account of the Antiquity of Hindu Medicine*. London: Baillière, Tindall and Cox, 1927.

Muthu, David C. "Some Impressions of Tuberculosis Problems in India." *British Journal of Tuberculosis* 17 (1923): 118–20.

Muthu, David C. "Some Points in the Treatment of Pulmonary Tuberculosis, Including Continuous Antiseptic Inhalation." *British Medical Journal* 2, no. 2702 (1912): 955–57.

Nandy, Ashis. *Alternative Sciences: Creativity and Authenticity in Two Indian Scientists*. Delhi: Oxford University Press, 2001.

Narayan, R. K. *The Painter of Signs*. New York: Penguin, 1983.

Nehru, Jawaharlal. *The Discovery of India*. New Delhi: APH, 2004.

Nelson, Diane. "A Social Science Fiction of Fevers, Delirium and Discovery: 'The Calcutta Chromosome,' the Colonial Laboratory, and the Postcolonial New Human." *Science Fiction Studies* 30 (2003): 246–66.

Newcombe, Suzanne. *Yoga in Britain: Stretching Spirituality and Educating Yogis*. Sheffield, UK: Equinox, 2019.

Nguyen, Vinh-kim. *The Republic of Therapy: Triage and Sovereignty in West Africa's Time of AIDS*. Durham, NC: Duke University Press, 2010.

Okeke, Iruka, Ramanan Laxminarayan, Zulfiqar A. Bhutta, Adriano G. Duse, Philip Jenkins, Thomas F. O'Brien, Ariel Pablos-Mendez, and Keith P. Klugman. "Antimicrobial Resistance in Developing Countries. Part I: Recent Trends and Current Status." *Lancet Infectious Diseases* 5 (2005): 481–93.

Ott, Katherine. *Fevered Lives: Tuberculosis in American Culture since 1870*. Cambridge, MA: Harvard University Press, 1996.

Packard, Randall. *White Plague, Black Labor: Tuberculosis and the Political Economy of Health and Disease in South Africa*. Berkeley: University of California Press, 1989.

Pandian, Anand. "Landscapes of Expression: Affective Encounters in South Indian Cinema." *Cinema Journal* 51 (2011): 50–74.

Pandian, Anand. "Tradition in Fragments: Inherited Forms and Fractures in the Ethics of South India." *American Ethnologist* 35 (2008): 466–80.

Patel, Geeta. "Risky Subjects: Insurance, Sexuality, and Capital." *Social Text* 24 (2006): 25–65.

Paul, Hugh. "Co-operation." *British Medical Journal* 1 (1938): 480.

Peterson, Indira V. "Campantar II.202 *Tirunirrup Patikam* (The Hymn of the Sacred Ash)." In *Poems to Siva: The Hymn of the Tamil Saints*. Princeton, NJ: Princeton University Press, 1989.

Petryna, Adriana. "Ethical Variability: Drug Development and Globalizing Clinical Trials." *American Ethnologist* 32 (2005): 183–97.

Petryna, Adriana. *When Experiments Travel: Clinical Trials and the Global Search for Human Subjects*. Princeton, NJ: Princeton University Press, 2009.

Phipson, Edward S. *Tribal Beliefs concerning Tuberculosis in the Hills and Frontier Tracts of Assam*. Shillong: Assam Government Press, 1939. British Library: ORW 1989 A375.

Pigg, Stacy L. "Languages of Sex and AIDS in Nepal: Notes on the Social Production of Commensurability." *Cultural Anthropology* 16 (2001): 481–541.

Pinto, Sarah. *Daughters of Parvati: Women and Madness in Contemporary India*. Philadelphia: University of Pennsylvania Press, 2014.

Pinto, Sarah. *The Doctor and Mrs. A.: Ethics and Counter-ethics in an Indian Dream Analysis*. New York: Fordham University Press, 2019.

Pomata, Gianna. *Contracting a Cure: Patients, Healers and the Law in Early Modern Bologna*. Baltimore, MD: Johns Hopkins University Press, 1998.

Porter, Roy. *Medicine: A History of Healing: Ancient Traditions to Modern Practices*. Collingdale, PA: Diane, 1997.

Porter, Theodore. *Trust in Numbers: The Pursuit of Objectivity in Science and Public Life*. Princeton, NJ: Princeton University Press, 1996.

Prabhakar, R. Letter. *Symposium on "Update on Imaging Technologies with Special Emphasis on Tuberculosis."* Tuberculosis Research Centre, Indian Council of Medical Research, Madras, 1995.

Prasad, Amit. "Ambivalent Journeys of Hope: Embryonic Stem Cell Therapy in a Clinic in India." *Health* 19 (2014): 137–53.

Prasad, Amit. "Resituating Overseas Stem Cell Therapy." *Regenerative Medicine* 12 (2017): 743–48.

Pritchett, Frances. "The Chess Players: From Premchand to Satyajit Ray." *Journal of South Asian Literature* 22 (1986): 65–78.

Rajya Sabha Official Debates. "Resolution Regarding Sterilisation of Adults Suffering from Incurable Diseases or Insanity." August 28, 1953. https://rsdebate.nic.in/handle/123456789/588290.

Ramanna, Mridula. *Health Care in Bombay Presidency, 1896–1930*. New Delhi: Primus, 2012.

Ramaswamy, Sumathi. *Passions of the Tongue: Language Devotion in Tamil India, 1891–1970*. Berkeley: University of California Press, 1997.

Rao, B. E. "Tuberculosis and Public Health Policies in the Madras Presidency, 1882–1949." PhD diss., Indian Institute of Technology Madras, 2007.

Rao, Menaka. "Bedaquiline Debate: Domicile Requirement for TB Patients to Get Live-Saving Drug May No Longer Apply." *Scroll.in*, January 21, 2017. https://scroll.in/pulse/827265/bedaquiline-debate-domicile-requirement-for-tb-patients-to-get-live-saving-drug-may-no-longer-apply.

Rao, Menaka. "A Domicile Rule Is Preventing an 18-Year-Old Girl from Getting a Life-Saving TB Drug." *Scroll.in*, January 6, 2017. https://scroll.in/pulse/826005/a-domicile-rule-is-preventing-an-18-year-old-girl-from-getting-a-life-saving-tb-drug.

Roberts, Nathaniel. *To Be Cared For: The Power of Conversion and the Foreignness of Belonging*. Berkeley: University of California Press, 2016.

Rolleston, J. D. "The Folk-Lore of Pulmonary Tuberculosis." *Tubercle* 22 (1941): 55–65.

Rosaldo, Renato. "Imperialist Nostalgia." *Representations* 26 (1989): 107–22.

Rosen, George. "Nostalgia: A 'Forgotten' Psychological Disorder." *Psychological Medicine* 5 (1975): 345.

Rosen, George. "Percussion and Nostalgia." *Journal of the History of Medicine and Allied Sciences* 27 (1972): 448–50.

Rothman, Jonathan. "China's Arthur C. Clarke." *New Yorker*, March 6, 2015. https://newyorker.com/books/page-turner/chinas-arthur-c-clarke.

Rothman, Sheila. *Living in the Shadow of Death: Tuberculosis and the Social Experience of Illness in America*. New York: Basic Books, 1994.

Rouse, Carolyn. *Uncertain Suffering: Racial Health Care Disparities and Sickle Cell Disease*. Berkeley: University of California Press, 2009.

Roy, Rohan D. *Malarial Subjects: Empire, Medicine and Nonhumans in British India, 1820–1909*. Cambridge: Cambridge University Press, 2017.

Salisbury, Laura, and Andrew Shail, eds. *Neurology and Modernity: A Cultural History of Nervous Systems, 1800–1950*. New York: Palgrave Macmillan.

Sambandar. "Stanza 18." In *Hymns of the Tamil Saivite Saints*, translated by F. Kingsbury and G. E. Phillips, 27. Oxford: Oxford University Press, 1921.

Sambandar. "Stanza 23." In *Hymns of the Tamil Saivite Saints*, translated by F. Kingsbury and G. E. Phillips, 33. Oxford: Oxford University Press, 1921.

Santosham, Mathuram. *Tuberculosis at a Glance*. Madras: Caxton, 1985.

Santosham, Mathuram. *What Everyone Should Know about Tuberculosis*. Madras: Crystal, 1952.

Schneider, Alexandra, ed. *Bollywood: The Indian Cinema and Switzerland*. Zurich: Museum für Gestaltung, 2002.

Scott, James. *Seeing like a State: How Certain Schemes to Improve the Human Condition Have Failed*. New Haven, CT: Yale University Press, 1998.

Seeberg, Jens. "The Event of DOTS and the Transformation of the Tuberculosis Syndemic in India." *Cambridge Anthropology* 32 (2014): 95–113.

Senn, Nicholas. *Away with Koch's Lymph!* Chicago: R. R. McCable, 1891.

Sennett, Richard. *The Fall of Public Man*. New York: Knopf, 1977.

Seth, Suman. *Difference and Disease: Medicine, Race, and the Eighteenth-Century British Empire*. Cambridge: Cambridge University Press, 2018.

Sethi, Aman. *A Free Man: A True Story of Life and Death in Delhi*. New York: Norton, 2012.

Shah, N. K. "Letter on Diagnostics." In *Symposium on "Update on Imaging Technologies with Special Emphasis on Tuberculosis."* Madras: Tuberculosis Research Centre, Indian Council of Medical Research, 1995.

Shapin, Steven, and Simon Schaffer. *Leviathan and the Air-Pump: Hobbes, Boyle, and the Experimental Life*. Princeton, NJ: Princeton University Press, 1985.

Shulman, David. *More Than Real: A History of the Imagination in South India*. Cambridge, MA: Harvard University Press, 2012.

Siddiqi, Majid. *The British Historical Context and Petitioning in Colonial India*. Delhi: Aakar, 2005.

Siegel, Benjamin. *Hungry Nation: Food, Famine, and the Making of Modern India*. Cambridge: Cambridge University Press, 2018.

Singh, Bhrigupati. *Poverty and the Quest for Life: Spiritual and Material Striving in Rural India*. Chicago: University of Chicago Press, 2015.

Singh, Jyotsna. "Why Aren't More TB Patients Getting the New Life-Saving Drug? Geography Is One Reason." *Scroll.in*, September 22, 2016. https://scroll.in/pulse/817140/why-arent-more-tb-patients-getting-the-new-life-saving-drug-geography-is-one-reason.

Singh, Saint Nihal. "An Indian Tuberculosis Specialist in England." *Modern Review*, May 1920, 531–37.

Sinha, Mrinalini. *Specters of Mother India: The Global Restructuring of an Empire*. Durham, NC: Duke University Press, 2006.

Sivaramakrishnan, Kavita. *Old Potions, New Bottles: Recasting Indigenous Medicine in Colonial Punjab, 1850–1945*. New Delhi: Orient Longman, 2005.

Solnit, Rebecca. *Hope in the Dark: Untold Histories, Wild Possibilities*. Chicago: Haymarket, 2016.

Sontag, Susan. *AIDS and Its Metaphors*. New York: Farrar, Straus and Giroux, 1989.

Southard, Barbara. *The Women's Movement and Colonial Politics in Bengal: The Quest for Political Rights, Education, and Social Reform Legislation, 1921–1936*. Delhi: Manohar, 1995.

Sprawson, C. A. "Tuberculosis in Indians." *Tubercle* 4 (1923): 481–88.

Srinivas, Smriti. *A Place for Utopia: Urban Designs from South Asia*. Seattle: University of Washington Press, 2015.

Staples, James, and Nilika Mehotra. "Disability Studies: Developments in Anthropology." In *Disability in the Global South: The Critical Handbook*, edited by Shaun Grech and Karen Soldatic, 35–49. New York: Springer, 2016.

Starobinski, Jean. "The Idea of Nostalgia." Translated by William Kemp. *Diogenes* 14, no. 54 (1966): 81–103.

Stead, William T. "Dr. Koch: Character Sketch." *Review of Reviews* 2 (1890): 547–51.

Stocking, George. *After Tylor: British Social Anthropology, 1888–1951*. Madison: University of Wisconsin Press, 1999.

Strathern, Marilyn. "Out of Context: The Persuasive Fictions of Anthropology." *Current Anthropology* 28 (1987): 251–81.

Strathern, Marilyn. *Partial Connections*. Walnut Creek, CA: Altamira, 2005.

Subramaniam, Banu. *Holy Science: The Biopolitics of Hindu Nationalism*. Seattle: University of Washington Press, 2019.

Sullivan, Timothy, and Yanis Ben Amor. "What's in a Name? The Future of Drug-Resistant Tuberculosis Classification." *Lancet Infectious Diseases* 13 (2013): 373–76.

Sunder Rajan, Kaushik. *Biocapital: The Constitution of Postgenomic Life*. Durham, NC: Duke University Press, 2006.

Sunder Rajan, Kaushik. "The Experimental Machinery of Global Clinical Trials." In *Asian Biotech: Ethics and Communities of Fate*, edited by Aihwa Ong and Nancy Chen, 1–55. Durham, NC: Duke University Press, 2010.

Sunder Rajan, Kaushik. "Experimental Values: Indian Clinical Trials and Surplus Health." *New Left Review* 45 (2007): 67–88.

Tarlo, Emma. *Unsettling Memories: Narratives of the Emergency in Delhi*. Berkeley: University of California Press, 2003.

Taussig, Michael. *Mimesis and Alterity: A Particular History of the Senses*. New York: Routledge, 1993.

Taussig, Michael. *Shamanism, Colonialism, and the Wild Man: A Study in Terror and Healing*. Chicago: University of Chicago Press, 1987.

Taylor-Brown, Emilie, Melissa Dickson, and Sally Shuttleworth. "Structures of Confinement: Power and Problems of Male Identity." *Journal of Victorian Culture* 24 (2019): 137–45.

Teira, David. "On the Impartiality of Early British Clinical Trials." *Studies in History and Philosophy of Science Part C* 44 (2013): 412–18.

Thapar, Romila. *Time as a Metaphor of History: Early India*. New Delhi: Oxford University Press, 1996.

Thapar, Romila, Ramin Jahanbegloo, and Neeladri Bhattacharya. *Talking History: Romila Thapar in Conversation with Ramin Jahanbegloo.* New Delhi: Oxford University Press, 2017.

Timmermans, Stefan, and Steven Epstein. "A World of Standards but Not a Standard World: Toward a Sociology of Standards and Standardization." *Annual Review of Sociology* 36 (2010): 69–89.

Tomes, Nancy. *The Gospel of Germs: Men, Women, and the Microbe in American Life.* Cambridge, MA: Harvard University Press, 1999.

Tresch, John. *The Romantic Machine: Utopian Science and Technology after Napoleon.* Chicago: University of Chicago Press, 2012.

Tripathy, S. N., and S. N. Tripathy. *Tuberculosis Manual for Obstetricians and Gynecologists.* New Delhi: Jaypee, 2015.

Tuberculosis Chemotherapy Centre. "A Concurrent Comparison of Home and Sanatorium Treatment of Pulmonary Tuberculosis in South India." *Bulletin of the World Health Organization* 21 (1959): 51–144.

Udwadia, Zarir, Rohit Amale, Kanchan Ajbani, and Camilla Rodrigues. "Totally Drug-Resistant Tuberculosis in India." *Clinical Infectious Diseases* 54 (2012): 579–81.

US Food and Drug Administration. "FDA Approves New Drug for Treatment-Resistant Forms of Tuberculosis That Affects the Lungs." FDA news release, August 14, 2019. http://www.fda.gov/news-events/press-announcements/fda-approves-new-drug-treatment-resistant-forms-tuberculosis-affects-lungs.

Valiani, Arafaat. *Militant Publics in India: Physical Culture and Violence in the Making of a Modern Polity.* New York: Palgrave Macmillan, 2011.

Valier, Helen. "At Home in the Colonies: The WHO-MRC Trials at the Madras Chemotherapy Centre in the 1950s and 1960s." In *Tuberculosis Then and Now: Perspectives on the History of an Infectious Disease*, edited by Flurin Condrau and Michael Worboys, 213–34. Montreal: McGill-Queen's University Press, 2010.

Valier, Helen, and Carsten Timmermann. "Clinical Trials and the Reorganization of Medical Research in Post–Second World War Britain." *Medical History* 52 (2008): 493–510.

Valmet, Aro. "The Making of a Pastorian Empire: Tuberculosis and Bacteriological Technopolitics." *Journal of Global History* 14 (2019): 199–217.

Valmiki. *Rama the Steadfast.* Translated by John Brockington. London: Penguin, 2006.

Van Boeckel, Thomas, Charles Brower, Marius Gilbert, Bryan T. Grenfell, Simon A. Levin, Timothy P. Robinson, Aude Teillant, and Ramanan Laxminarayan. "Global Trends in Antimicrobial Use in Food Animals." *PNAS* 112 (2015): 5649–54. https://www.pnas.org/content/112/18/5649.long.

Van Hollen, Cecilia. *Birth on the Threshold: Childbirth and Modernity in South India.* Berkeley: University of California Press, 2003.

Van Hollen, Cecilia. "Moving Targets: Routine IUD Insertions in Maternity Wards in Tamil Nadu, India." *Reproductive Health Matters* 6 (1998): 98–106.

Velayati, A. A., Mohammad Reza Masjedi, Parissa Farnia, Payam Tabarsi, Jalladein Ghanavi, Abol Hassan ZiaZarifi, and Sven Eric Hoffner. "Emergence of New Forms of Totally Drug-Resistant Tuberculosis Bacilli: Super Extensively Drug-Resistant Tuberculosis or Totally Drug-Resistant Strains in Iran." *Chest* (2009): 420–25.

Venkat, Bharat. "Awakenings." *Somatosphere*, May 25, 2016. http://somatosphere.net /2016/05/awakenings.html.

Venkat, Bharat. "Cures." *Public Culture* 28 (2016): 475–97.

Venkat, Bharat. "Iatrogenic Life: Veterinary Medicine, Cruelty and the Politics of Culling in India." *Anthropology and Medicine* (forthcoming).

Venkat, Bharat. "Of Cures and Curses: Toward a Critique of Curative Reason." *Public Culture* 30 (2018): 277–82.

Venkat, Bharat. "Scenes of Commitment." *Cultural Anthropology* 32 (2017): 93–116.

Venkat, Bharat. "A Vital Mediation: The Sanatorium, before and after Antibiotics." *Technology and Culture* 60 (2019): 979–1003.

Virdi, Jaipreet. *Hearing Happiness: Deafness Cures in History*. Chicago: University of Chicago Press, 2020.

Visvanathan, Shiv. "The Dreams of Reason." *Economic and Political Weekly* 48 (2013): 43.

Viswanathan, Gauri. "The Ordinary Business of Occultism." *Critical Inquiry* 27 (2000): 1–20.

Waksman, Selman. Speech delivered at inauguration of streptomycin plant. *Hindustan Antibiotics Bulletin*, 1962.

Waksman, Selman. "Successes and Failures in Search for Antibiotics." Audio recording. Lindau Nobel Laureate Meetings. 1969. https://www.mediatheque.lindau -nobel.org/videos/31464/successes-and-failures-in-search-for-antibiotics-1969 /laureate-waksman.

Weber, Hermann. "Remarks on Climate and Sea Voyages in the Treatment of Tuberculosis." *British Medical Journal* 3 (1899): 1321–24.

Wellin, Edward. "Water Boiling in a Peruvian Town." In *Health, Culture, and Community*, edited by Benjamin Paul, 71–104. New York: Russell Sage Foundation, 1955.

Wentworth, Blake. "Yearning for a Dreamed Real: The Procession of the Lord in the Tamil Ullās." PhD diss., University of Chicago, 2009.

Wilson, Caroline. "Thinking through CT Scanners." In *Development, Democracy and the State: Critiquing the Kerala Model of Development*, edited by K. Ravi Raman, 118–34. New York: Routledge, 2010.

Wilson, Erin. "The End of Sensibility: The Nervous Body in the Early Nineteenth Century." *Literature and Medicine* 30 (2012): 276–91.

Wilson, T. W. "On Tubercular Diseases in the East." *Indian Annals of Medical Science* 3 (1854): 182–98.

Wise, Alfred. *Alpine Winter in Its Medical Aspects: With Notes on Davos Platz, Wiesen, St. Moritz and the Maloja*. London: J. and A. Churchill, 1885.

Wolstenholme, Gordon. "Colonel E. S. Phipson, C.I.E., D.S.O., M.D., F.R.C.P., D.P.H., D.T.M.&H., I.M.S.(Ret.)." *British Medical Journal* 2 (1973): 720.

Worboys, Michael. "Before McKeown: Explaining the Decline of Tuberculosis in Britain, 1880–1930." In *Tuberculosis Then and Now: Perspectives on the History of an Infectious Disease*, edited by Flurin Condrau and Michael Worboys, 148–70. Montreal: McGill-Queen's University Press, 2010.

Worboys, Michael. "The Sanatorium Treatment for Consumption in Britain, 1890–1914." In *Medical Innovations in Historical Perspective*, edited by J. V. Pickstone, 47–67. Basingstoke, UK: Macmillan, 1992.

Worboys, Michael. *Spreading Germs: Disease Theories and Medical Practice in Britain, 1865–1900*. Cambridge: Cambridge University Press, 2000.

Worboys, Michael. "Tuberculosis and Race in Britain and Its Empire, 1900–1950." In *Race, Science and Medicine: 1700–1960*, edited by Waltraud Ernst and Bernard Harris, 144–66. London: Routledge, 1999.

World Health Organization. "Global Health Observatory Data Repository: Mortality Data by Country." Accessed June 4, 2020. https://apps.who.int/gho/data/view.main.57020ALL?lang=en.

Wujastyk, Dagmar, and Frederick Smith, eds. *Modern and Global Ayurveda: Pluralism and Paradigms*. Albany: State University of New York Press, 2008.

Yankovic, Vladimir. *Confronting the Climate: British Airs and the Making of Environmental Medicine*. New York: Palgrave Macmillan, 2010.

Zimmerman, Francis. *The Jungle and the Aroma of Meats: An Ecological Theme in Hindu Medicine*. Berkeley: University of California, 1987.

Britain, 55; David Chowry Muthu in, 36, 37, 252–54; E. M. Forster on, 78; T. J. Gallwey and, 87–88; tuberculosis in, 4, 87–88. *See also specific topics*
British East India Company, 43, 44, 56
British Medical Research Council (MRC), 138, 146; MRC team and antibiotic resistance, 143, 145–46; Tuberculosis Research Unit, 138; Wallace Fox and, 147, 153; WHO and, 148, 153
British Medical Research Council (MRC) antibiotic studies, 146; para-aminosalicylic acid (PAS) study, 145; research on streptomycin, 138–43, 145, 147–48, 150
British monarchy, 233–34
British Raj, 56
Bruns, Gerald, 19n53
Bryder, Linda, 8n21
Burma, 11, 59, 67; John Fiddes in, 104–9

Calcutta, 45, 92
Canguilhem, Georges, 43, 143n60, 180, 198nn80–81
caste, 19, 31–32nn20–22, 44, 44n68, 46, 50n91, 65
Chandni (film), 161n101
Chandran (god of the Moon), 168–72
Chennai. *See* Madras/Chennai
Chetpet hospital, 181, 186
cholera, 127, 128
Christianity, 31, 40, 44–45
Christian patients, 65
Church of Scotland, 31n20, 65
Clare, Eli, 10n27
clavulanic acid. *See* Augmentin
climate, 31, 36, 62, 98, 101; Alfred Wise on the effects of, 105n80; and British in India, 57, 87–88, 97; C. Fox and, 97–98; contributing to illness, 107; John Fiddes and, 107; unsuitable for treatment/recovery, 67, 84–85, 87, 170
climatic cures, 115

combination therapy, 145–47, 155
Condrau, Flurin, 8n21, 28n10, 35n27, 73n178, 86n16, 142n57
consumption, 14, 15, 91, 129, 170. *See also* tuberculosis
Consumptives Home Society, 31
coolies, 92–94, 95. *See also* indentured servitude
Coorg, 66, 67
Crombie, Alexander, 85
curative imagination, 4–6, 7n20, 11, 21, 22. *See also* imagination: of cure
cure rates, 143n62, 251

Daksha (god), 168–71
Damian Foundation, 178
Danenfels, sanatorium in, 86
Darwin, Charles, 2, 3
Dave, Naisargi N., 20n59
debility, 104, 105
delaminid, 249n1
Delhi, 228, 229, 233–36
Delhi Durbar, 233, 234
Delhi High Court, 229
DeZilva, I., 112, 113, 113n104, 115
Dharampur Sanatorium, 29, 31, 33, 36
diagnosis, 79, 90–92, 104, 184–87, 224; of John Fiddes, 104–6
diagnostic tools, 242; and prevalence of TB, 45–46. *See also* sputum microscopy; X-rays
Dongola (ship), 96f, 99, 100
DOTS (directly observed treatment, short-course), 183, 237–39, 244–45
Doyle, Arthur Conan, 133–35
drug resistance. *See* antibiotic resistance
Dube, Anandi Prasad, 63

East India Company, 43, 44, 56
Eliade, Mircea, 197–98
England. *See* Britain
eradication, 240–41
Evans-Pritchard, Edward Evan, 12, 13n32
Ewart, Joseph, 56–58

India Office in London, 104–5, 109, 110
Industrial Revolution, 38

Jack, W. M., 106–7
Jackson, Mrs., 99
jails, 58, 59f, 60. *See also* prisons
jail-sanatoriums, 61, 62. *See also* prisoners
Jain, S. Lochlann, 132n22
Jains and Jainism, 124, 126
Janssen, 227
Johnson & Johnson, 227, 228, 232

Kalanemi (sorcerer), 80
Kamalaswamy, T. V., 220–21
Kashmir, 65–68
Kaur, Amrit, 219
Khaparde, Sunil, 229
Kimball, G. V., 100–103
King Edward VII Memorial Tuberculosis
    Institute, 181, 186
Kipling, Rudyard, 4, 12; "A Bank Fraud,"
    98; "With the Night Mail," 4–6
Kleinman, Arthur, 13n32
Koch, Erin, xi–xii
Koch, Robert, 130f, 133–34; Arthur Conan
    Doyle and, 133–35; cholera and, 127,
    128; criticism of, 135–37; discovery of a
    microbial cause for TB, 4, 8, 51–53, 127–
    28; fame, 127; "A Further Communica-
    tion on a Remedy for Tuberculosis,"
    129, 131–33; life history, 127; plague and,
    128; sanatoria and, 137; and sanitary
    policy in India, 127; syringe used to
    inoculate patients, 133; TB cures and,
    123, 128, 133, 135, 136 (*see also* "Koch's
    lymph"); travels, 127, 128
"Koch's lymph," 128–29, 131–33, 135, 149.
    See also tuberculin
Krishnan, Nalini, 200
kshayarogam, 15–16
Kuhn, Thomas S., 141n53

Lakoff, Andrew, 243n63
Lakshmana, 80, 82, 83

Lankester, Arthur, 41n55, 45–48
latent tuberculosis, xi, 84
Latour, Bruno, 15n41
Lawyers Collective, 229
Laxminarayan, Ramanan, 230–32
Lévi-Strauss, Claude, 17–18
Levy, Dr., 135, 136
Liu, Cixin, 210
Lloyd, William Foster, 231
London: Bimal Gangooly in, 111–15; John
    Fiddes and, 104–6, 109, 110; Muthu in,
    37; Nirmal Chandra Sen in, 111, 112
London Medical Board, 104–6
Lucknow, 37–38, 45

Madras/Chennai, ix, 149, 162, 173, 192,
    200–202, 220; HIV clinic in, 201, 202;
    international research team based in,
    149; roadside diagnostic laboratories
    in, 187. *See also Milk and Fruit*
Madras government, 152, 181; David
    Chowry Muthu and, 74, 75; Tam-
    baram Sanatorium and, 74, 75, 152, 253
Madras Presidency, 65, 74
Madras Study, 1, 123, 161–62; drug-
    resistant strains and, 149; findings,
    154, 157, 232–33, 237, 250; in historical
    context, 146–48, 154, 156, 157, 162,
    183n44, 237–40; methodology, 123, 146,
    148, 149, 151–52, 154, 155, 157; purpose,
    123, 157, 238; Radhakrishna and, 149,
    150; ramifications, 194n69, 237; relapse
    and, 149; sanatoria and, 152, 237–39;
    and scientific imagination, 157, 159;
    Wallace Fox and, 147, 150, 155
Madurai, 124
magic: homeopathic and contagious,
    17; of juxtaposition, 16–20. *See also*
    witchcraft
Mahler, Halfdan, 141n54
Majumdar, A. C., 30–32
Malabari, Behramji, 30–31
Mantoux test, 192
Marriott, McKim, 50n91

sputum cultures, 141, 143, 240
sputum microscopy, 183, 186–88
Srinivas, Smriti, 71n168, 72
statistics, 56, 142–43, 143n62, 148
Stead, William Thomas, 131, 134
streptomycin, 215; Austin Bradford Hill and, 138–40; British Medical Research Council (MRC) research on, 138–43, 145, 147–48, 150; effects on lungs, 176, 177f; limitations, 142–43, 146; Mayo Clinic studies, 138, 141; para-aminosalicylic acid (PAS) and, 145; resistance to, 138, 143, 145; Santosham on, 175–76
Sultanpur Prison-Sanatorium, 61–64
Sushena, 80, 82
swadeshi, 216
Switzerland, 161; John Fiddes and, 105, 108, 109. See also *Milk and Fruit*
Symons, T. H., 62

Tambaram Sanatorium, 255; founding of, xiii, 74–75, 127; Madras government and, 74, 75, 152, 253; Muthu and, xiii, 74–75, 127, 253, 255; photograph of, 68f; Radhakrishna and, 152
Tamil Nadu, 200, 201
Taussig, Michael, 9n26, 17
Taylor, William, 84–87
TDR TB. *See* totally drug-resistant (TDR) TB
Tomes, Nancy, 49n87
totally drug-resistant (TDR) TB, 224–26
tragedy of the commons, 230–33
treatment cards, 183, 184
triage, 251
tubercular glands, 111, 112
tuberculin, 135–38. *See also* "Koch's lymph"
tuberculosis: epidemiology, xi; primary vs. secondary, 174–75; terminology, 14–15, 170. *See also specific topics*

Tuberculosis Chemotherapy Centre, 148, 151
Tuberculosis Research Centre (Chennai), 192
tuberculous meningitis, 203

Udwadia, Zarir, 222, 224, 225, 232–33, 241, 242; background, 222–23; bedaquiline and, 227, 228, 230, 232; drug resistance and, 222–26, 233
Umzinto (ship), 92, 93
Usmani, Shaukat, 61, 63, 64
utopianism, 70, 71n168. *See also* garden colony

vaccines, 82n4, 240, 241
Vijay, Dr., 186, 187n51, 202–6
Virdi, Jaipreet, 195n71
virgin soil, defined, 40
virgin soil epidemic, 40–41, 57
vitalism, 26, 36, 53–55, 71, 170, 171; Muthu and, 38, 39, 41, 54, 72, 254
von Bergmann, Ernst, 134; clinic, 134–35

Waksman, Selman, 138, 215–18
Wellin, Edward, 13n32
Wilson, T. W., 57
Wise, Alfred Thomas Tucker, 105–6
witchcraft, 9n26, 12–13
women missionaries, 45, 46
Worboys, Michael, 8n21, 8n24, 73n178
World Health Organization (WHO), 153
World War I, 109, 109n97
World War II, 11n28

XDR TB. *See* extensively drug-resistant (XDR) TB
X-rays, 159, 176, 177f, 181, 185–87

Zande, 12
zenanas, 44–49, 55, 64